THE MASTER MUSICIANS

VAUGHAN WILLIAMS

Series edited by Stanley Sadie

The Master Musicians

Titles available in paperback

Bach *Malcolm Boyd*
Bartók *Paul Griffiths*
Beethoven *Denis Matthews*
Berlioz *Hugh Macdonald*
Brahms *Malcolm MacDonald*
Britten *Michael Kennedy*
Bruckner *Derek Watson*
Grieg *John Horton*
Handel *Donald Burrows*
Liszt *Derek Watson*
Mahler *Michael Kennedy*
Mendelssohn *Philip Radcliffe*
Monteverdi *Denis Arnold*

Purcell *J.A. Westrup*
Rachmaninoff *Geoffrey Norris*
Rossini *Richard Osborne*
Schoenberg *Malcolm MacDonald*
Schubert *John Reed*
Schumann *Joan Chissell*
Sibelius *Robert Layton*
Richard Strauss *Michael Kennedy*
Tchaikovsky *Edward Garden*
Vaughan Williams *James Day*
Verdi *Julian Budden*
Vivaldi *Michael Talbot*
Wagner *Barry Millington*

Titles available in hardback

Chopin *Jim Samson*
Elgar *Robert Anderson*
Handel *Donald Burrows*
Liszt *Derek Watson*

Schubert *John Reed*
Richard Strauss *Michael Kennedy*
Stravinsky *Paul Griffiths*
Vaughan Williams *James Day*

In preparation

Dvořák *Jan Smaczny*
Mozart *Peter Branscombe*

Puccini *Julian Budden*
Shostakovich *Laurel Fay*

VAUGHAN WILLIAMS

James Day

OXFORD UNIVERSITY PRESS

1998

Oxford University Press, Great Clarendon Street, Oxford OX2 6DP

Oxford New York

Athens Auckland Bangkok Bogota Bombay
Buenos Aires Calcutta Cape Town Dar es Salaam
Delhi Florence Hong Kong Istanbul Karachi
Kuala Lumpur Madras Madrid Melbourne
Mexico City Nairobi Paris Singapore
Taipei Tokyo Toronto Warsaw

and associated companies in
Berlin Ibadan

Oxford is a trade mark of Oxford University Press

First published 1961 by J.M. Dent & Sons Ltd
© James Day 1961, 1964, 1998
Reprinted 1972, 1975

Third edition published by Oxford University Press 1998

The moral rights of the author have been asserted

British Library Cataloguing in Publication Data
Data available

Library of Congress Cataloging in Publication Data
Day, James, 1927–
Vaughan Williams / James Day.
p. cm. — (The master musicians series)
"The present edition is not just a revision, but a complete overhaul"—Pref.
Includes bibliographical references and index.
1. Vaughan Williams, Ralph, 1872–1958. 2. Composers—England—Biography.
3. Vaughan Williams, Ralph. 1872–1958—Criticism and interpretation.
I. Title. II. Series.
ML410.V3D4   1998   780'.92—dc21   [B]   97-33311
ISBN 0–19–816632–X
ISBN 0–19–816631–1 (Pbk)

1 3 5 7 9 10 8 6 4 2

Typeset by Hope Services (Abingdon) Ltd.
Printed in Great Britain
on acid-free paper by
J. W. Arrowsmith Ltd,
Bristol, England

*To Michael
and Charles*

Preface to the first edition

I do not claim that the biographical chapters of this book are in any way complete, but they are an outline of a long life in so far as the events of that life seem to me to be relevant to the music. I should like to thank Mrs Vaughan Williams, who is writing a full-length biography of her husband, for her help in correcting errors in the original draft, for supplying me with photographs, and for giving me permission to reproduce the manuscript of 'Bushes and Briars'. This acknowledgement should not be taken to indicate that she is responsible for any interpretation of facts or events set down here; any errors or misjudgements are my own.

Besides Mrs Vaughan Williams, I have been greatly helped by many others. The staff of the BBC gramophone library, and particularly Miss Britten, kindly allowed me to listen to records not commercially available to the public, and the staff of the Music Room in the Cambridge University Library have been most helpful on all the many occasions when I sought their assistance. The present editor of the R.C.M. Magazine and his predecessor have allowed me to quote passages from the memorial issue on Vaughan Williams, and thanks to the good offices of my father-in-law, Major-General H. J. Parham, and the editor of the Mosquito, a number of ex-Salonika veterans provided useful information concerning Vaughan Williams's army career. Messrs Novello, Curwen, Stainer & Bell, Boosey & Hawkes and the Oxford University Press have kindly granted me permission to quote from the works which they publish (in the case of the last-named, this extends also to quotations from Vaughan Williams's critical writings and to his published letters; here again, I am most grateful to Mrs Vaughan Williams and to Miss Imogen Holst for permission to quote from Heirs and Rebels). The Times Publishing Company have allowed me to quote from letters written by Vaughan Williams to The Times, and Lady Epstein has given me permission to qoute from her husband's autobiography, published by the Hulton Press. Messrs Harrap have also given permission for quotations from the late Hubert Foss's study of Vaughan Williams's music, published by them and Mr Frank Howes and Dr Percy Young have also allowed me to quote certain interpretations and comments from their studies of the composer's music. I should like, too, to mention one more useful 'crib': that is the phrase 'The Simple Kleptomaniac', which I have appropriated from Professor Herbert Howells—with permission.

My first revelation of Vaughan Williams's greatness came as a child of five at an Armistice Day memorial service in the Garrison church at Woolwich, when the strength and majesty of *Sine Nomine* created an impression on me that has never faded. Other, deeper qualities have since revealed themselves; not always immediately, but consistently and inevitably as one grew older. To study the music has been a rewarding experience; to submit to its impact, whether as a performer or as a mere listener, an unforgettable one.

James Day
Stapleford, Cambridge
Spring 1961

NOTE TO THE SECOND EDITION

I am most grateful to friends and reviewers for pointing out certain errors and omissions in the first edition—and especially to the Rev. Dr Erik Routley, Mr Michael Kennedy, Mr Keith Falkner, Sir Adrian Boult and Miss Diana McVeagh.

James Day
Stapleford, Cambridge
Autumn 1963

Preface to the third edition

The first version of this book was started not long after Vaughan Williams's death and went through a number of minor revisions over the years. The present edition is not just a revision, but a complete overhaul; and for it, Mrs Ursula Vaughan Williams has kindly allowed me to quote and paraphrase freely from her own indispensable biography of her husband. In expressing my gratitude to her for this kindness, I need hardly point out that any errors in or misinterpretations of the facts of RVW's life are my fault, not hers.

My thanks are also due in particular to Bruce Phillips and Helen Foster of Oxford University Press, to Julia Kellerman who has edited the text, and to Michael Kennedy who has read the script, made many valuable suggestions and corrections, and placed at my disposal his detailed and comprehensive catalogue of RVW's works. It will be clear that I have cribbed both consciously (with Michael's permission) and probably also unconsciously from his own extensive, always stimulating, highly readable, and meticulously-researched writings on Vaughan Williams and his music.

Others who have been of great help in pointing out inconsistencies, errors, and omissions include Hugh Cobbe and Duncan Hinnells, who has also drawn my attention to a number of new works on the composer, most notably the excellent and very recent *Vaughan Williams Studies* edited by Alain Frogley. It is a tribute to the international appeal of a composer whom we so often misguidedly think of as for our own insular consumption only that such a thought-provoking work should appear under the editorship of a professor based in the USA. Others to whose insight I owe much but to whom I can no longer offer my thanks personally include the late Hugh Ottaway and the late Deryck Cooke.

Now that a high proportion of Vaughan Williams's major works is available on CD, it is possible to study how they really sound, not just to infer from the printed page how they might sound if one were lucky enough to hear them played. The results are ear-opening, particularly when conductors of the calibre of Bernard Haitink, André Previn, and

Leonard Slatkin are involved. It is also amusing to remind oneself that on the very day when this preface was written, an article appeared in *The Independent*, ostensibly about Maurice Ravel, in which Mr Previn drew attention to the amazement expressed by a senior member of the Vienna Philharmonic Orchestra on learning that Vaughan Williams had composed not only the *Fantasia on a Theme by Thomas Tallis*, which he had just performed and by which he had been greatly impressed, but no fewer than nine symphonies. His response was to press Mr Previn to perform at least one of them with the great Vienna Orchestra. One hopes that this was more than just Viennese charm!

To mention distinguished overseas interpreters of RVW's music is not to denigrate our own musicians: Vernon Handley, Andrew Davis, and Richard Hickox, to mention only three of many, are now worthily carrying the torch handed down to them by Sir Adrian Boult, Sir John Barbirolli, Sir David Willcocks, and others. It has been stimulating and heart-warming to discover how many unexpected facets of RVW's musical personality have been revealed by the younger generation. Who knows: perhaps even one or other of our opera or ballet companies will one day break a lance for his operas or for *Job*. If this study strikes a chord in the mind of some imaginative producer or choreographer to bring this about, then its author will be truly content. And even if this does not happen, he is happy and privileged to have been asked once more to revise and expand what has always been a labour of love. For him, Vaughan Williams's music has stood the test of time remarkably well.

James Day
Cambridge, February 1997

Contents

Illustrations

Bibliographical abbreviations

Boult   *Music & Friends: Letters to Adrian Boult*, ed. Jerrold Northrop Moore (London, 1979)

Douglas   Roy Douglas, *Working with R.V.W.* (London, OUP, 1972)

Heirs and Rebels   *Heirs and Rebels: Letters written to each other and occasional writings on music by Ralph Vaughan Williams and Gustav Holst*, ed. Ursula Vaughan Williams and Imogen Holst (London, OUP, 1959)

Kennedy, *Works* 1   Michael Kennedy, *The Works of Ralph Vaughan Williams* (London, OUP, 1964)

Kennedy, *Works* 2   Second edition of the above (Oxford, 1980)

Lambert   Constant Lambert, *Music Ho! A Study of Music in Decline* (London, Faber & Faber, 1934)

National Music   Ralph Vaughan Williams, *National Music and other Essays*, second edition, ed. Michael Kennedy (OUP, 1987)

Ottaway   Hugh Ottaway, *Vaughan Williams Symphonies* (London, BBC Books, 1972)

RCM Magazine   *The R.C.M. Magazine*, Vol. lv, No. 1 (Easter Term, 1959)

VWS   *Vaughan Williams Studies*, ed. Alain Frogley (Cambridge, CUP, 1996)

UVW   Ursula Vaughan Williams, *R.V.W., A Biography of Ralph Vaughan Williams* (OUP, 1964)

Background and early life (1872–92)

If intellectual greatness can be inherited, then Ralph Vaughan Williams was surely marked out from birth for some kind of eminence in art, industry, scholarship, or science. His grandfather, his great-grandfather, and one of his paternal uncles were all notable and gifted lawyers; his mother was a descendant of Josiah Wedgwood and a niece of Charles Darwin. Three characteristics seem to have been common to both sides of his family: forthrightness, independence of outlook, and a capacity for sheer hard work. He inherited—or developed—a good measure of all three.

His father's family came originally from Wales. John Williams, Ralph's great-grandfather, was born at Job's Well in Carmarthenshire in 1757 and educated at Carmarthen Grammar School, later going up to Jesus College, Oxford, before becoming a scholar of Wadham in 1774 and a fellow in 1780. Distinguished both at the bar and as a legal historian and scholar, a Serjeant-at-Law in his late thirties and a King's Serjeant in 1804, he was responsible for highly valued editions of Blackstone's *Commentaries* and of the *Reports and Pleadings in the Court of King's Bench in the Reign of Charles II*. The latter in particular was valued for his shrewd and lucid notes.

John Williams married Mary Clarke of Forebridge in Staffordshire in 1789; and they had four sons and three daughters. Edward Vaughan Williams, the second son of the marriage and the composer's grandfather, was born in Bayswater in 1797. He was educated first at Winchester and then at Westminster, from which he won a scholarship to Trinity College, Cambridge, in 1816. His career as a lawyer was even more distinguished than that of his father: he established his reputation with an edition of his father's *Notes on Saunders's Reports*, and consolidated it with a treatise *On the Law of Executors and Administrators*, which appeared in 1832 and went into seven editions in its author's lifetime. Knighted in 1847 on becoming a judge, he gained a reputation as one of the most powerful constituents of the court *in banco*, well known throughout the profession for his profound learning, common sense, and remarkably keen judgement. His judgements were so reliable that fewer retrials occurred on grounds of misdirection attributable to those judgements than to those of any other judge of his time. When he pronounced judgement, his obituary says, his comments were 'short, accurate, and concise', a factor to be expected from one who, 'in his choice of words . . . was fastidious, and his delivery somewhat laboured and embarrassed'. Those who have heard a broadcast or a recording of his grandson giving short and emphatic shrift to what he considered to be some trendy and misconceived musical theory or practice will smile in amusement at this last choice of adjective. It would seem that this, too, was an inherited characteristic.

Edward Vaughan Williams married Jane Bagot, who could trace her ancestry back to that Bagot who appeared—not over-much to his credit—in Shakespeare's *Richard II*. They had six sons and one daughter. As a country house, they rented Tanhurst, on the slopes of Leith Hill, the highest point in the Weald, which enjoyed a fine view over towards the South Downs and afforded the chance to engage in outdoor sports and country walks. The house nearest to Tanhurst was the Wedgwood house at Leith Hill Place, originally built in the sixteenth century and modernized in the eighteenth. Set amidst woodlands, rhododendrons, and azaleas and within comfortable walking distance of the summit of Leith Hill itself, Leith Hill Place commanded an even grander view over the South Downs than Tanhurst. On a clear day, the two windmills above Hassocks in Sussex, some twenty miles distant, could easily be seen. There were even kangaroos in the grounds, as the Evelyns, the lords of the manor, were enthusiastic naturalists and had established a colony on the common.

Josiah Wedgwood III, whose grandfather founded the great pottery concern, had bought Leith Hill Place in 1847. At that time he was fifty-two and the father, through his wife Caroline, née Darwin, of three daughters, Sophy, Margaret, and Lucy. The Wedgwoods were by Victorian standards very enlightened parents. Discipline was strict, but not severe; class distinctions were observed, but snobbery and disrespect for servants and tenants severely discouraged; talent in the arts and sciences was encouraged and developed. The girls were certainly not expected to be seen but not heard. Charles Darwin wrote to his 'Lieutenant Lucy' asking her to check up on botanical references and from time to time issued courteous, friendly, and detailed hints to his nieces about observing and noting natural phenomena. As close neighbours, contact between the Wedgwood and the Vaughan Williams families was inevitable; and it was no surprise when the second Wedgwood daughter, Margaret, won the affections of Sir Edward Vaughan Williams's third son, Arthur. The match was a source of delight to both families. Lady Vaughan Williams had long wished that Arthur would marry Margaret; and the Wedgwoods were equally pleased. Josiah made a generous settlement on his daughter and urged the young couple to marry as soon as possible. They became engaged in September 1867 and were married at Coldharbour church, not far from Leith Hill Place, on 22 February 1868.

Arthur Charles Vaughan Williams was born in 1834 and entered Westminster School in 1846. His academic record was good, and he was elected a Queen's Scholar in 1849. He matriculated at Christ Church, Oxford, in June 1853, taking his BA in 1857 and his MA three years later. Ordained Deacon in 1860, his first appointment was as curate to the parish of Bemerton, near Salisbury, where the great poet George Herbert had been incumbent for many years in the seventeenth century. He enjoyed his time there, endearing himself not only to his vicar, but to the entire community, being especially praised for the care he devoted to the welfare of the children of the parish. In the year of his marriage, he was appointed to the Christ Church living of Down Ampney in Gloucestershire, near the borders with Wiltshire and Oxfordshire. His three children, two sons and a daughter, were born at Down Ampney; and it was at Down Ampney that Arthur Vaughan Williams died on 9 February 1875.

Ralph, his second son and youngest child, had been born just over two years previously, on 12 October 1872. On Arthur's death, the burden of raising the young family fell on Margaret; and it is plain that she possessed a full share of the Wedgwood strength of character. She returned to live with her parents and her unmarried sister Sophy at Leith Hill Place, and not long after her bereavement, her aunt Emma Darwin referred to her as: ' . . . a capital mother, very intelligent and yet firm enough to carry off little Ralph remorselessly when he screams, which he does on slight provocation. She says that he's so heavy that she will not be able to do so much longer, but I daresay it will not be needed.'[1] The passionate disposition and sudden accesses of anger (which always subsided as quickly as they arose) that so many friends and relatives noted in later years in the adult composer seem already to have been present in the child. Margaret handled such outbursts, or any other manifestations of childish obduracy, with tact and gentle firmness. Some time later, when Ralph was about ten or eleven and showing signs of promise on the violin, she asked him to play in front of some guests. He refused and left the room in a huff. Instead of punishing him, she simply went after him and said: 'Ralph, I told them you would play and you are making me look *such* a fool.' This appeal to his better nature had the right effect. He apologized, returned and, by his own account, 'played rather well'.[2]

Leith Hill Place is hardly a stately home; but it is a sizeable house, with farm cottages and pastures hard by. In Ralph's boyhood it was rather drably furnished; but the interior boasted a number of fine

[1] Ursula Vaughan Williams, *R.V.W., A Biography of Ralph Vaughan Williams* (OUP, 1964) (hereafter UVW), p. 10.
[2] Ibid., p. 13.

portraits by distinguished artists, including two of Josiah Wedgwood I by Reynolds, one by Romney of Joshua Wedgwood II's wife, Bessie, and a number of works by George Stubbs. Ralph was thus able to acquire early in life a knowledge of and love for arts other than the one in which he himself was to excel. Both music and painting were part of the life of the Wedgwoods and the Darwins—the drawing room at Leith Hill Place was hung with graceful water-colours by Ralph's Aunt Lucy—and it was within the family, from his mother's other sister, Aunt Sophy, that he received his first music lessons. She not only taught him the rudiments of piano-playing, but on the advice of a friend, decided to put him through a course in what in those days was called thorough-bass. This decision was the result of the boy's first attempt at composition, a four-bar piano piece written 'by Mr R Williams' when he was six and entitled ('Heaven knows why', as the composer put it in later life), *The Robin's Nest*. The tune has an arpeggio outline slightly reminiscent of the theme from the Andante of Haydn's 'Surprise' Symphony; it builds up to a nice melodic climax; and the bass part is founded on formidably solid tonic and dominant chords, but the little work can hardly be said to show any signs of precocious genius.

The Vaughan Williamses, the Wedgwoods, and the Darwins alike had traditionally been encouraged to accept things on their merits and not just according to fashion or convention. A Wedgwood aunt of an earlier generation had taken her acquaintances severely to task for confusing moral and aesthetic issues when judging Byron's poetry and condemning it because his private life was loose. Ralph was throughout his life a man of extreme moral probity and integrity, but it was never his practice to censure other artists of quality whose moral standards differed from or fell short of his own. The children were thus encouraged to form their own opinions rather than simply conform to those of others. They were looked after by a nurse, Sarah Wager, of whom Ralph was very fond and who demanded of them perfect table manners and courtesy towards others. Sarah's brother Henry was an organist and music teacher and helped the lad's musical education by answering queries about music. A letter has been preserved in which he goes into some detail about the range and qualities of the viola, which in later years became Ralph's favourite instrument.

Both Ralph's mother and Sarah instilled in the children a high standard of conduct and a code of manners that involved always treating others as equals (disrespect to the servants and tale-bearing were particularly frowned upon) and Sarah certainly also passed on to them her own radical ideas, which were in fact shared to a considerable degree by her employers. An amusing anecdote dating from 1881, when the boy was about nine years of age, attests to this outlook as well as to a certain slightly irreverent sense of humour, which he never lost. A by-election was to be held in Bournemouth which aroused more than purely local interest. The two candidates were the Liberal, Mr Davey and the Conservative, Mr Moss. Ralph and his cousin Diana Langton, later Lady Montgomery-Massingberd, a childhood playmate and a frequent guest at Leith Hill Place, promptly adapted a verse from the Sankey and Moody revivalist hymn 'Hold the Fort' as follows:

> Hold the fort, for Davey's coming;
> Moss is in the sea;
> Up to his neck in rhubarb pudding,
> That's the place for he![3]

It can safely be assumed that neither rhubarb pudding nor Toryism was ever much in favour with either of them, for they would still sing the 'hymn' together with gusto half a century and more later. Ralph used to claim in later life, in fact, that apart from one exception, he had always voted either radical or Labour.

At the age of seven, when he had made some progress on the piano, it was decided that Ralph should learn the violin 'with a wizened old German called Cramer', as he put it; and he quickly discovered that he much preferred the stringed to the keyboard instrument. Meanwhile, he also worked at the technique of composition, under the watchful eye of Aunt Sophy who had strong ideas about what did and what did not constitute good musical form. Waltzes, for example were vulgar; but Haydn was not. Little Ralph was distinctly puzzled to discover when he played Haydn's 'Drum Roll' Symphony as a piano duet with her that the infectiously rhythmic second subject of its first movement was in fact, if not in name, a waltz. He passed both preliminary and advanced grades in a correspondence course organized by Edinburgh University. Once again, the child was the father of the man: his handwriting was even at this age so illegible that he was allowed to dictate his answers to Aunt Sophy. He also worked his way through Stainer's *Harmony*, certainly a useful discipline, but one that had no real influence on his style: the juicy harmonies so prevalent in Stainer's own works hardly ever put in an appearance in those of the mature Vaughan Williams. The gift of a toy theatre stimulated him into sporadically composing music for it, but here, too, there is no real evidence of the greatness and the originality that was to come.

Childhood excursions and holidays were numerous, happy, and varied. They included visits to the seaside, to concerts at the Crystal Palace, where August Manns and his orchestra were showing remarkable enterprise in their choice of programmes and where George Grove provided the detailed and erudite programme notes (though Ralph, for all his intelligence and eagerness to learn was probably less interested in them than in a fascinating illustrated pictorial history of the Architecture of

[3] *The RCM Magazine*, Vol. lv, No. 1 (Easter Term, 1959) (hereafter *RCM Magazine*), pp. 20–1.

the British Isles, which his mother gave him as a Christmas present not long after his eleventh birthday). Other holidays took them to the Three Choirs Festival, where he heard major choral and orchestral works and where at about that time, a young man named Edward Elgar was gaining his first experience of orchestral playing under composer-conductors such as Antonín Dvořák. Ralph's first visit abroad came in 1882, when Margaret took her family to Normandy and Britanny. A visit to Mont Saint Michel made a particularly vivid impression on him, as did the thrill of climbing the cathedral tower in Rouen.

When he joined his elder brother Hervey at his preparatory school at Rottingdean in September 1883, he found the régime rather more spartan than that which he was used to at Leith Hill Place. The boys got up at 6.30 in the morning for an hour's prep, followed by music practice for those who were learning an instrument. Breakfast was at eight; and after morning school there was a fairly typical unimaginative boarding school lunch of such limited proportions that the boys used to go to a nearby shop to supplement it with kippers and cakes. According to Ralph, the headmaster's brother, William Hewitt, second master at Rottingdean, was a really fine musician; but he remembered with even greater gratitude his piano-teacher there, A. C. West, who introduced him to the music of his lifelong love, J. S. Bach; and his Manx violin-teacher, W. M. Quirke. The highlight of his public career as a performer came when he performed Raff's *Cavatina* at a school concert, 'double-stops and all', as he insisted, and on at least one occasion in later life demonstrated to a delighted audience of hardened professionals during the interval of a Three Choirs Festival rehearsal. The following year he again appeared in public as a soloist, this time playing the Gounod Meditation on Bach's First Prelude from the *Forty-Eight*.

During his time at Rottingdean, he was taken to a concert in Brighton partly, one assumes, because he was learning one of the pieces in the concert on the piano: Weber's *Invitation to the Dance*, which he heard in the Berlioz orchestration conducted by Hans Richter. He also heard the 'Eroica' ('which passed me by completely'), the Prelude to *Lohengrin* and the 'Ride of the Valkyries', both of which really thrilled him. This was presumably his first exposure to 'undiluted' Wagner, whose music also became a life-long love. He used to improvise on the latter to his friends at school, calling it 'The Charge of the Light Brigade'. He also got into trouble—nothing too severe, apparently—for playing his violin for the other boys to dance to in their shirts after lights out in the dormitory. Another musical escapade was the composition of a drinking chorus for a play one of his fellow schoolboys was writing on the subject of the rape of Lucretia. Perhaps fortunately, neither of the lads had any real idea of what the title meant; at any rate, the music got no farther than the chorus and even that has been lost. It is doubtful that Benjamin Britten would have had anything to fear from any possible comparison.

Later on, on the advice of a Vaughan Williams uncle, Margaret had an organ installed in the hall at Leith Hill Place for him to play. This action was not greeted with universal approbation. Even as a boy, Ralph had developed his lifelong custom of rising early and devoting some time before breakfast at 7.30 to music. In those days before the advent of electrical blowers, however, it was necessary for someone to be persuaded to pump the instrument for him. The servants had to find cogent excuses in order to go about their lawful business so that the routine of the house might continue undisturbed. It did not always do so, and on Sunday mornings, the adolescent Ralph was frequently the last member of the family to arrive for church, getting there just as the service was about to start.

In January 1887 Ralph joined Hervey at Charterhouse, then under the headmastership of William Haig Brown, the school's 'second founder' and a man of great will-power and foresight. It was under Haig Brown's direction that the school had been transferred from Smithfield to Godalming, where it reopened in 1872 with some 150 boys. By the time Hervey and Ralph were pupils there, the quality of the education and the environment offered had expanded the number to over 500 and a limit had to be placed on the size of the school. Haig Brown allowed his staff and the boys alike the greatest degree of independence compatible with good order and discipline. He was open minded in his attitude to change, though loyal to the school's traditions. His stern character was tempered by a friendly sense of humour and a knowledge of when to bend the rules.

Although in most respects a typical Victorian public school, Charterhouse was in no sense a philistine establishment where the arts were discouraged or disparaged. There was a school choir ('which practised during the time otherwise devoted to extra French and was therefore very popular') and an orchestra, in which Ralph played, to begin with among the second violins and later sharing the viola desk with one of the masters, Mr Stewart, 'whose chief business in life was to preside with complete inefficiency at "extra school" ', but who was a competent viola player. In addition, he took part in chamber music evenings during the school holidays with the family of his mother's friend Colonel Lewin and joined on Sunday afternoons during term-time with some other boys in tackling *concerti grossi* by Italian composers at the house of one of the masters, 'Duck' Girdlestone. Of these, he wrote in the school magazine, *The Carthusian*, in 1952: 'The performances were pretty rough ("Duck" himself was an execrable violoncellist) but I learned much from the experience.' Other masters who contributed to Ralph's musical development at Charterhouse were the organist. H. G. Robinson and the piano teacher, Mr Becker, who also played the horn in the school orchestra.

Haig Brown's 'friendly sense of humour' and ability to know when to bend the rules were now put to the test—and passed it. In August 1888, Ralph, aged nearly sixteen and a member of Haig Brown's own house, Saunderites, together with a friend, Vivian Hamilton, who played the piano, approached him in some trepidation and asked if they might use the school hall for a concert of their own music. A concert of works performed by schoolboy composers was something of a novelty; nevertheless, permission was granted, and a Piano Trio in G, by Williams, R. V., was offered to an audience of masters and their wives—and even some of the boys. Concerned perhaps that such a gathering might be rather more critical of his performing skills than the earlier one subjected to Raff's *Cavatina* had been at Rottingdean, the composer took the precaution of getting another boy to help out with the violin part. (A certain diffidence seems at that time to have been part of his make-up: another story dating from about the same period of his life tells of his fleeing blushing from the good-natured teasing of three beautiful young sisters at a Christmas dance, where he was considerably the youngest male guest present, when it was gleefully pointed out that he was standing under the mistletoe.) After the concert, the mathematics master, James Noon, told Ralph that he must go on composing. Perhaps fortunately, judging from the composer's own memory of the piece, the work has been lost, so we have no evidence on which to assess how apt Noon's encouraging comment may have been.

Possibly as a result of the success of this concert, Ralph was transferred in 1889 to Robinson's house, where he remained for the rest of his school career, becoming a prefect, a position he held for four terms, and, eventually, head of his house. Photographs from his schooldays show a self-composed, serious-looking boy, perhaps a little shy, with gentle and sensitive eyes but with a firm mouth and a quietly determined expression: the look of one who knows his own mind. It is more than likely that he already felt that music was his vocation, but he had not yet decided in what capacity. He was a promising viola player and in later years thought that he could have taken up the viola professionally. This, however, would have been quite out of the question in those days for one of his background, even for such an independently minded lad with such liberal family traditions. In the 1890s, English orchestral musicians were 'an overworked, hard-bitten proletariat', definitely falling into the category of players rather than gentlemen. Gentlemen musicians held academic posts or worked as cathedral organists; and the way to such a post led either through an articled apprenticeship or an academic training.

Ralph retained a lifelong affection for Charterhouse and had fitted in well there; but he was still not sure where his true gifts lay. After he left school in the summer of 1890, the family went on holiday to Bavaria, where he attended a performance of the Oberammergau Passion Play. He had already found at school that orthodox Christianity meant little to him and was by now a convinced atheist. Even as a spectacle, he found the play tedious and pretentiously solemn. Much more to his taste was his first exposure to a mature Wagner music-drama: *Die Walküre* in Munich. Unlike many of his contemporaries, he was not bowled over by the music. His reaction was rather different: 'that strange certainty that I had heard it all before. There was a feeling of recognition, as of meeting an old friend, which comes to us all in the face of great artistic experiences.'[4] He was to experience the same feeling when he first heard an English folk-song. Music, he had decided, was an essential part of his life; so it is not surprising that before going up to Trinity College, Cambridge, as his grandfather had done some seventy years previously, he now chose to devote two years to studying it at the recently-established Royal College of Music in Kensington.

[4] UVW, p. 30.

2

The student (1892–1902)

The Royal College of Music had been founded under the direction of Sir George Grove in 1883; and it is typical of the late Victorian era, the gathering twilight of the gentleman amateur, that its first Principal should have been not a professional musician, but a music-loving engineer. The appointment was none the less inspired. Grove was a man of authority and breadth of outlook; a bold planner and an efficient administrator; a distinguished scholar; an enthusiast for composers of high quality who he felt were underestimated, particularly Schubert; and a shrewd judge of men. His original staff included Arthur Sullivan, Charles Villiers Stanford, and Hubert Parry. Sullivan was famous, not just for the operettas that have lived on to this day, but for more ambitious choral and orchestral works. Stanford and Parry were regarded by some as suspiciously avant-garde figures who had made the pilgrimage to Bayreuth and were now preaching the new gospel of Brahms and Wagner in a country where the old dispensation of Handel and Mendelssohn still held powerful sway in many places.

It is not true to say that music was neglected in what was to be unjustly termed 'the Land without Music', nor even that its ruling dynasty was ignorant of the art. The Queen and some of her relatives (notably the then Duke of Edinburgh) were enthusiastic amateur musicians, and even Richard Wagner's music was regarded as acceptable in the royal family circle. That accomplished courtier Felix Mendelssohn (a ruthless judge of artistic pretension, even in royalty) had written with enthusiasm about the Queen's competence as a singer and her husband's as an organist. The problems with English musical life lay deeper. After the Restoration, the financial restrictions placed by parliament on the crown deprived the court of any opportunity to maintain and cherish a lavish musical establishment of the kind familiar in other, less democratic societies. Moreover, a country so suspicious of state interference in the body politic, one that had only recently (in 1870) established even a national school system, could hardly be expected to lavish public money on subsidizing the arts. The Royal College itself and its older cousin, the Royal Academy of Music, established in 1823, were overwhelmingly financed by donations and endowments, not out of tax revenue. The word 'Royal' may have graced the London opera house, but the Royal Italian Opera received no subsidy from court or state, and any thought of a publicly-funded Royal English Opera performing works by native composers in English was unheard-of.

The apparent dearth of genuinely original creative musical talent was to a considerable degree due to the lack of a proper career structure for trained musicians. The recognized way to musical eminence was through the Church and the universities; but not every talented young musician's bent was in either of those directions; and even if it was, appointment to a university chair sometimes involved the holder in so many administrative chores that creative talent withered and died. This was certainly the case, for example, with William Sterndale Bennett. If a church rather than an academic appointment fell to a creative musician, much of his time had to be devoted to choir-training and organ-playing. And although the daily offices of the Anglican Church offered considerable opportunities for music, a setting of one of the canticles or an anthem for performance at the appropriate place in the morning or evening service did not demand any great structural command or powers of extended invention, since the canticle settings rarely lasted for much more than five minutes.

When Ralph was a boy, concert-going was often either part of the social round or a charitable duty rather than something born of a genuine interest in musical experience. The principal London concert-giving body, the Philharmonic Society, founded in 1813, had slipped into an easy-going routine involving dull performances of repertory works, as foreign observers such as Eduard Hanslick were wont to point out. To play by invitation in the Society's orchestra was indeed a considerable honour; but it was not a full-time job. In fact, during Ralph's formative years, music-making in the capital had no central core, though there were plenty of concerts and regular concert series. Among these were the famous 'Monday Pops' at the St James's Hall, where an assortment of Lieder, chamber music, instrumental solos, drawing-room ballads, and other works was featured. There were also those at the enormous Crystal Palace at Sydenham, then a fast-growing residential middle-class suburb of London, where August Manns encouraged the performance of new works both from home and abroad. The Royal Choral Society, a thousand strong, performed major oratorios from its foundation in 1871 onwards at the Royal Albert Hall; and it was swiftly followed by the Bach Choir, formed by Otto Goldschmidt in 1875, which brought the major choral works of the great composer after whom it was named before the public at large.

Choral singing flourished in the provinces, especially in the great industrial centres of the Midlands and the North, at the two major universities and increasingly at the public schools. This was the aspect of music-making which Hubert Parry considered the most truly democratic because it was something that everyone might enjoy without having to undergo an expensive training or buy an instrument. In the industrial regions, the invention of an entire family of inexpensive valved brass instruments led to another democratic and very English form of music-making: the brass band, which enabled factories and mines to compete musically as well as at work or on the sports field and enlivened workers' festivals and open-air concerts with their bright sound.

But orchestral music and opera were another matter. Although Charles Hallé had founded what was to remain for many years the country's only permanent full-time professional orchestra in Manchester in 1858, concert-giving was all too often a case of too many institutions chasing too few adequate musicians for there to be permanent concert orchestras to which the players might owe their loyalty and much of their livelihood. Theatres, of course, maintained orchestras, but the standard of music they played and its relevance to the entertainment on offer varied enormously. At the Savoy Theatre, Sullivan, with his thoroughly professional training and his natural instinct for the orchestra, produced operettas that were not only ear-catchingly tuneful, with a fine sense of the rhythms and cadences of the English language, but also far in advance technically both in structure and scoring of the light stage pieces served up in Vienna or Paris. Elsewhere the standard was less secure. Opera meant opera in Italian: even early Wagner was performed in translation, though in 1876 Carl Rosa, like Manns a musician of German origin, had formed a company to take opera in English (sometimes even opera by British composers) to the provincial public. Even then, a figure as distinguished as Stanford could not manage to get either of his first two operas staged in Britain: they were put on in translation in Germany.

All these ventures needed a musical staff; but because there was no firm financial basis for them, the staff—and its professional training—was bound to be of a somewhat hit-or-miss kind. Unless he had a long-term engagement in a military or naval band, the life of the instrumental musician (and therefore of the composer whose works he might perform) was precarious and makeshift, which may be one reason why a fairly high proportion of those engaged in it were foreigners. So social convention, class distinction, and economic circumstances combined to oblige many of those who had a genuine talent for musical performance to pursue it as amateurs: a particularly interesting case of this was that of Arthur, the younger son of the Earl of Mornington, born just over a century before Vaughan Williams. As a young man, he had shown no talent for anything save playing the violin. It was considered unthinkable that a gentleman should earn his livelihood from playing an instrument, so his father (himself a distinguished academic musician) bought him a commission in the army, an action which the French in particular had cause to regret, for the young aristocratic violinist is better known today as the Duke of Wellington.

Yet a kind of law of supply and demand operates even in music; and it is no coincidence that this widespread diversification of large-scale music-making, the demand should arise for an increasingly large, fully professional body of musicians. The demand for performers was there. Was there also a demand for creative musicians; and if so, how were they to be trained?

First, of course, they had to study the theory of their craft. When young Ralph Vaughan Williams entered the Royal College in September 1890, he was placed under F. E. Gladstone, first cousin of the great Victorian Liberal statesman, an organist and a prolific composer of liturgical and organ music. Gladstone put the young student through the whole of MacFarren's *Harmony*, a technical discipline which may have seemed drudgery at the time, but which he regarded in later life as both salutary and necessary. He worked hard. Some of his exercises still exist, but they show no shred of evidence of the great composer who was to come. After two terms with Gladstone, he was able to pass Grade 5 in composition, which enabled him to achieve a cherished ambition and study under Hubert Parry. Parry maintained that a musician should write as his artistic conscience dictated; and he always tried to discover whether the music produced by his pupils had any individuality (to use his own favourite term, anything 'characteristic'). Not merely content, as so many teachers were and are, with pointing out faults, he also prescribed remedies for them which seemed to him to suit the student's personality, not just those dictated by the canons of the text-book.

Parry was a man of the highest ideals in conduct and in art. He had an alert and independent mind which never blinded him to originality simply because it was unconventional. Politically a radical, (he once maintained that the quality of the House of Lords would be improved by the admission of a few burglars), artistically he was receptive to new ideas while remaining faithful to what he considered the great tradition: that of Austro-German classicism and romanticism, from Bach to Wagner and Brahms. The very integrity of his artistic ideals and of those maintained by his colleagues at the College, did incline towards a certain priggishness in some respects, notably regarding French music in general and French opera in particular; but Parry was also aware of the great English tradition that had, he felt, been driven underground by the influence of distinguished foreign composers such as Handel and Mendelssohn (he might have added Brahms). Edward Elgar, who was virtually self-taught as a composer, none the less recognized the English feel of Parry's music, referring to him as 'the head of our art in this country' and holding him in great respect.

Vaughan Williams himself claimed in later life that a kind of priggishness was at this time infecting his own musical taste, but from this he was saved by such friends as Richard Walthew, who took him to *Carmen* and introduced him to Verdi's *Requiem*. They used to play piano duets together at Walthew's home and it was through this that Vaughan Williams got to know works such as Stanford's *Irish Symphony*, with its uncomfortable combination of folk-song melody and traditional academic development. His conviction that there are no canons in art except those of sincerity and integrity was reinforced by all these experiences; and he discovered something that he never forgot, even though it rarely affected his own music, namely that sentimentality, theatricality, even vulgarity and cheapness might nevertheless be qualities still to be found in a masterpiece and that they in no way diminished its artistic value provided that the composer's vision was sufficiently intense and profound. The fires of his admiration for Wagner were refuelled at the Royal Opera House in 1892, when a distinguished company from Hamburg, under the management of Augustus Harris and the conductorship of Gustav Mahler, performed *The Ring* and *Tristan und Isolde*. The latter in particular affected him so intensely that he was unable to sleep all night after the performance. Even Parry found this reaction a little excessive. 'That's a very strange young man,' he remarked to one of Ralph's fellow-students as he left the room after a lesson, 'He says he can't sleep at all for two nights after he's heard one of Wagner's operas.' He nevertheless lent Ralph the scores of *Tristan* and of *Siegfried* and introduced him to *Parsifal*. But for the moment, he required his young charge to study the late Beethoven quartets, 'as a religious exercise', an exercise that Ralph dutifully carried out, repugnant though he always found the Beethoven idiom to the end of his days.

Parry also lent his pupil the score of Brahms's *German Requiem*, which by Vaughan Williams's own account influenced him so strongly that many of his fledgling efforts consisted of variations on a passage near the beginning of that work. This is borne out by Michael Kennedy, who also cites an anthem, 'I heard a voice from Heaven', for tenor and organ, dating from the summer term of 1891, as possessing some of the melodic charm associated with such composers as Mendelssohn and Sterndale Bennett. 'There is nothing in these works', Kennedy comments tersely, 'to suggest the composer we know now.'[1]

In October 1892, Ralph went up to Trinity College, Cambridge, where he spent his first year in lodgings in Magdalene Street and the remainder of his undergraduate years in Whewell's Court, a nineteenth-century addition to the college. Pevsner describes it as:

> among the most satisfying of C19 Cambridge buildings . . . The best thing about Whewell's Court is the sensitive scaling of the three parts. The first court from Trinity Street is small, irregular in shape and flagged, . . . the second is no more than a strip of turf with herbaceous borders overlooked by the back windows of the two main courts. . . . Yet it acts visually as an extremely pleas-

---

[1] Michael Kennedy, *The Works of Ralph Vaughan Williams* (2nd edn; OUP, 1980) (hereafter Kennedy, *Works* 2), p. 15.

ant interlude. The other main court is much larger and squarer, with a turfed centre and two big towers as its main accents.[2]

In those days the medieval custom still prevailed that a student had to read for a degree in another subject in order to qualify for the course leading to the degree of Bachelor of Music. Vaughan Williams chose to read history, because lectures in it did not clash with Parry's teaching days at the Royal College of Music: the young man was obviously already determined that music was to be his life's work, whatever the outcome of his stay at Cambridge—and he emerged from it in 1895 with an upper second in history as well as his Mus. Bac.

Cambridge in those days was, as it still is today, a lively musical centre. The English tradition of doing it yourself is no modern invention. Neither town nor university was large enough to support a permanent professional musical establishment, but both made up for it by the quantity (and sometimes the quality) of amateur music-making. The energetic, volatile and irascible forty-year-old Irishman who held the Chair in Music, Charles Villiers Stanford, maintained musical contacts with most of Europe. When Stanford came up as an undergraduate a generation before Ralph, his assessment of musical life within the university was scathing. There was plenty of talent, he said, but no means of concentrating it for useful purposes.

Within a generation, this had largely changed. Already as an undergraduate, Stanford had by a combination of determination, showmanship, and cunning manoeuvring, both musical and otherwise, transformed the University Musical Society (then as now known as CUMS) by engineering the admission of women members. Under his régime it improved by leaps and bounds until, on 1 March 1877, CUMS rather than one of the larger London or provincial concert-giving organizations, had been responsible for the première in England of Brahms's First Symphony; and while Ralph was up, Stanford was largely responsible for organizing a splendid celebration of the Society's golden jubilee in 1893 by persuading the University Senate to award honorary doctorates in music to Tchaikovsky, Boito, Grieg, Max Bruch, and Saint-Saëns. (Verdi and Brahms had been approached, but had for various reasons declined.) The distinguished honorary doctors received their degrees in person and each conducted one of his works with the CUMS Orchestra; the occasion was brilliant, the concert a great success and even the reserved and gentle Tchaikovsky seems to have enjoyed the proceedings. When in Cambridge, Tchaikovsky stayed at the Lodge in Downing College, a college well known to Ralph because a friend of his family, Frederic Maitland, the Professor of the Laws of England, lived there and Ralph used to visit the house frequently for chamber-music sessions. Maitland's wife, Florence, was a member of the Fisher family that

[2] *The Buildings of England: Cambridgeshire* (Harmondsworth, 1954), p. 149.

15

produced a number of distinguished figures in academic and armed service life. She was beautiful and sensitive and a violinist good enough to perform together with her sister Adeline, who was a gifted pianist and a competent cellist, before the great Russian composer during his stay. Ralph's acquaintanceship with Adeline was soon to develop into something that went far beyond an interest in her purely musical gifts.

Stanford had surrounded himself with a number of gifted teachers, among them Charles Wood, a fellow-Irishman, who was Ralph's principal teacher for the Mus. Bac. Ralph was well aware of the quality of Wood's teaching: he described him as a superb technical instructor, unrivalled in teaching the craft of composition. One of the first scholarship students at the Royal College of Music when it opened in 1883, Wood had moved to the recently-founded Selwyn College at Cambridge five years later. In 1891, he had been appointed organist at Caius College and so settled in Cambridge for the rest of his life. Shy, retiring, but possessed of a strong sense of humour, he exercised a quiet and unobtrusive authority. He disliked brilliance for its own sake and detested any form of either personal or musical ostentation. This dislike is reflected in his own musical taste: he loved in particular the music of Handel, Haydn, Beethoven, and Schubert. It may well have been his influence that induced Ralph to investigate the Schubert masses, for which he formed a small choral society that used to rehearse on Sunday mornings.

It was in fact in the field of informal music-making that Ralph gained most from Cambridge in more senses than one. In addition to his Sunday morning choral society, he had the opportunity to hear church music in the architectural context of great buildings: King's College Chapel, the Chapel of his own college (attendance at Chapel was compulsory, even if you were a non-believer) and Ely cathedral, where he often used to attend the services despite his atheism. Then there were the CUMS and the University Music Club, which devotes its energies largely to the performance of chamber music and songs. It was there that Ralph had an experience of which he wrote with typically self-dismissive wit: In a male-voice quartet of his, one of the tenors got a bar out and stuck to his guns to the end. A repeat performance without mishap ensued. The audience, Ralph said, liked the piece even less the second time than the first. In those days, the Club's Saturday evening concerts were frequently followed by extempore performances of comic songs, in which, as in the more serious music-making, both dons and undergraduates were involved. Ralph enjoyed and remembered these concerts all his life and invariably remained for this part of the programme. Here, that sense of fun and of the absurd which had already been noticeable in his boyhood was stimulated by such sights as that of the venerable Trinity College scientist and amateur musician Sedley Taylor parodying Sullivan's 'Lost Chord' to words which began 'Batting one day at the Oval'.

Cricket, however, least of all the kind of cricket that could be musically portrayed through Sullivan's lugubrious ballad, was not one of Ralph's interests, though he loved the open air and used to walk and cycle a good deal, even, at the end of term, to London. On another occasion, when the Cam was frozen over, he was able to skate to Ely, making the return journey by train. He played tennis—mixed doubles being a favourite choice with one who was always very susceptible to feminine charms. Tall, handsome, serious-minded, somewhat reserved, and something of a dandy about his clothes, letting others speak before voicing his own carefully considered opinion and regarding personal relationships as a more important matter than a mere occasion for social pleasantries, he did not readily make friends, but when he did, the friendships lasted. Among his own particular circle of friends was his cousin Ralph Wedgwood, also up at Trinity. They had known one another as children and Ralph was a natural member of what he called Wedgwood's 'magic circle' of friends, a circle that included the philosopher G. E. Moore (later to become famous as the author of *Principia Ethica*), the lawyer and scholar Maurice Sheldon Amos, and the great historian G. M. Trevelyan. Some idea of their intellectual calibre may be gained from the fact that three of the five were awarded the O. M. in later life. Wedgwood himself was knighted in 1924, became a baronet in 1942, and ended his career as chief general manager of the London and North Eastern Railway.

It was with members of this group that he would engage in reading parties during their vacations in various parts of Britain, travelling as far afield as the Lake District, Cornwall, and the Isle of Skye, where he had an experience that made a lasting impression. He attended an open-air service conducted in Gaelic, of which he knew nothing. This enabled him to concentrate on the manner in which the preacher's voice was inflected as he grew more and more impassioned in his rhetoric. The melodic formulae that impressed themselves on his mind were to become startlingly familiar when he began to study and collect folk-songs not many years later.

In the Cambridge musical world, he was a close companion of the two Gatty brothers, Nicholas, who played the violin and composed; and Ivor, who played the horn. These two talented brothers were the sons of the vicar of Hooton Roberts, a quiet Yorkshire country village not far from Rotherham. Ralph became a frequent guest, paying regular visits both before and after his marriage and enjoying impromptu chamber music performances. It was at Hooton Roberts that Vaughan Williams's most popular song, 'Linden Lea', received its first public performance in September 1902. Somewhat older than them was another who was to become a lifelong friend: Hugh P. Allen, the Organ Scholar of Christ's College, a knowledgeable and frequent performer at the Music Club concerts and the conductor responsible for the performance with encore already mentioned of one of Ralph's part-songs.

Ralph also continued his studies on the organ, for which his teacher was Alan Gray. Like Charles Wood, Gray was saddened that a pupil so able and so enthusiastic was none the less so apparently unpromising. When after taking his degree Ralph, still unsure of his bearings musically, but still convinced that his future lay in music, was about to embark on a second stint at the Royal College, Gray wrote to Walter Parratt, the Professor of Organ at the RCM:

> I cannot tell [Vaughan Williams] that I think he is justified in going in for an organist's career which is his pet idea. He seems to me so hopelessly 'unhandy'. He has got to a certain point and sticks there. I can never trust him to play a simple service for me without some dread as to what he may do. And this he combines with considerable knowledge and taste on organ and music matters generally.[3]

Ralph re-entered the RCM in the summer of 1895 and during this stay, he made more important friendships, such as those with John Ireland, Thomas Dunhill, and S. P. Waddington, a first-rate pianist and a brilliant sight-reader who would play through Ralph's compositions for him.

But one friendship above all dating from this period was decisive in shaping Vaughan Williams's future development as a composer. Gustav Holst was twenty-one in 1895 when they met, and came from a quite different and considerably less affluent background from Ralph. Despite this, and despite—perhaps because of—an innate shyness on both their parts, they took to one another at once. Holst's family were professional musicians. He was two years Ralph's junior and had won a scholarship worth £30 per annum to the College, which he had to supplement by playing the trombone in various orchestras during the vacations, an activity that he often found utterly distasteful. His alert, enquiring mind, however, was not of the kind that is deadened by uncongenial activities; and his intimate knowledge of orchestral technique, partly gained during this period, was of invaluable aid to Vaughan Williams when, soon after their first meeting, they began their celebrated 'field days', on which they would together spend a whole day or part of it, at least once a week, studying and criticizing one another's latest work, as their published letters show, with a cordial frankness that would have caused offence to acquaintances of less mutual sympathy. The 'field days' continued until Holst's death nearly forty years later; and the two friends pulled no punches. 'I think the whole scheme of verses is bad',[4] Vaughan Williams wrote to Holst about the libretto to *The Youth's Choice*, before offering helpful suggestions as to how things could be improved.

---

[3] UVW, pp. 41–2.

[4] *Heirs and Rebels: Letters written to each other and occasional writings on music by Ralph Vaughan Williams and Gustav Holst*, ed. Ursula Vaughan Williams and Imogen Holst (OUP, 1959) (hereafter *Heirs and Rebels*), p. 6.

Writing from Berlin in 1903, Holst told his friend: ' . . . the voice parts of your opera are impossible. You must not do this sort of thing. Don't show them to a singer, but *get singers to sing them*.'[5] This was typical of the way they treated one another professionally; and it paid dividends for both of them in the years to come. Whatever the subject under discussion, whether the merits of a libretto, of a composer, or of a work, there was the same common sense, the same frankness, the same give and take between equals, the same affection unclouded by sentimentality.

One thread that runs through their early letters is a kind of frustrated bewilderment about the way forward for the young English composer of their era. They both knew that they had original things to say musically, but were unsure of whom to look to for guidance. As Holst put it, quoting his friend, they didn't seem to fit on to the great Austro-German tradition at all. But they were at a loss to know how to re-establish the tradition to which they felt they belonged. On one occasion, Holst suggested 'victimising' Elgar, a plan which, perhaps fortunately for both them and for Elgar, came to nothing. But they both eventually came to the conclusion drawn by Holst in a letter from Germany in 1903: 'I believe that really the only good that will last will be done by struggling away on your own . . . our business is to learn to please ourselves which is far more difficult as it is hard to find out what we want.'[6]

Straws were beginning to drift on the wind, however. In the autumn of 1895, the bicentenary of Purcell's death was due to be commemorated. Stanford had decided that the RCM students should stage *Dido and Aeneas* under his direction. Holst and Vaughan Williams were both involved, Ralph singing in the chorus; and the experience kindled a lifelong love in both of them for Purcell's music. Other 'extra-curricular' activities included delivering papers to the College Debating Society on Purcell, Bayreuth, The Rise and Fall of the Romantic School, and Didactic Art. But apart from the friendship with Holst, the main event of this second spell at the College was Ralph's contact with Stanford.

At this time, Stanford was at the peak of his fame. The best-known and most highly thought-of British composer after Sullivan, admired especially in Germany by such musicians as Brahms's champion Hans von Bülow, he was a conductor of ability, a composer of skill, and a teacher of genius. Prejudiced almost to the point of bigotry, quick-tempered, forthright and often wounding in his criticisms, thin-skinned, but gifted with a prodigious compositional technique and a born teacher's imagination, he sought to develop his pupils' minds rather than just their technical skill and to counteract what he saw as their faults by exposing them to new influences. Many of his students found his terse put-downs like his 'all rot, me bhoy', or his 'damnably ugly, me bhoy',

---

[5] Ibid., pp. 13–14.   [6] Ibid., p. 21.

forcefully delivered in his soft Leinster brogue, or his sometimes unpredictable surliness and quirky behaviour—'all crotchets and fads and moods', as Holst put it—too much for them. Vaughan Williams stood up to him and thereby gained his grudging admiration, if not always exactly his approval. Their lessons were surely a case if ever there was one of the irresistible force meeting the immovable object; yet Vaughan Williams retained a sincere and whole-hearted admiration for his teacher all his life. He himself wrote in his witty and informative *Musical Autobiography*:

> The details of my work annoyed Stanford so much that we seldom got beyond these to the broader issues, and the lesson usually started with a conversation on these lines:
> 'Damnably ugly, my boy. Why do you write such things?'
> 'Because I like them.'
> 'But you can't like them, they're not music.'
> 'I shouldn't write them if I didn't like them.'[7]

In later life, he regarded this obduracy as a mistake, advising later generations of students not to fight their teacher, as he had done with Stanford, but to keep, as he put it, a secret *eppur si muove* up their sleeve while conforming with their teacher's demands. But his attitude showed that he was a young man of solid convictions; and it led to at least one delightful ploy. Stanford felt that Vaughan Williams's work was rather too solemn, especially as he was addicted to the modes—this was some time before he discovered English folk-song in depth and detail. He told him to go away and write a Waltz. Ralph neatly turned the tables on his teacher by writing a modal waltz.

As important emotionally as the friendship with Holst was musically was his relationship with Florence Maitland's sister Adeline. The fifth of the eleven children of Mr and Mrs Herbert Fisher of Brockenhurst, she had developed into a young woman of singular beauty and charm, slenderly built, graceful in movement, with a cascade of fair hair and a warmth of character that her aloof bearing concealed from many people. The Fishers combined intellectual ability and good looks: Adeline's mother had been the model for G. F. Watts's *Una and the Red Cross Knight* and the strength of the likeness between mother and daughter can be seen if one compares a photograph of Adeline with the Watts painting. Five of Adeline's brothers were to achieve renown in fields as varied as those of military and naval warfare, banking, scholarship, and architecture.

The Fishers were a closely-knit family; and when Adeline became engaged to the shy young musician, who was two years younger than she was, some of the family's acquaintances felt that she was not

---

[7] *National Music and Other Essays*, ed. Michael Kennedy (2nd edn; OUP, 1987) (hereafter *National Music*), p. 185.

making a very good match. Even her father, on receiving the telegram announcing her acceptance of his proposal ruefully described the news as a *fait accompli*. This did not deter her in the slightest. Nor, it seems, did it worry some of her other closest relatives: one of her brothers commented in his letter of congratulation: 'I only know of one fault that he has or rather defect, and that is that he cannot discriminate between good and bad food. I don't know whether you intend to trade on this or cure it.'[8] Allied to Adeline's good looks were a discriminating shrewdness, abundant energy, a strong family loyalty, a keen sense of humour and, above all, an unshakeable faith in her fiancé's gift.

Ralph and Adeline were married at All Saints, Hove, on 9 October 1897. The officiating priest, it is tantalizing to note, was the famous Dr Spooner; and they set off for a prolonged honeymoon in Berlin, which was chosen for two reasons. The first was that the State Opera there was the only place apart from Bayreuth where *The Ring* was performed without cuts. The young couple prepared themselves for this pilgrimage by working through Wagner's tetralogy as a piano duo. The other reason was that Ralph wished to study there with Max Bruch—an unexpected choice, for Bruch was even more conservative than Stanford; and even Stanford thought that Ralph's music was too teutonically orientated, advising him instead to listen to opera at La Scala.

At the time of his marriage, Ralph has already been 'respectably' installed in the musical profession for some two years as the organist at St Barnabas's Church, South Lambeth, the only paid appointment he ever held in that capacity. He did not enjoy it. Once, when writing to Holst asking him to deputize for him, he referred to the men in the choir at the 'damned place' as 'louts' who 'make you mad' and 'slope into choir practice' half an hour late. Fortunately, perhaps, his atheist views and his refusal to take communion made him *persona non grata* with a new vicar shortly afterwards and he was able to resign.

Ralph's long apprenticeship was still to continue for some time. The period of study with Bruch began on 6 November and was fruitful in that at least Bruch gave him the encouragement that had been so sadly lacking in Stanford's teaching. His final testimonial from Bruch three months later described him as 'ein guter Musiker und ein talentvoller Komponist'. Ralph, quoting this to his cousin Ralph Wedgwood, went on to say that Bruch had complimented him on his original ideas but cavilled at his rather *too* original harmonies. He continued:

. . . it seems to me that the future of music lies between England and Russia, but the Russians must try to give up being original and the English being imitators. I very much believe in the folk tune theory—by which I don't mean that modern composing is done by sandwiching an occasional national tune . . . between lumps of the '2d the pound' stuff, which seems to be Dvořák's latest method.

[8] UVW, p. 49.

(Presumably this was a reference to works like the *New World* Symphony.)

> But that to get the spirit of his national tunes into his work must be good for a composer if it comes natural to him, in which case it doesn't matter if what he writes occasionally corresponds with some real 'folktune'. All this because in the last thing I wrote for him I used a bit of Welsh tune as my 'Haupt Thema'—unacknowledged of course, but then 'I made it my own'.[9]

Bruch himself had shown considerable interest in folk-music (*vide* his *Scottish Fantasia* for Violin and Orchestra, with its curiously Procrustean harmonization and adaptation of the tune of 'Scots wha hae', amongst a number of other works); and he noted Ralph's predilection for the flattened seventh and the modes.

Apart from a holiday with Adeline's family in Italy at Christmas, they remained in Germany, enjoying concerts, theatre, and opera-going, parties—and hard work with Bruch—until April 1898, when they returned to England and settled in in what Adeline described as a curious old panelled house at 16 North Street, Westminster, close to the Abbey. They didn't stay there long, moving to 5 Cowley Street after 'the landlady objected very strongly to [Adeline's] having influenza'. They remained at Cowley Street for a year before moving once again, this time to 10 Barton Street, Westminster.

For the moment, Ralph was busy polishing his composing technique with a steady stream of songs, chamber music, a serenade for orchestra that Adeline found 'rather Dvořák-y' (possibly because of the jovially folky second movement) and his Doctoral exercise, a setting for soloists, chorus, and orchestra of the text of the Mass. This he completed in 1899, proceeding to his degree in 1901. His formal musical education was now virtually complete; and though he was under no compulsion to earn his living from his compositions, having a small private income, he devoted his time to them in an intensely professional manner.

He eagerly attended concerts where new music was to be performed, being greatly impressed by the Enigma Variations and bitterly disappointed, not so much by the music as by the devastatingly poor first performance of *The Dream of Gerontius*. He lectured and wrote—sometimes provocative and always stimulating—critical articles. He was in demand as an editor (for example of two volumes of the *Welcome Songs* for the Purcell Society's comprehensive edition); and he contributed scholarly articles on 'Conducting' and 'Fugue' to the 1904 edition of *Grove*. Yet he was still vaguely aware that he had not found his proper voice as a composer. At various times he referred to himself in letters to Holst as 'stale', 'dried-up', and 'prematurely decayed and getting fat', to be roundly rebuked and gently encouraged by his friend. He and Holst

---

[9] Quoted in Christopher Field, *Max Bruch, His Life and Works* (New York, 1988), pp. 270–1.

attributed their misgivings to lack of tradition, lack of roots, lack of industry. Yet the real reason is hinted at in an article published in *The Vocalist*[10] in May 1902: 'What we want in England is *real* music, even if it be only a music-hall song. Provided it possesses real feeling and real life, it will be worth all the off-scourings of the classics in the world.'

Up till now, most of his works had been 'off-scourings of the classics'. A hint from Purcell (he noted with some delight in the preface to the second volume of *Welcome Songs* that Purcell had quoted the Playford dance tune 'Hey boys, up go we' note for note in the bass of 'Be lively and gay' from *Ye Tuneful Muses*), a possible thought sparked off by the relative ease with which he had produced a winner of a tune for the Dorset cleric and scholar William Barnes's gentle dialect poem 'Linden Lea', and possibly even a trace of William Morris's ideal of the artist basing his art on that of the cottage craftsman (Holst was a member of Kelmscott House, the Morris establishment in Hammersmith) may have prompted his next move. Ralph had already studied published English folk-songs in order to give a series of well-attended university extension lectures at Pokesdown in the winter of 1902. (They were popular enough to be repeated at Gloucester early in 1903 and at Brentwood in Essex in the autumn.) In doing so, he had discovered new and exciting aspects of the English musical tradition. It was at Ingrave, near Brentwood, where he was approached after one of his lectures on 3 December and asked if he would care to come to a tea-party at the vicarage for the old people of the parish, that his mind was, as he put it later, finally set to rest. At the party, Ralph was introduced to an elderly labourer, Charles Pottipher, who asked him to visit him the following day, when he would sing him some of the old songs. Thus on 4 December 1903, Ralph took down the first song of the total of over eight hundred that he was eventually to collect. It was called 'Bushes and Briars'.

[10] Reprinted in *Heirs and Rebels*, pp. 27–8.

3

The quiet rebel (1903–14)

The Folk Song Society had been founded in 1898 and by the time Vaughan Williams joined it in 1904, it had not exactly distinguished itself by its energy or its resourcefulness. This was despite—or possibly on account of—the erudition of its vice-presidents (one Scotsman, Alexander Mackenzie, one Irishman, Stanford, and two Englishmen, Parry and Stainer). Complaints were being voiced about the tempo and scope of its activities. The first fully co-ordinated body in England to be devoted specifically to exploring and preserving the national heritage of the people's songs should have had a well-planned and carefully thought out programme for doing this. During the first half-dozen years of its existence, about a hundred folk-songs were collected, an annual average that was by any standards singularly unimpressive. The belief might indeed have been forgiven that, as had sometimes been claimed, the English had no folk-music.

The spread of elementary education, the development of communications through a complex railway system, and the flight from the land to the great industrial towns are often held to have well-nigh destroyed indigenous musical culture in England. There is some truth in this, though when in the fifties of the twentieth century a further revival of interest occurred in folk-song and folk-song collectors turned their attention to what are nowadays called urban folk-songs, they found that despite radio, the gramophone, and the influence of commercial popular music, the old tunes and the oral basis of their transmission were still very much alive. They simply needed to be sought out and recorded for posterity.

The widespread lack of interest in our folk-music among the intelligentsia may well have been due, at least in part, to the fact that the country's national pride was focused on our Empire and the growth of our industrial power. There was no pressure to use folk-music and folklore, raised to the level of the symphonic poem or the epic music-drama, as a focus for sentiments of national unity, national pride, or national independence from foreign rule. Handel had already provided such a focus with his Old Testament oratorios. Moreover, with Britain's immense commercial wealth and political power came the opportunity for foreign musicians to seek their fortune here, bringing their own styles, tastes, and traditions: the Victorian leisured classes could afford to pay for the best, even if flashy charlatans also got through the net. The music of the people was peripheral to English nineteenth-century social history in a way that it was not in Germany, Bohemia, Italy, or Russia; and the rather dilettantish, almost kid-glove approach of the early membership of the Folk Song Society seemed to reflect this. One of its members, indeed, when asked what he thought about folk-song, declared grandly (and, as it happened, with no little accuracy) that *he* wrote the folk-songs of this country. As his name was Edward Elgar, he might perhaps be forgiven the jibe.

Yet the small band of enthusiastic pioneers who had initiated the process of collecting English folk-songs must have had some inkling of the riches that lay waiting to be discovered, though as in so many aspects of English national life in the nineteenth century, social convention and taste had inhibited developments. This may not in itself have been a disadvantage: academically trained musicians of the Victorian era might well have 'tidied up' any tunes they collected. The early collectors, from Broadwood in 1843 onwards, had necessarily been amateur members of the leisured classes rather than busy academic musicians, the clergy, such as John Broadwood himself and Sabine Baring-Gould, playing a significant part. Broadwood had a keen enough ear to notice that the scales and cadences of some of the songs he collected were unusual. Playing the tunes over on his flute to his parish organist, he found that the latter wanted to 'correct' certain inflections in the tunes to bring them into line with the major/minor key system. Broadwood resisted stoutly: 'I *will* have it as my singer sang it', he would say. But even when confronted with the evidence of their own ears, trained musicians sometimes remained unconvinced. One gentleman distinguished more for his priggishness than for his insight even came out with the classic comment when shown folk-song transcriptions that they must be wrong: nobody was going to tell him that an uneducated singer sang correctly in the Dorian mode when, as often as not, even our trained musicians didn't know what the Dorian mode was. And Stanford once told RVW that it was nonsense to think that a flat seventh was a feature of English folk-songs since they all descended to their tonic anyway. Even J. A. Fuller-Maitland's harmonization of 'Dives and Lazarus' in *English County Songs*, the pioneer collection he published with Broadwood's niece Lucy in 1893, though simple, effective, and straightforward, still ignores the modal implications of the tune in favour of casting it in E minor.

In the year that RVW joined it, the Society's comfortable complacency was shattered by a declaration from Cecil Sharp, who had been interested in folk-song and folk-dance for a number of years. Sharp claimed that it was not the business of members just to sit around in London sagely discussing folk-songs. Their duty was to go out into the field and collect the songs before they died out altogether. He gave immediate point to his argument by publishing a large collection of songs that he had gathered orally in the West country. They were a surprise and a revelation; and it is often forgotten that the first of them had been collected only some three months before Mr Pottipher had sung 'Bushes and Briars' to RVW.

Vaughan Williams knew such collections as had been published of folk-songs and folk-carols from childhood onwards. He had made his first contact with English folk-songs through Stainer and Bramley's *Christmas Carols New and Old* and John Broadwood's *Sussex Songs*. He was also aware of the pioneer work of collectors such as Baring-Gould and Frank Kidson, which appeared in print during his late adolescence and early manhood. And he knew of course *English County Songs*. His lectures on the Folk-Song at Pokesdown, Gloucester, and Brentwood had been illustrated from the latter: Lucy Broadwood herself had sung the illustrations at one of the lectures, the topic being 'The Characteristics of National Songs in the British Isles'.

Yet it is important to remember that right from the start, even before he actually went into the field himself, RVW saw folk-song not as a thing apart, an end in itself, but as part of a much wider national musical culture that would have to change in many important respects if we were to justify the claim that we were a truly musical nation:

> When England has its municipal-aided music, so that every town of decent size possesses its own permanent orchestra as is the case in Germany, we shall have conductors of our own, and with increased musical activity our composers will grow. Until the good time comes, the protest against foreign music and foreign conductors is futile.[1]

Developing a national musical culture was not just a matter of collecting and cultivating picturesque rustic melodies: it was part of the organized fabric of civilized social life, supported from public funds and available to all, not just the rich.

Moreover, he explicitly stated on a number of occasions that folk-song rhapsodies and a folky idiom were not the foundations on which a healthy national musical stylistic tradition could be established. The fact that he cast his first folk-song compositions in this conventional form should occasion no surprise. He had not yet found his feet as a composer; and the colour that he gives them—winding, interwoven lines of imitative writing often featuring solo instruments in a chamber-music-like texture—seems to show that there were forces tugging in different directions in his work: his academic training, his feeling for folk-song as the musical force that could conjure up in the mind's ear the atmosphere evoked by the landscape where the folk-song had been

[1] UVW, p. 63.

collected, and the harmonic momentum that could be generated by a linear orchestral texture. He had not yet cast off the trappings of the late-romantic tradition in which he had been brought up.

In the controversy that ensued after Sharp threw down the gauntlet before his fellows, Vaughan Williams was one of Sharp's strongest supporters. His own collection of folk-songs, mainly carried out over a period of about ten years and covering many parts of the country, such as Northumberland, Cumberland, Yorkshire, Derbyshire, Herefordshire, East Anglia, and the Home Counties amounted to 810 songs. His first full year as a collector, 1904, also saw his largest haul, with a total of 234; and it is no surprise that he was interested primarily in the musical content of the songs, not in their texts. Because of this, and because he dressed the songs, as it has been claimed, for concert performance by arranging them for choirs, providing them with piano accompaniments, or incorporating them into his own compositions, his contribution to the re-discovery of English folk-music has been dismissed by some latter-day socio-musicologists as 'fake-song'. This misses the point completely. Vaughan Williams is rightly remembered as one of the great folk-song collectors. He was also proud of the fact that he was—sometimes disparagingly—referred to as a 'folky' composer. The fact that he appreciated the virtues of English folk music, that he studied it so thoroughly and absorbed its essence into his own music should not cause us to lose sight of the equally important fact that folk-song was the spring that finally released his true musical personality, not a substitute for genuine style and inspiration. What he gained from it was a tonal freedom and a melodic idiom that fertilized his own creative imagination; what he made of it was the creation of his own genius.

It has sometimes been argued that his conscious effort to fertilize his musical idiom with elements from folk-song was an anachronism. It is difficult to see why. For one thing, RVW's interest in folk-music was not confined to that of his native country. Several of his early arrangements are of French and German folk and traditional melodies. For another, one might with as much justification accuse Olivier Messiaen of being even more anachronistic because he explored the exciting potential of birdsong. What matters in any kind of art is not just the manner in which something is expressed, but the matter that it expresses. And that depends on the quality of imagination of the artist.

At this particular period of his life, RVW spent every scrap of free time collecting folk-songs. During 1904, for example, he was at Herongate and Ingrave in Essex on 22 February, and between 14 and 25 April he spent more time in the same area. The end of May found him at work nearer Leith Hill Place, at Leith Hill Farm, at Forest Green, at Horsham, and at Hollycombe. In mid-July and August, a visit to Yorkshire yielded sixteen songs; and at the end of August and in early September, he was busy in Wiltshire. Further forays in Sussex and Essex followed in October. The week round about Christmas was particularly fruitful: before Christmas, he collected forty-seven songs in Sussex from two of his most prolific sources: Harriet Verrall and Henry Burstow. And the New Year began with possibly his most celebrated expedition of all, from 7 to 14 January to the Norfolk coast, where a visit to King's Lynn, Tilney St Lawrence, Tilney All Saints, and Sheringham resulted in a haul of no fewer than seventy-nine songs and dance tunes.

The spring of 1905 also brought him his first introduction to writing for the stage, when, with Holst's help, he prepared and conducted incidental music, some of it based on folk material, for the first performance of Jonson's masque *Pan's Anniversary* at Bancroft Gardens in Stratford. It was during this period that three other factors besides folksong collecting helped him to re-think his musical style. The first was a deepening interest in the poetry of Walt Whitman and the ideas for which he stood. The second was the commission to edit a new hymnal for the Anglican Church. And the third came from within his own family.

In 1904 the suggestion arose that a local competitive festival should be held for the villages in the Leith Hill area on similar lines to those that had already been successfully established in the North of England at places such as Morecambe and at Spilsby in Lincolnshire, where RVW's cousin Stephen Massingberd's wife Margaret was the driving force. It was for Spilsby that RVW's Rossetti part-song 'Sound Sleep' was specially composed.

The initial impetus to the Leith Hill Festival itself was provided by Lady Farrer and RVW's sister Margaret; and it was thus natural that he should be invited to conduct the evening concert and coach the choirs in the combined music beforehand. The first Festival, restricted to country parishes with a population not exceeding 3,000, was held on 10 May 1905 and lasted one day; the competing choirs came from seven villages and were organized into five classes: Full Chorus; Male Voices; Female Voices; Madrigals; and SATB quartets. Choruses from *Judas Maccabaeus* were performed at the evening concert; and the test pieces reflected the taste of the times: two by Mendelssohn, one by Brahms, one by Edward German. The madrigal was Edwards's 'In going to my naked bed' (prudishly bowdlerized into 'my lonely bed', something which, one suspects, may have occasioned a quiet, wry smile from the conductor). The Festival went from strength to strength, expanding in 1912 to two days and some years later to four; and soloists of national distinction, including among many others Peter Pears, Heather Harper, Astra Desmond, and Hervey Alan, and regular accompanists of the calibre of Leslie Heward, Eric Harrison, Arnold Goldsborough, Michael Mullinar, and Eric Gritton were among the many involved over the years in the concerts that crowned each year's music-making. After the First World War, the Festival was revived in 1920. Frances Farrer remained as Secretary until 1939, when she was succeeded (on a temporary basis that was extended for many years) by Margery Cullen.

There can be little doubt that the success of the venture owed a great debt to the enthusiasm and energy of the conductor and to his ability to inspire hosts of helpers to give of their best. Vaughan Williams conducted every Festival until his retirement in 1953, the year after his eightieth birthday, never missing a concert and missing very few rehearsals. His dedication to every aspect of the job was legendary, from helping prepare the parts to ensuring that the musicians felt welcome, comfortable and well looked after, whether on or off the platform, taking special care that new players were personally welcomed when they arrived. He set up a Trust Fund to provide meals for the professionals engaged for the performances, so that when they came to the end of the rehearsal there was no need for them to spend time searching for a suitable restaurant or pub for food: it was provided free for them in the Martineau Hall. Equally legendary were his loyalty to his players and his combination of frankness and teasing charm when dealing with queries: the distinguished harpsichordist Ruth Dyson, who regularly performed among the second violins, later took over as continuo harpsichordist and was for twenty-five years honorary orchestral librarian to the Festival, wrote:

> One year I was rather astonished to find myself in the first violins, and almost imagined there might have been some administrative mistake, though this was unlikely since he always planned the orchestra very meticulously. On asking him the reason for my apparent promotion I got the following characteristic reply: 'You'd better have the horrible truth—I've only got six second violins this year, and *they've all got to be good.*'[2]

RVW's successor, Dr William Cole, comments that in those days:

> the orchestra was very large and my first impression was that it never played below *mf* and did not always play well, but it did not seem to matter. Any imperfection was not unduly noticeable because the performances as a whole were so interesting and alive.[3]

By 1931, the Festival was able to move to the newly-completed Dorking Halls, which enabled performances to be mounted of large-scale choral works, such as Bach's *St Matthew Passion*, Brahms's *German Requiem* (of which RVW steadfastly refused to perform the fifth movement), and Elgar's *Dream of Gerontius*, which was broadcast on the BBC National Programme not long after the composer's death. *Gerontius* was a work RVW had always regarded as one of the major masterpieces of English choral music; his shrewd and appreciative comments on Elgar's orchestration and choral writing are evident from his

[2] Quoted from *The Leith Hill Music Festival: A Centenary Tribute*, ed. Barbara Yates Rothwell (Prologue Promotions, 1972).
[3] Ibid.

contribution to a memorial tribute to Elgar republished in the 1986 edition of *National Music and Other Essays*.

As the festival captured the local imagination, Dorking swarmed at festival time with singers bearing music and wearing rosettes, almost like football supporters. The choirs suffered the same worries as football teams, too: the Festival was competitive and there were fears of relegation or excitement about the prospect of promotion,—lightened by such occasions as when one gentleman of the chorus was so uplifted by the music that at the end he walked blindly out of a conductors' conference into the Farrers' fishpond and 'returned like a dripping merman to be clothed anew in someone else's trousers'. Or the misplaced loyalty of the chorus bass in one of the choirs who proudly informed his conductor that 'the Doctor took it all rather quicker than you, but I sang it at your pace all the way through'.

Leith Hill has never been and never set out to be a proto-Aldeburgh. The aims of the two festivals were quite different. But in its own way, it has provided music for a local community that has involved local performers and population, fostered a love and appreciation of music and developed a sense of community involvement in music and music-making. And, of course, it provided RVW with a platform for some of his most attractive *Gebrauchsmusik*.

The English Hymnal commission came as a bolt from the blue. He was at work in his study in his Barton Street house when a clergyman announced simply as 'Mr Dearmer' walked in and asked him to edit a new hymn-book, claiming that it would involve about two months' work. To Vaughan Williams's protests that he knew nothing about hymn-books, Dearmer replied that he had been recommended as musical editor by Cecil Sharp and Canon Scott Holland. This inclined him to accept; and he was finally won over when Dearmer shrewdly mentioned that if he refused, a musician with whose musical sympathies he emphatically did not agree, H. Walford Davies, would be approached.

The two people who so strongly recommended RVW for the job must have known that he was an atheist. But they must also have known that in other respects he was very much in sympathy with the kind of hymn-book the compilers had in mind, one that would restore clarity of language and a simple, vigorous musical style cleansed of chromatic clichés and would reflect the down-to-earth, socially-minded, humanistic High Church Christianity of the compilers. Percy Dearmer was an admirer of the Christian Socialist Charles Gore. At the time of his encounter with Vaughan Williams, Dearmer was secretary to the London Branch of the Christian Social Union. He and the other seven clerics who were compiling the book were dissatisfied with the layout, the theology, the social bias, the literary style, and the music of the revised edition of *Hymns Ancient and Modern* that appeared in 1904. At first, they had intended only to redress the balance with a supplement to that book; but they soon found that they had enough material for a complete hymn-book, eventually to be entitled *The English Hymnal*. Vaughan Williams found that the work took him two years and cost him £250 out of his own pocket (a tidy sum in the early twentieth century: Dearmer had somewhat ingenuously calculated—or perhaps disingenuously claimed—that it would cost him about £5 in expenses).

Vaughan Williams had here found an opportunity to improve musical standards at large in an area where many people were exposed to functional music who might never attend a concert or an opera performance in their lives; and he seized it with both hands. Despite the book's eventual title, he cast his net wide, taking in not only English tunes old, traditional, and modern, but raiding French, German, Welsh, Scottish, Swiss, Irish, Finnish, Hebrew, Italian, American, and Scandinavian sources. He re-introduced plainsong melodies, freeing them from metrical strait-jackets by ensuring that they were provided with free, flexible accompaniments. He persuaded friends like Holst, Martin Shaw, Nicholas Gatty, and John Ireland to contribute melodies. He slipped the chorale from Act I of *Die Meistersinger* in to fit the words of Thomas Parnell's 'Holy Jesus! God of Love!' and adapted a melody from *Parsifal* to fit the English translation 'O King Most High of Earth and Sky' of the seventeenth-century Ascension Day processional 'Supreme Rector caelitum'. He incorporated arrangements of sixteen of the splendid folktunes that he had collected on his various expeditions, naming most of them after the places where he had first encountered them. They included 'Monk's Gate', set to the discreetly watered-down version of Bunyan's sturdy Pilgrim's Hymn favoured by the compilers, 'King's Lynn', set to Chesterton's 'O God of Earth and Altar', and 'Forest Green', for 'O Little Town of Bethlehem', tunes which have become so popular as to need no introduction even to those who cannot put a name to them. And, perhaps most important of all, he recovered for liturgical use the magnificent Phrygian Mode Melody by Thomas Tallis that was to inspire him to one of his finest works.

Vaughan Williams was quite clear why he included these tunes. In 1956, the year of the hymnal's golden jubilee, by which time it had sold over five million copies, he remarked: 'Why should we not enter into our inheritance in the church as well as the concert room?' He might have gone further and quoted General William Booth: 'Why should the devil have all the good tunes?' but for the fact that it would have entailed associating his traditional folk-singers with the works of the devil. He also contributed four tunes of his own, increased to seven in the 1933 edition, attributing them to an anonymous composer. Two of these, the magnificent striding processional *Sine Nomine*, to Waltham Howe's 'For all the Saints' and the gently serene 'Down Ampney', for R. F. Littledale's translation of Bianco da Siena's Italian original ('Come down, O love divine') have become classics in their own right.

The lease on Barton Street having expired, Adeline and RVW had been living since 1 November 1905 at 13 Cheyne Walk, which was to be their home for some twenty years, and from where Adeline could easily visit her mother, who had moved to Chelsea. The new house also had the advantage of a fine view of the Thames and a small garden. The move came at a time when RVW was going through one of his several periods of self-doubt. This can hardly have been because concert-givers were fighting shy of putting on his works. In March 1904 alone, for example, his *Symphonic Rhapsody* was performed by the Bournemouth Municipal Orchestra; his three German folk-song arrangements 'Adieu', 'Think of Me', and 'Cousin Michael' were sung at the Steinway Hall, and his orchestral *Heroic Elegy and Triumphal Epilogue* was performed, where and when, we do not know, on 11 March. His folk-song-collecting expeditions, as we have seen, were bearing much fruit. In May 1906, the Journal of the Folk Song Society published sixty-one of the tunes he had collected; and a month's holiday at Meldreth in Cambridgeshire in July and August 1906 increased the tally by a further twenty-three from singers in Meldreth and nearby villages. He had finished a setting of Whitman's 'Toward the Unknown Region' that he dedicated to Adeline's sister Florence Maitland and used as a memorial tribute to her husband Fred, who had died at Las Palmas in December 1906. It proved to be the first of a long series of highly characteristic and highly successful Whitman settings; and it was well received at the 1907 Leeds Festival.

RVW owed his introduction to the poetry of Walt Whitman to a Trinity College contemporary, Bertrand Russell. It was some time before he came to grips with it as a source of inspiration and musical self-expression; but Whitman was a poet whose appeal never faded. It was not just the sentiments that Whitman expressed that found favour with RVW; the form of his poetry, with its metrical and rhythmic freedom, its exuberance and its energy stimulated him to develop a deeper and more ambitious approach to composition in general. The Wanderer of the Robert Louis Stevenson settings and the aesthete of the pre-Raphaelite ones had now found a poet whose verse enabled him to combine the outdoor strength of the one with the lyric introspection of the other; and the search for a suitable way of expressing in music the inner core of Whitman's thoughts and sentiments were a liberating challenge to which he was able to rise triumphantly in works like *Toward the Unknown Region* and, above all, *A Sea Symphony*.

He had now decided what his music needed. It was more colour, lightness, and air: a touch of French polish, as he himself put it. Various possibilities were suggested to him; he chose to go and work with Maurice Ravel. It was one of the most influential decisions that he ever made; and one of the shrewdest. In December 1907, he went off to Paris for three months and took rooms in the small Hôtel de l'Univers et du Portugal (a strange agglomeration of titles).

Ravel was three years younger than his new pupil, and the contrast between the two men could hardly have been more marked. RVW was tall, solidly built, and by now seems to have abandoned the slightly dandified appearance of his earlier years and acquired a somewhat tousled air. Ravel was tiny, neat, and elegant, yet, as RVW later discovered when providing him hospitality in England, remarkably sympathetic to many aspects of English life and even English food, such as steak and kidney pudding. RVW's musical development had been marked by the strongly teutonic bias of English late-Victorian academic musical training. Ravel, like his pupil, was open to new influences from Russia and of course from his contemporary Debussy. The new influences covered all aspects of musical style, especially scoring and harmonic procedures. The opening of RVW's musical horizons to these new approaches under a teacher who admired and encouraged him was just what he needed. And, as usual, he absorbed what he needed from the new impressionistic style of composing without ever becoming a fully-fledged impressionist composer: 'the first of my pupils who didn't simply write my music', as Ravel put it. He was careful, however, to hedge his bets by commenting that although RVW might have profited from his studies with him, on returning to England, he would find 'Sir Parry' or 'Sir Elgar' waiting for him on the quay, and then . . . The sentence was finished with a typically expressive Gallic shrug of the shoulders.

RVW's first encounter with Ravel on Friday 13 December 1907—certainly a case of the 'lucky thirteenth' as far as RVW was concerned—demonstrates how firm the usually so diffident young man could be when it was necessary. He showed his new teacher some of his work and was asked to go away and write 'un petit menuet dans le style de Mozart'. Vaughan Williams proceeded to tell Ravel in his best French (which was fluent and cogent: there had been a much-liked if sometimes histrionic French maid at Leith Hill Place and there are accounts of him holding forth in French Society debates at Charterhouse) that that was precisely what he was *not* going to do. He studied mainly orchestration with Ravel, taking four or five lessons a week and scoring piano pieces by mainly Russian composers new to him. Ravel was shocked to find that he had no piano in his rooms with which to invent new harmonies, but Vaughan Williams was quite capable of using old harmonies in a completely original context, as his work was soon to show. What he did learn from Ravel was how to let flecks of colour and subtle changes of light into his scoring (the results are seen at their most effective in works like the *London* and *Pastoral* symphonies) and, above all, that he had not, as he feared, reached a dead end in composition. Ravel's own motto, 'complexe, mais pas compliqué' was carefully remembered, even if not invariably followed.

RVW returned to England in March 1908 and resumed his activities as a conductor, adjudicator, and folk-song collector, in addition to going to Cambridge in June to conduct *Toward the Unknown Region*. A new friendship arose out of a folk-song collecting expedition in Hereford that July, when he accompanied Ella Leather, the wife of a Weobley solicitor and a distinguished amateur local historian in her own right. Mrs Leather had discovered a number of traditional singers when hop-picking in the fields; and the harvest they gathered was rich in music as well as hops. RVW incorporated many of the tunes in *The Oxford Book of Carols* nearly twenty years later. He found a further outlet for his energies and enthusiasm when Gustav Holst, who had been appointed Musical Director at Morley College in South-East London, asked RVW to give a course of extension lectures on the theme 'From Haydn to Wagner', the music having been requested by the students themselves.

Composition was not neglected, however. A number of songs was written this year as well as the delightful String Quartet that quite erroneously caused a friend to remark that he had been having tea with Debussy. There is certainly a new harmonic freedom and a lightness of texture about this work as well as a melodic charm that makes one regret that he did not publish more music in this medium; and gramophone companies sometimes acknowledge its mild indebtedness to Ravel's teaching by coupling it with Ravel's own essay in the form. The real first result of his time spent with Ravel, however, can be heard in the Housman song-cycle *On Wenlock Edge*, which reached performance on 15 November 1909, a week after the Quartet had done so. Vaughan Williams's choice of texts was changing markedly in emphasis. A harder, bleaker realistic pessimism on the one hand and an aspiring agnostic idealism were gradually supplanting the scented lyricism and half-nostalgic, half-escapist *Wanderlust* of some of his earlier choices of text. With this came the first signs of full stylistic maturity, which is not to say that he had reached the end of his 'apprentice' period: there were more experiences to be gone through and absorbed yet. But it does mean that the trappings of post-romanticism were being discarded in favour of a tougher and more sharply-etched idiom.

It was during April 1909 that Ravel accepted an invitation from his pupil to visit London. He enjoyed his stay. RVW and Adeline proved to be perfect hosts even though Adeline had been seriously ill with influenza not long before his visit. He even enjoyed English food, despite the fact, as RVW had discovered in Paris, that he took the subject of food very seriously. RVW accompanied him to what he called 'Vallasse', rightly construing this as meaning the Wallace Collection. A busy summer followed, including a visit to Woodhall Spa to try and ease the pain that Adeline's developing arthritis was causing her; and on 28 September they both attended the first (and only) Festival held by the newly-established Musical League. All the great names in English music, including Elgar, Delius, Bantock, and Arnold Bax, were associated with this venture, but it failed to attract either notice or support and collapsed in obscurity. The work of RVW's that came up for performance was his early Rossetti cantata *Willow Wood*, which had lain unperformed since 1903 and was composed in a style that he had by now outgrown. Much more characteristic of his mature style was the delightful incidental music composed for a performance of Aristophanes' *The Wasps* at Cambridge on 26 November. It was a success from the start and he soon extracted a concert suite from it.

The horizon, it seemed, was gradually brightening for the English composer. The renaissance of English music had involved a renaissance of English orchestral playing and the rise to fame of conductors who not only performed English works, but performed them with sympathy and care, such as Thomas Beecham and Henry Wood, the latter of whom Vaughan Williams and Holst particularly admired. And at Christ Church Oxford, an undergraduate was acquiring a reputation as a thoughtful and serious young musician who was already bent on becoming an orchestral conductor at this early stage of his career. He was to become one of the most sympathetic interpreters of RVW's music throughout his life, as he was of the music of Elgar, Holst, and William Walton. His name was Adrian Boult.

In 1910, two major works of RVW's had their first festival performances, one of which is a *sine qua non* of any anthology CD of his music and has gone into the repertory of many of the great orchestras in Britain and the United States. When editing *The English Hymnal*, RVW had come across Thomas Tallis's great tune that he set to Addison's hymn 'When rising from the bed of death'; now admiration developed into inspiration and he used it as the basis of a fantasy for double string orchestra. It was performed at the Three Choirs Festival on 6 September under the thirty-seven-year-old composer-conductor, who looked, as Herbert Howells wrote nearly half a century later: 'magisterial, dark-haired, clear-cut of feature; a physically magnified version of the then Sir Edward Grey. . . . Two thousand people were in Gloucester Cathedral that night, primarily to hear *Gerontius*. But there at the rostrum towered the unfamiliar magnificent figure. He and a strangely new work for strings were between them and their devotion to Elgar.'[4]

There is nothing sensationally original about the *Fantasia on a Theme by Thomas Tallis* of the kind that might have been invented by Ravel, or even by RVW himself, on a keyboard. Yet it is unquestionably the first work by Vaughan Williams that is recognizably and unmistakably his and no one else's. The influences have all been absorbed and fused into a rich, warm, and powerful style. The textures, whether tenuous or full, have a radiance that was new even in a tradition that had recently absorbed such fine works for strings as Elgar's *Introduction and Allegro*; the craftsmanship and the uniquely convincing form of the piece were as

---

[4] Obituary, *The Sunday Times*, 31 August 1958.

old as the Elizabethan and Jacobean fantasias that RVW knew so well, yet as new and as fresh today as they were when the solemnly passionate piece was presented to that first audience. It probably did not occur to many of them that in *Gerontius* and the *Fantasia* they were listening to two of the finest manifestations of the English musical renaissance, works of which any country with a rich musical tradition could be proud.

At Leeds, a month later, on 12 October, his thirty-eighth birthday, RVW conducted the first performance of his *Sea Symphony*, whose long gestation of some seven years perhaps shows in a lack of coherence in the finale and some uneven writing elsewhere. None the less, Hubert Parry was right to note in his diary that it was 'big stuff—with some impertinences'. It is, of course, the 'impertinences' that are the most original and characteristic parts of the work to a modern listener.

Holst's galvanizing energy had made Morley College a centre of the revival of English music; and RVW was delighted to be involved in the first performance of Purcell's *Fairy Queen* since the seventeenth century, the manuscript having been rediscovered in 1910. It was mounted by the College at the Victoria Hall, and RVW acted as the link-man between the numbers. It was at about this time, too, that he got to know a number of personalities in the dance world beyond that of Folk Dance, where he had been elected a committee member of the Folk Dance Society in 1911. He was more captivated by Isadora Duncan and her style of dancing than the tradition represented by the Russian ballet, which at this time was bringing forward the early Stravinsky ballets and dazzling western audiences with the skill and elegance of such dancers as Nijinsky. A project whereby RVW might have composed a score for Diaghilev foundered because no agreement could be reached about whether the score or the scenario (by Gordon Craig) should come first.

The idea of writing for the operatic stage now began to arouse his interest. He had wanted for some time to tackle an operatic subject; he wanted it to be a truly 'English' one and to include an on-stage prize-fight. Harold Child of *The Times* became his librettist, and RVW began work on the opera in the summer of 1911 when on holiday with Adeline at Freshwater in the Isle of Wight. Considering that *Hugh the Drover* was the first venture both of librettist and composer into the field of opera, it is remarkable how successfully it turned out, despite its undoubted shortcomings. Had there been a more consistent tradition of writing for the 'serious' musical stage, with skilled writers who knew how to construct a libretto, pace the action, and vary the verse rhythmically, the story of English opera might have been very different. Walton and even Britten were to experience similar difficulties with their librettists when they came to the task of operatic composition. *Hugh the Drover* was not to see the stage until the mid-twenties, but much of the work on it was done sporadically in the years immediately before the First World War.

Other works, some to commissions, took precedence. The *Five Mystical Songs* were performed at the 1911 Three Choirs Festival. The *Fantasia on Christmas Carols* followed in 1912, the year in which he was first invited to arrange and conduct the incidental music for F. R. Benson's season at Stratford-upon-Avon. He followed up his Quartet with a Phantasy Quintet composed at the request of William Cobbett, who did so much to encourage the development of modern English chamber music. He worked on a wide range of folk-song arrangements for schools and other bodies. The most striking and elaborate of these is certainly the set of *Five English Folk Songs* published in 1913. But the most important of the new works that came to performance in these years is the one that shows most emphatically how well he had absorbed the lessons from Ravel while remaining his own highly personal self. This was *A London Symphony*, which was first performed at Queen's Hall on 17 March 1914 under Geoffrey Toye.

The idea of composing a symphony was suggested to him by George Butterworth, a gifted young musician some thirteen years younger than RVW, who had been a scholar at Eton and, after finishing his studies at Oxford had been a journalist, public-school master, and student at the RCM, where he had abandoned his course in favour of collecting folk-songs in Sussex. Vaughan Williams was already working on a large orchestral tone-poem with London as its subject—perhaps a cockney counterblast to Delius's *Paris* and an investigation into more sombre aspects of London than the cheerful, brilliant surface of Elgar's *Cockaigne*. He re-cast his ideas in the form of a four-movement work and took the first night audience by storm.

His reputation was growing in France, where Marcel Xavier Boulestin had warmly praised his work in the January 1913 issue of *La Revue Musicale* and where *On Wenlock Edge* was, according to Ravel, a revelation at its first public performance. True to his beliefs, he had found himself as an Englishman and was now attracting attention elsewhere. More traditionally-inclined critics such as Ernest Newman were not impressed. Newman observed tartly in the *Birmingham Daily Post* on 16 February 1914: 'The truth simply is that M. Boulestin is insensitive to the greater English music [whose?] because it is not French, and he prefers some of the minor English music because it coquets with the modern French idiom.' As Newman himself said in the same article: We live and learn! Or rather, most of the critics did.

How little Newman understood what Vaughan Williams was trying to do as a composer can be seen by comparing this comment with Vaughan Williams's own in his article 'Who wants the English Composer?' published in No. 1 of Vol. ix (1912) of the *RCM Magazine*. Its main point was that music alone of the arts was judged by standards which severed its connection with everyday life, and that as long as British composers continued to base their work on these artificial standards, they would remain unwanted and unready:

> We English composers are always saying, 'Here are Wagner, Brahms, Grieg, Tchaikovsky, what fine fellows they are, let us try and do something like this at home', quite forgetting that the result will not sound at all like 'this' when transplanted from its natural soil. It is all very well to catch at the prophet's robe, but the mantle of Elijah is apt, like all second-hand clothing, to prove the worst of misfits.

He recommended 'cultivating a sense of musical citizenship', urging composers to live with their fellows and make their art an expression of the life of the whole community. This meant sharing the community's experiences for good or ill; and it was not very long before he was to be presented with an opportunity to do this in the most drastic manner possible. On 4 August 1914, war was declared on Germany, and Vaughan Williams, like the heroes in many of the folk-songs he loved so much, felt it his duty to 'go for a soldier'.

4

Gone for a soldier (1914–18)

The call to arms in August 1914 was immediately answered by a flood of volunteers from all social classes. Many people thought that it would 'all be over by Christmas'; others thought in terms of a war lasting at least three years and called for volunteers to create for the first time in Britain's history a large-scale citizen army. For whatever reasons, the romantic sense of high-minded adventure, the feeling of taking part in a crusade, simple patriotism, or a sense of civic duty, thousands of young men enlisted, many of them the cream of the country's intelligentsia. This war, it turned out, was the first totally industrial and mechanized war in the history of the world; when it began, few can have foreseen the carnage that it would involve.

The effect on English musical life was profound. There was a sad feeling in many quarters that in some way the Germans had let down not merely their friends and admirers in Britain, but their own noble and high-minded heritage. It seemed impossible that the culture that had produced Beethoven, Schumann, Mendelssohn, and Brahms could be the same as that which unleashed the terrors of chemical and unrestricted submarine warfare. The understandable anti-German reaction in some cases reached almost hysterical proportions: the complete banning of German music was advocated by some misguided patriots. Sir Thomas Beecham relates how, when a rich financier threatened to boycott some of his performances involving German compositions, he pointed out that the gentleman possessed some fine German paintings. If he would destroy them, then he, Beecham, would agree to ban German music from his programmes. Stanford composed a fierce anthem, 'O Lord, arise!' calling upon God to destroy his enemies, in which the energetic organ part sounds distinctly like a sardonic perversion of the 'Ride of the Valkyries'. Even Hubert Parry, perhaps with a slight sense of guilt, discovered merits in French and Russian music where before he had found few and confessed to having sailed rather too closely to the Teutonic bank of the stream of musical progress.

Concert life continued, though on a reduced scale and with a considerably higher proportion of charity concerts in aid of countries over-run by the Central Powers and the refugees from them, or of the armed services of the crown. Music by British composers featured more prominently in concert programmes, though any long-term permanent effect on concert audiences seems to have been limited. Composers produced works that reflected both their desire to provide some kind of escape from wartime austerity and horror, or else to reflect their national pride and their human sadness. Elgar, for example, did both. A comparison between *The Starlight Express* and *For the Fallen* demonstrates the duality (which is not of course the same thing as ambivalence) of his feelings about the war; but the elegiac nature of the last chamber works and the Cello Concerto is surely a stronger clue to his deepest sentiments about the passing of the old way of life that it entailed.

The middle and younger generation of composers were caught in a conflict between their art and their patriotism. Some, like Frank Bridge, were pacifists and horrified by what they felt was misguided and unnecessary destruction of human life and values. Others felt that they had a duty to help shoulder the burden of the conflict by enlisting. Among those who volunteered were George Butterworth, F. B. Ellis, Geoffrey Toye, and RVW's future brother-in-law R. O. Morris, who was to marry Adeline's elder sister Emmie in February 1915. All of them were under thirty. RVW was over forty, yet he soon decided what he ought to do.

The day after the outbreak of war, RVW and Adeline had gone to stay at Margate with RVW's mother. Military service was not the only way of course in which musicians could put themselves rather than their art at the disposal of their country. Elgar, then fifty-seven years of age, volunteered for the Special Constabulary; and when RVW returned to London with Adeline later in the month, he followed suit, soon being promoted Sergeant. But this was only a stop-gap. Before very long, he volunteered for Army service in the Royal Army Medical Corps, joining a Territorial Army unit, the 2/4 Field Ambulance.

Many people must have been slightly puzzled by the apparent quixotry which impelled him to enlist. He would in no way have been eligible for any form of compulsory military service. Conscription was not introduced to fill the ranks of Britain's armed forces until 1916 and even then the upper age limit was 41. Vaughan Williams was only a few weeks off his forty-second birthday when he volunteered, so there would have been no question of his call-up even then. Hubert Parry's reaction must have been fairly typical of what many of his acquaintances and colleagues thought. It was not noticeably sympathetic. Early in the new year, he expressed his sentiments forthrightly and forcefully:

As to your enlisting, I can't express myself in any way that is likely to be serviceable. There are certain individuals who are capable of serving their country in certain very exceptional and very valuable ways, and they are not on the same footing as ordinary folks, who if they are exterminated are just one individual gone and no more. You have already served your country in very notable and exceptional ways and are likely to do so again: and such folks should be shielded from risk rather than exposed to it. We may admit the generosity of the impulse and feel—I will not say what.[1]

All that can be said by way of comment was that RVW always had a strong sense of personal and professional duty. The RAMC was a regiment whose professional aim was to heal wounds and to save life, friend and foe alike, not to slaughter and destroy. He and Adeline had no children, nor were they likely to have, since she was two years older than he; and he must have felt that by volunteering for service in the medical arm, he could serve his country's cause at the risk of his own life without any thought of taking the lives of others.

To begin with, however, he was in no great danger of featuring in one of the casualty lists that were already growing alarmingly as the opposing armies settled down to the war of attrition in the trenches. On account of his flat feet, he had been found fit for duty only as a waggon orderly; he now found that there were as yet no waggons. His first billet was near home—the Duke of York's HQ at Chelsea, after which, on 1 January 1915, the unit was posted to Dorking: again a stroke of good fortune, as it was not far from Leith Hill Place. RVW was a conscientious soldier, though he can hardly have been considered a smart one. Tall enough to have been a guardsman, his broad shoulders and his flat feet precluded him from either looking or moving like one. He was always in trouble with his puttees and invariably required assistance when expected to dress in a smart and soldierly manner. To some of the wags of the unit he was the object of some mirth whilst under training, yet, as was invariably the case in all human contacts with him, his frankness, his sincerity and his self-deprecating humility caused him to be respected at the same time.

Because there was still no sign of the much-needed waggons and the horses to draw them, the unit's training at Dorking during a very severe winter involved long route marches and stretcher drill up the slopes of Box Hill. On one occasion they had waited at Epsom for two hours in heavily falling snow to be inspected by Field Marshal Lord Kitchener, who practically alone amongst the British high command had realized that the war would be a long one and had called for an army of three million men. It is most unlikely that he realized that one of his country's leading musicians was on parade before him that day.

One compensation of this posting was that it was easy for Vaughan Williams to visit his family on short leave passes or for Adeline to visit him. Adeline also found a place and a post at Cheyne Walk for the young wife of a refugee Belgian miner, who was grateful to live in a household where French was understood and spoken. RVW in the meanwhile was making (and in some cases lifelong) friendships with

---

[1] UVW, p. 117.

members of his unit from backgrounds totally different from his own. Among these was Harry Steggles, more than twenty years younger than RVW, who played the mouth organ well and helped him with the more problematic aspects of military dress and the care of equipment. They teamed up as a kind of music-hall duo, with Harry singing popular music-hall songs and RVW accompanying him on the piano. Their party piece, much called for, was a version of 'When Father Papered the Parlour', which must surely have raised a wry and sympathetic smile from the accompanist. RVW also played the organ occasionally at the garrison services, amusing Harry, who often blew the organ for him and instantly recognized when he was improvising a voluntary on music-hall favourites such as 'Make your mind up, Maggie MacKenzie' as the unit was filing solemnly into the church. If challenged, RVW would almost certainly have protested that this was in no way different in principle from Bach's adaptation of secular melodies as fugue subjects. As a case in point, he might even have cited the Great G minor Fugue, which is said to be based on a Dutch folk-song, but it also shows the same irreverent wit as the trick he played on Stanford by writing modal waltzes or his ribald childhood adaptation of 'Hold the Fort'. It must surely have had an element of tongue-in-cheek about it, however sincerely he could have reconciled it with his precept of giving the people back their music.

In April 1915, the unit moved to Watford, where he heard from Ravel, who was serving in a French artillery regiment pending what he hoped would be a transfer to the Air Force. In May, the Unit was posted to Saffron Walden, where he was able to practise on the organ in the magnificent perpendicular church. During this posting, he and Harry, together with another Private who had sung at the Palladium in peacetime days, became friendly with a Bishop's Stortford family called Machray. The Machrays had a lively interest in music; and on Sunday evenings, there was regular music-making. Mr Machray played the viola, sometimes lending his instrument to RVW, one of his sons the trumpet, two others, one of whom was in RVW's unit, the clarinet, one daughter the violin and another the piano. Harry contributed by singing, playing his mouth organ and improvising a jazz-drummer's outfit from flower-pots, fire-irons and a drum borrowed from the unit band. The music naturally covered a wide range of styles, but RVW made sure that he introduced his hosts to Morris and country dance tunes.

The next move was to Sutton Veny, near Warminster on Salisbury Plain; and on 22 June 1916, the unit sailed for France. They took up quarters in outhouses round a large country house at Ecoivres, where a field dressing station had been established. Ecoivres was close to the front near Beaumont Hamel, where so much bitter fighting was to take place during that summer and autumn. They had barely settled in when the ten-day barrage began that was to prelude the disastrous British attack on 1 July, an attack that cost Kitchener's new army some 60,000 casualties on the first day of fighting alone. RVW wrote to Holst: 'all parades and such things cease. I am "waggon orderly" and go up the line every night to bring back wounded and sick in a motor ambulance'.[2] He must have had to deal with hundreds of them; and as the course of the battle unrolled, the work of the RAMC must have been grim and relentless. It was here, he told his second wife Ursula in later years, that what was to become *Pastoral Symphony* began to incubate in his mind, as he went up night after night to bring in the wounded. The combination of a wonderful Corot-like desolate landscape in the sunset, the terrible, perhaps meaningless suffering that the soldiers in the line were enduring, the fact that, to quote Harry Steggles 'He was more at peace with himself in the fighting areas for we were getting on with the war, not forming fours in squad drill.'[3] Even the chance occurrence of a bugler practising and hitting the seventh of the scale instead of the octave, all contributed in the long run to the fabric of what was to become one of his most personal, most thoughtful, and most misunderstood works. Harry continued: 'The trenches held no terrors for him—on the contrary, he was thrilled one day when he was allowed a peep at the German front line trenches.' If ever there was a case of emotion recollected in tranquillity, it was *Pastoral Symphony*.

Music-making was not neglected. He had formed a choir in the unit at Saffron Walden; and they continued to practise whenever possible, even so close to the front, though their duties and the fatigue parties that are an inevitable part of clearing up when the action is over took up much of their spare time.

The year 1916 was one of great personal losses for RVW, as it was for hundreds of thousands of others. Adeline's brother Charles was killed at the Battle of Jutland; F. B. Ellis and George Butterworth were killed in action. This was a particularly severe blow for RVW. He wrote to Holst:

I sometimes dread coming back to normal life with so many gaps—especially of course George Butterworth. . . . I sometimes think now that it is wrong to have made friends with people so much younger than oneself—because soon there will be only the middle-aged left—& I have got out of touch with most of my contemporary friends—but then there is always you & thank Heaven we have never got out of touch & I don't see why we ever should.[4]

In the autumn, the unit was moved; it was rumoured that they were to move even closer to the main Somme battlefield. They marched south-eastward to Longpré-les-corps-saints, where they were loaded into cattle-trucks for a long rail journey to Marseilles. Here, they took ship for Salonika.

RVW enjoyed the sea-voyage: the weather was calm and warm and the unit proceeded unharmed first to Dudular and then to Vromeri,

---

[2] UVW, p. 120.   [3] *RCM Magazine*, p. 22.   [4] Ibid., p. 16.

where they were stationed in a sector of the front where the allies were expecting an attack. They lived on a hillside near Katerini that over-looked the Pelikas Valley, dominated by Mount Olympus, in bivouacs that were somewhat smaller than a double bed. These makeshift abodes had neither doors nor windows. The entrances were hung with old sacks or groundsheets, which afforded the occupants little comfort but ample ventilation, something that on the cold, cloudless December nights they could well have done without. They were usually heated by means of primitive stoves improvised out of old oil-drums, mud, stones or bricks, fed with tree-roots or charcoal. Into such a 'bivvy' RVW and Harry packed all their worldly goods, among which were the indispensable Isaiah and Jeremiah, two empty pineapple tins filled with charcoal, so christened by RVW. The procedure for warming the 'bivvy' was sim-plicity itself. They would light Isaiah and Jeremiah and swing them vig-orously around outside until they were sufficiently alight to rush into the 'bivvy', all air intakes sealed up as far as possible and sit by them in moderate discomfort: 'I think we slept more from our rum ration plus carbon monoxide from Isaiah and Jeremiah than fatigue,' commented Harry Steggles over forty years later. The discomforts of such an exis-tence had their compensations. There were wine shops in Katerini; and RVW and Harry tried their wares without acquiring much of a taste for resinated wine. They also watched Greek soldiers doing their folk-dances. RVW took down the tune, but seems not to have made any fur-ther use of it. On Christmas Eve, on a clear, starlit night, against the picturesque backcloth of Mount Olympus, RVW conducted his choir in a carol-singing session that included some of the carols he had collected in earlier days.

The unit was moved to the Dojran sector, on the Serbian border, the scene of heavy fighting, where the British positions were completely overlooked by a strongly-entrenched enemy; and RVW took advantage of his musical knowledge to breach security regulations in a rather novel manner, informing Adeline on a postcard where he was by writing out a Dorian scale on it. Despite the military action, the unit could be found little to keep them occupied other than anti-mosquito precautions, fill-ing in puddles. This at any rate was useful even if boring; and RVW did not object to doing it, but when they were reduced to such activities as washing red bricks to be laid out in the form of a cross in order to ward off German air attacks, he felt that enough was enough. 'I will do any-thing to contribute to the war,' he said, 'but this I will *not* do', so he volunteered for training as an officer in a combatant regiment: the Royal Garrison Artillery, the heavy branch of the Royal Artillery that in those days handled the large permanently-mounted siege guns and howitzers rather than the lighter and more mobile field guns. He was told to return to England and report to the War Office for further instructions. This was apparently the result of a message given to a staff officer who had been enjoined to 'do something about Vaughan Williams' and had repeated the phrase when lying semi-conscious after being thrown by his horse. The powers that were did indeed 'do something about Vaughan Williams'. On arrival in England, he was rushed to London and told of his new posting.

During his final three weeks in Salonika, in June 1917, he was engaged on latrine fatigues at Summerhill Camp, a very unpopular transit camp some six miles from the town of Salonika itself. This unpleasant duty was the lot of all potential officers awaiting posting back to England; and it was better not to complain about it, as anyone rash enough to do so was instantly returned to his unit. Even though this particular duty was more or less inevitable, RVW could, had he so wished, have avoided the others. Members of concert parties (there were two of these, the *Roosters* and the *Barnstormers*, either of which he could almost certainly have joined) were excused fatigues. So were those in the divisional theatre group. His reason for not joining any of these was that he felt with his usual diffidence that they were managing very well and that his participation could not possibly have improved their standard of performance.

Nobody could ever accuse him of shirking unpleasant tasks. Nor could anyone accuse him of conforming too closely to military conventions. He detested the standard army phrase 'officers and men', for example; and when leaving the Medical Corps for his Gunner course, he had caustically informed the officers of his unit, standing stiffly to attention before them, that his greatest regret was that on leaving it, he would cease to be a man on becoming an officer. A similar comment resulted from his observation on the voyage back to England that the officers and the nurses were cordoned off from the 'common herd' of other ranks and occupying the fore part of the ship.

His gunner training began in August 1917 when he was sent on No. 32 Siege Course at No. 2 RGA Officer Cadet School at Maresfield Park, near Uckfield in Sussex. Once again, he was much older than most of his fellow cadets; and once again the problems of correct military dress irritated him. He wrote to Holst mentioning the stupidity of wearing white gloves on ceremonial parades in the middle of a war. Parry had written to him when he was still in Salonika with encouraging news of the public's reception of *A Sea Symphony* at a Bach Choir Naval concert at Queen's Hall and wondering whether he might be able to extract something from his war experiences. And—perhaps the best news of all from a personal point of view—the Carnegie Trust had undertaken to publish *A London Symphony*. This was a source of particular gratification to Stanford, for of the works chosen for publication that year, one was by Stanford himself, his opera *The Travelling Companion*, and five of the other six were by pupils of his. He sent an exuberant postcard to Herbert Howells, one of the other beneficiaries under the scheme, with a diagram of the hen (CVS) and the five 'chicks'.

45

Meanwhile, RVW was doing his best to master the abstruse science of siege gunnery and to cope with 'the proper arrangement of straps and buckles and all those things on which the sergeant major is so keen', as a fellow-cadet, John Tindall Robertson, put it. He managed to achieve a certain privacy for his gunnery studies by taking a room in a cottage outside the camp grounds (which was against regulations) and coming and going to it through a camouflaged hole in the hedge that surrounded the grounds, so that he could avoid the sentries. He also learned how to manage a motor-bike, though he never seems to have made any use of this skill in later years.

In November 1917, he passed out as an officer cadet and after a short leave, went to Lydd on the Romney Marshes for a firing course, which ended just before Christmas. Three weeks' leave followed; and in January 1918, Second Lieutenant Vaughan Williams, R., was posted to Bordon awaiting his first posting overseas as an officer. On 1 March 1918, he sailed from Southampton to join his new regiment, which caused him to wonder at the army's administrative methods: he had been trained on motor-drawn 6-inch howitzers and found that he was to join a battery (141 Heavy Battery) equipped with 60-pounder horse-drawn guns. His comment to Holst was: 'The war has brought me strange jobs—can you imagine me in charge of 200 horses! That's my job at present, I was dumped down into it straight away, and before I had time to find out which were horses and which were waggons I found myself in the middle of a retreat.'[5] The retreat in question was necessitated by the great Hindenburg/Ludendorff March offensive, which drove General Gough's Fifth Army back over the wasteland of the Somme battlefield and nearly cut off the entire British Expeditionary Force from its French allies, occasioning Haig's famous 'backs to the wall' order. RVW was put in charge of the horse lines; and part of his task was to go up the line with the ammunition waggons. Even so, in what little spare time he had with all the confusion and disorder of a retreat, he tried to organize vocal concerts by and for the troops. He was respected throughout the battery as a kind, firm, and considerate officer.

Not long after the battle front was stabilized in the early summer of 1918 and the allied armies began to advance, RVW was appointed Director of Music to the First Army of the BEF, with its headquarters at Valenciennes. His task was to seek out and exploit the musical talents of the soldiers, organizing choral societies, orchestras, and music classes. By February 1919, when he was demobilized, he had organized nine choral societies, three classes, an orchestra, and a band. He himself took responsibility for the HQ Choral Society, recruiting members and training them. He even attempted to reconstruct an organ (with what degree of success we are not told).

[5] *Heirs and Rebels*, p. 46.

Throughout his war service, he never forgot those who had been left behind to carry the torch of English music-making, particularly Holst. He felt that this was the real England and that they were keeping it alive for the day when peace should return. Holst had been unable to take part in active war work because of his health, but he had not spared himself lecturing, conducting, and teaching; and in 1918, he was offered the post of Musical Organizer in the Educational Department of the YMCA in the Near East. He was in Salonika when RVW left the army, but had been able, thanks to the generosity of H. Balfour Gardiner, to hear his large-scale orchestral suite *The Planets* performed under the up-and-coming young conductor Adrian Boult before he left. Like Vaughan Williams, he too had now completely found his feet as a composer; and now that the tumult and the shouting had died and the captains and the kings departed, they both had to sort out what kind of a society it was to which they would return, what kind of musical culture it would support and to what extent there would be any prominent place for the English composer in that culture.

5

Not without honour (1919–34)

The orgy of self-destruction in Europe between 1914 and 1918 intensified the powerful reactions already in train before the war to forms, styles, and artistic doctrines that had held sway for generations. Blinkered nationalism above all was regarded as one of the root causes of the war; and the eager interest—and apprehension—generated by the enormous social experiment that took place following the Russian Revolution in October 1917 rested partly in the hope that an internationally-minded classless society would arise to banish warfare and lead to a world in which artistic and social progress would march hand-in-hand.

Even where the political involvement of the arts in national movements was played down, reactions developed against the direct expression of emotion in music. In many cases experiments took place that deliberately bordered on (or crossed into the territory of) the bizarre and the absurd, even if these were frequently nothing more than further developments of pre-1914 tendencies. Sir Osbert Sitwell's phrase 'amiable debility', used of Lytton Strachey, seems in retrospect to sum up many of the now forgotten 'daring' works of the period. At their best, these now seem chic and witty. At their worst, they were slick, epicene, and absurdly self-important.

Romanticism in any form was felt by some to be out of place, and 'romanticism' became all too often a kind of meaningless vogue word implying 'something-of-which-I-do-not-approve'. 'Classicism' and 'objectivity' became catch-words, romanticism in some way being considered as an outworn by-product of the decadent mental climate of the pre-war era. The place of art and the artist in society was also under scrutiny. Some thought that any new forms of art should be for the benefit of a cultured elite, as seemed to be the belief of those who followed the lead of a number of white Russian émigrés centred on Paris or the Bloomsbury set in England. Others looked to the time when they would take the form of a kind of art for all, based on folk and popular cultures (such as the exciting jazz music that was sweeping in from across the Atlantic).

Vaughan Williams quietly went his own way. He was never one of the 'smart', fashionable composers of the twenties, nor did he ever lose his belief that art should be rooted in the moods, the traditions and the culture of the artist's native country; but his artistic nationalism had never been associated with any aggressively narrow, exclusive, jingoistic viewpoint. He was always aware that the artist, in the Western world at any rate, was part of a tradition that transcended national barriers. His kind of musical nationalism was misunderstood—perhaps wilfully in some cases—and sniped at by those who may sub-consciously have been seeking a more elitist as well as an internationalist kind of art. What many of his critics overlooked was that he, too, was re-thinking his style and idiom. His style, however, expanded from what had previously served him so well: it did not contract by jettisoning elements of it. The interruption in the flow of his creative writing occasioned by his work on *The English Hymnal* and his studies with Ravel had already helped him to consolidate and expand his style. Those experiences had exposed him to a greater variety of styles, a wider range of idioms and, in the case of Ravel, to new approaches to compositional technique.[1] In a similar but subtle different manner, his return to creative work after the wartime break seems to have been broadened and deepened by his wartime experiences.

At first, this stylistic expansion was masked by the fact that a number of his works that came up for performance and publication after the close of World War I had been written but not performed before it broke out. These included *The Lark Ascending*, first performed in 1920 and published in 1926, the *Four Hymns* for Tenor and Orchestra, written in 1914, but not performed until 26 May 1920 in Cardiff by Steuart Wilson and the London Symphony Orchestra under Julius Harrison; and *Hugh the Drover*, which did not reach the stage until 1924. Such works of the 1920s as *Pastoral Symphony*, *Sancta Civitas*, and *Flos Campi* revealed a new side to his musical character. Much of the music that he composed during the twenties and thirties has a clarity and power that was latent but never fully realized in his work before 1914; and certainly his bold development of new forms, approaches, and textures in works such as *Flos Campi* surprised even those closest to his musical thinking, such as Holst. Partly this was the result of a 'back-to-the-past' approach that paralleled but differed basically from that of Stravinsky's works of this period, partly of his own reaction to contemporary experiments with polytonality and new thinking about the role played by metre and rhythm in musical form and style. But he was certainly neither reactionary in his attitude to the present nor nostalgic towards the past; and any comments attributed to him about 'the maddest polytonalities of the

---

[1] It is slightly ironic that Stanford had at one time wanted him to broaden his musical outlook by studying opera in Italy instead of going to Berlin. Ravel did indeed provide him with 'just what he needed'—but probably not in the way that Stanford expected or even desired.

maddest central Europeans' need to be taken with a very large grain of salt. His own polytonalities (or rather polymodalities) were certainly not mad; but they were unquestionably there. To some contemporary developments, such as the fashionable flirtation with jazz engaged on by such composers as Bliss, Walton, and Lambert in England or Milhaud, Kurt Weill, and even Stravinsky and Shostakovich abroad, he seems superficially to have turned a deaf ear: yet the bite, the galvanic energy, and the restless syncopated rhythms that are a significant component of the jazz idiom are to be found in his work, too, even if they assume a slightly different guise. They develop from tendencies already inherent in his earlier style and are rooted in a culture older than the transatlantic musical idiom that gave its name to a whole generation.

RVW was demobilized in February 1919. For a time, he and Adeline lived in furnished rooms at Sheringham, on the Norfolk coast, where Adeline was looking after her invalid brother Hervey. He died in May 1921 and his death was a severe blow, but it did mean that RVW and Adeline could now return permanently to Cheyne Walk. Adeline herself had been for some years gradually falling prey to arthritis, which by this time and despite various attempted cures was causing her considerable pain and was eventually to cripple her completely. They remained at Sheringham throughout the spring and summer of 1919; and it was there that RVW revised *A London Symphony* for a performance under the auspices of the newly-founded British Music Society on 4 May 1920. He also orchestrated *Hugh the Drover* and set to work on *Pastoral Symphony*. It remains in many ways the most elusive and enigmatic of his symphonies, yet it is also perhaps the most truly individual and personal. It is surely significant that it is the tranquillity so evident in the music rather than the elegiac emotion also recollected in it that affected early listeners most. Because the violence and manic brutality of twentieth-century warfare are totally absent, the work was regarded as a rapt, almost escapist dream. His reaction to the more unpleasant aspects of war was to come later, particularly in works like *Dona Nobis Pacem*. *Pastoral Symphony* reflects more the eerie, disconcerting calm and monumental aloofness of the natural landscape which formed the backcloth to his wartime experience.

In the years following the Armistice, a number of organizations were founded to further the cause of English music. Several of them flaunted their aims in the titles. Besides the British Musical Society, there were the British National Opera Company and the British Symphony Orchestra. The British Musical Society had been set up in August 1918 and incorporated as a society in November 1919, largely thanks to the zeal of A. Eaglefield Hull, its first honorary director. It promoted not only English music, but music-making in the country in general; its office became the headquarters of the International Society for Contemporary Music; and it chose *A London Symphony* as the chief native work for performance at an important Queen's Hall concert on 4 May 1920, when a revised version was performed under Albert Coates that involved Vaughan Williams making several sizeable cuts in the finale. The British National Opera Company was set up in 1922 and performed in London and on tour for a number of years, with a repertory that included Debussy, Holst, Ethel Smyth, and of course Vaughan Williams, as well as Wagner, Mozart, and Verdi. The British Symphony Orchestra was founded in 1919 from professional musicians who had served in the First World War, and its first principal conductor was that same young musician, Adrian Boult, who had first 'caused *The Planets* to shine in public' and who was from then onwards to be strongly associated with RVW's work.

In the autumn of 1919, RVW took up an invitation made by Hugh Allen to teach at the Royal College of Music. Allen had succeeded Hubert Parry as Principal after Parry's death in 1918; and between that time and 1920, he appointed no fewer than twenty-six new teachers to the College staff, including Holst as well as Vaughan Williams and Vaughan Williams's brother-in-law R. O. Morris, who shared the house at Cheyne Walk with RVW and Adeline. These three were mainly responsible, together with Stanford, for the teaching of composition; and it is clear that the methods and aims of the younger teachers were somewhat at variance with those of the older. There had, of course, been a reaction during the war against the Germanic tradition which Stanford and Parry had sturdily upheld—a reaction that, as has already been mentioned, had in some cases been expressed in somewhat extravagant and ridiculous terms—but the new musical art of which Holst and Vaughan Williams were two of the foremost representatives was too much for Stanford. The composer Arthur Benjamin related how Stanford almost pathetically begged him not to 'go mad', as all his 'lovely pupils: Holst, Goossens, Vaughan Williams, Bliss' had done. RVW did not consider himself to be in Stanford's league as a teacher, but there is no doubt that many of the new generation of students found him more sympathetic to some, at any rate, of the main contemporary musical developments.

His teaching methods were not orthodox: he taught what has been described as not a style but an attitude towards composition. If he was convinced that a student had talent, but that he was unable to develop that talent, as was the case for example with Constant Lambert, he spared no pains to find him a teacher who could. His attitude was based on the precept 'to thine own self be true'. He encouraged his pupils to get together with their peers, on the analogy of his own 'field days' with Holst, play one another any compositions they had on the stocks and criticize them frankly immediately afterwards. He discouraged them from any conscious attempts to be strikingly original, rightly and shrewdly telling them that if they really were original, it would show itself in their work; and if they weren't, no amount of technical jugglery would make them so.

Certain of his pupils have commented succinctly on his approach. Gordon Jacob wrote that in those days

> he had a horror of professional skill and technical ability. As he grew older, he came to realize that these qualities did not necessarily add up to superficial slickness and his later pupils were put through the mill or, as he put it, 'made to do their stodge' methodically.[2]

He had, wrote another of his pupils, Elizabeth Maconchy:

> no use for ready-made solutions: he had worked out his own salvation as a composer and he encouraged his pupils to do the same. Technical brilliance for its own sake he despised, and this perhaps made him rather too distrustful of brilliance in any form—though he overcame this distrust to some extent later.[3]

With his distrust of anything second-hand, he did not believe at that time in making pupils work through text-books packed with synthetic theoretical examples, even though he himself had learnt much as a student in that way. When studying counterpoint, for example, he maintained that they should study contrapuntal music by great composers. This approach had the further advantage of giving the students a sense of history and traditions of their art as well as a solid grounding in the fundamentals of the craft in which it had to be rooted.

He was now in his late forties and acknowledged as a leading figure in English musical life. The new quarterly periodical *Music & Letters*, started by A. H. Fox Strangways on a suggestion from Cecil Sharp, acknowledged this with a drawing of him by William Rothenstein and an article by Fox Strangways on RVW's music in its second issue (the first, published in January 1920, had been largely taken up with a tribute to Elgar). The issue also included RVW's piece 'The Letter and the Spirit'; and he contributed an essay on Holst to a later edition that year. The first of these pieces contains the following passage:

> What the musical composer, in effect, says to his performers is: 'I desire to produce a certain spiritual result on certain people; I hope and believe that if you blow, and scrape, and hit in a particular manner this spiritual effect will result. For this purpose I have arranged with you a code of signals in virtue of which, whenever you see a certain dot or dash or circle, you will make a particular sound; if you follow these directions closely my invention will become music, but until you make the indicated sounds my music *does not exist*.[4]

The first sentence is significant. Throughout his life, Vaughan Williams stuck to the belief that the object of 'putting black dots down on paper' was to create a spiritual effect in the listener. This led to complications when speculation arose about the precise spiritual effect that certain sequences of black dots, notably those of some of his later symphonies, were intended to produce.

---

[2] *RCM Magazine*, p. 31.   [3] Ibid., p. 34.   [4] *National Music*, p. 124.

Both personal and practical recognition swiftly followed. On 19 June 1919, the University of Oxford conferred an honorary Doctorate of Music on him. The ceremony was followed by a performance by the Oxford Bach Choir under Hugh Allen of *A Sea Symphony*, which also commemorated the 250th anniversary of the opening of the Sheldonian Theatre. Allen's commitments at the College were now heavy; and this persuaded him that he could no longer conduct the London Bach Choir. On 9 March 1921, the conductorship was offered to RVW. He held it for some five years; and he was determined not to limit the choir's experiences to Bach alone, though his first concert was devoted entirely to Bach cantatas. His venturesome programmes later included works by Byrd, Holst, Dvo rák—and Vaughan Williams. Some of the programmes were brought before a newer public at the People's Palace in the Mile End Road, surely one of the many ways in which Vaughan Williams was returning the people's musical heritage to them.

The Leith Hill Festival had been revived on an even larger scale after the wartime break, with twelve choirs now participating instead of the eight that had been involved previously. It not only stimulated RVW to compose two part-songs for performance by the competing choirs but also sparked off the idea for a similar festival organized by Diana Awdrey at Stinchcombe in Gloucestershire, which RVW helped to launch in 1922.

A disappointing visit to Amsterdam to hear a large-scale performance of the *St Matthew Passion*, interpreted on principles almost diametrically opposed to what RVW considered appropriate, had at least one positive aspect: a meeting with Percy Grainger, whom RVW had known well before the War and who was also in Holland. But the most significant visit abroad was RVW's first stay in the United States in May and June 1922. This was at the invitation of Carl Stoeckel, the wealthy son of a Bavarian *émigré* musician who had become Professor of Music at Yale University and who had established a summer festival at Norfolk, Connecticut in 1907. RVW was to rehearse and conduct his recently-composed *Pastoral Symphony* with the New York Symphony Orchestra. He enjoyed his visit immensely, especially the associations with Walt Whitman, the white-painted clapboard New England houses, the New York skyline and the Woolworth building, which impressed him more even than the Niagara Falls. He fretted somewhat, however, at the customary and at times slightly overpowering expansiveness of transatlantic hospitality. Adeline, who accompanied him, wrote to her sister Cordelia on 8 June:

> The Stoeckels are very dear people—only we have to do just what Mr Stoeckel plans for us and Ralph feels a little restive from a surfeit of kindness! . . . They live in the *ancien régime*, beautiful horses instead of motors, Swiss maids, an English gardener and an English parlour-maid! a very happy feeling in the house. Meals are too rich and wine flows all the time![5]

[5] UVW, p. 144.

Returning to England, he was able to see a performance at the Royal College of Music of his recently-completed one-act opera *The Shepherds of the Delectable Mountains* on 11 July before he and Adeline spent a summer holiday at her sister Cordelia's house at Tetsworth, near Thame in Oxfordshire. Despite RVW's agnosticism, *The Pilgrim's Progress* retained a fascination over him that was to be fully realized only some thirty years later: a voyage into an unknown region as depicted in a literary masterpiece he had known from childhood. The radiant, intimate, visionary atmosphere of this work is recognizably from the same mind that was responsible for *Pastoral Symphony*, yet the mood is subtly different: a mind at ease with itself and serenely in tune with its subject. There is no undercurrent of disquiet or regret, for all that the musical idiom is superficially so similar. It was, however, works like this that induced some critics to think that Vaughan Williams had succumbed to an escapist vision of some imaginary and sentimental placid rural landscape. Nothing could have been further from the truth, as later works of the twenties were to show.

Vaughan Williams's interest in the musical stage stimulated him to a number of ventures during this decade, none of them remotely like *The Shepherds of the Delectable Mountains*. They included three operas, *Sir John in Love*, *Riders to the Sea*, and *The Poisoned Kiss*; but the first of them to achieve performance was the relatively unimportant ballet *Old King Cole*. This was staged in Cambridge. He had composed it for the local branch of the English Folk Dance Society and it was first performed in Nevile's Court of his old college, Trinity, in June 1923. It must have sounded ghastly. RVW, Cyril Rootham, and Boris Ord (who conducted) spent the whole night before the performance correcting errors in the orchestral parts of a score that RVW himself found difficult enough in all conscience when he came to perform it with a professional orchestra. What the CUMS amateurs of the 1920s made of it beggars description. The kind of dancing that he came to favour in presenting his works for the stage was much more in keeping with the folk-dance tradition in which this work was cast: more down-to-earth than the style favoured by traditional ballet groups; and this attitude to dance was to colour the style that he wished to see used when his greater and spiritually more ambitious work for the dance stage, *Job*, came to be composed not long afterwards.

In the meantime, other works based on folk music appeared in various kinds of arrangements. The most ambitious, and possibly the best-known, was the suite for military band based on traditional folk-songs written for the Royal Military School of Music at Kneller Hall. He enjoyed this, particularly as he had formed a rather low opinion of some of the military band music he had been exposed to during the war and wanted to provide something better for them. He had a particular detestation of the RAMC regimental march 'Her Sweet Smile Haunts Me

Still', regarding it as a sentimental left-over after the fighting regiments had appropriated all the best tunes. It is plain that he was just as much at home providing utility music of a less exalted kind as he was when realizing more intense and serious projects. In the folk-music field, these included *Six Studies in English Folk Song*, written in 1927 for and dedicated to the cellist May Mukle; and the *Fantasia on Sussex Folk Tunes* that he composed for Pau Casals in 1929.

A springtime holiday in Venice and the Dolomites in 1923 was followed by a summer stay in a furnished house at Danbury in Essex. It was here that he set to work on a piece that sums up most powerfully what might be termed his agnostic faith: the oratorio *Sancta Civitas*. The intensity with which he expressed the apocalyptic vision in the text must surely have some roots in his experience of the war. *Sancta Civitas* is the other side of the medal of *Pastoral Symphony*; he was always fond of the work, but it is typical of Vaughan Williams's down-to-earth attitude to his craft that when H. Walford Davies confessed to writing his famous *Solemn Melody* on his knees, he was met with the curt rejoinder: 'I wrote *Sancta Civitas* sitting on my bum.' He would doubtless have made a similar comment on his setting of the Mass for a cappella chorus, dedicated to Holst and his Whitsuntide Singers and received and performed with enthusiasm by the dedicatees:

> Dear R
> It arrived on Wednesday but I only got *It* yesterday and shall not be able to look at *It* properly until tomorrow morning. . . . How on earth Morleyites are ever going to learn the Mass I don't know. It is quite beyond us but still further beyond us is the idea that we are not going to do it. I've suggested that they buy copies now and then when we meet in September I'll sack anyone who does not know it by heart![6]

Holst was not the only conductor to enthuse about the Mass. A performance in Leipzig at the *Thomaskirche*—Bach's own church—on 16 November brought a letter from the conductor of the *Thomanerchor* expressing his admiration for the work.

He was broadening the repertory of the Bach Choir by introducing it to works by Holst and others; and he may well have startled some of its more hidebound members by insisting that Holst's *Ode to Death* should be performed twice in one concert, both at the beginning and the end of a performance on 19 December 1923, to give the audience a chance to assimilate properly what was for most of them a new and possibly controversial work. Holst was delighted and wrote to RVW suggesting that he be contracted to conduct every first performance Holst got over the next ten years or so. His conducting of more traditional Bach Choir fare, such as the *St Matthew Passion* and the B Minor Mass elicited praise from Stanford in the case of the *Passion* and from RVW's predecessor,

---

[6] *Heirs and Rebels*, p. 59.

Hugh Allen, when RVW gave his first performance of the Mass with them on 13 May 1924. Both Allen and Holst commented in letters on the improvement in the choir's tone since RVW had taken it over; and those who think that brisk performances of Bach's faster movements are a product of the 'authentic' tradition that has grown up in recent years will be amused to learn that Allen commented on RVW's performance of the Mass: ' . . . I never heard them double along as you made them in the Osanná. It's the first time I've ever known angels to be hustled.'[7]

These tributes give the lie to the assertion that his approach to conducting was in some way amateurish. It was not. As a recording made late in his life amply shows, he approached the *St Matthew Passion* from the point of view of a great music-drama. He insisted on his choristers knowing the story in any narrative work, such as the Bach *Passions* so that they could see their contributions in context; and he even timed the pauses between movements so that every single second that elapsed from the moment the performance began contributed to the total impact of the work. He expanded the continuo part where it accompanied emotive or expressive phrases in the text, leaving it as dry chords where the words implied action or dramatic tension and took care to bring out expressive inner parts in the string orchestra accompaniment to Christ's words, as, for example, at 'The same shall betray me'. He was always aware of the intimate relationship between text and music, which perhaps explains why he was able to make a body of three hundred singers perform with the flexibility of a small madrigal group: indeed, to get them actually to perform madrigals themselves. At times, during the Leith Hill Music Festival, he would put down his stick after a few bars, secure in the knowledge that the choir was sure of itself, resuming conducting only for the closing passage. He may not have been the most polished of conductors technically, but he knew what he was aiming for and seems in most cases to have achieved it. He was able to rely on a witty tongue and a great ability to explain in simple terms what he was driving at; and although he sometimes exploded in a vehement outburst of rage, such outbursts were always over quickly and always followed by a gentle, sincere apology. English professional orchestral players are usually, and rightly, regarded as hard-bitten; and they are almost invariably quick to detect charlatanry on the rostrum. They played willingly and affectionately for RVW; and they never let him down because he never let them down.

RVW did not conduct the first performance of *Hugh the Drover* in July 1924, but he was certainly involved in the preparation for the student performances at the Royal College of Music (conducted by S. P. Waddington), which were followed less than a week later by the professional staging of the work at His Majesty's Theatre by the British

<hr />

[7] UVW, p. 154.

National Opera Company. One of the RCM performances was graced by the presence of Queen Mary, who left RVW at a loss for a rejoinder by asking him why the hero and heroine had not used the church that figured prominently in the stage backcloth to get married in before leaving for their life together. Another surprise came at the woefully under-rehearsed BNOC performance when RVW discovered that Malcolm Sargent, who conducted, had recruited most of the RCM choral singers to boost the professionals. According to the HMV record producer Fred Gaisberg, the 'racy folk opera' was 'cheered to the echo' and Sargent had to take at least a dozen curtain calls. RVW's version of the opening night was rather different; he claimed that Sargent had 'saved it from disaster every few bars, and pulled the chestnuts out of the fire in a miraculous way'. Such were only some of the obstacles facing English opera composers not so long ago.

After this hair-raising experience, RVW and Adeline left for a holiday in the country. RVW set to work on two compositions featuring a string soloist, the Violin Concerto, which he christened *Concerto Accademico*, and the remarkable and intensely passionate work for viola, small orchestra, and wordless chorus, *Flos Campi*. This latter work in particular puzzled many people, including even Holst, who wrote that he 'could not get hold of it at all', but realized that the rapt bitonality used to convey the work's searing passion represented a new and highly expressive departure in his output. The composer himself was greatly amused that the Queen's Hall Orchestra, who with Lionel Tertis as soloist gave the first performance under Henry Wood on 10 October 1925, referred to it as 'Camp Flossie': witty, but rather wide of the mark.

Two other events in 1924 were to affect RVW's career and reputation. One was his work on *Songs of Praise*, Percy Dearmer's fine new hymn-book, for which he again invited RVW to edit the music, assisted by Martin Shaw. RVW said that there wasn't a single tune in the book of which he was ashamed, something that could not quite be said even of *The English Hymnal*. *The Oxford Book of Carols*, involving the same basic editorial team, followed in 1928. The other was the establishment of Oxford University Press's Music Department under the twenty-five-year-old Hubert Foss. The first work of RVW's to be accepted was *The Shepherds of the Delectable Mountains*, and from then onward, OUP published nearly all his works.

RVW was now not just a figure of national, but of international musical consequence. When he received an honorary doctorate from the University of Swansea on 22 June 1930, Walford Davies presented him to the Chancellor with the comment that he uttered what he loved with musical intensity and had become the unconscious leader of national musical thought and idiom. This was no mere *hywl*, it was nothing more or less than the truth. The same could be said of the comment made by the Public Orator at University College, Liverpool, when RVW was awarded an honorary Doctorate of Laws on 18 December 1931: 'His melodies and harmonies are not less original for being comprehensible. He is no mere imitator. He is the author of many works . . . and they are all unmistakably his own. But his novelty is based in antiquity; growing freely, though rooted in the past.'[8]

The works by which his reputation was being established abroad were by no means those that were most readily associated with any contemporary 'wrong-note' trend or movement. But nor were they the most obviously 'folky' ones. *Pastoral Symphony*, for example, was performed in Prague in May 1925 at what RVW whimsically referred to as the 'Freak Festival', i.e. a festival organized by the International Society for Contemporary Music. RVW claimed that the audience hated it. A letter from Adeline to her sister Cordelia indicates otherwise. What he did particularly enjoy on this occasion was his first chance to see Janá cek's *The Cunning Little Vixen*. It is still sometimes thought that he was something of a musical old fogey; and he sometimes deliberately—even sedulously—fostered that impression. In fact, any music that 'spoke' to him, from whatever source, came in for praise, whether it was Stravinsky's *Les Noces*, or his *Symphony of Psalms*, or certain works by central European composers whose aims he appreciated, like Bartók and Kodály.

The years since his demobilization had seen much change and development in his own idiom. There is a new sinewy toughness about some of his music at this time that was to become even more evident in the 1930s; and this is especially so in two works on which he was engaged in 1925. One of them, the oratorio *Sancta Civitas*, came to performance fairly soon with the Bach Choir. The other, his setting of J. M. Synge's terse little tragedy *Riders to the Sea*, had to wait several years for its first staging. Early rehearsals of the oratorio were held at Oxford in February, where RVW and Adeline stayed at New College with Adeline's brother, H. A. L. Fisher, the distinguished historian who was Warden of New College. The première, by the Oxford Bach Choir and the Oxford Orchestral Society, conducted by Hugh Allen, was in the Sheldonian Theatre on 7 May 1926. RVW himself conducted the first London performance with the Bach Choir just over a month later. Later on that year another stage work, a 'Masque with dancing, singing and miming freely adapted from Dickens's *A Christmas Carol*' was staged in Chicago by the Bolm Ballet. RVW had produced a quodlibet of folk tunes and country dances to fit this lively half-hour ballet. It took some years for this work, too, to reach the English stage. A suite from it was performed on 17 December 1929 at a concert of the New English Music Society; but it was not actually staged until 29 December 1935.

Many of his holiday breaks at this time were still spent on relaxed but invigorating walking tours, usually in Wiltshire or Dorset. On one

[8]   UVW, p. 189.

holiday, during a chance stop at the village of Chitterne in the Wylye Valley, near Warminster, RVW was directed to a cottage where he was to stay the night and was recognized from a wartime photograph. The young woman of the house's brother heard and recognized his voice and came down to greet and talk to him for hours on end, regardless of the fact that he had retired early to bed because he had to be up very early to go to his work as a farm labourer.

RVW's typical willingness to help friends out in any capacity that he could is charmingly illustrated by an anecdote about a performance of *The Taming of the Shrew* at the Forest School in Sussex. He and the headmaster's wife, Margot (née Gatty) shared a viola desk. Margot remembered his enthusiasm as being such that in a very vigorous passage, the point of his bow would slip under the bridge, causing endless amusement to Adeline, who would be sitting in the front row. Another regular holiday engagement was as a lecturer and choral conductor at the English Folk Dance Society summer courses.

RVW's term of office with the Bach Choir was coming to an end, not for any musical reasons, but for purely practical ones. He resigned in February 1928 because the house at Cheyne Walk was becoming difficult for Adeline to cope with physically; and they had decided to move to somewhere in the country not far from London to a house where stairs would not be a bother to her. She had had a bad fall in October 1927 and had to spend several months in plaster, and they were much occupied in the summer of 1928 looking for a suitable house. Eventually, after spending some months until just after Christmas at what RVW called the 'perfectly appalling address' of Glorydene, they settled on a bungalow called Chote Ghar, near Dorking, which they renamed The White Gates.

He was as busy as ever, despite the problems associated with moving house, and was able to go to Malines in October 1928 to hear the Cathedral choir sing his Mass. He wrote a Te Deum for the enthronement of Cosmo Gordon Lang as Archbishop of Canterbury on 4 December 1928 and what Adeline described as a 'very fierce' setting of the Benedicite for town choirs to sing at the Silver Jubilee of the Leith Hill Festival in 1930. Two other works were also composed for this occasion: a setting of the Hundredth Psalm for the Second Division choirs and three Choral Hymns for the choirs from the First Division. The *Fantasia on Sussex Folk Tunes* for Pau Casals was performed at the Royal Philharmonic Society's concert on 13 March 1930, the orchestra being conducted by the young John Barbirolli, himself a fine cellist and later to be one of the most sympathetic interpreters of RVW's music. RVW had also completed another stage work, begun in 1924: the Falstaff opera *Sir John in Love*. It was finished that winter and first performed under Malcolm Sargent at the RCM on 21 March 1929. Even when tackling familiar texts, he struck out on new paths. A Magnificat for the Three Choirs' Festival of 1932 was an avowed effort to get the words out of the smug atmosphere with which they had become associated. He thought of the text within the context of its first appearance: the song of an awe-filled young woman anticipating the birth of a child of unprecedented character, not simply as a well-worn canticle text.

In 1927, the centenary of Blake's death, Maynard Keynes's brother Geoffrey and RVW's cousin Gwendolen Raverat had devised a ballet scenario derived from Blake's illustrations to the Book of Job and they asked RVW to write the music. He responded with enthusiasm, stipulating that the style of dancing should be suitable to the subject: no *sur les pointes*, and a thoroughly straightforward approach to a vivid and profound story that touched on far more than purely aesthetic matters. Diaghilev was approached with a view to producing the piece, but he thought it was 'too English'. RVW was not downcast; in fact, he thought that the Diaghilev company, with their 'over-developed calves' would have made an unholy mess of it; and having started work, he found that he had to go through with it, whether or not it ever reached the stage. The causes of his intense interest in the subject are self-evident. The story as he knew it is couched in the majestic prose of the Old Testament. It asks basic questions about man's whole place in the universe rather than centring round a pretty fairy-tale. The totally individual visionary potential implicit in Blake's engravings, and the thought of developing a genuinely English style of stage dancing must also have appealed greatly to him. It is clear that *Job* remained in his view primarily a theatre rather than a concert piece and one that he took very seriously. He made numerous suggestions for modifications to the original scenario, and Holst and he spent field day after field day going over the work. It was ready for concert performance by 1930 and was first performed at the Norwich Festival on 23 October of that year. Finally, through Holst's persistence, the Camargo Society took it up.

The society arose out of a lunchtime conversation between the ballet critic Arnold Haskell and Philip Richardson, editor of the *Dancing Times*. Like most people in the world of ballet, they had been greatly saddened by the death of Diaghilev in August 1929. Many thought that ballet had died with him. Haskell and Richardson disagreed. They knew there was now a knowledgeable and reliable public for ballet in London. Not wishing to see it disintegrate, they decided to assemble all the British dancers who had made their reputations with Diaghilev (in many cases adopting Russian names) to see if a new and equally enterprising company could be formed. It was called the Camargo Society after the first modern French ballerina.

The management committee of the new society included Maynard Keynes as treasurer, his ballerina wife, Lydia Lopokova, dancers such as Anton Dolin, Marie Rambert, and Ninette de Valois. Its original aim was to present four ballet performances a year to a subscription audience. The brilliant young conductor/composer Constant Lambert, who for a short time had been a pupil of RVW's at the Royal College of Music, was engaged as resident conductor; and it was to Lambert's energy, knowledge, enthusiasm, and flair for ballet conducting that the outstanding success of the company was largely due, laying the foundations of the whole tradition of English ballet.

Lambert's policies were eclectic and enterprising, even when he did not always fully sympathize with the works that he loyally conducted (*Job* was certainly not one of these: in his astringent, hard-hitting and devastatingly witty book *Music Ho!* he singled out *Job* as one of Vaughan Williams's finest works). His policy was that the music and the ballet that it carried should be effective on stage and worthy of the attention of a company with basically serious aims. Thus, in the first few seasons ballets such as *La Création du Monde* and *Façade* were presented alongside familiar works like *Giselle*. For *Job*, he had to reduce the scoring so as to suit the small orchestra pit at the Cambridge Theatre. The whole thing was run on a shoestring: the total cost of the orchestra was £100; and the dancers were paid £1 per performance. But the important thing was that it worked as a stage spectacle. Contemporary accounts state how Anton Dolin, as Satan, danced with unforgettable impact and *élan*. These performances convinced people who knew something about ballet that the music 'worked'. On seeing *Job* at the theatre, Lydia Lopokova, for example, was completely converted from her initial scepticism about the project and the music. Writing in August 1931 to Geoffrey Keynes, she described how the composer 'bowed and looked like a nice bear', and commented on the work itself:

> I went to Oxford to see Job and was much impressed, much more than on the wireless, when I thought the music was a noble, but a *dreary* way to spend an hour. But it had much more grandeur with scenes, costumes, and moving creatures. Job was truly a thing for the theatre, which I used to doubt. I congratulate you on your obstinate efforts without which Job would be never performed . . . My chief pleasure was that it differed from the Russian Ballet tradition—the most important merit of Job. Pat [Dolin] surpassed himself—so perfectly devilish. Ninette [de Valois] had the most difficult task for, except for Satan, the music is not dancing—but her name, since Job, is quoted by managers. With more time and rehearsals it will stand up better.[9]

The last sentence tells a whole story of its own. Among those early audiences was a young ballet student at the Old Vic called Ursula Lock. She was quite overwhelmed by the power and grandeur of the music; and she was to play a supremely important role in the composer's life later on.

By this time, some of the 'tougher' works that were to come before the public in the next few years were taking shape in RVW's mind, such

[9] Quoted in 'From Parry to Britten', *English Music in Letters, 1900–1945*, ed. Lewis Foreman (London, 1987), p. 148.

as the Piano Concerto and the Fourth Symphony. There is a peculiarly English kind of rage that finds expression sporadically in our literature and painting—in King Lear's tirades, for example, in the vehemence of a Dickensian moral outburst, or in the intensity of certain of Turner's apocalyptic visions, such as 'The Slave Traders'—a rage that is born not so much of the urge to destroy or deceive as of frustration and a sense of impotence in the face of injustice or cruelty. In music, it is surely found in such contexts as the amazing 'Roman' episode of Elgar's *In the South,* or the 'Dead, dead, long dead' episode of his Second Symphony, but its most forceful expression musically is surely in these works of RVW's. The splendid ambiguity of music has enabled commentators to relate such works as these to this type of rage, on both a cosmic or an individual scale. But the intensity of that rage and the power and calibre of the personality that expresses it are unmistakable.

Both RVW and Holst were invited to lecture and teach in the USA in 1932. RVW's stay was at Bryn Mawr, Pennsylvania, in October and November, where he was invited to deliver six lectures under the auspices of the Mary Flexner Trust. Adeline was by this time so crippled that she was unable to accompany him. The lectures were published under the title of *National Music* in 1934 and are really a positive and more detailed development of the provocative article he had published in 1912, incorporating a number of ideas contained in other occasional writings of earlier years. The two main arguments he adduced in favour of a 'national' school of composers can best be shown by two quotations:

> . . . the St Matthew Passion, much as it is loved and admired other countries, must mean much more to the German, who recognizes in it the consummation of all that he learnt from childhood in the great traditional chorales which are his special inheritance . . . Is it not reasonable to suppose that those who share our life, our history, our climate, even our food, should have some secret to impart to us which the foreign composer . . . is not able to give us?[10]

which approaches his theme from the point of view of the consumer, i.e. the listener, and:

> It is by synthesis that the student learns. Early Beethoven is 'synthetic' Haydn. Early Wagner is 'synthetic' Weber, and I believe that for a student to do a little 'synthetic' folk-song writing is a better way of arriving at self-knowledge than imitation of the latest importations from Russia and Spain which after all only cause him to write 'synthetic' Russian or Spanish folk-song, and that at second hand.[11]

which does so plainly from that of the producer, i.e. the composer. Over-simplified the argument may be: but cogent it certainly is.

Whilst in the States, he celebrated his sixtieth birthday. He also had the chance to hear three of the great American orchestras in quick

[10] *National Music*, p. 9.   [11] Ibid., p. 46.

succession: the Boston Symphony, the Philadelphia, and the New York. Though he felt that there was a suspicion of things being 'too much organised', he was delighted to hear the magnificent string section of the Boston Orchestra under the virtuoso Russo-American conductor Serge Koussevitzky (who was later to declare that RVW was one of the 'really great' composers of all time, especially in his fifth and sixth symphonies) perform the *Tallis Fantasia*—and caused some baleful glances from two Boston matrons seated at the opposite end of the row of seats from him. Completely lost in the music, he rose and fell with something of a bump in the more strongly accentuated passages. This in itself would have been distracting enough; what was worse was that the seats were attached to the floor only at the far end from RVW. The implied affront to the matronal dignity can well be imagined. Unfortunately, there is no record of the ladies' reactions when the bulky, ill-mannered philistine who had aroused their displeasure went up to join Koussevitzky on the platform after the performance.[12]

But if the inter-war years were a period of increasing recognition and one that saw the appearance of new friends, such as Foss, Cecil Forsyth, and Gordon Jacob (a former pupil) they were also a period of loss. His teachers, Parry, Stanford, and Charles Wood had already died, Parry in 1918, Stanford in 1924, and Wood in 1926. Elgar, with whom RVW had been on friendly though never intimate terms for some years, died in February 1934. But 1934 was to bring one further loss which affected him as man and musician far more than any of these. On 25 May, Gustav Holst, who had been ill for some months and had had to abandon a course of lectures at Harvard University on account of his illness and return to England, died suddenly at the age of fifty-nine.

---

[12] Archibald T. Davison in *RCM Magazine*.

6

Uncrowned laureate (1935–45)

It is hardly surprising that the death of Holst affected Vaughan Williams profoundly both as man and as artist. His sense of personal loss was expressed in a letter to his friend's widow and daughter: 'which ever way I turn, what are we to do without him—everything seems to have turned back to him—what would Gustav advise or do—'[1] and his sense of professional loss was summed up some sixteen years after Holst's death in his own *Musical Autobiography*:

> Holst would spend hours bringing his mastery, his keen vision, and his feeling for clear texture to bear on my work especially in those clumsy places where I was continually getting into holes and could not find the way out. He would not rest till he had found a solution for the problem which not only satisfied him, but one which my obstinacy would accept. This was all the more wonderful because Holst, I know, found it difficult to appreciate the amateurish attitude of mind; his absolute sureness of purpose inclined him to be unsympathetic to the vacillations of human nature.[2]

The equation of 'the vacillations of human nature' with 'amateurishness' is typical. It underlines the eternal difficulty of the liberal temperament, with its willingness to see a problem from a number of different points of view, when faced with the uncompromising attitude of the single-minded. In someone less open-minded than Holst such an attitude could easily have led to fanaticism and bigotry rather than the professionalism that Vaughan Williams discerned in it.

RVW was determined that Holst's memory should be worthily preserved. He acted as the energetic chairman of a committee to raise funds for the construction of a small hall in memory of Holst at Morley College; and two months after Holst's death he wrote more in consternation than in protest to Adrian Boult at the BBC when he heard that the 1934 Proms were not to contain a concert devoted to Holst's music. He also suggested that the Scherzo from a symphony left unfinished at Holst's death might be included in a BBC Symphony concert. (The work was in fact performed at a BBC concert on 5 February 1935.) Frank and honest as ever, though, he was by no means uncritical of all Holst's out-

---

[1] UVW, p. 200.   [2] *National Music*, pp. 193–4.

put. When Boult proposed taking the *Fugal Overture* to Salzburg in 1935, where he was due to conduct a concert of English music with the Vienna Philharmonic, he consulted Vaughan Williams as to whether his new F minor Symphony or *Job* should be included. RVW wrote back apropos the whole programme:

I feel that *Job* is less like what they are accustomed to, which I feel is what we ought to give them . . . I am not quite happy about the rest of the programme— but I daresay that is inevitable. Could you not do Bax 3rd Symphony instead of *Tintagel* and *The P[erfect] F[ool]* Ballet or *Egdon Heath* or *Hammersmith* instead of the *Fugal Overture*—which is not one of my favourite works.[3]

The hint was taken, at least in part. The *Fugal Overture* was replaced by the music from *The Perfect Fool*, but Boult retained *Tintagel* instead of substituting the Bax Third, probably because the longer work would have overloaded the programme and the rehearsal schedule.

It has sometimes been suggested that after Holst's death the quality of RVW's works fell off somewhat, particularly in matters of shape and scoring. The charge is groundless. However much he missed Holst's help and guidance, and there can be no doubt that he did, the loss had no effect on the quality of his output. Such works as the *Five Tudor Portraits*, the Fifth, Sixth, Seventh, and Eighth Symphonies, the Second Quartet, the Violin Sonata and the late songs, to mention but a few, all show that he was still full of ideas for striking and unusual instrumental effects, while the forms of his later symphonies show an imaginative willingness to experiment equal or indeed superior to that of his earlier ones. The suggestion that having lost Holst, he no longer had a friend on whom to rely to help him judge how to improve passages in new works with which he was not satisfied also implies that he now rushed works into performance without checking what would and what would not do. This is belied by the reminiscences of many friends and acquaintances, nearly all of them experienced and practising performing musicians. He would refer new works that had been sketched out completely enough to listen to a play-through to a 'jury' who would pass judgment on them; and while he would always accept criticisms or suggestions about passages that dissatisfied him, no amount of persuasion would make him change anything that he felt was as he wanted it. He could be just as single-minded (and hence 'professional') as his friend when he knew that what he had written was what he meant.

In June 1933, RVW had been laid up for some time with a cracked fibula, sustained after a fall when walking home across the fields from Dorking station one night after a day in London; and a short time after Holst's funeral service in Chichester Cathedral in June 1934, he was again laid up for eight weeks with a poisoned abscess on the foot of the

[3] *Music & Friends: Letters to Adrian Boult*, ed. Jerrold Northrop Moore (London, 1979) (hereafter Boult), pp. 117–18.

same leg. The first indisposition had led to a course of somewhat unproductive clarinet lessons while he was convalescing. To his unconcealed delight and relief his teacher turned out to be not the forbidding dragon he had been expecting, but an extremely attractive though still very demanding young lady teacher, Elizabeth Darbishire. The second meant that he had to withdraw from participating in the Abinger Pageant in July 1934, for which he had arranged the music. It also caused him to miss the opening season of Glyndebourne and the 1934 Three Choirs Festival, but he was able to conduct both *A London Symphony* and a new work, *The Running Set*, based on English folk dance tunes, at a Henry Wood Promenade concert on 21 September. His new Suite for Viola, composed for Lionel Tertis, who was in no small degree responsible for rescuing the viola from its Cinderella position as a solo instrument, was first performed by Tertis at a Courtauld-Sargent concert on 12 November.

That same winter, he was elected to the Collard Life Fellowship of the Worshipful Company of Musicians, left vacant by Elgar's death in February. At the 1934 Leith Hill Festival he had for the first time conducted *The Dream of Gerontius*, a work that he fervently admired for its craftsmanship and inspiration, possibly in spite of its theological content. The performance had been planned before Elgar's death and was broadcast on the BBC National programme. Elgar's friend W. H. Reed led the orchestra, and both Reed and Elgar's daughter, Carice Elgar Blake, were deeply moved by the performance. There is a delightful story of RVW's lead cellist, Arthur Kennedy, who, playing golf the next morning, was asked by an acquaintance if he liked music. On replying that he did, he was then asked if he had listened to the wireless the previous evening. No, he replied; he had been otherwise engaged, whereupon he was greeted with the response: 'Pity. You missed a very good performance of *Gerontius*.'

The publication of his Bryn Mawr lectures occasioned Vaughan Williams mild amusement as well as quiet satisfaction. It is completely typical of the attitude of even the cultured English middle classes of his time that friends and relatives were highly impressed by the fact that 'Ralph had written a book' whereas for over a quarter of a century the performance of his many major compositions had raised little or no comment.

One work that did arouse a good deal of comment received its première on 10 April 1935. This was the F minor Symphony. One can only wonder how carefully those who thought it to be a completely new departure had been attending to his works since at least *Sancta Civitas* nine years previously. While it had been taking shape, even Adeline had been slightly unsure of it: 'The symphony is emerging—and now I couldn't bear you *not* to hear it!' she wrote to her sister Cordelia '—last week I thought I cdn't bear anyone to hear it! It was wonderful to get the Ist movement going this morning. It's powerful—I ought to have had more faith.'[4] Cecil Sharp's colleague Maud Karpeles described it as 'tremendous' and wrote of 'the feeling of some huge force at work, driving us to fight and struggle, which may eventually shatter us to pieces'. Adrian Boult, who conducted the first performance and who, in RVW's words '*created* the slow movement' spoke of RVW 'foreseeing the whole thing', meaning the conflagration of 1939–45. Henry Wood wrote of Vaughan Williams 'beating the moderns at their own game', but with a far greater musical effect. Elizabeth Trevelyan found in it 'a vastly wider and profounder emotional range than your other work', while the composer's widow likens it to a Rembrandt self-portrait done in middle age. The press were divided. Edwin Evans described it as vigorous and uncompromising; Eric Blom, in the *Birmingham Post*, who clearly *had* been taking careful note of RVW's development over the years, called it 'harsh and grimly uncompromising', adding that it was 'tremendously strong, convincing and wonderfully devised' and rightly pointing out that the new vein that it seemed to open up had in fact been gradually emerging in *Sancta Civitas*, *Job*, and the Piano Concerto. Even Ernest Newman praised its 'combination of ardour and concentration . . . and the profoundly reflective beauty that is often attained'. Neville Cardus wondered whether it would take its place in the works that go beyond national boundaries, commenting—rightly—that it had stopped short of a post-war freedom of rhythm and a post-war harshness of dissonance and that there was a big nature behind every note and—wrongly—that its technique was old-fashioned and that the 'big nature' did not immediately realize itself in expression. Holst had been puzzled by the early sketches of this formidable work and, according to RVW himself, 'disliked the rest'.[5] Bearing in mind 'Mars', *Egdon Heath*, and 'Uranus' it is surely not too fanciful to believe that he would have understood and appreciated it as it finally appeared. Its dedicatee, Arnold Bax, was guardedly grateful, referring to it in a thank-you letter as 'an ever-to-be-honoured present' and 'the finest tribute of affection and comradeship' that had ever been paid him, but making no comment on the content or the design of the music itself.

RVW himself seems at times to have been slightly puzzled by what he had produced and there are a number of stories associated with the piece, such as the famous comment that if that was modern music, he didn't like it and his response to the orchestral player querying a particular note: 'It's B flat. It *looks* wrong and it *sounds* wrong; but it's right!' Yet this was the only symphony of his that was commercially recorded under his own baton; and the sheer energy and explosive force of the performance is an object lesson in how it should be interpreted: with the gloves remorselessly off.

---

[4] UVW, p. 205.   [5] See letter to Adrian Boult of 19 August 1934.

He also managed during 1935 to attend performances of Holst's *Savitri*, Stanford's *The Travelling Companion*, and Walton's First Symphony and to be present with Adeline, whose arthritis, though severe, was still not severe enough to prevent her travelling with RVW in the car to such ceremonies, when Delius's ashes were buried in Limpsfield churchyard. Ursula Vaughan Williams describes her at about this time, or slightly later, as follows:

> She was very thin; the cool beauty of her youth had changed to gaunt and austere age. Her back was straight, her head beautifully set on her shoulders, and her heavy eyelids in their deep sockets lifted to show pale blue eyes where amusement could flash or fury blaze, though she usually looked at the world with gentle irony. Pain had taught her stillness and she had a quality of heroic endurance that could be intimidating. Though she could melt into friendliness there were tremendous barriers of reserve that froze between her and people she did not like.[6]

On 17 May 1935, RVW received a letter from Sir Clive Wigram offering him the Order of Merit. Neither he nor Adeline was at all keen on official honours, but this was different. There was no whiff of party politics about it or of kow-towing to officialdom. It was a personal honour conferred by the sovereign himself on the recipient as the representative of his art and it was restricted to twenty-four holders at any time. King Edward VII had instituted the order in 1902 and Elgar had been one of the earliest recipients; it was presumably to replace him as the most eminent musician in the Order that it was offered to RVW. After considerable reflection and discussion with Adeline, he accepted. In a sense he may be said to have returned the compliment when George V died early in 1936 with the funeral tribute 'Nothing is here for tears', a simple setting of a text from Milton's *Samson Agonistes*, composed in twenty-four hours at the request of the Master of the King's Musick.

His candour in expressing his opinions was in no way curbed by the award; nor was it always appreciated. At the Musicians' Company dinner on 24 March 1936, he returned to a theme that crops up at intervals throughout his life with some observations to the effect that the average Englishman hated English music. This was taken to be a plea for a greater regard for the contemporary English composer, which drew a letter from RVW stating that all he wanted to imply was that there was something wrong either with the average Englishman or with the current situation. He had always maintained that a composer should be able to stand on his own feet without being coddled, and in this instance he was merely drawing attention to a fact rather than begging for sympathetic consideration (which he, at any rate, did not need). What he continued to stress was that the composer should not live in an ivory tower; and he was to prove this yet again later in the year.

[6] UVW, p. 208.

There was another example of this forthrightness when he character-istically took issue with *The Times* on the matter of a work by the Swiss composer Willy Burkhard performed at an ISCM concert at Queen's Hall in June 1938. The work—*The Vision of Isaiah*—had been ponti-fically declared to be unfit for consumption by a Three Choirs audience, *The Times* described it as 'eschewing all ameliorating harmonies', the composer as 'decorating his chant only with dissonant orchestration' and scornfully dismissed the 'ungainly fugue' that formed part of the piece. Vaughan Williams retorted:

SIR:

Your unfavourable notice of a choral work by Willy Burkhard at a contem-porary music concert at Queen's Hall last Friday prompts me to venture to express my opinion that we have here a remarkable, often beautiful and often deeply moving composition. It seemed to me that evening to stand out amid a waste of arid note-spinning as a genuine and deeply felt expression.

I ought perhaps to add that in case my opinion should cause the composer to lose face among his fellow 'contemporary' musicians that he is fully as cap-able of inventing lacerating discords as any of them. But the discords seemed to me to come from a genuine emotional impulse and not from a desire to out-shine one's neighbours in hideosity.

I hope that one of our choral festivals will perform this work, having previ-ously revised the present English translation.

Yours faithfully,
RALPH VAUGHAN WILLIAMS.

The 'waste of arid note-spinning' included works by the Ferrarese com-poser Riccardo Nielsen, Roberto Gerhard, Aaron Copland, and Hindemith; and the substance of the letter—including the reference to 'lacerating discords'—is fully consistent with what Vaughan Williams preached and practised throughout his life.

Meanwhile, there was something of a stirring of interest in his stage works; and the two that now came up for performance made his point far better than any words might do. The romantic musical-comedy extravaganza *The Poisoned Kiss* was put on by a largely amateur cast at the newly-opened Cambridge Arts Theatre, conducted by Cyril Rootham, and transferred for one night with the same cast, this time under the composer's direction, to Sadler's Wells Theatre in London six days later. (It had been offered, without success, to the Theatre Royal, Drury Lane, in 1934.) For the première, it had had to be cut quite severely so that the performance could start at 8.30 (giving the dons time to recover after Hall) and end before 11.30 (so that the undergraduates could be back in College bounds by midnight). It went down well with the Cambridge audience, but the press were generally lukewarm, more, admittedly, about the text than the music. The *Manchester Guardian* likened the piece to an end-of-term charade, which on the occasion of its première it more or less was; and most of the other critics were equally guarded. Richard Capell, in a generally appreciative review in the *Daily Telegraph*, described the music as 'good and at the same time popular', but also (alas rightly) commented that the choice of libretto was all too uncritical. *The Poisoned Kiss* remains the only one of RVW's stage works not so far to have received a proper professional production (apart from a BBC studio broadcast). Another work that had germinated in the twenties and been published in 1936, *Riders to the Sea*, was at last staged in public for the first time at the Royal College of Music under Malcolm Sargent on 1 December 1937. Terse and powerful, with not a note wasted, it remains one of the most striking operatic achievements by a British composer of the twentieth century and, like Holst's *Savitri*, may well have helped pave the way for the intimate kind of chamber opera that Benjamin Britten was to exploit so imaginatively at the height of his creative powers.

On 14 September 1936, RVW attended a Prom devoted to his works; and eleven days later, on 25 September, he conducted the work commissioned by the 1936 Norwich Festival. Unpredictable as ever, he had chosen to set five racy poems by Skelton. A chance remark by Elgar, who always enjoyed exploring the byways of English literature and who had suggested making an oratorio out of *The Tunning of Elinor Rumming*, had put him on to this poet. In the 1930s such a ribald choice of subject-matter from so highly respected a composer was to say the least unexpected; and at the first performance, there is a well-authenticated story of the elderly Countess of Albemarle rising in the middle and leaving the hall with a loud hoot of 'Disgusting!' RVW reacted afterwards when his contralto soloist Astra Desmond told him of the incident by commenting on the evident quality of the choir's diction and reflecting that it was a pity that the Countess had not seen some of the lines he hadn't set. There was another rather different incident at this Festival, reported by the soprano Sophie Wyss,[7] who was singing the solo in Britten's *Our Hunting Fathers*. This was performed on the same day as *Five Tudor Portraits*, so the more staid members of the Norwich audience must have felt that they had been exposed to what a later generation was to refer to as a 'double whammy'. Beecham's élite London Philharmonic Orchestra, who had been engaged for the Festival, became somewhat restive at what they considered the young avant-garde composer's extravagant and unconventional orchestral writing, and began playing him up at rehearsal. Vaughan Williams ticked them off. They took the hint and there was no more trouble.

A week later came the première of a choral work of totally different hue: *Dona Nobis Pacem*, composed for the centenary of the Huddersfield Choral Society on 2 October. This work was no rumbustious celebratory paean. It was composed under the growing shadow of the Second

---

[7] In a letter to Ursula Vaughan Williams soon after RVW's death.

World War. The Civil War in Spain, Hitler's persecution of the Jews and his march into the Rhineland, and Mussolini's aggression in Abyssinia showed all too plainly the direction in which Europe was heading. If Britten and Auden had made their own political statement in *Our Hunting Fathers*, Vaughan Williams was issuing an unmistakable warning here, based on personal experience in the trenches, as well as expressing the hope that conflict could be averted and the blessings of peace enjoyed.

Family illnesses and ailments clouded the autumn and winter. First Adeline broke her arm and then RVW's mother fell ill. It looked as if the illness might be her last, but she recovered enough after several anxious weeks to return to Leith Hill Place and manage the household for RVW's elder brother Hervey. Hervey had troubles of his own: his wife, Constance, had died on 3 December after being knocked down by a bicycle and he had been looked after in the meantime by RVW and Adeline at The White Gates. RVW's mother continued to be active for much of 1937, but finally died on 20 November at the age of ninety-five. At such an advanced age, the loss was hardly unexpected; but RVW and Adeline still felt it keenly. It was mainly thanks to his upbringing at her hands that as well as being revered as an artist, her son was loved and respected as a person. Just five weeks later, on Boxing Day, came the death of Ivor Gurney, one of the saddest of the musical casualties of the First World War, who had been driven insane by his experiences and who had received frequent visits and letters from RVW and Adeline during his stay in the mental hospital. RVW wrote a simple and sincere tribute to him for *Music & Letters*.

For the Coronation of George VI in June 1937, RVW was commissioned to write a number of works, including the *Flourish for a Coronation*, somewhat inappropriately performed for the first time on 1 April and involving not just a chorus singing a text drawn from the Old Testament, Chaucer, and the Agincourt Song manuscript, but an orchestra of Straussian proportions, so that as many musicians as possible could be involved—and paid for their services. At the service itself, his contribution was a festival setting of the Te Deum, based on traditional themes. Besides being at the ceremony, he was invited down at the end of May by Adeline's brother, Admiral Sir William Fisher, C.-in-C. Portsmouth, to see the Coronation Review of the Fleet. He enjoyed himself greatly, despite arriving home at 4.30 in the morning in pouring rain, but his memories of the day must have been saddened by the fact that the admiral died hardly a month later.

During the summer of 1937, he was informed that the University of Hamburg wished to award him its Shakespeare Prize. Bearing in mind his strongly held views about the National Socialist régime, it is easy to understand that the acceptance of this honour must have caused him severe misgivings. Indeed, his first thought was to refuse. Eventually, after much thought, he accepted, though making sure that acceptance did not associate him in any way with a government he detested and a social system he deeply mistrusted:

> You have answered me that this honour is offered purely in the cause of art by a learned body to a member of the English musical profession; that it implies no political propaganda and that I shall feel free as an honourable man, if I accept, to hold and express any views on the general state of Germany which are allowable to any British citizen.[8]

On receiving the prize on 15 June 1938, he was regaled with performances under Eugen Jochum of the *Tallis Fantasia* and *A London Symphony* and took the opportunity in his speech of thanks to remind his audience that *das Land ohne Musik* possessed a number of other talented composers besides himself. He was also highly critical, though not overtly and not so rude as to be so on this particular occasion, of those who would regard everything English, including our executant musicians, as *ipso facto* inferior to those from the continent. In an essay on Beethoven's Ninth Symphony, which must have been taking shape in his mind at about this time, for it was written down in 1939/40, we find this passage:

> But is this music [i.e. the finale of the *Ninth*], so unsingable? Toscanini and Bruno Walter have proved to us that with an English choir, at any rate, a performance can be thrilling, brilliant, and musical, and there need be no (apparent) throat strain. Our English soprano soloists have also taught those dignified German ladies who were, till lately, considered the high priestesses of the Beethoven cult, that there is no necessity in those difficult high quavers of the Second Variation to make a noise like a dog being run over by a motor car.[9]

Performance of his music in other countries besides Germany gives the lie to the view that his music was so 'English' that it did not 'travel'. He had not only established a link with his country's musical past; he was part of the European tradition.

But as the Munich crisis showed, nationalism in politics was quite another matter from national traditions in the arts; and as war drew nearer, he decided that he must do something to help the hundreds of refugees entering Britain from the Fascist dictatorships. The Dorking Committee for Refugees from Nazi Oppression was formed to administer to their needs; it started work in December 1938 and RVW was able to contribute much to its success because he understood the nature and the needs of ordinary people. Nor did he forget that suffering does not necessarily ennoble the spirit. When an indignant welfare worker complained about the ingratitude shown by a German refugee who protested that the hostel where he was billeted in Dorking was far worse heated than houses in his own country, RVW's response was: 'How right he is!

---

[8] UVW, p. 217.   [9] *National Music*, p. 89.

And how excellent that he should still remember the good things in his country!' Nevertheless, according to one of Adeline's letters, his music was banned in Germany 'owing to his anti-Nazi propaganda'. The paranoid dictatorship had taken offence at his support of such humanitarian ventures.

On 31 March 1938, RVW first met and soon became friends with a young poet and writer who was later to play an increasingly important part in his life. Ursula Wood, as she had now become, had been a student at the Old Vic. and had been completely bowled over by *Job* when she saw the Camargo Society perform it during its 1932/3 season. She had since married an officer in the Royal Artillery, Captain Michael Forrester Wood. At this time, they were stationed in the Isle of Wight. Ursula Wood retained a lively interest in drama and stage works; and in 1937, she sent one of her ballet scenarios to RVW. He sent it on to Douglas Kennedy of the EFDS, who offered to turn the script into a dance scenario for which Vaughan Williams might provide the music. Ursula met him over lunch to discuss the project and it gradually took shape over the ensuing months, eventually—and, as it much later turned out, prophetically—bearing the title *The Bridal Day*. The work was ready for performance (featuring Ursula in the principal role) in the autumn of 1939, but the outbreak of war intervened and it was not heard in public until 5 June 1953, when it was revised and broadcast on BBC Television.

A friendship of longer standing brought another unusual musical tribute. The sixty-nine-year-old Henry Wood celebrated his golden jubilee as a conductor on 5 October 1938; and Vaughan Williams hit upon the imaginative idea of composing a piece that would involve sixteen well-known British singers who had long been associated with the veteran conductor. The result was the *Serenade to Music*, one of his loveliest occasional pieces. It was more than just a sincere tribute to Wood. The voice parts were tailor-made for the singers involved; from the very opening, the music creates the spellbinding atmosphere of a heady summer night in a Mediterranean garden, matching Shakespeare's magnificent poetry (which in those days when men still believed that the universe was held together by the unheard music of the spheres must surely have been intended to be understood quite literally) and creating in its lyric dignity exactly the right mood for celebrating the work of one whom Vaughan Williams himself described as having 'none of the affectations of the virtuoso, no swaggering in with his head in the clouds, no temperamental hysteria; stern business is the order of the day, the expert craftsman doing his job.'[10] The *Serenade* itself exactly matches this description of the man for whom it was composed, both in spirit and in workmanship, but it is also shot through with an extra dimension of

[10] Ibid., p. 268.

stately serenity, respect for Wood's strong points as a conductor, and warm human affection.

Yet another and rather less well-known work of an unusual kind resulted from a visit to Christ's Hospital, which in 1902 had moved from the City of London to West Horsham, not far from Dorking. Inspired by the example set by Clement Spurling at Oundle, the Director of Music there, Craig Sellar Lang (universally known among fellow-musicians as Robin Lang), had built up a considerable repertory of arrangements for massed unison voices for use in conjunction with the normal choral forces. Thus that section of the school not in the choir was able to become involved in the performance. Lang had, in fact, developed the school's massed singing to such a remarkable degree that he even arranged a simple and effective part for the five hundred or so 'school' singers in certain choruses from *Messiah*, as Spurling had done with Bach's B minor Mass. Vaughan Williams was much impressed by this sensible and effective method of interesting the 'average' boy in musical performance. It appealed to his own belief that the English were at heart a musical nation. Like Vaughan Williams, Lang had been a pupil of Stanford's, and his own compositions for the school chapel may without disrespect be described as Stanford for the masses. He involved the massed body of school singers in his own settings of the Jubilate Deo, the Magnificat, the Nunc Dimittis, and the Te Deum; and it is likely that hearing one of these settings, probably the Jubilate, the composer's own favourite, spurred RVW to write for the school. The outcome was a complete set of canticles: morning and evening service and a communion service, involving unison voices, choir, and organ, 'for C. S. Lang and his singers at Christ's Hospital'. Lang, for his part, tempered his own musical conservatism with a cautious admiration for RVW's music. (When rehearsing his *Te Deum* he would proudly refer to the passage at 'Thou art the King of Glory, O Christ: thou art the everlasting Son of the Father' as 'pure Vaughan Williams').

In 1938 Vaughan Williams retired from his post as composition teacher at the Royal College—part of a process of gradually withdrawing from regular musical activities of a more formal nature—but he continued to give private lessons and to work hard for the Leith Hill Festival. During the summer months, he would be busy compiling the schedule. In December and January, he would attend the conductors' conference, when a few singers from each of the competing choirs would work through the festival music under his guidance. Later on in the season, he would take the combined choir rehearsals; and, when the festival was due to take place, the orchestral ones as well. His kindness and consideration showed itself in numerous ways, ranging from his practice of starting the full rehearsal with five minutes' playing 'to see if you have room to play' to his friendly reminder to individual members that there was a meal provided for them after the rehearsal.

On 13 May 1939 he was at Sadler's Wells where *Hugh the Drover* and *Job* were given as a double bill. Further honours came his way, such as the honorary doctorate awarded by Trinity College Dublin in June 1939; and new works continued to flow from his pen. One that gave him particular trouble (but which in its original form appealed both to Adeline and to the Menges Sextet who gave its première) was the Double Trio, which remains unpublished in its original form. RVW was not satisfied with it and recast it a number of times, eventually publishing it in 1948 as the Partita for Double String Orchestra. One that certainly did not give him trouble was the *Five Variants of 'Dives and Lazarus'*, conducted for the first time by Adrian Boult in New York on 10 June 1939.

When war broke out in September 1939, RVW busied himself with menial but essential tasks such as collecting salvage and addressing envelopes (in his unique and almost illegible hand), occupying some of his time with the completion of a provocative and deeply interesting essay on Beethoven's Ninth Symphony, a by-product of a projected Leith Hill Festival performance of the work, scheduled for 1940, that the war had caused to be cancelled. But the war was soon to bring him into contact with a new form of *Gebrauchsmusik* already familiar to some of his younger contemporaries such as Walton, Bliss, and Britten.

Early in 1940, Muir Mathieson, the director of music for London Films, rang him up and asked if he would be prepared to write the music for a feature film, mentioning that he would have four days in which to produce the first batch. Ever since Arthur Bliss had been called upon to compose the music for the film of H. G. Wells's *Things to Come* in 1935, British film studios had shown considerable enterprise in their choice of composers, taking their lead from our documentary film groups. The film in question, *49th Parallel*, was an exciting adventure story about the attempt of the survivors of a sunken German submarine to escape from Canada into the then neutral United States. Both the film and the music were a considerable success; and the opening title music was adapted and words were set to it by Harold Child, the librettist of *Hugh the Drover*. It became the stirring unison song *The New Commonwealth*. RVW was invited to provide music for a number of films after *49th Parallel* and this enabled him to contribute personally and in a highly effective manner to the war effort. He rose to the challenge with enthusiasm and took considerable pains to ensure that his music was not just hackwork. Some of it, in fact, was later adapted and used in other works, notably the Sixth Symphony and the *Sinfonia Antartica*.

Film music was not his only preoccupation during the war years. The BBC commissioned six choral songs to sung in time of war, all to texts by Shelley, chosen by the composer with Ursula Wood's help. The summer of 1940 saw a visit to his old school for the ceremonial opening of the new music school there—a bold and enlightened gesture when the country was fighting for its survival and an occasion memorable for a performance of the *Toy Symphony* directed by the Headmaster, Robert Birley, in which the most distinguished living old Carthusian member of the musical profession 'solemnly, and, moreover, artistically' played the cuckoo. During the summer of 1940, he was busy learning to operate a stirrup-pump and 'digging for victory', as the contemporary slogan had it. This he did, his widow wrote, 'with zeal and fury'; and he kept his mind alert with omnivorous reading and writing both occasional journalistic pieces and works such as the delightful *Household Music* for four instruments, playable by any group of four musicians who could muster a couple of treble instruments, a tenor one and a bass one. But wartime inevitably brought losses, not all of them through enemy action. Dorothy Longman, a fine violinist and a friend of many years' standing for those wedding Ralph had played the organ in November 1915, died in June 1940 and Maurice Sheldon Amos shortly afterwards; and on 2 September, his well-loved niece Honorine, who for many years before her marriage acted as RVW and Adeline's chauffeur, was killed in an air-raid. Later that year, H. A. L. Fisher, the historian, Adeline's brother, also died; and so did a good friend of encyclopaedic scholarship and technical skill from his own profession: Donald Tovey.

RVW was appointed chairman of the Home Office Committee for the Release of Interned Alien Musicians; and his quiet work behind the scenes resulted in a number of useful releases. He organized and acted as *compère* at fortnightly concerts for the forces at the White Horse Assembly Rooms in Dorking and also arranged concerts of a more 'popular' nature at the Toc H depot behind the Red Lion Hotel, which combined with a happy informality popular pieces chosen by the audience and more unusual music selected by the organizer. He wrote articles and radio pieces, such as 'The Composer in Wartime', broadcast in 1940, the stirring piece on 'Nationalism and Internationalism', published in 1942 and that published in the *Manchester Guardian* in 1943 on William Shrubsole, the composer of the fine hymn-tune 'Miles Lane'. And, of course, he continued to compose.

He had found that it was possible after all to organize a Leith Hill Music Festival for March 1940 and the choirs performed *Elijah* and *Judas Maccabaeus*. The Festival acquired a new Secretary, Margery Cullen, as Lady Farrer was heavily involved in her full-time work for the Federation of Women's Institutes. The Dorking Halls had been requisitioned by the Meat Marketing Board; and Miss Cullen was given permission to use them for the Festival provided that the meat storage equipment was dismantled before the concerts and re-assembled (at twenty-four hours' notice if need be) after they were over. Eventually, however, somewhere else had to be found to house the Festival music-making, so until 1947, performances were given in St Martin's Church. It was there that in 1942, the regular annual performances began of Bach's *St Matthew Passion*, which later became an indispensable feature of the Festival, using RVW's own specially prepared 'piano concerto' continuo version.

A rather more hilarious musical episode that year was vividly described after RVW's death in a letter to Ursula Vaughan Williams by the CO of the 2nd Battalion of the Welsh Guards, Colonel Price. This involved Dame Clara Novello Davies, mother of the light music composer Ivor Novello. RVW had been invited to adjudicate at a regimental Eisteddfodd at Pirbright camp, near West Byfleet, where the Battalion was stationed, and had conscientiously rehearsed the entrants in their music. As President of the Eisteddfodd, Mme Novello Davies had composed a song for the occasion. In Colonel Price's words:

> Behind the stage the curtains parted. We beheld Madame Clara now sheathed from head to foot in tight gold lamé, a wreath of gold leaves in her hair and carrying a baton of gold leaves presented to her, we afterwards learned, by some long-forgotten President of France. As she advanced to conduct her song, the ranks of massed choirs in battle-dress parted in amazement. The train of her dress had caught in a nail on the Pirbright floor, the music of her song had been placed upside-down on the music stand and, the butterfly screw being loose, it gave way under her as she appeared to lean on it for support and down she went in deep but involuntary obeisance to the audience.[11]

Worse was to follow. After a long eulogy of her son, she launched into the performance of her song. It was a fiasco; and ' . . . oblivious of Vaughan Williams at her feet, of the audience and indeed of the occasion, she rapped out "You don't know it. Stand up!" ' and proceeded to drill them intensively until the Regimental Sergeant-Major saved the day by calling for three cheers for Madame Clara. One imagines that RVW joined in the cheering as heartily as anyone.

In 1942, RVW celebrated his seventieth birthday. Constant Lambert dedicated his beautiful and uncharacteristically pastoral *Aubade Héroique* to him to mark the occasion; and Gerald Finzi his fine cycle of Shakespearean songs *Let us Garlands Bring*. Among the hundreds of letters of congratulation there was one particularly prophetic passage in one from his cousin Ralph Wedgwood: 'The last Rembrandts were the best, the last Titians the most surprising—the arts often give to old age its finest moments, those which look over the edge of the world which surrounds them into the future.'[12] The widespread celebrations, despite wartime conditions, drew the country's attention to the quality of its leading composer. He did not rest on his laurels. Besides various wartime works, such as the choral song *England, my England*, two of the *Five Wartime Hymns* to words by Canon G. W. Briggs, and 'The Airmen's Hymn', he was busy on what many people at the time assumed would be the last of his symphonies: the Fifth. By 31 January 1943, it was ready for a two-piano play-through; and on 25 May, the London

[11] UVW, p. 238.   [12] Ibid., p. 251.

Philharmonic Orchestra played it through at the BBC's Maida Vale Studios. He conducted them in its first performance at a Promenade concert on 24 June; and it seemed to many of its first listeners and commentators to be some kind of valedictory vision. Visionary it may have been, for some of the music was drawn from an unfinished opera on *The Pilgrim's Progress*. Valedictory it certainly wasn't: four more symphonies were yet to come.

The White Gates offered shelter and accommodation for many friends and relatives during the war, including R. O. Morris and, from time to time, Ursula Wood, whose husband had died of a heart attack and who had a flat in London from which she was offered refuge by Adeline and RVW when the bombing got too fierce. More film music, incidental music for a broadcast performance of Shakespeare's *Richard II*, some informal pieces, such as the *Winter Piece*, for Genia Hornstein, a refugee friend, and the *Fantasia on 'Linden Lea'* for John Parr of Sheffield were composed, as well as more substantial works such as the charming oboe concerto for Leon Goossens and the String Quartet composed as a birthday gift for Jean Stewart, the viola-player of the Menges Quartet. (RVW's asking price for the dedication was 1,000 kisses!)

RVW also worked hard on behalf of his fellow musicians whom he considered had been misunderstood or unfairly treated by the authorities. Among these was the left-wing composer Alan Bush, whose music had been banned by the BBC. RVW wrote protesting about what he called 'this victimisation' and retaliated by returning the fee for a choral song commissioned by the Corporation and demanding the return of his MS. The same sense of fair play inspired him to act on behalf of Michael Tippett in June 1943 when he testified (unsuccessfully, unfortunately) in court on Tippett's behalf when there was the threat of his being sent to prison for refusing to do war service as a pacifist conscientious objector. What mattered to Vaughan Williams was that although he disagreed strongly with Tippett's views, Tippett held them out of conviction and that his work as a composer of 'very remarkable' music which he considered 'a distinct national asset', and as director of music at Morley College was increasing Britain's prestige in a manner that more orthodox war work would not have done. RVW judged people by such criteria as personal integrity, sincerity, and moral convictions. Tippett's views met these criteria; and that was enough to guarantee him Vaughan Williams's unstinted support.

By 1944, victory was in sight and relief and optimism were in the air. But 1944 was also saddened for RVW by the deaths of Henry Wood and of RVW's elder brother Hervey. At one stage of the year, Adeline, too, was very ill with pleurisy and pneumonia. Hervey left RVW Leith Hill Place, which he had inherited when their mother had died. RVW almost immediately made arrangements for it to be presented to the National Trust.

Thus things were for those who knew him and were of his family circle. But far beyond that circle, he became during the war years a kind of embodiment in music of the wartime spirit of Britain. The directness and simplicity of his art, the strength of will and quiet but firm patriotism that underlay it and that it seemed in some way to symbolize—these qualities reflected the 'real' Britain that emerged during the war years after the shifting improvisations and evasions of the 1930s. His music seemed to say with deeper and more immediate effect what he himself had written in 1942:

> I believe that love of one's country, one's language, one's customs, one's religion, are essential to our national health. We may laugh at these things, but we love them none the less. Indeed, it is one of our national characteristics and one which I should be sorry to see disappear, that we laugh at what we love. This is something that a foreigner can never fathom, but it is out of such characteristics, those hard knots in our timber, that we can help to build up a united Europe and a world federation.[13]

Those virtues that show the British at their best, more obvious perhaps in time of war when the survival of the nation itself is at stake, when illusions can lead to fatal errors and the truth, however harsh, must be faced seemed to be part of the fabric of his music. They struck a responsive chord in wartime audiences and revealed to the British how great a composer their foremost musical patriot was.

[13] *National Music*, p. 154.

7

The final years (1945–58)

In anticipation of the allied victory in 1945, the BBC had commissioned a work from Vaughan Williams entitled *Thanksgiving for Victory*, for speaker, chorus, and orchestra, which was recorded on 5 November 1944 and broadcast after the Nazi surrender as part of a special thanksgiving service on 13 May 1945. Vaughan Williams himself chose the words with care from familiar sources: the Bible, the Apocrypha, a few lines from *Henry V*, and Kipling's *Puck of Pook's Hill*.

It was certainly not inconsistent with his avowed agnosticism that he should have chosen texts with so many overtones of prayer to and reliance on God. First of all, the Thanksgiving was a special commission for a national rather than a personal celebration. It therefore had to take account not just of the composer's own beliefs, but of those held by other people. Secondly, Vaughan Williams could not possibly have chosen a text without considering its suitability for setting to music, and the moods the words projected as well as their relevance to a national act of thanksgiving. Thirdly, the texts he chose would have strong resonances amongst those brought up within the Christian tradition, even if like him they had rejected the theological foundations of Christianity. And fourthly, there is a great deal in the text with which no humanist or agnostic could take issue, such as for example the edited verses from Isaiah 61, (used in their full form by Elgar in the opening of the Prologue to *The Apostles*), where Vaughan Williams has deleted the reference to preaching the gospel but retained those to the proclamation of liberty to the captives and the opening of the prison to them that are bound. His re-ordering of the verses from Isaiah is also noteworthy, first enjoining a dedication to the task in hand of reconstruction and then foretelling that reconstruction shall take place and violence cease. What is notable is the tone of the text: humility, gratitude, and a firm statement of the justice of the cause, pledging the participants (and therefore the nation) to a just and charitable social order: in Kipling's words, 'an undefiled heritage', marked by

> . . . the strength that cannot seek
> By deed, or thought, to hurt the weak

and

> . . . delight in simple things,
> The mirth that has no bitter springs
> Forgiveness free of evil done,
> And love to all men 'neath the sun.[1]

Kipling's words expressed principles by which RVW had always lived and continued to live; and here again he had, it seemed, judged the mood of the nation, and particularly of many in the armed services, better than many politicians and not a few prelates.

RVW also gave firm and specific instructions as to the kind of voice he wanted, should the work be performed, as he intended, on other occasions just as *A Song of Thanksgiving*. Some of these are worth quoting:

> This work was originally designed for broadcasting. For concert and church use certain modifications are necessary. This is especially the case in the accompaniment to the speaker's voice. For broadcasting this should be performed poco forte, but 'faded down' so as to form a background to the voice. In the concert room this must be represented by the softest pianissimo so that the speaker's voice may absolutely dominate.

> The soprano part should be sung by a powerful dramatic voice, but there must be no vibrato. On no account should the part be sung by a single boy's voice, though in case of necessity it may be sung by several boys' voices in unison.

> The children's part must be sung by real children's voices, not sophisticated choir boys . . . [2]

Vaughan Williams therefore clearly had very definite ideas about how this music should sound; and if this is so of an occasional piece of this kind, it must surely be so of other works on a grander scale. A similar indication of what he wanted in a quite different context is provided by the little congratulatory speech he made to Sir Adrian Boult and the London Philharmonic Orchestra tacked on to the end of an early Decca recording of his symphonies, in which he drew attention to the eerie sustained pianissimo 'so full of tension' in the finale of the Sixth. Nor was he above gently but firmly and publicly rebuking performers at rehearsal if they tinkered about with his music. Yet he was prepared to give *carte blanche* within reason to a conductor such as Adrian Boult or John Barbirolli whom he trusted implicitly.

It was an appropriate coincidence that the season of Henry Wood Promenade Concerts that took place when the war with Japan was in its closing stages should have been the first to include all his five symphonies, though few people, the composer perhaps least of all, can have thought that the final tally was only just over half-complete. His

---

[1] *Puck of Pook's Hill*, The Hymn.
[2] Michael Kennedy, *The Works of Ralph Vaughan Williams* (OUP, 1964) (hereafter Kennedy, *Works* 1), pp. 575–6.

reputation and the veneration in which he was held were now such that he was asked to lend his name and presence to all sorts of gatherings and organizations. Any bodies who thought to exploit his name so as to glorify their own soon found that he invariably took his duties as chairman or president very seriously. He thus became a busy and conscientious member of many boards connected with musical, educational, cultural, and humanitarian projects. Among them was the Committee for the Promotion of New Music, formed in January 1943 with himself as president. Though he supported the committee's work enthusiastically, he was not always equally enthusiastic about the discussions that followed the play-throughs, given gratis after careful rehearsal by distinguished musicians. Under his presidency the committee grew from what he himself called 'thirty or so composers more or less taking in one another's washing' to an important element in the assessment and performance of contemporary music, giving its hundredth recital on 5 October 1948. Though not particularly sympathetic to some developments in modern music, he never failed to give encouragement to any 'wrong-note composer' as he called them, whom he felt to possess a real musical gift. On Sir Hugh Allen's death he succeeded him as President of the British Federation of Competitive Music Festivals, a task that he probably found more to his liking.

Some idea of the nature of everyday life at The White Gates during and after the war can be gained from a description set down shortly after his death by his 'niece' Mary Bennett:

> All its activity was contained in a single large room which, with galleries and inglenooks, seemed to be full of false old oak. The piano stood at one end, the dining table at the other; Robin Darwin's childhood sketch of R.V.W. conducting hung side by side with a bad reproduction of Van Gogh's chestnut tree on the walls; an exceptionally large cat slept in the warmest patch. Here Aunt Adeline would sit with her silver hair and long black dress, immobile in her high chair and infinitely welcoming; Uncle Ralph would come lumbering in from rolling the lawn or taking a practice for the Leith Hill Festival—or sitting to Epstein; as a treat there might be played a worn record of Noel Coward singing 'The Stately Homes of England', which reduced both to helpless laughter; there would be a delicious tea to which, when she could no longer use her crutch, Uncle Ralph would move Aunt Adeline, chair and all, with the greatest skill and delicacy. They were never alone. There was a student, perhaps, who needed quiet to prepare for examinations, a refugee, someone who happened to be homeless or convalescent, the little great-niece who sent a jet of fresh life spurting through the house as one of its wartime residents.[3]

'They were never alone'. Scores of those who knew Ralph and Adeline well bore witness to their hospitality. Visitors and guests were frequent at The White Gates. Adeline was a formidable correspondent, keeping in touch with friends and family alike; and Ralph too was extremely

[3] *RCM Magazine*, p. 20.

conscientious about answering letters, especially to the young. A nine-year-old lad, Tom Whitestone, had written to Sir John Barbirolli prais-ing a Haydn symphony played by the Hallé and adding that he had not liked Vaughan Williams's Eighth Symphony at the same concert. Barbirolli sent it on to the composer, who wrote back to the boy:

Dear Tom,
Sir John Barbirolli has sent me your letter to him—I am glad you like Haydn. He was a very great man and wrote beautiful tunes. I must one day write a tune which you will like.
Yours affectionately, R. Vaughan Williams[4]

Vaughan Williams almost invariably used the word 'tune' when refer-ring to one of his compositions. 'Tunes' kept pouring forth from him for the rest of his life, even though some slackening of activity would surely have been considered pardonable in a septuagenarian. In 1945, for exam-ple, he had composed the score, making use of Italian folk music, to the film *The Stricken Peninsula*, set in and dealing with the liberation and rehabilitation of Southern Italy. The following year saw the composition of the music to *The Loves of Joanna Godden*, a semi-tragic story set on Romney Marsh about the love-life of two contrasted sisters. It was the first time, Vaughan Williams remarked, that he had ever been asked to write music about an outbreak of foot-and-mouth disease. He managed to complete the score before the film itself was finished, a fact that Ealing Studios' shrewd and witty director of music, Ernest Irving, care-fully concealed from the directors, 'who must not', he wrote to RVW, 'be approached from windward'. He might have added the same about RVW on certain issues: the composer was most displeased when he found that an inappropriate Cornish carol had been introduced into a film set in Kent. The first proper professional performances of *Sir John in Love* and preparation for the first professional production of *The Shepherds of the Delectable Mountains* also took place in 1946, both at Sadler's Wells. So did the first play-throughs of the sketched version of the Sixth Symphony (Michael Mullinar heroically managing four in one day!). During that summer, RVW was also engaged on arranging his Piano Concerto for two keyboards.

Despite Adeline's growing indisposition, he was able—usually in charming and attractive female company, such as that of Ursula Wood or Genia Hornstein ('on the razzle again', as Adeline once put it in a let-ter to her sister Cordelia)—to attend important new works such as *Peter Grimes* and *The Rape of Lucretia*, both of which he admired; to visit inter-esting art exhibitions, such as those featuring Van Gogh and Paul Nash; and to keep up with new films, such as Eisenstein's *Ivan the Terrible*, with its stirring Prokofiev score. He was awarded the honorary freedom of the Worshipful Company of Musicians, formed a special choir in

[4] Kennedy, *Works* 2, p. 335.

Dorking to perform Bach's *St John Passion*, busied himself with the preparations for reviving the Leith Hill Festival in full for 1947 and was frequently in demand to conduct his works at concerts all over the country. Some prospective commissions even he had to turn down, however. He tactfully declined Boris Ord's request for a set of evening canticles for the choir of King's College Cambridge, and with characteristic frankness ('it seems ungracious after your splendid letter to make a grouse', he wrote, by way of a warning shot over the bows) added a sting in the tail of his letter by gently reproving Ord for not including enough English carols in the annual broadcast Christmas Eve service of Nine Lessons and Carols. Ord was not the only recipient of such a rebuke. The same thing happened when RVW wrote to congratulate Cecil Cochrane, Robin Lang's successor at Christ's Hospital, on the standard of performance of his choir's end-of-term carol service broadcast in 1950.

The revived full Leith Hill Festival in 1947 was a notable success, the choirs tackling Bach's B minor Mass for the first time in an English version prepared by Vaughan Williams himself. That year, at the first Edinburgh Festival, when the choice of programme was left open to each conductor, all five of the major orchestras participating (three British, one French and one Viennese) offered the *Fantasia on a Theme by Thomas Tallis* in their programmes. It was allotted to the Vienna Philharmonic under Bruno Walter, as their programme had been received first. On 9 October, he and Adeline celebrated their golden wedding; and three days later, his own seventy-fifth birthday. The celebrations included broadcasts of a personal selection of his music (*Flos Campi*, *Sancta Civitas*, and the *Four Hymns*), a party at Cecil Sharp House, a concert including *A Sea Symphony* and *Five Tudor Portraits* at the Dorking Halls, followed the next day by a birthday party at which a conjuror performed, at the guest of honour's special request. Three days later, RVW conducted the BBC Symphony Orchestra in his *London Symphony*.

This symphony was a favourite with him; he conducted it at intervals almost to the end of his life; and although his hearing was now beginning to deteriorate, which limited his ability to pick out and solve problems in such a delicate and colourful orchestral texture, he was so revered by orchestral musicians that they invariably gave of their best for him. In later years, he amassed a veritable battery of hearing aids, the largest of which was a formidable affair that he referred to as his 'coffee-pot'; and there are striking photographs of him with it listening, perhaps, to some new work or other at one of the numerous festivals of music, new and old, in which he continued to take a lively interest.

In 1948 came what was probably his most impressive film score and the one that seems to have involved him most deeply on a personal level, that to *Scott of the Antarctic*. He did his homework thoroughly on the background to the expedition; and he was appalled by much of what he learned about the inefficient preparations for the expedition and of the unnecessary exposure of its members to fatal risks. Other works of this period included two arrangements of German traditional carols, the *Introduction and Fugue* for two pianos, also composed for Cyril Smith and his wife Phyllis Sellick, the motets *The Souls of the Righteous*, composed for the dedication of the Battle of Britain Chapel in Westminster Abbey on 10 July 1947, and *The Voice out of the Whirlwind*, adapted from 'Galliard of the Sons of the Morning' from *Job* to words from the Book of Job. But most important and most arresting of all was the Sixth Symphony, first performed by the BBC Symphony Orchestra under Sir Adrian Boult at the Royal Albert Hall on 21 April 1948. The impact on the audience was profound. Among those present was the musicologist and critic Deryck Cooke. He wrote

> Rumour said it was a sort of cross between the Fourth and the Fifth, being neither as violent as the one, nor as serene as the other. Nothing could have been further from the truth.
> The effect on the present writer, at the first performance, was nothing short of cataclysmic . . . [5]

Cooke was by no means the only listener who was shattered by the work. Amongst probably thousands of others, a small group of normally voluble music-loving national servicemen at the Royal Signals War Office transmission station at Droitwich were reduced, despite unreliable reception on an extremely low-fi NAAFI recreation-room radio, to a prolonged and awestruck post-performance silence by the impact of the rampaging opening, the great flowing melody at the end of the first movement, the relentless trumpet and drum patterns in the second, the jazzy saxophone solo in the third and what seemed the utter desolation of the finale. Within a year it had achieved nearly a hundred performances, by no means all of them in the English-speaking world. It was plain that, like Verdi, he was full in his old age of new and unpredictable musical ideas.

This meant in turn that he was in demand for commissions. Sometimes these were fulfilled with an alacrity a little disconcerting to his collaborators. Having been asked to provide a tune for the Scottish supplement to *The English Hymnal* to an as yet unwritten hymn about St Margaret, he asked Ursula Wood if she would provide the text, adding that there was no hurry. When next she visited him a few days later, having carefully done her homework on the subject, she was greeted with an apology and the news that he had written the tune that morning and to the metre of 'The Charge of the Light Brigade' to boot. (The hymn is No. 748 in *Hymnal for Scotland*: 'Praise God for Margaret'.) As he told her on another occasion, when they were collaborating on *The Sons of Light*, 'where there are difficulties it is the librettist's part to yield

[5] Deryck Cooke, *The Language of Music* (OUP, 1959), p. 252.

gracefully, to accommodate, to alter, to adapt, and generally to be tractable', so, as the poet herself puts it, 'I knew my place exactly'. Another 'occasional' work of this time is the *Prayer to the Father of Heaven*, a Skelton setting in quite a different vein from *Five Tudor Portraits*, first performed in Oxford on 12 May 1948 and dedicated 'to the memory of my master Hubert Parry'. He re-clothed the *Double Trio* for strings in orchestral garb as the *Partita for Double String Orchestra*.

Outings to music festivals continued unabated—often, like that to the Three Choirs Festival of 1948, involving a whirlwind round of parties and excursions as well as the concerts to be heard and works to be conducted. So did visits to the theatre and the cinema. A theatre outing that he particularly looked forward to was the first ever production of *Job* using the original full score. This was at Covent Garden, and the work's dedicatee, Sir Adrian Boult, who in his younger days had conducted regularly for the Diaghilev ballet, was in charge of the orchestra. Though Robert Helpmann was superb in the role of Satan, the production, despite effective choreography, did not entirely please the composer. The original score contains detailed stage directions, many of which were simply ignored; and this vitiated some of his most dramatic *coups de théâtre*. The age of the producer whose ego-trip fantasies take precedence over and often conflict with those of the creative artist had already dawned, it seems.

The great sculptor Jacob Epstein had for some time wanted to make a bust of Vaughan Williams; and early in 1949, the sittings were arranged. Epstein wrote in his autobiography:

> Here was the master with whom no one would venture do dispute. He reminded one in appearance of some eighteenth-century admiral whose word was law. Notwithstanding I found him the epitome of courtesy and consideration, and I was impressed by the logic and acuteness of everything he discoursed upon and was made aware of his devotion to an art as demanding as sculpture.[6]

Epstein's bust has not met with universal favour as a complete portrait of the subject: the 'eighteenth-century admiral' aspect of his sitter seems to dominate the end-product, but it undeniably catches the immense rugged power, the solidity, and the dignity that are so much part of RVW's character and his music. Yet the phrase is both telling and apt, when one considers the combination of whimsical banter, self-effacing charm, and forthright, at times almost cussed bluntness that characterized many of his public utterances on subjects other than music and often on music itself. What it misses is the wit, the gentleness, the serenity, and the 'courtesy and consideration' that Epstein himself mentions.

Epstein was not the only artist wishing to portray Vaughan Williams. The renowned portrait photographer Josif Karsh—Karsh of Ottawa, as

---

[6] Jacob Epstein, *Autobiography* (London, 1955), p. 171.

he was universally known—spent a day, uninvited, photographing him in the summer of 1949, brooking no protests that RVW had work to do and peremptorily insisting that his subject should shave and put on a tie for the occasion. The photographs when they came out fully justified the unceremonious treatment RVW had to put up with: they reveal the warmth, the sly, twinkling wit, and the strength of his character admirably. Sir Gerald Kelly, commissioned by the RCM to paint a portrait of RVW in June 1952, was less peremptory but equally eager to paint him. In fact, so impressed was he by his sitter that six years later, he remarked that RVW was so much more beautiful at eighty-five than he had been at eighty that he felt the need to paint him again. So he did. Again, the results are both striking and true to character.

Later in 1949, when his old school celebrated its quatercentenary, he wrote a masque for the occasion, incorporating the School Song into it. (The school returned the compliment some three years later by arranging a special celebration for his eightieth birthday.) The Festival of Britain, commemorating the centenary of the Great Exhibition of 1851, was by now in full preparation; and Vaughan Williams set to work completing the project that had been at the back of his mind ever since his early days as a young composer: the morality/opera *The Pilgrim's Progress*, which was to be put on at Covent Garden as part of the Festival.[7] None of his major works caused him so much anxiety, pain, and grief. It did not go down well. RVW had insisted that the conductor should be involved in every stage of the preparation, which meant that none of the 'opera house hacks' as he called them, was available. This was probably just as well, for even Erich Kleiber, shrewd and experienced 'opera house hack' as he was, dismissed the work with the off-hand comment 'Nothing much you can do with it, is there?'

The conductor at the first performance was the comparatively unknown Leonard Hancock, who was so self-effacing that Sir Thomas Beecham, with that grand-seigneurial arrogance so typical of his wit at its least appealing, loudly remarked after being introduced to him 'Does he breathe?' Hancock did a competent job, but it may well be that he was too good a team man and lacked the force of personality to press the claims of the score in the face of a production whose costumes and lighting were by all accounts unimaginative and unappealing, Apollyon being presented as 'a cross between an Assyrian figure and the Michelin tyre advertisement'. The composer was bitterly disappointed. 'They won't like it, they don't want an opera with no heroine and no love duets—and I don't care. It's what I want and there it is.' And there matters rested for the time being. What could be done with it, under a forceful and sympathetic conductor, with a carefully-planned production and an enthusiastic, committed, and talented cast was proved, first at the

---

[7] Some of the music had been written for a radio version in 1942.

Cambridge Guildhall in 1954 by the Cambridge University Musical Society under Boris Ord, with Denis Arundell as producer and—even more effectively, as the CDs show—in March 1992 at the Royal Northern College of Music under Igor Kennaway, with Joseph Ward producing.

RVW was asked to compose a work for children's voices as part of the celebrations. Protesting his ignorance of such works, he persuaded Ursula Wood to write the poem for him and on 6 May 1951, *The Sons of Light*, a substantial piece lasting some twenty-five minutes, was performed at the Royal Albert Hall by a massed choir of over 1100 voices from the Schools' Music Association of Great Britain, who had commissioned the piece.

Pilgrim and *The Sons of Light* were the last works of her husband that Adeline was to experience. She died on the afternoon of 10 May, when RVW had been at a rehearsal by the London University Choral Society of *Toward the Unknown Region*.

As Elgar had been when his wife died, Vaughan Williams was distraught; but his reaction was totally different from Elgar's. After the funeral, he refused to look back in anger or regret, let alone virtually abandon his craft, but plunged into a round of relentless professional and domestic activity. He attended a wide range of performances, not just of his own music: they included one, for example, of Britten's *Spring Symphony*. Britten, like Walton, or like Elgar, for that matter, was a composer whose work he respected and admired rather than loved, but he had no doubts as to the quality of any of the three as artists. Other younger composers whose work appealed to him included among others Edmund Rubbra, Michael Tippett, Herbert Howells, Gerald Finzi, Elizabeth Maconchy, and Richard Rodney Bennett. Even when he was not on the same wavelength as the composer, he usually took the trouble to go and talk to him afterwards, encouraging him if he felt that he had something to say musically, as was the case, for example, with Peter Racine Fricker.

His musical tastes remained consistent, though not unchanging, throughout his life and his respect was always engaged when he felt that the composer took his craft seriously, if his own imagination was sufficiently involved. Certain composers went 'off the boil', as he put it; but he recognized and acknowledged the greatness of others, such as Beethoven, whose music did not appeal to him. Gustav Mahler, whose music he did not like, he judged 'a tolerable imitation of a composer' because of his intensely professional attitude to his craft. It was only when 'putting the black dots on the paper' seemed to him merely a matter of completing a sterile and meaningless pattern that his distaste and disapproval were aroused. Most of Stravinsky, apart from *Firebird*, *Les Noces*, the Suite for Violin and Piano, and the *Symphony of Psalms*, and all that he knew of Bruckner bored him; Sibelius, Janáček, and Bartók seemed of his contemporaries to attract him most. He dismissed the

atonalists as practitioners of 'the worst kind of German music', meaning the strict observance of pedantic rules that crippled imagination by
excessive attention to technique. This was something from which he had
been fighting to free English composers all his life and which he now
saw as sneaking in through the back door through the advent of atonal-
ism among the youngest generation. In his contribution to a *Music &
Letters* symposium on Arnold Schoenberg, he commented with curt
frankness: 'Schoenberg meant nothing to me—but as he apparently
meant a lot to other people I daresay it is all my own fault.'[8] This, it
may well be imagined, did not endear him to the pundits of musical solid
geometry who were to dismiss even Schoenberg as old hat later on.

During the early summer that followed Adeline's death, he set about
revising *The Pilgrim's Progress*. Ursula Wood, whom he had asked to
manage his domestic affairs on a three-day-a-week basis, provided the
words for a new song for Lord Lechery in the Vanity Fair scene. Not
having had a holiday away from home since 1939, he went with her for
a few days to Romney Marsh, where he insisted on climbing the church
tower at Rye—at the age of seventy-eight—to admire the view. He also
took advantage of the holiday to re-read *Lavengro*: Borrow was one of
his favourite authors, along with Whitman, Matthew Arnold, and Blake.
It was at this time that a visit to Stratford-upon-Avon on the return journey from the Three Choirs Festival at Worcester sparked off a project
to re-read the entire canon of Shakespeare's plays.

Needless to say, there were numerous visits to the opera. In 1951
alone, he was able to compare two different productions of *Sir John in
Love*, one by the students of the Royal Academy of Music and one by
the Clarion Singers of Birmingham. He travelled to Oxford to see Egon
Wellesz's *L'Incognita* and went to both the dress rehearsal and the first
night of *Billy Budd* as well as to Tchaikovsky's *The Queen of Spades*.
Another outing was to see Holst's *Savitri* at the St Pancras Town Hall,
conducted as part of a triple bill that included Mozart's *The Impresario*
and Menotti's *The Telephone*, by the rising young opera conductor Colin
Davis. In 1952 he even attended the dress rehearsal and first performance
at Covent Garden of Berg's *Wozzeck*, which he was glad to have seen
without particularly enjoying it, but he baulked at the offer of compli-
mentary tickets for Strauss's *Elektra*, which he had seen—and disliked—
as a young man before the First World War.

On 14 December 1951, he became the first honorary Doctor of Music
of the University of Bristol, receiving his honour from the University's
chancellor, Winston Churchill. After the ceremony, he paid a visit to an
old friend, Arnold Barter, whose amateur choir had given performances
of *Toward the Unknown Region* and *A Sea Symphony* when they had been
new and pioneering works.

---

[8] *Music & Letters*, Vol. xxxii, No. 4.

Causes close to his heart continued to arouse his sympathy—and his ire against those who seemed to him obstructive, obtuse, or short-sighted. When the Bournemouth Council threatened to disband the Municipal Orchestra, which under Rudolf Schwarz, and after him Charles Groves, had reached a higher standard of performance than ever before in its history, RVW wrote a formidable letter to the *Bournemouth Daily Echo* castigating the proposal: 'Up to the present, largely owing to its Symphony Orchestra, Bournemouth has been a civilised town. Are your Council prepared to let their names go down to posterity stigmatised with the disgrace of allowing the town, for whose welfare, spiritual as well as material, they are responsible, to lapse into barbarism?'[9] The Orchestra survived, but as the Bournemouth Symphony Orchestra, not the Municipal Orchestra, still generously supported by the municipal authority. Similarly, when it was proposed to close down the Crown Film Unit, which had commissioned much fine incidental music from promising young British composers, he wrote to *The Times* describing the decision as 'a sentence damaging to our colleagues at home and our prestige abroad'. He came sturdily to the defence of his old teacher, Stanford, when on the occasion of his centenary, the same newspaper criticised his *Stabat Mater* (a work that Elgar had thought highly enough of to insist on its performance at the Three Choirs Festival when he and Stanford were not even on speaking terms) on stylistic grounds. He informed an International Folk Music Council Conference in London in July 1952 that there was too much of a tendency, not confined to Britain, to admire foreign products at the expense of home-grown ones. And in 1953, when much hot air was generated by reactions to the style and subject-matter of Britten's fine coronation opera *Gloriana*, given its first performance before an audience which, as has been remarked, would probably have found Edward German's *Merrie England* musically taxing, he voiced his own opinion in *The Times* with tact and frankness, at the same time indirectly rebuking those who had dismissed the work outright for various reasons, most of them totally irrelevant to its merits as an opera:

> I do not propose, after a single hearing, to appraise either the words or the music of *Gloriana*. The important thing to my mind, at the moment, is that, so far as I know, for the first time in our history, the Sovereign has commanded an opera from these islands for a great occasion. Those who cavil at the public expense involved should realize what such a gesture means to the prestige of our music.

Such words, coming from one who knew full well what public neglect of his own operas implied, went completely over the heads of most of the other participants in the correspondence.

---

[9] UVW, p. 322.

Other topics, such as the inadequacy of royalties paid to composers on sales of gramophone records, the curtailment of the Third Programme and the future of John Nash's elegant terrace houses in Regent's Park, also called forth trenchant comment and usually vigorous action from him. When Rutland Boughton, whom he liked and respected both as a man and a musician, tried and failed to gain his support for a communist-inspired Peace Manifesto, he got very short shrift indeed:

> I am not afraid to have the finger of scorn pointed at me because I refuse to be taken in by all these bogus 'peace' moves which I think have duped even you.
>
> Ever since I had a vote I have voted either Radical or Labour except once, after the last war when I was so disgusted by what I considered the mean trick of the Labour party in forcing an election.
>
> I voted Labour in the last election though in my heart of hearts I wanted the Tories to get in, but the old spirit of opposition crept up and with all the country shouting for the Tories I determined to be on the other side; so I assure you my spirit remains what you call 'generous'. I believe in freedom and that is why I will not be bullied by Nazis, Fascists or Russians.[10]

RVW was equally forthright (and sometimes wilful) in condemning with a Johnsonian forcefulness other contemporary trends of which he disapproved. 'Authentic' performances of eighteenth-century music on an intimate scale on reconstructed instruments, for example, were anathema to him: he even disliked the sound of the harpsichord, preferring a piano for the continuo part. He dismissed the revival of early nineteenth-century Italian *bel canto* opera as 'shaking the dead bones of *Norma*'; and for the 'bubble-and-squeak' tone of the baroque organ he entertained a contempt worthy of the Great Cham himself. Misguided or not, he was always sincere in his firmly-expressed opinions, always direct and never mean or petty.

In *Cakes and Ale*, Somerset Maugham drew the somewhat cynical conclusion that longevity was more or less an essential of genius in England. While it is true that the massive figure of the veteran composer was revered on account of the 'character' which the public saw and heard of, the compositions of his old age generally belie any thought that it was simply on account of his age that he was admired. When, for example, the Royal Festival Hall was opened in June 1951, it went without saying that his then latest symphony, the Sixth, should be included in one of the two inaugural concerts. Arturo Toscanini, no less, was the conductor invited to direct the BBC Symphony Orchestra in the concert, but he was unable to accept—a pity, for it is fascinating to conjecture what the great Italian would have made of the work. In the event, the programmes were taken over *en bloc* by Sir Malcolm Sargent. At the more formal and musically less substantial concert that had commemorated

---

[10] Ibid., p. 323.

the ceremonial opening of the hall, the *Serenade to Music* had been performed in its choral version with a special orchestra under Sir Adrian Boult.

In October 1952, he celebrated his eightieth birthday. Concerts at Dorking and at the Royal Festival Hall brought home to him how respected and beloved he was by musicians and the general public alike; and one of the ways in which he chose to celebrate a birthday treat himself was a visit to see Gershwin's *Porgy and Bess*. That same year, he was asked by *The Sunday Times* to list his books of the year. He must have surprised many readers with his choice: Eric de Maré's *Times on the Thames*, A. P. Herbert's *Why Waterloo?*, Cecil Day Lewis's *Poems*, and his cousin Gwen Raverat's *Period Piece*, in which memories of himself as an undergraduate were described with obvious affection, a certain awe, and gentle amusement.

He also continued to surprise the critics, the public, and possibly even himself with his later compositions. Once, indeed, he so surprised himself that he even denied all knowledge of the work. This was a 1949 documentary film called *Dim Little Island*, which used some of his folk-song music and in which he himself spoke part of the commentary, describing the way in which the higher reaches of British musical life depended on the grass roots activities of folk-singers and amateur musicians. His remarkable memory for once betrayed him here: he vigorously denied any connection with the film when it was pointed out that no mention of it was made in cataloguing his film scores for *Grove's Dictionary*. The film certainly seems to have been somewhat nondescript: another of the participants, Osbert Lancaster, told Michael Kennedy that until Kennedy reminded him of the film's existence and of Vaughan Williams's involvement with it, he had forgotten all about it.

A much more memorable film was *Scott of the Antarctic*, some of the music from which was reworked into a seventh symphony, the *Sinfonia Antartica*, dedicated to Ernest Irving, musical director of Ealing Films, and first performed in Manchester on 14 January 1953 under a conductor for whom RVW's growing admiration eventually knew no bounds: John Barbirolli. 'Glorious John', as RVW christened him, was to receive the dedication three years later of its successor, the Eighth, in which he experimented not only with captivating new sonorities but new forms.

A man so involved in public activities and so vigorous in the practice of his own art was not surprisingly equally vigorous in his human and personal relationships. The great (such as Kathleen Ferrier, whom he met at a dinner party given by the Barbirollis and took to at once) and the little, the old and the young, all received forthright and kindly advice and criticism from him when it was required and deserved. In one case a long-standing friendship developed into something deeper. The poet and writer Ursula Wood, widowed during the Second World War, had sporadically written texts for him to set ever since they had first met in

1938. After Adeline's death, she became a frequent companion, accompanying him on holidays, such as his first visit to France for many years in 1952, to festivals, concerts, and theatre visits. She it was, for example, who wrote the poem 'Silence and Music' for his contribution to a symposium tribute *A Garland for the Queen* by British composers to the second Elizabeth (a direct, intentional and, it must be confessed, far less exhilarating parallel to the *Oriana* madrigals for the first). On the evening of 13 January 1953, before going up to Manchester to hear Barbirolli première the *Sinfonia Antartica*, they went to Covent Garden to hear him conduct *Tristan und Isolde*. It was certainly not just the intoxication of the music that prompted RVW to propose, nor his companion to accept him; and on 7 February 1953, they were quietly married in the vestry chapel of St Pancras church—so quietly, indeed, that when RVW asked Margery Cullen to take a Leith Hill rehearsal of the *St Matthew Passion* for him scheduled for that day because he had 'another engagement' none of the singers knew what the other engagement was. The honeymoon journey, delayed until May because of the bridegroom's very full diary, was spent in Italy, taking in Bergamo, Desenzano, Sirmione, Verona, Padua, Venice, and Milan, where a shortage of cash in those days of meagre currency allowances for trips abroad and the unavailability of tickets precluded a hoped-for visit to La Scala. That year's Leith Hill Festival was his last as conductor. The newly-weds had decided to live in London, which meant his having to resign from the conductorship, so in August 1953, The White Gates was put up for sale and they moved to 10 Hanover Terrace, NW1, in Regent's Park, where he lived for the rest of his life.

In June 1953 came the Coronation, for which Vaughan Williams had composed the exquisite anthem *O Taste and See*. He also arranged the 'Old Hundredth' for congregation, choir, and orchestra, drawing on the setting of the psalm on which it was based that he had composed nearly a quarter of a century previously for the Leith Hill Festival. Both of his contributions were supremely suited to the occasion, though the intended impact of the hymn, he claimed, was somewhat marred by some members of the huge congregation at Westminster Abbey who either got the rhythms wrong or joined in when they were supposed not to.

Just before the coronation, on 26 May, came a sad personal blow, the death of Hubert Foss who had for so long helped see many of RVW's works through the press. One work that Foss died too early to advise on was the Christmas cantata *Hodie*, for which Vaughan Williams and his wife had arranged the text. It was first performed at the Worcester Three Choirs Festival on 8 September 1954 under the composer's direction; and it was perhaps with the reception of *Hodie* that something of a reaction can be discerned against the pre-eminent place he occupied in English music. In the April and May 1955 issues of *Musical Opinion*,

Donald Mitchell, later to become Professor of Music at Sussex University, referred to the piece as 'grossly over-praised and grossly under-composed', commenting on its 'clumsy technique' and its 'downright unacceptable and damaging primitivity' yet acknowledging his 'very real and personal genius', which would, he said, 'keep his music alive'. Such comments were by no means new. In the 1920s similar things had been said about RVW by critics such as Cecil Gray; and throughout his career he had in general been treated somewhat patronizingly by other well-known critics, including Ernest Newman.

It was felt by some that his strong sense of national musical pride was in some way narrowly insular. Nothing could have been further from the truth. When addressing a lunch given in his honour by the Manchester branch of the Federal Union, he had repeated almost verbatim the words he had written in 1942 about love for one's country being the foundation on which a united Europe and a world federation should be built. He never wavered from those beliefs, least of all in his attitude to his own art. But he never lost sight of the wider vision of that art being part of the great Western cultural heritage. He was in this respect very similar to the great German poet and dramatist, Goethe, who had brought German literature to an unprecedented peak of excellence that was none the less based on an awareness that it was part of a common European heritage. The parallel with Goethe is perhaps worth pursuing further. Both of them kept major works—in Goethe's case, *Faust* and in Vaughan Williams's *The Pilgrim's Progress*—by them all their long lives until they were ready to give them to the world. Both of them were men whose classic calm and dignity concealed a vigorous, even volcanic temperament which is not always evident in their work. Both were extremely versatile and willing to tackle almost any form. Both continued to work energetically until the very last days of their lives; and both owed much to the advice and critical stimulus of a younger friend whose acquaintance they had made when quite young and who died considerably earlier than they did themselves: Schiller on the one hand and Holst on the other. Both lived a busy public life, but neither forgot his calling as an artist. When he was eighty-one years of age, Goethe wrote:

> Diese Richtung ist gewiss,
> Immer schreite! Schreite!
> Finsterniss und Hinderniss
> Drängt mich nicht zur Seite.[11]

To no one do these words apply with greater force than to Ralph Vaughan Williams.

---

[11] 'This direction is certain: keep pressing on! keep pressing on! Neither darkness nor obstacle will force me aside.'

Whatever the critical response to *Hodie*, Vaughan Williams continued to pour forth works either to commission or simply because he felt the urge to compose them. A concerto for the London Symphony Orchestra's tuba player on the occasion of the Orchestra's golden jubilee in 1954 broke new ground both for the composer and for the repertory. A set of variations was composed as a test piece for the 1957 National Brass Band Championship at the Royal Albert Hall (which he attended and where he presented the prize to Munn and Felton's Band, the eventual winners). *The Times* considered this 'unquestionably the best piece ever written for this unwieldy medium'—a clumsy compliment to a movement that had encouraged popular music-making in a form that was both subtle in sound and texture and capable of bringing out the musical potential of the ordinary Englishman. His later years also brought a remarkable violin sonata, a number of songs, music for the British Transport Commission's film *The England of Elizabeth*; and of course, the Eighth and Ninth Symphonies: his output would have been remarkable in a man half his age.

His appetite for travel remained insatiable. Early in 1954, the baritone singer Keith Falkner, who had been living for some time in the USA, was lunching at Hanover Terrace, when Vaughan Williams chanced to remark that he had never visited Rome nor seen the Grand Canyon. What should they do about it? His wife suggested that they should see them both; and in May of that year, an Italian holiday that included stays in Pisa, Florence, Siena, San Giminiano, and Rome enabled him to realize one ambition. As for the other, Falkner pointed out that a visiting professorship at Cornell University might be a useful springboard for an American tour. So, late in September 1954, he and Ursula arrived at Ithaca, NY, for the beginning of his third and last visit to the States. It lasted four months. As usual, his energy seems to have left everyone else save himself physically exhausted. After a hectic day seeing the sights of New York, for instance, he insisted that the whole party should go to the top of the Empire State Building to see the sunset. Fortunately, the lifts were working, but even had they not been so, it would probably not have deterred him.

His Cornell lectures developed a similar theme to the earlier American course published as *National Music*, and they in their turn were published in 1955 under the title *The Making of Music*. During this visit, he conducted and attended performances as well as lecturing and wherever he went, his robust vitality, his kindness, and his humour deeply impressed everyone he met. Everyone, that is, with the possible exception of the unfortunate young Cornell student who played over to him on the piano a movement from a somewhat dissonant quartet, at the end of which he simply peered down his glasses and observed: 'If a tune *should* occur to you, my boy, don't hesitate to write it down.' The comment might have come from Stanford himself; the bantering tone in which it was

95

delivered such that no offence could possibly have been taken. This was typical: 'Even when he is telling you you are wrong,' Michael Kennedy quotes a friend as saying, 'you feel "What a pleasure!"'

The visit was a triumphal progress across a huge country. The University of Michigan at Ann Arbor, where he celebrated his eighty-second birthday, organized a special concert of his music that included *On Wenlock Edge* and the *Serenade to Music* in his honour. At Indiana University, which he also visited, they had recently performed *Five Tudor Portraits*; and at UCLA he was able to experience something quite out of the ordinary: *Riders to the Sea* performed, first as a play and then as his opera. At Yale, he received the highest award that the University can bestow: the Howland Memorial Prize. At Buffalo, he conducted the Tallis Fantasia before Josef Krips, the Buffalo Symphony's principal conductor, and performed *Sancta Civitas* before an ecstatic audience of 3,000. At Cornell, he was able to conduct the same orchestra in *A London Symphony*, having to use an unfamiliar unmarked score because his own had somehow got locked in the piano, his visible irritation at the mishap adding a special edge and verve to his conducting and to the performance. The Grand Canyon was duly visited, but no descent was attempted: RVW felt that the donkeys would be unable to support his weight. But he still maintained that nothing in the States equalled as a spectacle the New York skyline.

Further holidays, described in loving and entertaining detail by his wife, took him in 1955 to Greece (including a swim in the Aegean and a return journey via Venice, Solèsmes, and St Malo) and Ireland, to Majorca in 1956, to Austria in 1957, and to Italy, where he and Ursula were able to spend a month with Sir William and Lady Walton at their island home on Ischia, in 1958. Life at home took in an almost incessant round of concerts, festivals, and other functions, including the regular 'Singeries' that he and Ursula had inaugurated at Hanover Terrace not long after their marriage. Groups of friends were invited to sing madrigals (always conducted by the host), enjoy copious food and drink and—if they were young and pretty, as most of the lady guests were—be vigorously kissed by the conductor. But for all the jollity, nobody was allowed to lose sight of the fact that the primary purpose of the singery was to explore seriously and with care the rich treasures of the Tudor and Jacobean repertory.

By this time, RVW had become not just a beloved national institution, but a musical elder statesman of international repute. Thanks to broadcasting and long-playing gramophone records, his music was known far beyond his own shores. (Michael Kennedy points out that between September and November 1957, the Eighth Symphony alone, to say nothing of several works that he mentions, was performed in Helsinki, Malmö, Houston, Hilversum, and Cape Town, twice in Rotterdam and no fewer than ten times in Boston.) The National Arts Foundation of

America had voted this 'Miltonic figure', as it called him, the outstanding musician of 1953, describing his music as 'full of splendour without tinsel'. (One wonders whose music among his contemporaries might have been characterized as 'tinsel' if the last two words were intended to convey any sub-text.) In Germany, the editor of Schumann's *Neue Zeitschrift für Musik*, Dr Heinrich Lindlar, published a highly appreciative article on his symphonies, shrewdly taking the scherzos as starting points for a perceptive discussion of their structural strength, depth, and range. In November 1955, he became the first musician ever to receive the Albert Medal of the Royal Society of Arts. He had every reason to rest on his laurels and bask in his fame.

He didn't. When death quietly and unexpectedly overtook him on the night of 25/26 August 1958, he had been at work on another opera, *Thomas the Rhymer*, to a libretto by his wife, based on two English folkballads. He also left sketches for a Cello Concerto, for a number of songs, for a piece for Vibraphone, for a string quartet, and for a long-cherished opera on the subject of Belshazzar.

His funeral service in Westminster Abbey on 19 September included, in accordance with his wishes, Maurice Greene's 'Lord, let me know mine end' and Bach's Fugue in E flat. His own work was represented by *Five Variants of 'Dives and Lazarus'*, by 'Rhosymedre', by 'O Taste and See', and by his coronation setting of the 'Old Hundredth', by 'Down Ampney' and by the 'Pavan of the Sons of the Morning' from *Job*. Craftsman and artist, visionary and common man, the rich diversity of his musical character was well represented by this choice. This 'tremendous figure', as Benjamin Britten called him in a letter to his widow, who showed 'wonderful, uncompromising courage in fighting for all those things he believed in', things, Britten added, that he personally believed to be some of the most important in life, had once told Herbert Howells shortly after the end of the Second World War, that all he required was a little time to glean his mind. The 'gleanings' had included four symphonies, some remarkable songs, an opera, a concerto, and a cantata. He had left one uncompleted work, a masque called *The First Nowell* to a text arranged from medieval plays by Simona Pakenham, the author of a recently-published and highly discerning study of his music. The time he required had been allotted to him; he had not wasted it.

8

The simple kleptomaniac

A favourite word in Vaughan Williams's vocabulary was 'cribbing'. He had no qualms, he claimed, about deliberately basing a theme or a movement on an idea lifted from some other composer; and he seems rather to have enjoyed projecting an image of himself as a man of little originality who plundered his predecessors and contemporaries, helping himself to whatever was of use to him. This, as we have seen, he regarded as a perfectly legitimate way of developing a characteristic style. He kept good company: Handel, for example, was one of the greatest and most effective 'cribbers' of all time. In the obituary notice quoted in chapter 3, Herbert Howells called him a 'great original [who] liked to be thought a simple kleptomaniac let loose harmlessly among his creative peers—or inferiors'. What goods he pilfered and how he blended them into his own characteristic musical merchandise are a measure of his own originality.

In *National Music*, he states with approval: 'The best composers store up half-fledged ideas in the works of others and make use of them to build up perfect edifices which take on the character of their maker because they are ideas which appeal to that special mind.'[1] Of nobody was this statement more true than of Vaughan Williams himself. He often pointed out where he cribbed certain themes and ideas: Satan's Dance, from *Job*, is a development of an idea first put on paper in the scherzo of Beethoven's F major quartet, Op. 135—recognizably so; and the composer admitted as much. Similarly, the opening of the Fourth Symphony has been said to be derived either from a 'freak work' performed at some contemporary music festival of which he had read an account, or, by the composer's admission, from the grinding dissonance at the opening of the finale of Beethoven's Ninth. Much more interesting, however, are the cases where, consciously or unconsciously, he adapts a scheme that another composer had used before and explores its meaning in a different and sometimes more profound manner.

Two of the most striking cases of this are the Fourth and Sixth Symphonies. The former might be described as a nightmare version of

---

[1] *National Music*, p. 27.

Beethoven's Fifth. The superficial features of this can be seen in the grop-
ing lead into the finale from the explosive Scherzo (itself a kind of updated
version of that of the Beethoven, with its 'Leith Hill Rocket' built up from
a chain of superimposed fourths and its grotesquely capering trio). There
is the same build-up of top-heavy harmony over a reiterated figure in the
basses, the same powerful crescendo and the same rhythm of three ham-
mered minim major chords at the beginning of the new movement. But
the differences show how Vaughan Williams has gone beyond Beethoven:
not 'improved on him', but simply used a device of his to express something rather different. Beethoven's three triumphant tonic C major chords
and the great march that follows represent a release from the almost
unbearable tension of the first and third movements. His reference to the
Scherzo later on in the movement now has all the menace drawn from it.
But Vaughan Williams's three triads (F major, A major, D major) and his
marche macabre are nothing of the sort. Thrown into the dissonant turmoil, they simply constitute an element of 'reculer pour mieux sauter': the
tension does not relax; it is screwed up to an almost intolerable degree. A
possible and quite different parallel in another work occurs towards the
end of the Tallis Fantasia, where a series of four massive, grinding chords
leads eventually to the serene final recapitulation of the opening and the
main theme. Here, the (unconscious?) model may be the similar series of
chords in the funeral march of the 'Eroica' (bar 150 *et seq.*), where the
tables are reversed: Beethoven screws up the tension, whereas Vaughan
Williams resolves it.

The parallel between Beethoven's Fifth and Vaughan Williams's
Fourth is useful in other respects, even if it is completely unintentional
and totally coincidental. Whether or not he was portraying in the Fifth
Symphony some kind of personal crisis overcome, Beethoven of all composers seems to express most intensely in music the widespread sense of
hope and liberation experienced in the immediate aftermath of the
French Revolution. Again, whatever impelled Vaughan Williams to put
down on paper the black dots that eventually constituted the Fourth
Symphony, the work is an amazing expression of passion and explosive
rage, such as was felt by many people in the 1930s as they contemplated
the inevitable drift to war and the brutality of the regimes that would
have at some to be confronted if liberal democracy was to survive. Both
the musical designs and the context of moods run parallel. This is not,
however, to say that 'he [RVW] foresaw the whole thing'. It is the purely
musical and formal factors that are under consideration here; and while
it is an absurd exaggeration to claim that Vaughan Williams explores
the implications of Beethoven's Fifth more profoundly than Beethoven
did himself, it is certainly true that, wittingly or unwittingly, he translated it into appropriate modern terms in more senses than one.

Michael Kennedy has summed up RVW's character as that of an
'extraordinary ordinary man'. As the man was, so was the musician. He

was ordinary in the sense that he ostensibly fitted in effortlessly to the social environment in which he was brought up and never rejected the values that he absorbed at home, at school, and at university. These included a sincerely-held and consistently-practised code of conduct based on the chivalrous ideals of high-minded Romantic agnosticism that still accepted the altruism of the Christian ethic while rejecting its supernatural element. He was extraordinary in that he subscribed to this code not just because it was the 'done thing' to do so, but because he had thought it through and really and sincerely believed in it. He was a visionary perfectly at home amongst the staid and conventional. Just as Elgar looked like an army officer or a country gentleman, so Vaughan Williams, particularly in his middle age and later, when his tall frame was becoming solid and bulky, looked like a yeoman farmer. He certainly showed all the sturdy positive attributes of the traditional English yeoman: rugged independence, forthrightness, self-reliance, a strong but not puritanical sense of duty, and personal integrity.

Yet there was far more to him than that. He was a bundle of paradoxes: a lifelong agnostic who found powerful inspiration in the words of the Holy Bible, the prose of Bunyan's *Pilgrim's Progress*, and the verse of great Anglican poets such as George Herbert. Quotations from the Bible and from Bunyan, surely absorbed from his intensive reading and home and school background, pepper his writings. He was a true gentleman who liked to conceal his extreme sensitivity; self-deprecating and self-critical, yet utterly devoid of false modesty. He held strong opinions and varied between diffidence and forcefulness in expressing them (a phrase that constantly recurs in his correspondence and his public communications is St Paul's 'I speak as a fool', when he surely knew he was doing nothing of the kind). He was as far as possible from the conventional picture of the self-absorbed garret-bound genius waiting for inspiration and writing in a *furor poeticus* once it had come upon him; and his rather ponderous, rough-hewn outward 'Englishness' concealed a sharp wit and a shrewd, penetrating, and well-read mind. A favourite poem of his, Matthew Arnold's *Scholar Gypsy*, was often cited as an example of one who waited so long for inspiration that it never came. He never fell into that trap.

He was both extremely attracted by and attractive to beautiful women, yet a kind of chivalrous innocence as well as a strong moral code precluded his giving anything more than light-hearted expression to his feelings. He must surely have known that some of his admired musical colleagues, such as Edward Dent, Tippett, and Britten, were homosexual, but that did not cloud his respect for them or their work, even though he did refer scathingly in a letter to Michael Kennedy in May 1957 to 'the young pansies who run the BBC'. Imbued with a strong sense of good form, he was also possessed of a teasing, irreverent, and sometimes mildly Rabelaisian sense of humour.

Taken too seriously, his bantering comments on people and professional relationships led more than once to irritating misunderstandings. A symptomatic and highly revealing case was his collaboration late in life with Roy Douglas, whom he would casually introduce to strangers with some such phrase as 'the man who writes my music for me'. Douglas was indeed a gifted composer in his own right, a skilled orchestrator who had been responsible amongst other things for the best-known and most effective version of the ballet *Les Sylphides*, based on Chopin piano pieces. He was also a member and the librarian of the London Symphony Orchestra.

For some time before he met the composer, Douglas had been involved with the tidying up of Vaughan Williams's scores for performance. In 1942, he was asked to prepare the parts for RVW's music for the film *Coastal Command*—'make the scores more readable' was the official euphemism. The appointed studio copyists had refused to undertake the task because there had been complaints about mistakes in the band parts they had prepared for *49th Parallel*. In fairness to the unfortunate copyists, Douglas's own words deserve quotation:

> When I looked at the scores of *Coastal Command*, I was considerably dismayed: this was my fight sight of V.W.'s manuscript, and my eyes goggled and my mind boggled more than a little. After a while I decided that the only way to make the score 'more readable' would be to write the whole lot out again after deciphering them; but there was not time to do this . . . So I embarked on the only practical course: copying out all the band parts myself.[2]

Douglas first met RVW in December 1942, when he was invited to The White Gates to advise him on scoring for a film sound track, but it was not until nearly two years later that he first really collaborated with the composer. This was in connection with a reduced scoring of *A Song of Thanksgiving* so that it could be performed by forces rather less lavish than those envisaged for its ceremonial guise as *Thanksgiving for Victory* at the end of the Second World War: what Douglas himself termed 'de-orchestration'.

This was the start of virtually fourteen years of close collaboration, though it was not until February 1947 that Douglas was next invited to work with RVW. It was typical of the composer's self-effacing and slightly whimsical way of referring to his music to write in the following terms:

> Dear Douglas,
> I have been foolish enough to write another symphony [No. 6 in E minor]. Could you undertake to vet and then copy the score? If in the course of this you have any improvements to suggest I would receive them with becoming gratitude . . .[3]

[2] Roy Douglas, *Working with R.V.W.* (OUP, 1972) (hereafter Douglas), p. 4.
[3] Ibid., p. 9.

This letter makes perfectly clear the parameters of Douglas's involvement in Vaughan Williams's work. To ask someone to 'vet and copy' a score is by no means to give him *carte blanche* to tinker about with it as he will; and to say that any suggested improvements would be received with 'becoming gratitude' is by no means to say that they would actually be incorporated in the score.

Douglas now became what he called the 'mid-husband' to the authentic versions of many of Vaughan Williams's later works, 'washing their faces', as the composer put it, and preparing the score for performance. The reason was simple. Douglas has always been adamant that the music simply poured from VW in such abundance that his mind worked well ahead of his pen: hence the Beethovenian illegibility of his musical handwriting. He was equally adamant that whatever suggestions he himself might have made about interpreting correctly what Vaughan Williams had written, only one person was responsible to the end of his life for the substance, the shape, and the scoring of the music: the composer himself. Douglas's involvement in the preparation of the scores was such that, as Michael Kennedy has made plain:

> the only trustworthy full scores of most of the later large-scale works [are] . . . those in the handwriting of Roy Douglas and the printed scores which were engraved from these. . . . It is obvious, therefore, that the full scores in Vaughan Williams's handwriting, most of which are now in the British Museum, do not represent these works as the composer wished them to be performed.[4]

The process continued long after RVW's death. OUP would send Douglas copies of the full score from their library for 'face-washing' before committing them to the engraver. These ranged from early works such as *In the Fen Country* and the one published *Norfolk Rhapsody* to late ones such as *Hodie*, and included *Dona Nobis Pacem*, *Five Tudor Portraits*, and *Riders to the Sea*. It is obvious, therefore, that the responsibility for Vaughan Williams's music was entirely his own: Douglas was responsible for preparing the scores for accurate part-copying and accurate publication where the composer's own manuscript could have led (and quite often did lead) to ambiguity and confusion.

The case of Roy Douglas is symptomatic because both with Vaughan Williams's personality and with his music it is often all too easy—and always all too misleading—to take the self-deprecatory self-portrait for the true likeness. This means that all too often a superficial reading of the music, too, can lead the listener badly astray. Ostensibly, works like *Pastoral Symphony*, for example, are placid, totally given over to reflection and utterly lacking in tension or drama. But, in Alain Frogley's phrase, 'Vaughan Williams's pastoral vein is nearly always shot through with a painful sense of loss and of man's ambivalent place in a fallen world.'[5] This 'fallen world' in which we live and the ambivalence is

---

[4] Kennedy, *Works* 2, pp. 289–90. . [5] *BBC Music Magazine*, July 1993, p. 33.

caused by all the shortcomings of human behaviour and their violent expression in such activities as mechanized and chemical warfare. Vaughan Williams had experienced them at first hand. He had lost a number of close musical friends in World War I. He had worked with casualties on military service and seen the devastating effect that war had on the mind of the gentle Ivor Gurney.

For Vaughan Williams, the natural world itself, whether the tranquil world of *The Lark Ascending* or the elegiac evocative soundscape of *Pastoral Symphony*, is simply there. It must be accepted on its own terms. Neither it nor any vision of another world is to be treated simply as an escape-route. Man must seek his own salvation. There is no act of faith to inspire the hope of redemption either of man or of the world in which he lives through some kind of divine intervention or divine self-immolation. Prayers, however intense (and there can be no mistaking the intensity of the prayers in a work like *Dona Nobis Pacem*) are a projection of man's hopes and fears, nothing more. For Vaughan Williams the man, this is so even if the prayers are taken from poems by a writer who genuinely believed in their efficacy, such as Herbert or Bunyan. But that does not, in his view, invalidate the power and resonance of the religious and particularly biblical symbolism employed by these writers and by others to whose imagery he was attracted.

Vaughan Williams so frequently chose to set biblical or Christian texts, firstly because that was the imagery most familiar to the educated listeners in the world in which he grew up. But he showed equal enthusiasm for setting such writers as Whitman and Housman, who could in no sense of the term be considered as Christian. And finally, although he was an agnostic, he held that, to use his own words: 'The object of art is to stretch out to the ultimate realities through the medium of beauty . . . ' This statement totally begs the question as to what he, as an agnostic, meant by 'ultimate realities'; but it recurs constantly, expressed in differing terms, throughout Vaughan Williams's writings. It seems that he found some of the most potent symbols for these ultimate realities, in which he clearly believed, in the Bible and in writers like Herbert and Bunyan: grace, love (or charity), a sense of awe, of the transcendent, and the idea that life on earth was a voyage with a goal that each man had to find for himself. These he must have considered landmarks on the internalized moral chart by which every individual may or may not choose to steer his way through life. He found this quest most tellingly defined by the agnostic Whitman in his phrase 'the unknown region'. Perhaps the most powerful expression of it, however, comes in a passage from F. J. Church's translation of Plato's *Phaedo* that prefaces *Sancta Civitas*:

> A man of sense will not insist that things are exactly as I have described them. But I think he will believe that something of the kind is true of the soul and her habitations, seeing that she is shown to be immortal, and that it is worth

while to stake everything on this belief. The venture is a fair one and he must charm his doubts with spells like these.

The last sentence is particularly significant, as Byron Adams has remarked:

> By employing this excerpt, the composer clearly sets aside a Christian interpretation of the biblical text that follows, while pointing towards a reason for its selection. While the inscription from Plato is meant to distance the composer from the literal meaning of the biblical passages he has chosen, it also serves to guide performers and listeners of *Sancta Civitas* towards his symbolic intent. . . . By combining textual and musical symbolism, the composer gave his listeners the freedom to find their own meaning for both words and music.[6]

The doubts were there; and they were powerful. At times, the doubts are so strong as to hint that the quest is meaningless, after all. Those doubts may be heard at their most powerful in *On Wenlock Edge*, perhaps at the end of *A London Symphony* and certainly at the end of the Sixth. Yet again and again, 'spells like these' occurred to him as a peg on which to hang his musical ideas. The nature of the quest, particularly in a work like *Sancta Civitas* with its apocalyptic imagery of violent war in Heaven leading to the descent of the City of God, *Job*, with its bold confrontation of the problem of evil and unjustified suffering, or the Fourth and Sixth Symphonies, might sometimes be expressed in musical language forceful to the point of brutality; but they could still find what Vaughan Williams believed to be beautiful expression. Beauty is truth and truth beauty, a phrase from Keats that Holst set in his *Choral Symphony* and that RVW quoted back at him as 'all [he] need[ed] to know'; and even if the truth was harsh and painful to contemplate, the act of contemplating it and reducing it to a pattern of appropriate black dots on paper created beauty out of it. Sometimes, as has already been pointed out in the case of the Fourth Symphony, he was not sure that he liked the beauty that he had created; but he was still convinced that it *was* beauty, even if it was not of a placid, lyrical, idealized, or ruminative kind. His conception of beauty undoubtedly expanded as he grew older, yet the 'old' Vaughan Williams of the pre-World-War-I era is liable from time to time to break into even such late works as the Ninth Symphony. This was not nostalgia; nor was it the outcome of inconsistency or lack of imagination. The original vision had not faded. It had simply been absorbed into a broader and more comprehensive one.

Similarly, his music is all too often dismissed by the unsympathetic as homespun and unsophisticated, partly perhaps because he was by his own admission so much influenced by the melodic contours, the moods and the rhythms of English folk-song. Such shallow dismissals totally ignore the fact that he underwent a thorough academic training and that

---

[6] 'Biblical texts in the works of Vaughan Williams', in *Vaughan Williams Studies*, ed. Alain Frogley (Cambridge, 1996) (hereafter *VWS*), p. 111.

at least one of his many doctoral titles was earned the hard way: through submitting an exercise that satisfied the rigorous standards of the Cambridge examiners. It also ignores the period of study spent with Ravel, his knowledge of works outside the Austro–German stylistic tradition, his study of the works of earlier English masters, notably of the Tudor period, and his love for and intensive study of the music of Bach and Purcell. Much of the trouble was his own fault. His correspondence and his published utterances are peppered with quite sincere and totally unjustified references to his clumsiness and amateurishness as compared with those he admired, like Holst, or those who trained him, such as Wood and Stanford.

It is perhaps worth pointing out in this context that Benjamin Britten, whose compositional technique was surely second to that of few if any of his contemporaries, always regarded it as a failing on the part of music critics that they could never discern when in any of his works his inspiration had faltered for a moment, leaving him to rely on sheer technique to maintain the momentum and shape of the piece. Vaughan Williams, on the other hand, tended to harp so much on his lack of technique that it is all too easy to read faults into passages in his works that on closer examination prove to be a logical and inevitable feature of the total fabric of the music. This is often true whether one considers his solid, chunky scoring, his heavy, galumphing rhythms, his sudden harmonic shifts of gear, his meandering passages where one feels something ought to be happening and nothing apparently is, his part-writing that doesn't quite fit in text-book terms, the massive heartiness of some of his musical ideas, the strings of apparently unmotivated consecutive triads, and so on. The reason why these features seem sometimes to be technical flaws is often (though not of course always) not because his imagination or his technique has failed, but because the performers or the listener have misread his instructions (notably about dynamics and rhythmic emphasis) or not properly thought through what he is aiming at.

Perhaps the most telling demonstration of the truth of the above thesis is Deryck Cooke's remarkable analysis of the Sixth Symphony. This should be read in full to understand how Cooke demonstrates conclusively that the whole work holds together as a unity; and its cogency makes it all the more regrettable that Cooke was not spared in health to write a book that he had in mind about Vaughan Williams's musical language.

Yet even in this closely-argued musical texture, there is an element of the 'crib'. It comes from Holst's *Planets*, particularly in its second and fourth movements. The menacing, swirling string passages in octaves that occur in the Moderato movement and the terrifying trumpet and drum figure that appears, as it were, from outer space, though it is really derived from a phrase of the main theme and merges with that theme when it recurs, are, intentionally or not, a crib from 'Mars'. Vaughan

Williams's use of this material is, however, quite different from Holst's. Similarly, the tenuous web of sound, pianissimo throughout, and ending in an indeterminate cadence, which constitutes the finale, is somewhat like 'Neptune'; but again, on account of its context, the impact of the music is totally different. The relationship between the two friends bears musical fruit here some twelve years after Holst's death.

Vaughan Williams is not usually included among that group of composers, such as Walton, Bliss, and Lambert, who were much influenced by jazz; though he did warn his American audience that they were wrong in despising jazz or jazz-influenced American composers such as Gershwin. The 'smarmy saxophone . . . drool[ing] a kind of doodling . . . swing music' (Deryck Cooke) in the Sixth Symphony's third movement has many of the superficial characteristics of a jazz 'riff': the repeated changes of stress, the insistence on the repetition of one small phrase with minor variations, the quasi-improvisatory nature of the whole theme, for example, all point to a case of the composer exploiting the popular music of his era for a most effective end. And when, at the end of the movement, the theme is pounded out in augmentation by the full orchestra with something of the brutal bravura of the last movement of the Fourth Symphony, the effect is electrifying. A molten torrent of unorganized trivial sound has solidified into a series of brutal, violent hammer-blows; the 'jazz' element has fulfilled its purpose of acting as the raw material of the horrifying finished product.

Vaughan Williams's own musical tastes have been comprehensively summed up by Michael Kennedy and can be amply documented from his own writings. He developed a marked but always guarded respect for Beethoven, whose music he found repugnant as a young man and to whose style he remained what he called temperamentally allergic all his life. Other composers for whom he had either a great regard or a highly respectful admiration included Wagner, Verdi, some of Elgar, such as *Gerontius* and the Enigma Variations, Parry, Stanford, Haydn and some Mozart, Purcell, the Elizabethans (especially Byrd, the madrigal composers, and Tallis), Debussy, particularly *Pelléas et Mélisande*, and the piano works of his teacher Ravel. Of his contemporary countrymen, he admired the work of Tippett and Rubbra and spoke with appreciation of certain of Britten's works, notably *Les Illuminations* and *Peter Grimes*. His opinions of other Britten operas that he is known to have seen, such as *Billy Budd* and *Gloriana*, are not extant; but as a composer of opera himself and as a pupil of Stanford, he must surely have been pleased that here at last was an English composer of genius making his presence felt in the professional opera theatre. It would be bold to claim that Vaughan Williams 'cribbed', consciously or unconsciously, from any of these composers; yet traces of most of them, as well as of less likely influences, such as Shostakovich and Prokofiev, can be found at some place or other in his output.

At one time, he was fond of the music of both Schumann and Schubert, but, as he put it, they went 'off the boil'; and his 'prentice works are sometimes coloured by the Brahmsian bias of his teachers at the Royal College. He seems to have considered Dvořák a greater genius than composers such as Liszt and Berlioz, whose music he cordially detested. Holst and Bach were in a class apart, so to speak, but his appreciation of Bach was of a kind that would raise purist eyebrows nowadays. Even some of his own friends and contemporaries looked askance at certain of his performance practices, which were based on intuition, perhaps even prejudice, rather than the scholarly and painstaking research of which he was quite capable, as *The English Hymnal* shows, to give but one example.

His mind remained open and receptive to the end of his life, yet he could occasionally be cussed, not to say blinkered. He was very firmly against employing a harpsichord continuo in the Bach *Passions*; and even so staunch a champion of his music as Sir Adrian Boult roundly dismissed some of his ideas about the performance of the classics as 'quite ridiculous', remarked on 'the most extraordinary things' that he required the pianist to play in the *Passion*, but added 'He didn't expect people to agree with him, but that was just how he felt it'. Other anathemas included what he contemptuously referred to as the 'bubble-and-squeak' tone of the baroque organ and the use of the viola da gamba ('I WILL NOT HAVE a viola da Gamba inside the building', he once wrote to Michael Kennedy).

Dr William Cole, who succeeded RVW as conductor of the Leith Hill Festival in 1954, put it rather differently from Sir Adrian:

> As a hero-worshipper, I copied all his marks into my own score and tried to follow them implicitly. As I grew older I realised that V.W.'s interpretation of this work was unique in the sense that it was part of himself and its essence could never be outwardly transferred to another person. I have been eternally grateful to him that he gave me such a positive, although personal, interpretation.[7]

Personal or no, RVW's interpretations, whether of other composers' works or of his own, never settled into a stereotyped formula: even when he had conducted a work many times, he re-thought it and studied it anew. But when he was satisfied with something, he did not take well to others tinkering with it uninvited. At a rehearsal of *Pastoral Symphony* in the 1930s at Queen's Hall, when the young Malcolm Sargent[8] was making well-meant adjustments to the scoring of the third movement, he was interrupted by a stentorian vocal thunderbolt from the balcony: 'What do you think you are doing, young man? I know

[7] Rothwell (ed.), *The Leith Hill Music Festival*, p. 22.
[8] Charles Reid, *Malcolm Sargent: A Biography* (London, 1968), p. 405; R. Temple Savage, *A Voice from the Pit* (Newton Abbot, 1988), pp. 46–7.

what I wrote!' The bass clarinettist Richard Temple Savage tells a similar story about the same conductor rehearsing the *Flourish for a Coronation*.

Neither Vaughan Williams nor his art was quite as simple, and certainly nowhere near as homespun, as his detractors often make out. Direct, forthright, and rooted in the traditions of his country they certainly were. But beneath the rugged surface lay a sensitivity, a cosmopolitanism, and a sophistication that have all too often been overlooked, ignored or simply misrepresented.

9

Songs and other small-scale works

Vaughan Williams first attracted attention as a song-composer and he continued writing songs and part-songs at intervals throughout his long career. If we are to take seriously his claim that the last two bars of his first extant part-song, a setting of 'The Willow Song', were almost certainly composed by Hubert Parry, then that must date from about 1891 and count as his first preserved and actually published composition. Another part-song, a setting for male voices of 'Music, When Soft Voices Die', was performed at the Cambridge University Musical Club on 18 November 1893. This was presumably the celebrated occasion when the first tenor got a bar out, enabling the conductor to organize a repeat performance on the spot (see p. 16).

Tennyson's 'Crossing the Bar', which dates from 1892, is RVW's first surviving song for voice and piano. His last was composed sixty-six years later, not long before his death in 1958. If in the general category 'songs' we include part-songs, folk-song arrangements, hymn-tunes and unison songs, the total of his compositions in this field exceeds 150, not counting *On Wenlock Edge* and the three Chaucer roundels *Merciless Beauty*. These may be included among his chamber works because they require an instrumental ensemble for performance. This is admittedly a far cry from Schubert's total of over 600 original accompanied songs, composed over a much shorter period, but it still constitutes a considerable corpus.

The manner in which Vaughan Williams's songs expand in range and sensibility can be judged from the changes in his choice of poets. The early songs reflect a fairly conservative taste in poetry, albeit one of a high literary standard, from Vaux and Herrick to Romantic and pre-Raphaelite poets, such as Coleridge, Browning, Tennyson, Swinburne, and the Rossettis, and a fairly conventional range of subjects. None the less, characteristic musical fingerprints may be found even here. One cadence in 'To Daffodils' (text by Herrick) prefigures the modality that was to become a feature of Vaughan Williams's style when he reacted musically some years later to the stimulus of English folk-song; and Stephen Banfield says that the setting of Thomas Vaux's 'How can the tree but wither?' is virtually a re-creation in contemporary terms of the pre-baroque English ayre, with 'elastic phrase-lengths, hemiola, *style brisé* embellishments, interrupted cadences . . . and a period melancholy that suggests he may have written it for incidental performance in a play'.[1]

Ironically, it was his very first song actually to achieve publication— 'Linden Lea'—that eventually became Vaughan Williams's greatest and most lasting commercial success. It appeared in 1902 in the first issue of *The Vocalist*, a magazine devoted to the art of singing and to the encouragement of new songs; and no self-respecting CD recital featuring RVW's songs would ever risk excluding it. Small wonder: the gentle imagery of William Barnes's poem evokes an idyllic mood that never degenerates into sentimentality, underlining the positive aspect of the countryman's admittedly hard lot—his independence. Vaughan Williams matches these sentiments with a simple, straightforward, well-nigh (but not quite) pentatonic melody that has never lost its appeal; and the opening passage of the accompaniment, with its imitative entries, has enough of the feel of a pre-baroque English ayre about it to counterbalance its plainness. (The composer himself used on occasion to hold it up self-deprecatingly as an example of what an accompaniment should *not* be like.)

It is strange to think that *The Vocalist* found that 'Linden Lea' did not sell as well in the first year of publication as either VW's companion Barnes song, 'Blackmwore by the Stour', or his setting of Stevenson's 'Whither must I wander?' which was later incorporated into the song-cycle *Songs of Travel*. It has lasted better than either, or indeed than any of the three Tennyson settings: 'Crossing the Bar', 'Claribel', and 'Tears, Idle Tears'. These are notable only for a kind of plainsong touch in 'Claribel'; the last of the three was acclaimed for its beauty by *The Times* and *The Globe* when Francis Harford and Evlyn Howard-Jones first performed it on 5 February 1903, but it is difficult to disagree with Banfield when he dismisses it as maudlin and heavy in texture, save for the effective exploitation of 'Tchaikovskian throbs of pathos, propelled by a "symphonic" four-note motif which recurs in many of his later works'.

The most important of the early songs for solo voice are the song-cycles *The House of Life* and *Songs of Travel*. Holst put his finger on the salient merit of Vaughan Williams's idiom at that time when he wrote in a letter from Berlin in 1903:

You have never lost your invention, but it has not developed enough. Your best—your most original and beautiful style or 'atmosphere' is an indescribable sort of feeling as if one was listening to very lovely lyrical poetry. I may be wrong but I think this (what I call to myself the *real* RVW) is more original than you think.[2]

[1] Stephen Banfield, *Sensibility and English Song* (Cambridge, 1985), p. 77.
[2] *Heirs and Rebels*, p. 15.

The *real* RVW was indeed more original than perhaps the composer thought; and certain passages in these two song cycles amply demonstrate Holst's acumen both in his criticism and his praise.

Vaughan Williams had already tackled Christina Rossetti's verse in the delightful but lightweight 'If I Were a Queen', whose ingenious simplicity and catchy rhythm exactly capture the mood of the childlike poem. *The House of Life*, by Christina's elder brother, Dante Gabriel Rossetti, demanded a much more sophisticated approach. The cycle was published in 1903 and comprises six numbers: 'Love-Sight', 'Silent Noon', 'Love's Minstrels', 'Heart's Haven', 'Death in Love', and 'Love's Last Gift'. Rossetti was a gifted painter; his imagery tends therefore to be either atmospheric or visual. It is not, consequently, of the kind that inspires a Lied-style setting, where the piano part can be structured to seize on a key image in the poem, find an appropriate figure for it and exploit that as a unifying illustrative rhythmic device which will give life to the supporting harmonies while the voice projects the expressive emotion of the text. 'Love's Last Gift', for example, mentions 'glistening leaf', 'rose tree', 'apple tree', 'flowers to the bee', 'golden shafts', 'secret grasses', 'filtering channels of sunk reef' in the octave—hardly the stuff, one would think, to spark off onomatopoeic or even harmonically illustrative musical imagery. Nor do the rosy blooms, the kingcups, the cow parsley, and the visible silence mentioned in 'Silent Noon' seem to offer much for the musician to latch on to.

Vaughan Williams, however, is adept both at catching musically the voluptuousness of the verse and at balancing the longing, the ecstasies, and the sorrows of love that it expresses. The scale is not remotely Wagnerian, but there is surely a carefully contained touch both of the searing longing and of the sense of luxurious fulfilment of *Tristan und Isolde* in this music (as at the thundering climax of 'Death-in-Love' to the words 'and I am Death'). The melodic line has as yet no echoes of folk-song, but it is very English in its successful expression of powerful passion held in by dignified restraint: witness the incomplete cadence of the final vocal phrase in 'Love-Sight', to the words 'The winds of Death's imperishable wing', so gently rounded off in the piano postlude. (There is also, incidentally, an interesting foretaste of *Sine Nomine* in 'Love's Last Gift'.)

The sonnet form, with its octave/sestet division, is always a problem for the musician to handle. Vaughan Williams tackles it with considerable skill and resourcefulness. In 'Silent Noon', for example, he balances the form of the song by replacing the initial gently throbbing rhythm of the piano part by a more flowing texture during the central part of the poem that describes the lovers' bliss and contentment, only to resume it at the words, 'So this wing'd hour is dropt to us from above. / Oh! clasp we to our hearts, for deathless dower, / This close-companion'd inarticulate hour,' sung to a variant of the song's opening strain, as they realize its significance. 'Heart's Haven' contains dramatic writing of a kind that makes it sound almost like an early sketch for the operas that were to come. But the most interesting of these songs is undoubtedly 'Love's Minstrels'—significantly, a setting of the one sonnet that exploits explicitly musical symbols—instruments—rather than Rossetti's more usual visual imagery. Vaughan Williams takes up the challenge of representing the oboe (symbol of love's ardour) and the harp (symbol of its worship) in the piano part. He also rejects tonal harmony for modal and strict barring and conventional harmonic progressions in favour of a certain metrical freedom and bold harmonic shifts. It doesn't quite come off, partly, one suspects, because the rest of the cycle remains within more conventional terms of musical reference, partly because the devices are applied a little self-consciously. *The House of Life* does not quite achieve greatness, nor does Vaughan Williams thrust greatness upon it, but it does have personality and it does express sincere, powerful emotion, however discreetly.

The *Songs of Travel* show the composer at his early best, representing a new stage of Vaughan Williams's musical development. The theme of the restless search for an unknown ideal is there; some of the stylistic fingerprints are there; and hints of what the composer was looking for and what he was to gain from the discovery of English folk-song and his study with Ravel are also there. What is lacking is the consistent welding of these personal elements into a recognizable coherent personal style.

For many years, the cycle was incomplete: the intended final song, 'I have trod the upward and the downward slope', was discovered by the composer's widow only after his death. When originally published, the songs had to be re-cast into two sets, fragmenting a genuine cycle into two collections of attractive but disparate tunes, one extrovert, the other more reflective and sophisticated. 'Whither must I wander?' was not included in either set: it had already been published separately. Unfortunately, the gap of some two years between the publication of the two sets and the omission of 'Whither must I wander?' with its quasi-modal cadences, masked the originality that was already there and left the listener to infer that it was a later development. The publishers' decision implies that they considered the public unprepared to appreciate the more impressionistic side of Vaughan Williams's style that is so apparent in the original second set: these songs show that what Ravel did as a teacher was to help RVW make explicit features already latent in his developing style. Such prudence may have been prompted by comments like that in a *Manchester Guardian* review of Plunket Greene's recital on 3 February 1905, which included five of the *Songs of Travel*: '[Vaughan Williams's] melodies curvet according to the most approved tenets of modernity, while his accompaniments prance about like a very Mazeppa.'[3] (At least the critic had noticed that Vaughan Williams had

---

[3] Kennedy, *Works* 2, p. 62.

broken away from hymn-tune-like four-part accompanimental writing.) As so often in early Vaughan Williams, the whole is undoubtedly greater than the sum of its parts: it tells a poignant story in clear and imaginative but not always consistent musical terms, with thematic cross-references between the songs, as in *The House of Life*, and some vivid and generally effective accompanimental writing. Some of these songs are in fact much closer to the tradition of the German Lied than either Vaughan Williams's other early songs or the works of many of his English contemporaries. This is hardly surprising. At this stage in his career, Schubert and Schumann ranked high in his pantheon of song-writers. The hero of the *Songs of Travel*, indeed, is a rather less self-pitying cousin to that of *Winterreise*: just as introspective but tougher and more resilient. Moreover, we get some idea of what he has to offer in the way of emotional attraction to the girl: we actually hear him woo her before he goes on his way. She does not reject him: he regretfully leaves her in favour of an unfettered independent lifetime of wider and not always happier experience.

Many stylistic features of these songs show the emergence of the *real* RVW, as Holst put it: the relentless onward stride of 'The Vagabond'; the graceful urgency and modal touches of 'Let Beauty Awake'; the coaxing, wheedling effect of the lingering stress on 'I' at the opening of 'The Roadside Fire'; the gently hovering accompaniment of 'Youth and Love', like drifting leaves in an autumn breeze; the caressing chromaticism of 'In Dreams'; the rapt remoteness and fluent, irregular phrasing of 'The Infinite Shining Heavens'; the contrasting modal chill of 'Whither must I wander?'; the D major cadence leading without warning into a chord of E flat in 'Bright is the ring of words' to prepare for the chill of 'After the singer is dead'; ('Damnably ugly, me bhoy', Stanford probably thought); and the exhausted yet fulfilled calm of 'I have trod the upward and the downward slope', a tentative prototype (unless the song itself was a later afterthought) of the reflective epilogues that are so marked a feature of Vaughan Williams's larger-scale works, especially the symphonies.

It is in the accompaniments that Vaughan Williams faced the most difficult challenge in his early songs: one is often left, even with such a splendid song as 'Linden Lea' with the impression that the early songs win acceptance despite rather than because of their accompaniments. Often there is too much unnecessary doubling of the melodic line in the top part of the piano harmony; one feels that the piano is there, *faute de mieux*, simply to fill out a hymn-tune-like texture. Even some of Vaughan Williams's earlier folk-song arrangements tend to this fault, though where, as in 'The Unquiet Grave', he brings in the violin as well, it is a different story. Yet it is probably no coincidence that his first substantial vocal work after his study with Ravel, *On Wenlock Edge*, signalled his full maturity as a song-writer and shifted the emphasis between vocal line and accompaniment. His accompaniments had already become more detailed and illustrative; he now became much more versatile in the way he shaped them. Detailed discussion of *On Wenlock Edge* is given in the chapter on chamber music; all that needs to be said here is that in addition to showing a new freedom and imagination in handling the accompaniment and giving it more prominence in both the structure and the atmosphere of the music, it brings a new poet on to the scene: A. E. Housman. It is an over-simplification to say that Romanticism and pre-Raphaelites were now 'out' and Georgian lyrics 'in', but it is certainly true that under the combined influence of the discovery of English folk-song, the detailed work done on *The English Hymnal*, and the period of study with Ravel, Vaughan Williams had found himself as a composer and this in turn markedly affected his future choice of poets, and of musical forms.

The more sophisticated kind of accompaniment, for the most part pared to essentials rather than developed at extensive length, is found in the *Four Poems by Fredegond Shove*, published in 1925. Fredegond Shove was a niece of the composer's wife. Even as perceptive and sympathetic a commentator as Michael Kennedy seems to feel that the composer found these poems somewhat intractable to set, almost implying that he set them out of duty rather than from a genuine compelling urge. 'Motion and Stillness' sets him some real challenges with its imagery of sea-shells 'cold as death', its clouds 'like a wasted breath', its sleeping cows (small chance for Straussian pictorialism here, even if Vaughan Williams had wished to indulge in it!) and its ships 'like evanescent hopes'. Vaughan Williams contrives to solve them by basing his setting on hollow fourths and fifths in the accompaniment, anchored first to F in the bass and then to D flat before the first (and ambiguous) triad occurs at 'The cows sleep on the tranquil slopes': the chords drift along, forming a more static, but thinner and less substantial line than that familiar from *Pastoral Symphony*.

Of the other songs in this group, 'The Water Mill', reminiscent of a Dutch painting in its loving attention to the small details of the scene, simply cries out for a quasi-illustrative Lied-like setting and duly gets it. The piano part gently picks out little allusions from the poem—the rhythm of the mill-race, the clock ('very tall and very bright'), the twilit pool; even the cat. 'Four Nights' avoids the lower reaches of the keyboard for most of the first section of a poem in the setting of which Vaughan Williams telescopes two lines of text into one phrase of music. The vocal line is folky and somewhat square but not facile: an instance of avoiding the obvious occurs when Vaughan Williams slows up the regular rhythm of the phrase for the last (and most important) words of the line, minims weighting the rhythm of a line predominantly consisting of crotchets. Again, both the manner in which the poem divides into associations of the four seasons and the actual imagery—the text mentions scythes swinging in the second verse, tangled winds, and armoured knights riding the skies in the third—invite (and receive) illustrative attention. The glum semi-recapitulation of the final verse, with its complete contrast to the others, dies away into an enigmatic cadence based on a rhythmic variant of the same chords of D flat and C flat major in the right hand against B flat minor and E flat minor in the left that formed the prelude to the voice's entry, to evaporate into a single note of A flat. 'The New Ghost' is the best known of the four, a kind of English 'Doppelgänger', with supernatural sweetness and love in place of an essay in the grim and the macabre. The dramatic picture of a soul's flight to its Lord after the death of the body that formed its sheath is enhanced by the rich lightness of the accompaniment, which lies entirely in the treble stave until the words 'late spring'. As befits the subject, the final cadence reaches out into remoteness.

The three Whitman settings, also published in 1925, are simpler still, as if Vaughan Williams were seeking a kind of austere, self-imposed clarity of expression, underlining rather than actually setting the words. Death is the central theme. 'Nocturne' develops from a shadowy, wandering quasi-ostinato in octaves low down in the piano, out of which emerges a drifting vocal line and sombre minim chords: a simple effect in a noble setting. 'A Clear Midnight' is a kind of *Sine Nomine* in slow motion, with minims in the bass slowly descending in solemn dignity, and the overall effect is of a sterner and more mature version of 'The Infinite Shining Heavens'. 'Joy, Shipmate, Joy!', is a sacred shanty on the familiar and time-honoured of life as a sea voyage, ends triple *f* on a chord of G with no third.

Other settings from the same period also show this search for clarity. The pleasing Shakespeare songs limit the accompaniment to unobtrusively supporting the vocal line and so they stand or fall by their melodic interest. *Two Songs by Seumas O'Sullivan* pare the accompaniment so much that it is actually optional. 'The Twilight People' has a certain fey charm, pointing backwards to *Hugh the Drover* in its 'folkiness' and forward to *Riders to the Sea*, sounding in its sombre strength and Celtic shadows almost like a study for the opera itself.

Even more interesting examples of Vaughan Williams's quest for clarity in integrating voice and accompaniment as equal partners are the eight Housman settings (from about the same period though not published until 1954) for voice and violin. There were originally nine, but the setting of 'The Soldier' was scrapped. As a collection, they take their title and their general mood from the second of their number: 'Along the Field', as if Vaughan Williams wishes to recall a love or a friendship now lost for ever. The elaborate impressionistic apparatus of *On Wenlock Edge* is eschewed here in favour of a stark and delicately interwoven tracery of song and accompaniment. This is sometimes, as in the hypnotically beautiful 'Along the Field' itself, almost medieval in effect, though rather more chromatic than would be the case in any medieval composition. The main technical problems lie firstly in the fact that the violin is essentially a melodic rather than a harmonic instrument and secondly, of course, in its tessitura: its downward range extends no lower than the open G string. In most cases, Vaughan Williams tackles these problems by requiring the violin to play a kind of descant to the voice part, possibly in the manner of folk-musicians that he may have heard, sometimes blending with and supporting the vocal line. But the use of double stops and the hints now and then of a drone-bass add spice and variety to the settings, especially as the double stops are often of a kind that no folk-fiddler would countenance: in musical terms, indeed, he might consider them 'outway rude'. So although the style of some of these songs is folky, both the mood of the vocal line and the handling of the accompaniments that shadow and supplement the voice are not. What happens is that the accompaniment often provides the 'foreground' mood of the poem, while the voice delves deeper into the subtext: a more sophisticated approach than one might reasonably expect of all but the most gifted and sensitive folk-duos.

The majority of the poems Vaughan Williams chooses to set here are gently elegiac: one wonders if the songs were in any way intended as a memorial to friends such as Butterworth and Ellis, killed in the First World War. Some of the violin postludes arch very movingly upwards in a kind of nostalgic aspiration; others (notably the spritely pay-off to 'Goodbye', with its cheeky pizzicato ending) are witty. On occasion, however, Vaughan Williams supplies chords that fill out an implied—and sometimes dissonant and ambiguous—harmony, and in both 'Goodbye' and 'Fancy's Knell' he catches at the implications of the text by juxtaposing a spirited dance-tune in counterpoint with the voice part. In the latter song, in fact, there is a fascinating contrast between the lively accompaniment and the more deliberate and reflective vocal line, which seems always to have the closing lines in mind:

> Tomorrow, more's the pity,
> Away we both must hie,
> To air the ditty,
> And to earth I.

This could be the motto for the entire cycle.

Towards the end of his long life, Vaughan Williams began work on two song cycles for voice and piano to words by his wife Ursula and completed a set of ten to words by Blake for voice and oboe. The title *Four Last Songs* given to the songs with piano that he actually completed between 1954 and 1958 inevitably raises the spectre of Richard Strauss; but Vaughan Williams's four songs (three of them suitable for male voice) are as far from Straussian territory as could be imagined. Here there is tenderness without nostalgia, austerity of expression but not of feeling, the passion of the early Rossetti settings seen through the eyes (or rather heard through the ears) of long experience, a return to port after a long spiritual voyage, promising not just 'the mixture as before', but a new lucidity. The restlessness in the first of them, 'Procris' a subtle study in understated impressionism with a basically linear piano part that carries no chords until the phrase 'flowers that spring', portrays not just the open-air imagery of the poem, with its breezes, trees bending towards the rushes and eyes (musically flickering in delicate cross-rhythms)

> . . . so lit by love that everything
> burned, flowed, grew, blossomed,
> moved on foot or wing
> with the guessed rhythm of eternity

but the gnawing jealousy of the wife who wrongly suspects her husband of keeping a rendezvous with his mistress and is killed by his unerring spear. 'Tired' is a (subjective?) love lyric suffused with tender affection. The composer responds with a gentle lullaby rhythm in the bass as a basic component of an accompaniment sounding at times as if the song was conceived as a latter-day lute-song. 'Hands, Eyes, and Heart', the only one of the four that has to be sung by a woman, is simple, touching (again subjective?), and rhythmically supple: a kind of secular prayer. 'Menelaus' has a much more elaborate and illustrative accompaniment than the other three songs and is particularly memorable for the sudden and highly characteristic stasis at the phrase: 'Forgetting the place you are in / [where the cold seawinds] . . . '

The Blake Songs show similar artistic economy to the songs of *Along the Field* in limning the substance of the poems. The challenge is even more severe here. There are very few oboists who can manage to produce double-stops on their instrument! In some (for example Nos. 4, 'London', 6, 'The Shepherd', and 9, 'The Divine Image') this is achieved entirely by the creation of an expressive melodic vocal line, the songs being entirely unaccompanied. These are not folk-songs; but the manner in which Vaughan Williams rhythmically modifies very similar melodic cells derives from a folk-song tradition. This is most readily seen (or heard) in 'The Shepherd', which is virtually strophic: the pitch of the notes of each verse is identical, but the rhythm varies subtly from one verse to another. The tune itself is almost a folk-tune in its own right save for the melisma on 'filled', in verse 1, which is split up between 'know' and '[when their] Shepherd' in verse 2. The same could be said of 'Divine Image', which could almost, and quite appropriately, be a hymn-tune, but it would have to be one from pre-baroque days: the rhythms are free and flexible.

In others, such as No. 5 'The Lamb', a poem that Vaughan Williams detested, yet a tune for which forced itself into his mind, so that for all his protestations, he had to set it, the oboe is skilfully woven as a pastoral background into the texture of the setting. In all of them the octogenarian composer shows a remarkable sensitivity to the spoken rhythms and inflections of Blake's verse, yet the writing remains consistent with his familiar style, the oboe lines being in their way as expressive (though not perhaps as virtuosic) as those in Britten's *Metamorphoses*. The melodic line in 'Infant Joy', the first of the songs, is almost, but not quite pentatonic. There is considerable subtlety in the way Vaughan Williams adapts the rhythm of a phrase to provide question and answer, or statement and allusion (Ex. 1).

Ex. 1

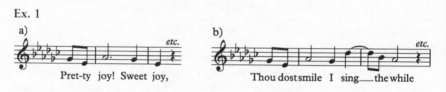

a) Pret-ty joy! Sweet joy,

b) Thou dost smile I sing——the while

The manner in which the glum little tune of No. 2, 'A Poison Tree', expands out of the apparently self-contained opening phrase is typical of Vaughan Williams's organic manner of developing melodic material, while the way in which he undermines the major-key implications of the tune at 'smiles, / And with soft deceitful wiles' by the false relations between the voice and the oboe can be compared with Britten's quite different but equally effective treatment of this text in his magnificent *Songs and Proverbs of William Blake*. The sinuous wavering tonality of this little masterpiece shows how two great British composers of different generations could each in their contrasting way illuminate different aspects of the same poem. A similar almost oriental tortuousness can be found in No. 8, 'Cruelty has a human heart', where the message of the poem is conveyed by the augmented fourth between the voice entry on E (ostensibly the tonic) and the oboe on B flat and in the cadence at 'Secrecy the human dress'. An enigmatic and hauntingly effective song.

Of the songs requiring more complex forces, the earliest mature solo songs with orchestra (though they can be performed with piano only) are the *Five Mystical Songs* of 1911, first performed at the Three Choirs Festival in Worcester that year. *Pace* the young Benjamin Britten, who wrote scathingly about them to RVW's pupil Grace Williams when he heard them on the radio in January 1935, they are in places admirable examples of RVW's early style. Britten's comments on what seemed to him to be technical incompetence are not entirely unfair, however. The songs *are* a trifle mannered. The Elgarian opening that Michael Kennedy rightly notes of the orchestration of 'Easter' on 'Rise, heart', (but surely the thematic material rates the same comment), flatters only to deceive. The authentic RVW voice *is* heard once or twice, however, for example at 'as at his death', with its shadowing of the vocal line deep down in the orchestral basses. 'I got me flowers' is a disappointment, despite the beautifully balanced Berliozian 'Enfance du Christ' wood-wind interpolations. Vaughan Williams seems curiously hesitant to underline the detailed imagery of the poem, yet he doesn't really catch its general atmosphere either. Again, in 'Love bade me welcome' there is no real sense of catching the undertow of guilty diffidence of the poem, despite the fluent inevitability of much of the word-setting. The touching sweetness of the overall mood is unmistakable, but it seems to hark back to Vaughan Williams's 'pre-Raphaelite' days, an impression underlined by the rather flaccid choral vocalizing on 'Ah' at the end. Vaughan Williams's mastery of the use of the wordless chorus in later works merely emphasizes his comparative inexperience here. 'The Call' is far and away the best of the set, with its haunting major/minor harmonic inflections and its swaying melody pivoting about the fifth degree of its scale. Such inspired simplicity as this reflects anything but the 'pi' and 'artificial mysticism' censured by Britten (whose comments Grace Williams sturdily and loyally rebutted in her reply), but one has a feeling that his uncharitable comment was much closer to the mark when applied to the others in the set. The last of the songs, 'Antiphon', in particular, is noisy and hearty rather than genuinely energetic, with a rhetorical ending that, as Vaughan Williams said of Delius, is addition, not multiplication; the whole is all too redolent, dare one suggest, of the muscular Christianity that may have been preached at and rejected by the composer in Charterhouse chapel. On the positive side, there is throughout the songs a flexibility in the vocal line, making it a kind of enhanced recitative. The *Mystical Songs* are serious, thoughtful works by a composer whose idiom seems not yet to have been fully capable of expressing the moods underlying Herbert's virtuoso craftsmanship and beautifully chosen imagery. Or was Vaughan Williams on 'automatic pilot' when he composed some of them? Certainly, the direct vision of the Transcendent to which they aspire and which Herbert so tenderly expressed was later to find much fuller and more penetrating expression in *Sancta Civitas*.

How quickly Vaughan Williams was maturing as a composer can be seen if the *Five Mystical Songs* are compared with the *Four Hymns* for tenor, viola, and orchestra of 1914, which were not performed in public until 26 May 1920. Here, the idiom is fully developed. The viola threads a reflective descant through the texture. The intimate nature of these songs in fact entitles them far better to the description 'mystical' than the earlier set. There is none of the mannered ecstasy here of 'Love bade me welcome': a comparison of that song and 'Evening Hymn', the last of the four, shows what a remarkable development had taken place in a mere two years or so, a development that was to lead in due course to *Pastoral Symphony* and *The Shepherds of the Delectable Mountains*.

A type of *Gebrauchsmusik* that is peculiarly English is the unison song for massed voices, of which Vaughan Williams composed a considerable number. With the encouragement in the inter-war years of the singing of folk-songs in state schools and the tradition of singing hefty, swinging melodies on occasions of patriotic display, and even the custom of bursting into unison community songs at cup finals (or at rugby internationals if you are Welsh!) there is a fine opportunity open to any composer capable of writing a broad, simple melody with a diatonic outline and straightforward rhythm. The ancestry of this kind of unison song can be traced back to Purcell. (There is no claim here that Purcell wrote such airs, but simply that a number of his finest melodies, such as 'Fairest Isle' or 'Come if you dare' fit the bill admirably.) Arne, Parry, and Elgar in their turn were able to turn these qualities to good account; and so was Vaughan Williams. Although none of his unison songs has captured the heard of the nation to the extent that 'Rule, Britannia!', 'Jerusalem' or the trio melody of the First *Pomp and Circumstance* March has, such melodies as 'Famous Men', 'The New Commonwealth', or 'Land of our Birth' constitute a worthy contribution to what is after all an aspect of our musical life. In keeping with the age in which they were composed, both music and texts are more subdued than Elgar's, but the characteristics of the melodies are the same: strength, simplicity, and dignity. Moreover, in such a song as 'Famous Men', Vaughan Williams exploits some of his salient stylistic features without placing the music beyond the bounds of either what is suitable or what is practicable for such compositions.

Vaughan Williams's numerous folk-song arrangements for voice and piano or for choruses of various kinds show that he loved the material with which he was working and that whatever the shortcomings that some find in his piano-writing, he knew exactly what kind of harmonic background to provide for the tunes. It is pointless to look in his accompaniments for the sophistication to be found (and censured by some— but not by him, as is pointed out elsewhere) in Britten's or even Holst's folk-song accompaniments. He rarely sought to illustrate details of the text or to provide a graphic or dramatic accompaniment, nor did he use the song as a basis for the exercise of his own creative reaction to the music and the words: he was concerned to make known to the widest possible public the treasures that he and others had discovered. And, as he said, it was possible to enter into our musical heritage elsewhere than in the concert hall. Both *The English Hymnal* and *The Oxford Book of Carols* provide examples, not only of his own composition, but also of characteristic arrangements of folk-songs (many a congregation might blush if they knew the original words to some of the tunes, as the composer must have known).

His treatment of the tunes was for the most part straightforward, but one of the most famous of all of them owes its widespread popularity at least as much to the collector/arranger as to the qualities of the original; and it is worth mentioning what RVW did to it. The tune itself was collected at Monk's Gate, Sussex, on 22 December 1904 from Mrs Harriet Verrall; and it is quite appropriate that as a hymn-tune it has become universally known as 'Monk's Gate'. Vaughan Williams used it to provide music for the updated and adulterated version of Bunyan's famous 'Pilgrim's Hymn' supplied by the editors of *The English Hymnal*.

As it stood, Mrs Verrall's somewhat irregular but sturdy tune did not fit Bunyan's words. The original words—the song is entitled 'Our captain calls'—dealt with a theme common in folk-verse: the parting of a sailor from his beloved, and her reactions. The verses in the folk-song have eleven syllables to each of their four lines and the tune has an ABBA structure to fit them. Bunyan's verse form is slightly different. Its first two lines run 6.5.6.5., which fits the tune. But then comes a pair of 'rogue' lines: 6.6., before the final couplet, which returns to a 6.5. structure. Moreover, Bunyan's metre could be scanned either as three in a bar ('Who would true 'valour see; 'Let him come 'hither'—which is how Vaughan Williams himself scans it in the original tune of his own that he uses in *The Pilgrim's Progress*), or, as fits Mrs Verrall's tune, as a martial four in a bar: ''Who 'would true 'valour 'see, 'Let 'him come 'hither'. But to do this, the rhythm of the music has to be altered; and to fit Bunyan's verse scheme, both the structure and the rhythm of the music have to be altered slightly.

Vaughan Williams solves one structural problem neatly by repeating not the 'B' strain of the tune, as in the original, but the 'A' strain in its place. He also lengthens the up-beat and slows up the movement of the tune by changing it from a quarter bar of even quavers to a half bar consisting of a dotted crotchet and a quaver. The 'B' strain itself he slightly alters so as to fit Bunyan's verse, lengthening the note values of the cadential phrase, which again imparts a steadier, more martial rhythm to the tune. Mrs Verrall's tune is also rather unusual in that the last line consists almost completely of new musical material. Vaughan Williams clinches his tune by tightening the rhythm of the final line, dropping the 5/4 bar. So what was in itself a slightly wayward but melodically interesting tune has become a sturdy processional hymn (see Ex. 2), a kind of English cousin to his much-loved 'Lasst uns erfreuen', a tune that he himself adapted and used in *The English Hymnal* for Hymn 519 and one that, as Michael Kennedy has pointed out, seems to have influenced his own melodic idiom.

His own hymn-tunes, like all his other compositions, display a very considerable range, from the rather recondite harmonic experiments of 'Mantegna' to the simple serenity of 'Down Ampney', with its surreptitious false relation. The contributions to *The Oxford Book of Carols* range from the dullness of 'The Snow in the Street' to the unsentimental grace and charm of 'Wither's Rocking Hymn'.

Ex. 2

'Our captain calls' (Mrs Verrall, Monks Gate, 22 Dec. 1904)

'Monks Gate' (transposed)

Bars 1/2 ... becomes ... [NB Bars 1–4 repeated in 'Monks Gate']

Bar 4 ... becomes

Bars 4/5 ... Bars 8/9 ... becomes ... [NB Bars 4–8 NOT REPEATED as in Mrs Verall's tune]

Bars 10/11 ... Bars 10/12 ... becomes

Bar 14 ... becomes

His other small-scale works not involving voices are at their best captivating and at their worst insipid. Vaughan Williams was never a pianist of the calibre of Britten; and his experience as a church organist depressed rather than inspired him. Yet he managed to produce at least one work involving each instrument that reflects his genius, if not at its greatest, at any rate at its most charming. *Three Preludes on Welsh Hymn Tunes* must be well known even to many who cannot put a name to them. The tunes are all used in the main body of *The English Hymnal* itself. They are well known, but not traditional: the composer can be traced for each of them. 'Bryn Calfaria' is by W. Owen (1814–93). Presumably remembering the words with which he had associated it in *The English Hymnal*, Vaughan Williams treats it rather in the manner of a baroque toccata, with brilliant flourishes and imitative entries leading to a final grandiose climax. 'Rhosymedre' is by D. Edwards (1805–95). It figures in the Hymnal as the tune to 'Author of Life Divine' (No. 303) and is certainly the best known of the group, a delicate embellishment of the simple, rather square tune that stands comparison with some of the more meditative chorale preludes of Bach's *Orgelbüchlein*. 'Hyfrydol', by R. H. Pritchard (1811–87), is familiar as the tune of 'Alleluia, sing to Jesus' (*EH* No. 302). Here, steadily moving crotchet inner and pedal parts transform a graceful lilting tune into a solemn processional melody of considerable power. The *Three Preludes* are unambitious pieces, yet their quality is such that they have entered the repertory of countless organists, whether from village church, university college, or mighty cathedral.

The *Introduction and Fugue* for two pianos is probably the most worth while of his other keyboard works. It combines rhythmic vitality and a remoteness of atmosphere—notably in the Prelude—which is oddly reminiscent of a late Beethoven slow movement without being in the least derivative from that source: perhaps Bela Bartók's keyboard writing provides a link. The hymn-tune prelude on Gibbons's Song 13 also deserves a mention, as does the tranquil *Lake in the Mountains*, arranged from part of the music to *49th Parallel*. But even so, there is enough for which to be grateful.

Choral music (1)

'Write choral music as befits an Englishman and a democrat.' Vaughan Williams remembered Hubert Parry's advice all his life. Parry surely wanted his young student to devote his main attention to large-scale works composed for massed amateur choruses. Underlying this may well have been the aim, apocryphally attributed to Handel, not merely of entertaining them, but of 'making them better': music performed by the people, for the people's moral good. Festival cantata and oratorio, in fact.

Many of Vaughan Williams's choral works were truly 'democratic', but not always quite in the sense Parry probably intended. Those composed for his singers at the Leith Hill Festival were surely music for the people, performed by the people. This holds good not just for the competitive part-songs, but for more ambitious accompanied works for concerted performance at the festival concerts. At times, they were music of the people in another sense, too, based as some of them were on genuine folk-melodies. Then there were the numerous occasional pieces for use in wartime, at celebrations and on great state occasions such as the Coronations both of George VI and of his daughter Elizabeth II. But although he came to artistic maturity in an age when a critic could accuse Parry himself as 'sickening for another oratorio', Vaughan Williams, unlike his distinguished mentor, wrote only one oratorio as such; all his other major choral works are given such titles as 'Cantata', 'Song for Orchestra', etc. One, indeed, is actually called a symphony and will be discussed under that heading. And a large-scale festival commission like *Five Tudor Portraits* could hardly be described as providing moral uplift, though it is certainly most enjoyable.

His earliest sizeable choral work is the setting for soprano, chorus, and orchestra of Swinburne's 'The Garden of Proserpine', which dates from 1897, remains unperformed and unpublished and is considered by Michael Kennedy to be superior to the Rossetti cantata *Willow Wood*. *Willow Wood* was composed in 1903 and first performed in its choral version in 1909, by which time Vaughan Williams had outgrown his 'pre-Raphaelite' phase. It is perhaps slightly cheating to include this work as a choral one, as the chorus of women's voices merely vocalizes while the baritone soloist wrestles with the Rossetti sonnets that form the text. Be that as it may, the work, originally for low voice and piano, was orchestrated and performed in its revised form on 25 September 1909 at a festival mounted by the short-lived Music League. The composer wrote on the MS score 'Complete flop', but for all that, the work got as far as publication in 1909. That seems to have been about as far as it did get.

By the time Vaughan Williams composed *Toward the Unknown Region*, he had forsaken Rossetti for Whitman as a textual source: an interesting and significant change. The text and the title of the work proclaim in unmistakable terms the challenge that he had set himself. Yet according to the composer's own account, its origins lay in a contest between himself and Holst as to who could set Whitman's poem the more effectively. They agreed that his setting was the better of the two. The shadow of the Brahms *German Requiem*, and in particular of its third and sixth movements, hangs fairly heavily over this fine work, which is understandable and not particularly regrettable, for even if the style might have been described by Stanford as 'Brahms and water, me bhoy', at least there is plenty of Brahms, and good Brahms at that, and precious little water. The post-Romantic chromaticism of the inner parts is used to impart a surge and onward flow to the music, not to thicken the texture or render it voluptuous, nor, as would quite possibly be the case in mature Vaughan Williams, to imply some kind of evil or morally ambiguous presence. The very first bars, with their hint of modality and their melodic foreshadowing of a mature characteristic Vaughan Williams phrase that became almost a cliché are also worth noting, while the Elgarian (or more probably, Parryesque) spaciousness of the work, and in particular of its aspiring final pages, is full of a majestic strength and confidence.

The *Fantasia on Christmas Carols*, first performed at the 1912 Hereford Three Choirs Festival, has remained a favourite with choral societies—and with good reason. Neither learned nor profound, it is, as would be expected, tuneful, singable, and immediately recognizable stylistically. The text is deftly arranged to tell the story of the Fall of Man and Christ's redemption of the fallen world and to rejoice in and reflect on it, both as a narrative and in musical terms. An indication of the shape of things to come is the way in which the solo cello introduction unwinds itself, a fragment of its first phrase (Ex. 3a) evolving via a small rhythmic change, in the manner familiar from such works as *In the Fen Country*, into Ex. 3b, and finally, by a kind of musical pun, into the carol 'The Truth Sent from Above'. Vaughan Williams unobtrusively draws attention to the family resemblance between two of his chosen tunes by juxtaposing and contrasting 'Come all you worthy gentlemen' and 'Here we come a-wassailing' (the first from Somerset, the second from Yorkshire) and introduces another carol that he himself had collected, 'On Christmas night all Christians sing', which is in turn

Ex. 3.

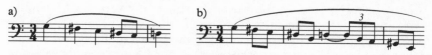

intertwined with 'God bless the master of this house', 'A Virgin Unspotted', and 'The First Nowell'. Critics of this unambitious, lively yet often surprisingly reflective work seem to attack it for being what it can never have set out to be. It is not a kind of solemn attempt to force the unsophisticated folk-tunes into unnecessary clever-clever ceremonial displays of learned counterpoint. There is simply just enough 'academic' treatment of the material to demonstrate the kinship of the tunes and to integrate them into a loose but satisfying design. And the quiet ending, after all the jovial festivities, reaches out into the starlit depths of the winter sky as—to quote Michael Kennedy[1]—'the wassailers' voices vanish into the distance, across the snow-covered fields into the night', as if to indicate that there is a greater meaning to the Christmas story than just an occasion for wassailing and a 'good sing'.

More ambitious than this work is what is certainly the most telling product of Vaughan Williams's pre-first-world-war folk-song collecting activities: the *Five English Folk Songs* of 1913. Latter-day purists (if that is the correct term) who prefer their folk-songs ground out over a series of primitive strummed chords on a guitar with a cracked, toneless, out-of-tune yokel-colour 'authenticity' and a nudge-nudge-know-what-I-mean emphasis on the more prurient innuendos of the texts will dismiss these arrangements as unspeakably middle-class 'fake-song'. Yet they were clearly made with a love and a care for the true nature of the tunes far outweighing any sense that there may be of dressing them up for proud presentation by some ambitious local choral society. They are a joy to sing and to listen to, given a chorus-master who tries neither to paint the lily with genteel 'expression' nor to treat them merely as a rousing vocal exercise.

This unaccompanied choral sinfonietta, for that is in effect what it is, opens with a comparatively straightforward treatment of 'The Dark-eyed Sailor'. It is followed by the pastoral calm of 'The Springtime of the Year' a gorgeous tune taken down in April 1908 from a Mr Hilton of South Walsham in Norfolk. Vaughan Williams seems to have been the only collector to have gathered it orally. He has transmuted it into music of the kind that Holst would surely have called the *real* RVW, though he has disregarded the story, another tale of the separation of a seaman from his beloved, in favour of using only those verses that contribute to a purely lyrical atmosphere.

[1] Kennedy, *Works* 2, p. 135.

'Just as the Tide Was Flowing' he turns into a display piece for the singers, contrasting male and female voices with regard more to their differing expressive qualities than to the dialogue nature of the text, which he slightly emasculates, both in fact and in implication. He concentrates more on building the tune up into a riot of energetic imitative counterpoint that illustrates the tide of the 'rolling river' in the first verse instead of underlining or overtly expressing the phrase's erotic associations, which are certainly clear enough in the original text. The poignancy of 'The Lover's Ghost' derives equally from the haunting modal tune and from Vaughan Williams's treatment of it. He turns it through imitative entries, stately harmonic rhythm and a kind of cantus fermus treatment into what is virtually a madrigal rather than a part-song. In places, indeed, it sounds more like a full anthem or a study for the Mass in G minor. The choral texture is perhaps not as exuberantly elaborate as that of 'Just as the Tide Was Flowing' but is certainly more profoundly expressive.

Dare one detect a 'crib' from the opening of Beethoven's Ninth Symphony with the overlapping fragmentary imitative entries building up to the tune itself at the beginning of 'Wassail Song'? If so, what follows is certainly more akin in its rough, good-natured vigour to a Beethoven scherzo than to the glowering grandeur of the Ninth's first movement. The end, after the rousing climax, is most poetic: a mini-epilogue such as was by now characteristic of the composer.

The motet 'O clap your hands', published in 1920 is, as Michael Kennedy rightly says, 'in the composer's church-going "Ward the Pirate" mood'. Its air of hearty, slightly self-conscious three-in-a-bar jubilation, similar to that of 'Antiphon', is straightforward and rather redolent of the school chapel or morning assembly. Perhaps that is what it is best suited to in performance terms. The composer goes deeper with 'Lord, Thou has been our refuge', published in 1921, using both the tune ('St Anne') and the words ('O God, our Help in Ages Past') Isaac Watts's well known paraphrase of the psalm he sets (Psalm 90) as a kind of gloss on the original. The rhythmically free yet metrically firm declamation of the baritone solo's part looks forward to the lead role in *The Pilgrim's Progress*; and sonorous brass recapitulation towards the end of Croft's tune *without* Watts's words as the chorus declaims forte what the baritone had introduced piano shows imagination of a high order. This work, with its conflict between the modal restlessness of the opening psalm setting and the strong diatonic assurance of 'St Anne', sounds as if it might have been the first of Vaughan Williams's musical reactions to his recent experiences at the battle front.

There is no hint of any such reaction in the Mass in G Minor (which is, incidentally, apart from the opening Kyrie, noted for the sake of convenience mainly in a kind of G major). Only in its duration is this is a small work. It is compact and succinct in idiom and in the way

Vaughan Williams handles the text. It is a striking indication of the manner in which an atheist or an agnostic with imagination can look at the text of the Mass starting from first principles, as it were. But Vaughan Williams also had stored within him half a lifetime's study and experience of great liturgical music and his setting of the Mass is both liturgically apt and a vivid evocation of the meaning behind the words. The soft, melancholy richness of *Pastoral Symphony* is blended with the massive power and solidity of the Tallis Fantasia in the service of the liturgy, and a stylistic excursion is made into the remote musical past in order to create something quite new—impressionistic in its exploitation of archaic techniques rather than aiming at any kind of historicism, suffused with a glowing serenity (notably in the Kyrie and the Sanctus) that is reminiscent of one of the great Renaissance masters, notably Byrd, without ever being derivative from them. The false relations free the sometimes Debussyesque sequences of triads from the realm of mere sonic solid geometry, facilitating modulations that would have been quite out of court in the sixteenth century. They also enrich the texture and add piquancy to the harmony, either as an element in a progression or as an immediate sensation. As with modern devices, so with old ones: Vaughan Williams always employs them as a starting-point, to expand his technical range of expression, not as a finishing-post, which is essentially a limitation of technique.

The choral textures of the Mass may sound archaic at first hearing; and most of them can certainly be found in mass settings from the great period of unaccompanied choral liturgical music. In fact, however, they are much more varied than those to be found within any one a cappella mass setting from the sixteenth century. And certainly Vaughan Williams's use of the contrast between soloists and chorus is in the best twentieth-century practice. The Mass is a compendium of stylish unaccompanied choral writing from the age of organum to the age of impressionism, leaving out, it is true, the *galant* and romantic idioms and ignoring as far as possible the classical and the baroque, though he does nod in the direction of setting the 'Cum sancto spiritu' as a fugue by treating it in imitative canonic entries. Yet the work is not a ragbag of styles, but a congruent entity. The communal experience of three centuries of west European musical evolution is here read back into liturgical music of the purest and least theatrical kind imaginable: music as aural incense rather than as part of a dramatic action.

The main formal problem with any setting of the Mass lies in unifying the diversity of the Credo; and this Vaughan Williams achieves first of all by using the same music for 'Patrem omnipotentem' as he does for 'Et resurrexit', (with its unprepared leap at the beginning from a cadence in a modal F to a modal D major)—thereby perhaps symbolizing that it was the same force that created the world as raised Christ from the dead, and possibly symbolizing also that the resurrection was as signifi-

cant a demonstration of divine power as the creation itself. Overall unity
is further strengthened by using the same phrase for the opening of
'Miserere nobis' in the Agnus Dei as for the Kyrie. Another unifying
device is the familiar Vaughan Williams procedure of developing an initial motif set to different words as it expands from a similar opening
phrase—the method of the Tudor and baroque fantasia, in fact. This in
the 'Et in spiritum sanctum' section of the Credo, the phrase shown in
Ex. 4 introduces 'Spiritum sanctum' in the soprano, 'et vivificantem' in
the tenor, 'qui cum patre et [filio]' in the bass, 'simul ador[atur]' in the
soprano (with a slightly altered rhythm), 'qui locutus est' in the soprano
again, 'et unam sanctam ca[tholicam ecclesiam]' in the second chorus,
and so on, each time leading to something slightly different.

Ex. 4

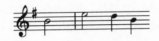

There are many striking touches in this fine work but lack of space
precludes the mention of more than a few. Two of the most effective are
the introduction of the chord of A flat major into the 'Et incarnatus',
which transforms a trite tonal progression into one with a veiled radiance that exactly suits the mystery of the text to which it is set; and the
gently undulating and interweaving lines of the Sanctus, the aural
equivalent of incense being wafted gently up from slowly swinging
censers to the tinkle of liturgical bells. The motif familiar from the
'Alleluia' of *Sine Nomine* recurs once more in the Benedictus.

The Mass is emphatically not 'democratic'. It may make some impact
in the concert hall, but it really belongs in the church or the chapel,
preferably as part of the liturgy. Designed as it was for Holst's
Whitsuntide Singers, it requires a sensitive choir with a really sympathetic conductor. It is not enough just to get the notes right, the entries
firm, and the intonation correct. It may be *Gebrauchsmusik*, yet it is not
merely an adornment of the service, but a revelation of its meaning.

After the Mass, a new element seems to have entered Vaughan
Williams's approach to choral music. His emotional range, his style, and
his conception of what a choral work could convey, democratic or no,
seem to have expanded. The expansion went in two directions. From
Sancta Civitas onward, a new toughness is found in his choral writing.
The breadth, lyric intensity, and rhythmic vigour already evident in his
earlier works were more and more to erupt into a visionary incandes-
cence on the one hand and a low-life zest on the other that exhilarated
and sometimes puzzled his friends and admirers and often exasperated
his critics.

11

Choral music (2)

Sancta Civitas, the composer's own favourite among his choral works, was the only work to which Vaughan Williams gave the title 'oratorio'; and his choice of such an apocalyptic text leads to the conjecture that the music was at least in part influenced by his experiences of Armageddon in 1914–18. So it is hardly strange that some of the work's most convincing interpreters have gone through the experience of the battlefield themselves. It is also mildly surprising that RVW was quite unaware that the projected third part of Elgar's huge trilogy of which *The Apostles* and *The Kingdom* formed parts I and II was to be on the subject of the Last Judgment. In fact, when Elgar congratulated RVW after a Three Choirs performance of *Sancta Civitas*, he added that he had at one time considered setting those very words, but that he would never do so now; and that he was glad he hadn't, because RVW had done it for him. To which RVW characteristically replied that he regretted Elgar had not set them himself.

Sancta Civitas, with its combination of shattering power and dazzling radiance, is certainly one of his most profound and concentrated works. Hubert Parry as well as Elgar would surely have appreciated its grandeur, scope and intensity, even if he might not have approved some of its 'impertinences'. For impertinent it certainly is in its attitude to the oratorio tradition. Here is no stately and not too disturbing exposition of one of the gorier prophetic stories from the Old Testament, but a mighty depiction of the new heaven and the new earth which the text claims are to come. It is white-hot in its intensity, spine-chilling (and, for some, hackle-raising) in its almost indecently ferocious energy. The Unknown Region has at last been reached; and this is a vision of what it might be like:

> . . . a country far beyond the stars,
> Where stands a winged sentry
> All skilful in the wars[1]

though in this case, 'sweet peace' certainly does not sit, above noise and danger, crowned with smiles.

[1] Henry Vaughan (set by Hubert Parry in *Songs of Farewell*).

The remoteness of the opening, indeterminate in key, exactly catches the sense of being 'in the spirit', as the first words of the text set the scene. There is a feeling of total dissolution of any sense of the material at the two dissonant flute chords merge into one another, high up over the awesome murmur of the lower strings, when the semi-chorus enters. Gradually the mists dissolve as the distant chorus comes in with a rapt bitonal effect and the action begins to yet another characteristic RVW fanfare call-to-arms.

One of RVW's favourite Bach movements was what he called the 'battle' chorus[2] 'Und wenn die Welt voll Teufel wär' from *Ein' feste Burg*. It is surely not fanciful to think that he was here emulating his supreme musical hero. Emulating, not imitating. The spirit may possibly be that of Bach; the fierce, athletic manner is much closer to a kind of impressionistic re-thinking of Beethoven in his most dynamic, elemental mood, as in the *Grosse Fuge*. But the energy is less wilful than Beethoven's: not onward-thrusting counterpoint, but rugged and powerful block chords in a ponderous and highly characteristic rhythm that exactly matches the mood of the verbal context. The veil is drawn aside, the heavens open and battle is joined between the forces of Good and Evil—in 5/4 metre. The 'angel standing in the sun' strikingly foreshadows the tremendous second movement of the Sixth Symphony; the accompaniment builds up to a gigantic chord of G minor on the word 'fierceness' and then evaporates abruptly, leaving the ecstatic chorus supported by the timpani 'beating like some supernatural pulse', as Michael Kennedy graphically puts it. The 'mighty howl of savagery' (Kennedy) at 'slain', as the account of the overthrow of Babylon the Great is narrated, provides an interesting contrast with Walton's setting of a similar text in *Belshazzar's Feast*. But here there is a kind of heart-aching regret, a sadness at the heart of the savage triumph that is totally alien to the exultant relish with which Walton narrates the Old Testament story. What Babylon the Great symbolized for Vaughan Williams we can only guess. Perhaps it stood for the Germanic culture against whose background his musical education had taken shape, product as it was of a socio-political system overthrown by military defeat in 1918 and further undermined by an aesthetic reaction in the post-war period. The composer uses his bi- and tri-planar harmonic technique to telling effect in the imitative choral writing at this point: the same technique as dominates the first movement of *Pastoral Symphony*, but this time applied to a choral texture.

The New Heaven and the New Earth are ushered in with a wonderful flowing metrical freedom by a solo violin over a bass line in the lower strings that is in fact a variant of the very opening of the work. Vaughan Williams's unmistakably characteristic rhapsodic violin writing is here

[2] See, for example, the mention in *National Music*, p. 116.

put to a totally different use from that in a piece such as *The Lark Ascending*. That was union with the natural world of field and sky: man may be a mere dot on the landscape, but he is there. This is beyond the natural. It is a timeless skyscape inhabited not so much by men and women, less still by birds and beasts, as by awesome angels of a transcendent Being. One is tempted to say that when he wrote this music, Vaughan Williams willingly suspended his unbelief. It is eerie and serene at the same time. Its background of ambivalent chords at such passages as 'Clear as crystal', when the composer is depicting the precious stones of the Holy City, creates a remote, shimmering radiance, like that of a host of distant nebulae (Ex. 5). This celestial city shines with a quite different light from that projected in *The Shepherds of the Delectable Mountains*: the musical radiance is much less intimate, much less transparent; and the mood is one of almost oriental splendour.[3]

Ex. 5

The sure hand with which the composer builds up the tension from 'And the city had no need' to the whispered choral unison at 'And they shall see His face', the startling distant trumpets (surely another reminder of the Flanders battlefield), the great blaze of cloudy choral glory at 'Heaven and earth are full of thy glory', with the brass striding in and out of the rich choral texture, and the setting of 'Holy, holy, holy'—a moment worthy to place alongside the great climax before 'Take me away' in *The Dream of Gerontius*—are all highly memorable. But more memorable still is the manner in which the vision fades, leaving the semi-chorus, trumpets, and timpani to lead back into the remote immensity of the opening. The introduction of the tenor for his brief solo is another master-stroke: a voice from outside the confines of the resources used so far is essential to link the unearthly vision experienced with the material world. It *was* a vision, after all, just as *The Pilgrim's Progress* is in the similitude of a dream; but for the time being, we have been caught up in it. Atheist or not, of this work at least, the composer

---

[3] Michael Kennedy points out (*Works* 2, p. 215) that this passage was originally intended for an unpublished setting of Whitman's 'Nocturne', dating from 1908, but had been waiting in Vaughan Williams's mind for its proper consummation.

might claim 'We beheld His glory', as the prologue to the Fourth Gospel has it.

The sequel and complement, as it were, to *Sancta Civitas*, is *Dona Nobis Pacem*. But in the eleven years that lay between it and *Sancta Civitas* came a whole host of smaller choral works and one significant and totally unexpected larger one. The larger one was *Five Tudor Portraits*. The smaller ones included a setting of the Te Deum for the enthronement of Dr Cosmo Gordon Lang as Archbishop of Canterbury in December 1928, four works for the silver jubilee of the Leith Hill Festival in 1930: the *Benedicite*, The Hundredth Psalm, the *Three Choral Hymns* and *Three Children's Songs for a Spring Festival*, each containing suitably rewarding technical challenges to the skill of the various choirs involved; the Magnificat, composed for the 1932 Three Choirs Festival; 'O How Amiable', composed for the Abinger Pageant of 1934, and *The Pilgrim Pavement*, for the dedication of the pilgrims' pavement of the Cathedral of St John the Divine in New York in the same year.

Of these works, most are either slight or unsophisticated; but the Magnificat is something more. Vaughan Williams sets out to underline not merely the semantic meaning of the all-too-familiar text, but to illustrate its historical significance, 'trying', as he put it, 'to lift the words out of the smug atmosphere which had settled down on it from being sung at evening service for so long'.[4] This he achieves by setting the text proper in its gospel context of an astonished young woman experiencing puzzlement, rapture, and finally apprehension lest she prove unworthy of the great charge laid upon her.

This impressive scena for mezzo-soprano and female chorus, written with Astra Desmond in mind for the solo part, could almost be called Vaughan Williams's counterpart to Purcell's *Blessed Virgin's Expostulation*. As a footnote to the vocal score rather unnecessarily points out, it is not intended for liturgical performance. It is dramatic and mystical without being theatrical, expressing the young mother-to-be's direct access to the Godhead through the messenger Gabriel and the power of the Holy Ghost. It effectively conveys the ecstatic outpouring of the conflicting emotions felt by a humble young woman to whom has been unexpectedly revealed the greatest mystery of time and eternity: the 'Incarnatus' of the Mass is experienced from the inside, not mindlessly ground out within the context of a routine office. The other-worldly atmosphere is conveyed at the outset by the swaying Holstian chords (unconsciously or even perhaps deliberately cribbed from *The Hymn of Jesus*) and the melismatic flute solo, almost a kind of *Prélude à l'après-midi d'une demoiselle élue*, to adapt an apt phrase from Christopher Palmer. The voluptuous scoring, too, is much more in line with *Flos Campi* (of which there is also a hint in the passage illustrating 'He hath

---

[4] *Heirs and Rebels*, p. 79.

showed strength with His arm'). Mary's astonished joy is evident in her florid, melismatic vocal line. At the end of the work the favourite device of a quiet epilogue after a big climax is used to bring audience and performers back to earth, to Mary's meek humanity after her heavenly vision: once again, the comment 'we beheld His glory' is not out of place.

A similar attempt to bridge the gap between routine and reality is found in the *Benedicite*. Here, however, the attempt is less successful, the music all too often falling into a hearty rumpty-tumpty metrical squareness that makes it fun to sing but embarrassing to listen to. The *Three Choral Hymns*, with texts by Miles Coverdale, one for Easter, one for Christmas, and one for Whitsun, are more successful. The broad main tune of 'Easter Hymn', punctuated with approving 'Alleluyas' and with appropriate outbursts of joy from the orchestral 'heavies', is suitably reminiscent of early Tudor church music. 'Christmas Hymn' starts off as a lullaby in the composer's best 'Oxford Book of Carols' vein, a more sophisticated version of a tune like that used to 'Wither's Rocking Hymn'. The predominantly close choral texture opens out at the words 'Eternall lyght doth now appeare', the women's voices providing a kind of halo above the men's 'To the worlde both farre and neare'. The 'Whitsunday Hymn' harks back to the *Four Hymns*, but differs from them in that apart from the two introductory bars, it is entirely unaccompanied. The changes that RVW rings on the choral layout of the combination of Alleluyas and main text are particularly enchanting, as when the women's voices declaim 'O holy fyre and comforthe moste swete' to the men's Alleluyas, the full chorus combining to sing the same text only with the final verse.

The setting of Psalm 100 is notably mainly for its introductory fanfares—appropriated for RVW's 1953 Coronation service setting of 'All people that on earth do dwell'—and for the way in which it side-slips into the tune of 'The Old Hundredth' at the words 'O enter then His gates with praise', first in the orchestra, then in the chorus, to be suitably varied in following triplets worthy of his beloved Bach in his best pastoral vein. The words of the 'Old Hundredth' as well as the tune are thundered out for the final doxology.

It was to a rather less high-minded Tudor source than Coverdale that Vaughan Williams turned for his next major choral work. John Skelton was no mean scholar. Respected enough to be appointed poet laureate both by Oxford and Cambridge Universities, he was the young Henry VIII's tutor and at least an acquaintance of Erasmus. Appointed rector of Diss in Norfolk somewhere about the end of the fifteenth century, it was while he was there that he composed at least two of the five poems set by Vaughan Williams. Their vigorous, bouncy metres ('pure jazz', said Elgar, who introduced RVW to these particular poems) terse lines, speed of movement, facile but imaginative rhyme-schemes, and combination of lyric charm, childlike pathos and downright ribald satire found a ready musical counterpart in the racy, robust musical humour and gentle warmth that RVW was able to bring to them. The verse is short-winded but long-limbed, proceeding in jerky macaronic lines cast in breathless, lengthy paragraphs. It lacks any kind of polish or elegance (indeed, the poem chosen by RVW for his finale explicitly mocks such qualities) and enables the composer to exhibit the reverse side of the medal of which the Scherzo of the F minor Symphony constitutes the obverse. The whole suite is aflame with passion and feeling, whether tender (as in 'Jane Scroop'), sarcastic (as in 'Jolly Rutterkin') or splenetic ('Epitaph on John Jayberd of Diss'). The visionary of *Sancta Civitas* descends from his apocalyptic heights and, rather than carving out massive soaring vaults, sets his musical chisel to work hewing out with glee three human gargoyles and sketching with loving care two tender misericords.

The pulse of the movements is for the most part heavy but rapid. The angular opening of 'The Tunning of Elinor Rumming' sets the tone for the odd-numbered movements. The cunningly contrived (or marvellously inspired) opening motif, with its downward cascading augmented fourth opening—Vaughan Williams emulating (but again not imitating) the thunderbolt opening of the Scherzo of Beethoven's Ninth Symphony, which he greatly admired—in its curt, emphatic rhetorical two-note descending semitonal phrases repeated a fifth apart and telescoped into a thumping two-quaver-plus-crotchet pay-off, gets the movement off to an unmistakably grab-you-by-the-scruff-of-the-neck start. Once set on its course, the music goes crashing on its way, as in the Fourth Symphony, but here the irresistibility of its momentum is the outcome, not of brutal and explosive violence, but of sheet impetuous *joie de vivre* (and later, in the case of 'John Jayberd', of *joie de haïr* as well).

Two other great English composers lurk in the background of this masterly score. First, and most appropriately, there is Elgar, to whom RVW pays the sincerest flattery, as he himself might have put it, of re-creating the musical climate of *Falstaff*. He does so, not only by (surely unconsciously) compressing and rhythmically distorting Falstaff's own main theme into the harmonically ambiguous opening motif of 'Elinor Rumming' and by the (probably much more intentionally) bibulous scoring and melodic high spirits of the 'drunken Alice' episode, but also by evoking a reminiscence of Falstaff's dream sequence in the texture, chording, and scoring of 'Pretty Bess' and the shambling gait of Falstaff's rag-tag-and-bobtail army that characterizes certain parts of 'John Jayberd'. Then there is the Waltonesque vitality of 'Rutterkin', a *tour de force* of jazzy rhythmic verve and orchestral brilliance, its themes providing a suitable cross-reference to those of 'Elinor Rumming' ('What now' is related to 'With a hey and a ho', and the bumpy jauntiness of the main tune is first cousin to the angular motif which permeates the first section of the first movement). There are reminders of Ravel, of Mahler even, in the wonderfully delicate scoring of 'Jane Scroop', too. Yet every note is pure Vaughan Williams, and vintage Vaughan Williams into the bargain. There is no question of cribbing.

'Elinor Rumming' is a large-scale patter-ballad for full chorus and orchestra, but far rougher-mannered than most patter-songs in opera or operetta. The ale-house commotion of the opening, coarse or cantabile by turns, carries the music along in one vast sweep, either in a beer-mug-thumping three-in-a-bar or a more graceful landler-like one-in-a-bar, until the procession breaks into a rampaging scherzo at the change to 9/8. All the rudest instruments of the orchestra are given their heads—no wonder the Countess of Albemarle left the hall in disgust. For once I feel that Michael Kennedy[5] is wide of the mark when he describes the rabble that enter towards the close of the movement after Drunken Alice has fallen into her slumbers as outstaying their welcome by several bars. And even if he is right, don't uninvited guests do precisely that, anyway? The party comes to disreputable life again, with pipe, bowl, and rustic, Breughelesque high spirits, suddenly breaking off with an abrupt close after a rumbustious semi-fugato that seems to be cocking a snook at the one in Weber's *Euryanthe* Overture.

The brief and charming intermezzo, 'Pretty Bess', shows Skelton in an unexpectedly tender vein. It is a charming love-song for the solo baritone, with the male chorus gently but eloquently supporting his plea. Two epitaphs follow. 'John Jayberd' is sarcastic and uncouth, both words and setting undermining rather than underlining the old saw: 'de mortuis nil nisi bonum'. Skelton's splenetic outburst, carefully couched for the most part in Latin, is matched by Vaughan Williams with a kind of up-market racy male-voice rugger-song, culminating in a raucous trill, with the tenors and basses an augmented fourth apart. Howes calls it 'a skit on the clergy and their ways'. That's putting it mildly; there is far more malice than skit about this text, though Vaughan Williams's tongue-in-cheek setting somewhat draws its sting by clothing it in music of cheerful savagery.

The lament for Jane Scroop's pet sparrow, Philip, is the only number in the suite devoid of any hint of parody and its pathos is all the more marked after the bitterness of 'John Jayberd', since it underlines the fact that the little girl feels her pet's death far more acutely than anyone does John Jayberd's. The attempt to recapture the feelings of childhood, the land of lost content, is a marked feature of the music of two of our other great composers: Elgar and Britten; but they value childhood for its lost sense of wonderment on the one hand or its lost innocence on the other. Vaughan Williams rarely looks back to childhood; and here, it is not so much lost innocence that he is mourning as the genuine and profound

[5] Kennedy, *Works 2*, p. 270.

loss of a companion. Delicacy, as opposed to sensitivity, is not a trait habitually associated with his music, but it is most marked here, especially in the orchestration. Those who think that his music went into a decline after the death of Holst would do well to study this movement.

The lament is headed 'Romanza', a title that RVW applied only to movements where he felt the emotions expressed were both lyrical and intense. Like Skelton, he takes little Jane's grief seriously. Even the quotation of the *Dies irae* has no hint either of parody or of the macabre about it. Whereas in 'John Jayberd', all went at a rasping allegro, her movement is marked 'Lento doloroso'. His tunes and their harmonization were jagged and brutal; hers flow and the inner parts are often marked by expressive chromatic inflections. (Here, there is no association of chromaticism with evil.) His obituary is bawled out in Latin by the men; hers is half-crooned by the women and given personal point by the mezzo-soprano. His is short and perfunctory, for all the length of the text. Hers is considerably the longest movement in the suite. The scoring of his movement is spiky and close-textured. That of hers is tender, picturesquely illustrative, transparent, and like chamber music. Instances of this abound. One might single out perhaps the miniature tone-painting at the 'Poco più mosso' for 'Sometimes he would gasp / When he saw a wasp', with its piccolo, horns, and muted trumpet (rather different from and much less blatant than the good-humoured buzzing of the opening of *The Wasps* Overture!) or the minuscule details used to paint in the characters of the various birds mentioned in Skelton's procession at Philip's funeral as summoned by Jane to mourn her pet and perform a given function at his funeral. Vaughan Williams loathed the music of Liszt and was ambivalent about Mahler's. None the less, the delicacy of the 'Gretchen' movement from the *Faust* Symphony and of a Mahler movement such as 'Von der Schönheit' (*Das Lied von der Erde*) or 'Ich bin der Welt abhanden gekommen' (from the *Rückertlieder*) come to mind as parallel examples where innocence and ingenuousness evoke similar moods and inspire a similar approach to scoring.[6]

The scoring of *Five Tudor Portraits*, in fact, is one of the hallmarks of the work's and its composer's versatility, for with the first bars of the brilliant finale, 'Rutterkin', we are back in the world of satire. It is, however, quite a different world from that of 'Elinor Rumming' or 'John Jayberd'. This crisp Scherzo has for its target a swaggering and dandified trendy; and the rhythms, the scoring, and the melodic contours of the music differ accordingly from anything we have had before. The headlong syncopations and cross-rhythms of the opening ('pure jazz', did Elgar say? Vaughan Williams certainly took him at his word in this

[6] Michael Kennedy has suggested to me that the end of this movement was written with the Angel's Farewell in *Gerontius* in mind, and is therefore perhaps a tribute to Elgar, who had died in 1934.

movement, at any rate) set the tone of the piece. The manner in which the first five bars of the soloist's first entry bounce repeatedly from B flat to E flat and back, as if he cannot get away from admiring his own image, is musical characterization of the simplest and most effective kind; and the interchange of roles between soloist and chorus at the compressed recapitulation underlines still further the character's conceit—and what Skelton and Vaughan Williams think of it. What had been scathing objective comment has now become the expression of pure self-absorption. But there is no malice here, as there had been with Jayberd. Rutterkin may be a fop; he is no hypocrite.

Dona Nobis Pacem, which, like *Five Tudor Portraits*, calls for one male and one female soloist, chorus, and large orchestra, was first performed a mere week after *Five Tudor Portraits*; and the contrast could hardly have been greater. Here, the composer came right down into the political arena. To adapt Gilbert Murray's fine phrase: whereas *Five Tudor Portraits* had mainly displayed the snook-cocking rebel against smug choral respectability, *Dona Nobis Pacem* shows us the heir to the great tradition of choral uplift. This was music with a message; and Parry would certainly have approved. The work was commissioned to celebrate the centenary of the Huddersfield Choral Society, but instead of setting some kind of paean in praise of the great Yorkshire choir, he chose to remind the performers and audience of the all-too-evident threat to peace. 'All that a poet can do is warn', to quote Wilfred Owen. Those who read messages about World War II into the F minor Symphony or about the threat of nuclear warfare into the E minor were hardly to be blamed when the composer so explicitly centred a work commissioned for such an occasion round such a theme.

There are six sections, the texts drawn mainly but not exclusively from the Bible on the one hand and Whitman on the other. The first is a prayer for peace, the text taken from the Requiem Mass, declaimed by the solo soprano, a voice above the battlefield, as it were, 'leading the forces of apprehensive humanity . . . in their quest for peace'.[7] It starts gently and with a sober anguish, but suddenly becomes an almost panic-stricken cry—the choral ecstasy of the climax of *Flos Campi* turned to quite different ends—the two versions, pathetic and anguished, alternating until the approach of the menacing drums of war beneath the soprano's sobbing cry surfaces as a vivid objective portrayal of the brutality of war and its effect on the community. The text is taken from *Drum Taps* in which Whitman writes of the American Civil War, the first of those all-or-nothing mechanized wars in which the whole populace was involved in a conflict that may have started over a political issue but ended up by becoming ideological. Nobody is spared: not the scholar, nor the newly-wed, neither the townsman nor the farmer, the

---

[7] Christopher Palmer, sleeve-note to the Hyperion recording (CDA 66655).

old nor the young, nor even the congregation worshipping in church. Vaughan Williams matches Whitman's stark rhetoric with music of a brutal, almost frenetic intensity, with its terse, declamatory choral writing and jagged, strident scoring that cannot fail to remind the listener of the F minor symphony.

The persistent triplets and fanfares of the opening subside into a gentle syncopated rhythm, and the key shifts from a Phrygian E minor to a serene E major (which underlines the fact that Vaughan Williams's abrupt transitions in other works were the result of deliberate policy, not clumsy craftsmanship). The tumult and the shouting die, the rhythm slackens and leads into the next Whitman poem, also from *Drum Taps*, 'Reconciliation', which opens in what would be Vaughan Williams's best nocturnal *Serenade to Music* vein if the *Serenade* had not still been nearly two years in the future. Several commentators have pointed out the similarity in mood between the text of this section and that of Wilfred Owen's 'Strange Meeting', so finely set by Britten in the last movement of the *War Requiem*. But Whitman is less personal than Owen, though as in the *War Requiem*, the soldiers are symbols of a common humanity bound together by the common tie of death in battle.

The most moving sections of *Dona Nobis Pacem* are the elegiac 'Dirge for Two Veterans'—Vaughan Williams in his most Elgarian (or perhaps Parryesque) vein—and the opening of the last section of all, where one theme rises from below and the other, a modified inversion of it, floats down, as it were, from the sky to meet it. The 'Dirge' emphasizes the pathos and eeriness of death, rather than its glory or nobility, though there is a splendid solemn climax at the words 'And the strong dead march enwraps me' that foreshadows Elgar's 'For the Fallen' (the 'Dirge' setting in its original form pre-dates World War I). The rather over-hearty jubilation of the faster section of the finale, the weakest part of the work, rather lets down the quiet grandeur of its opening and seems to be based on wishful thinking rather than genuine conviction; but the last word is most effectively left with the unaccompanied chorus, breathing its anxious prayer for peace.

The Coronation of George VI in 1937 brought two works from Vaughan Williams. The three-movement *Flourish for a Coronation* is a setting, not of some flatulent jingoistic ode, but of texts chosen by the composer from the Old Testament, Chaucer's *Lake of Stedfastnesse* and the Agincourt Song respectively. Scored for an enormous orchestra, it is notable for its Handelian swagger, spiced up, as Michael Kennedy has pointed out, by a dash of Waltonesque rhythmic angularity and, in the second movement, for a broad and memorable tune. The *Festival Te Deum* based on traditional themes, composed for the actual coronation service, sounds as if RVW were on automatic pilot.

If that assertion is true of the Te Deum, it is certainly not so of the glorious *Serenade to Music* composed in 1938 to celebrate Henry Wood's golden jubilee as a conductor. The well-known passage from *The Merchant of Venice* on which Vaughan Williams drew for his text refers in fact to the ancient doctrine of the Music of the Spheres: that divine music, inaudible to human ears, that was believed to hold the cosmos together in eternal harmony and of which human music was but a pale reflection. This was not mere imaginative fantasy to Shakespeare: he was writing a good century before the formulation of the law of gravity. It is interesting that Vaughan Williams, for whatever reason, pruned the text as he set it of all such references.

The tribute extends far beyond the occasion for which the work was composed. It is just as much a tribute, as the title makes clear, to the art that Wood had served so faithfully and to the vocal art of the sixteen fine English singers that RVW had in mind when laying out the piece. The sopranos come off especially well: the radiant purity of Isobel Baillie's voice and the rich, Italianate sonority of Eva Turner's in particular are associated with memorable and superbly apposite solos.

The sheer lyric appeal of the *Serenade* reduced Sergei Rachmaninoff to tears at the first performance. He if anyone would have been in sympathy with this work: there is an almost voluptuous feel about the orchestral textures and the melodic curves of the piece that have caused some commentators to think of Delius. The parallel, I would suggest, lies rather further back. In 1937, RVW had been adapting Antonin Dvořák's Te Deum for performance at the Leith Hill Festival; and the opening of the *Serenade* bears distinct traces of the open-air freshness of parts of that work as well as of the moonlit tranquillity of the central section of the *Carnival* overture. There is even a slender reminiscence of Dvořák's 'Nature' theme in the outline of the opening orchestral phrase; and the violin solo is considerably more Dvořákian than Vaughan Williams's usually are. That Vaughan Williams admired the great Czech master is evident from a passage in his tribute to Elgar, published in January 1935:

> I lose patience with those people who try to put up Berlioz as a great composer because he interpreted Shakespeare, because he could give literary reasons for his beliefs, and do not see that a composer like Dvořák, a reed shaken by the wind, is far the greater man of the two because the wind was the divine afflatus.[8]

In the *Serenade*, the composer is, in fact, revisiting his early Dvořákian pre-Raphaelite territory, but applying all the wisdom and experience he had gained in the thirty years that had elapsed since the days of *The House of Life*. What Holst would at that time have called the *real* RVW emerges in the work's unobtrusive originality.

An unexpected aspect of the 'democratic' Vaughan Williams is to be found in the sturdy set of canticles that he wrote unprompted 'for Dr.

---

[8] *National Music*, p. 251.

C. S. Lang and his singers at Christ's Hospital'. Vaughan Williams, as might be expected, did not write down to the boys. The angular, sometimes apparently meandering modal melodies, strings of consecutive triads, and juxtapositions of unrelated keys are typical fingerprints. The haunting melody of the Benedictus, the thrilling effect of the canonic imitation between the massed voices and the choir at the words 'Holy, holy, holy' in the Te Deum and the fact that the choral tenor part is skilfully kept as far as possible below F so that the boys' voices are not strained to reach the higher notes, are three touches of many that might be cited to show that this was no mere academic exercise born out of duty, but a labour of care and enthusiasm, perhaps even of love. It is a pity that these fine works cannot be better known, but it is also worth noting that other distinguished English composers from Britten to Maxwell Davies have followed RVW's lead in providing characteristic music for young people without in the least writing down to them.

World War II brought a commission from the BBC for a further exercise in musical democracy: the *Six Choral Songs—To be Sung in Time of War*. They are for unison voices with pianoforte or orchestral accompaniment; and it is notable that, helped by Ursula Wood, he went to one of his favourite 'rebel' romantic poets, Shelley, for the texts rather than to a more obviously 'patriotic' source. Two of the texts were from *Prometheus Unbound* and one from *The Revolt of Islam* and none of them can be regarded as sabre-rattling or jingoistic. The mood of the nation and the character of the composer called for something deeper and more aspiring. The music is surely of a kind that would have appealed immediately to Parry: forthright, melodious, straightforward, and eminently singable, like most of RVW's unison songs. The same may be said of his two contributions to the five settings of Canon G. W. Briggs's *Five Wartime Hymns*. They date from 1942 and are entitled 'A Hymn of Freedom' and 'A Call to the Free Nations'.

The *Song of Thanksgiving*, as it is now known, composed in 1944 in anticipation of the allied victory in World War II that came in 1945, is worth remembering for the implied statement of Vaughan Williams's patriotic (not chauvinistic) creed in its text. Its musical merits, as opposed to any actual stylistic originality, are considerable. They include the arresting opening on the solo trumpet—thematic, not just introductory—and the shock effect both of the timbre and the tonality of the children's choir entering in a quite unexpected and radiantly pure D major. Here once more is a 'democratic' composition, reminding participants and listeners alike in forceful terms what true democratic freedom and real patriotism are all about.

A number of slighter works deserve passing mention on account of their directness and lack of pretension. These include 'The Souls of the Righteous', a solemn motet composed for the dedication of the Battle of Britain chapel in Westminster Abbey on 10 July 1947; 'The Voice out of the Whirlwind', appropriately adapted from the 'Galliard of the Sons of the Morning' from *Job*; the 'Prayer to the Father of Heaven'—a moving tribute to the memory of RVW's beloved teacher Hubert Parry with a text by Skelton in his stately rhyme-royal rather than his more scurrilous vein; the *Three Shakespeare Songs* of 1951, composed as the attractive but challenging test piece for the British Federation of Music Festivals National Competitive Festival; the part-song 'Silence and Music', RVW's measured yet passionate contribution to *A Garland for the Queen*, with its haunting, indeterminate final cadence drifting back into the silent slumber from which the music had originally emerged; and, above all, the disarmingly simple yet tenderly moving 'O Taste and See', written for the 1953 Coronation service.

Of the larger choral works of his final years, the most substantial is the Christmas cantata *Hodie*: where the story really started, so to speak, as opposed to *Sancta Civitas*, which portrays how it may all end. It is highly appropriate that the original cover of the vocal score of the work should contain a reproduction of a Piero della Francesca painting, for *Hodie* has exactly that ingenuous vitality and childlike delight in celebrating the Nativity that seems to have been such a feature of early Renaissance Italian art. Childlike, not childish, for *Hodie* is a wide-eyed 'once-upon-a-time' child's view of the Nativity told with all the wit and self-assurance of a seer of much experience who has a clear understanding of what lies behind the story, even if he does not believe in it literally. Once again, the risk is honourable.

The solid rejoicing of the prologue, for example, projects a mood of a kind expected from a man of twenty-two rather than eighty-two. Perhaps the choice of text helps. Taken from the vespers for the Christmas festival, its final Alleluia, culminating in the tangy tritones and faintly jazzy off-beat chords of the angels' light-footed choral dance, it adds just the right sense of rejoicing round the crib to the cheerful atmosphere. The mellifluous stylized narration—back to a kind of folky Schütz in an unexpectedly jovial mood rather than to Bach, enhances the early Renaissance feeling. The melismatic incantatory recitative, over a comparatively static and totally un-Bach-like chord formula, is gentle and matter-of-fact, almost deadpan, the dramatic strokes being reserved for such points as the fanfare of consecutive triads on the brass at the mention of the word 'Jesus'. The settings of George Herbert, Hardy, and Milton, skilfully introduced at appropriate places in the narrative, show a fine sensitivity to the speech-rhythms and—more important still—to the natural spoken intonation of the poems; and the splendid 'March of the Three Kings' belongs more to the pantomime theatre than to the church.

Donald Mitchell's contention that the work is seriously undercomposed is understandable, if unfair. It is a child's view of the Christmas story, told by one whose long experience and agnostic outlook have not blunted his perception of what the story means to the innocent: Jane Scroop, perhaps, or one of RVW's numerous 'nephews' and 'nieces'. Childlike, in fact, without any regrets for lost innocence or a lost sense of awe, where it might be (and often wrongly is) construed as childish. This is shown by the epilogue: the mystery of the opening chapter of St John's Gospel is blended with the jubilation of Milton's 'Ode on the Morning of Christ's Nativity', and the work ends in a blaze of exuberant, ingenuous sound.

Of the other late choral works, the cantata *Folk Songs of the Four Seasons* is once more truly 'democratic' music. Asked to provide a work for the Federation of Women's Institutes festival at the Albert Hall in June 1950, he wrote of the commission:

> I set my mind to find some unifying idea which would bind the whole together. It was not long before I discovered the necessary link—the calendar. The subjects of our folk-songs, whether they deal with romance, tragedy, conviviality or legend, have a background of nature and its seasons.[9]

Thus, each movement refers to one of the seasons of the year and the musical material is based on appropriately seasonal folk-songs. Knowing that the choir would be roughly divisible into three sections, a large body for unison singing, a smaller one for part singing and a smaller number for an unaccompanied passage, and that they would all be women, he laid out his work accordingly. The work is in many ways a larger, more mature and more comprehensive secular version of the *Fantasia on Christmas Carols*, with four movements instead of one, but less elaborate movements in structure.

The Sons of Light, for the Schools Music Association, is direct and uncomplicated, lively and cheerful. Once more, Vaughan Williams shows his understanding of what urges children to sing out heartily— just as Britten does in *Noye's Fludde* and the *Spring Symphony*. *An Oxford Elegy*, taking the concept of a recitation with orchestral accompaniment, as in *A Song of Thanksgiving*, a stage further, sounds almost at times like a sadder, if not wiser, companion to *Flos Campi*, the choir being used very sparingly and often wordlessly, with a prominent part for solo viola. Just as he paid tribute to the landscape north of Cambridge so many years previously in *In the Fen Country*, so here he paints in gentle colours that surrounding Oxford.

Song for a Spring Festival was his final tribute, composed in 1955 to words by his wife, to the Leith Hill Festival. As it is intended for performance there and nowhere else, it is only fair simply to mention but not to discuss it. Other 'occasional' pieces of his later years, such as the attractive *Three Gaelic Songs*, translated by his wife, of 1954 or the *Choral Flourish* for the 21st anniversary of the National Federation of Music Societies and *A Vision of Aeroplanes*, both composed in 1956,

[9] Kennedy, *Works* 1, p. 585.

show unflagging vigour even if it is unfair to look for anything new in them. And it is surely fitting that his last almost completed work, the nativity play *The First Nowell*, to a text adapted from medieval pageants by Simona Pakenham, the author of one of the most perceptive and enthusiastic studies of his music, should include a significant chorus part composed and arranged from traditional tunes. For over half a century, he had remained faithful to Parry's charge.

12

Stage and film music

All his life, Vaughan Williams was interested in the theatre, and for much of it in the cinema as well. Overtures to plays whose titles, alas, were both more tantalizing and more ambitious than their musical content are listed among his childhood efforts. The plays were presumably performed in the toy theatre that entertained the Vaughan Williams children at Leigh Hill Place. At his prep-school at Rottingdean, as has been related above, (p. 6), he began work on a promising-sounding drinking chorus intended for a play by a fellow-pupil on the rape of Lucretia, but this potential forebear of Drunken Alice's cohort from 'The Tunning of Elinor Rumming' has also sunk without trace. No theatre music survives either, if any ever existed, from his days at Charterhouse; and his surviving student works from the RCM and Cambridge do not seem to include either any exercises in stage music for his teachers or music for college or university stage productions.

It was not, in fact, until he was thirty-two, in April 1905, that he wrote his first music for the stage. This was for Ben Jonson's masque *Pan's Anniversary* for a production at Stratford-upon-Avon. There were twelve movements, eight by Vaughan Williams and four by Holst. The full orchestra involved is of modest but solid dimensions: single wind, two horns, two cornets, one trombone, timpani, and strings. Some of the movements make use of folk-songs and these are allotted to a smaller ensemble comprising a piccolo, a clarinet, and a side-drum. A note to the score baldly states that in the music of the choruses, of which there are four, 'certain characteristic phrases from English folk music have been inserted'.

Both the subject-matter and the music of a work dating from 1906 are of considerable interest. This was the music composed for a performance at Reigate Priory of an adaptation of *The Pilgrim's Progress*. The forces involved are soprano and contralto soloists, mixed four-part chorus and strings. As with the opera/morality of forty years later, the Prelude is based on the hymn-tune 'York'. This recurs in the finale and in the epilogue music; and of the other movements, it is noteworthy that after the fight between Christian and Apollyon, there is a song for the contralto soloist to the words 'Whoso dwelleth under the defence of the

Most High' (Psalm 91), later adapted for the setting of the same text in *The Shepherds of the Delectable Mountains*.

The next commission came in his mid-thirties, from the Greek Play Committee in Cambridge in 1909. It was for music to a production of Aristophanes' *The Wasps*. The cast list for this production includes a number of names later to become famous on the 'straight' or the musical stage, such as W. M. (Miles) Malleson, F. D. (Dennis) Arundell and J. S. (Steuart) Wilson. There were eighteen numbers in the original score; and it was on them that Vaughan Williams drew for the familiar orchestral suite. The bright and tuneful overture is probably one of RVW's most popular works, conceding only the opening impressionistic flourishes in the strings to the title of the play, but based for the most part on skilfully worked 'folky' material, with themes that, as Tovey aptly put it, combine in rowdy counterpoint. Some of the other movements have been known to turn up unacknowledged as incidental music to radio dramas of a suitable kind. The glum theme of the 'March Past of the Kitchen Utensils' exhibits a vein of saturnine wit; the two entr'actes are charming; and the scurrying romp of the final tableau really does seem to foreshadow a more genteel 'Elinor Rumming'.

The Wasps is not the only Greek play for which Vaughan Williams provided music. In 1911, for example, he set parts—mainly choruses, with orchestral accompaniment—of *Iphigenia in Tauris*, *The Bacchae*, and *Elektra*, in Gilbert Murray's translations. Much of the music to all three survives, but only one item was considered worth publishing. This was the duet 'Where is the Home for Me?' published in 1922 as one of a series of vocal duets for class singing by Edwin Ashdown Ltd. Of some interest is the composer's comment on how the choruses in *Iphigenia* are to be sung:

> These choruses must be sung throughout with due regard to the true declamation of the words and the metre of the poetry. The note values of the voice parts are, for the most part, only approximate. The solos may be divided among the members of the chorus according to the compass and nature of their voices.[1]

The reference to the 'only approximate' nature of the note values in the voice parts is evidence of the composer's sensitivity to the difference between spoken and sung rhythms, however precisely the latter may be notated.

In 1913, Vaughan Williams received a number of commissions for stage music. Most, but not all of them were for Shakespeare productions at Stratford-upon-Avon for a season by F. R. Benson's company. The plays concerned were *Richard II*, *Richard III*, *Henry IV part 2*, *Henry V*, and *The Merry Wives of Windsor*. In some cases the music has been almost entirely lost, but thirty-two numbers for *King Richard II* have

---

[1] Kennedy, *Works* 1, p. 453.

1. Leith Hill Place

2. RVW with Ralph Wedgwood ('Randolph')

3. Sir Hubert Parry in 1898

4. Sir Charles Stanford

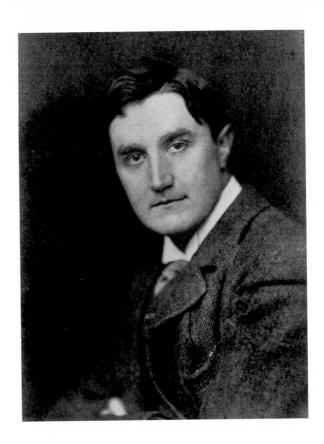

5. RVW in his early thirties

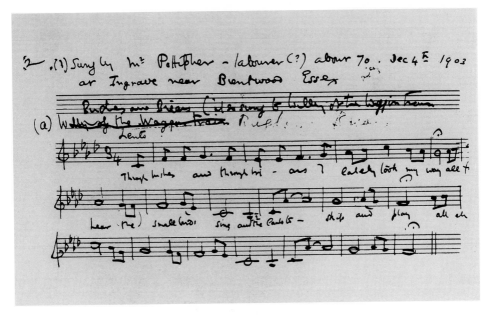

6. RVW's first collected folk-song: 'Bushes and Briars'

7. George Butterworth in his twenties

8. Ralph and Adeline Vaughan Williams, 1918

9. RVW rehearsing for the Leith Hill Festival at the Drill Hall, Dorking

10. RVW and Holst on a walking tour, September 1921

11. The opening of RVW's F minor Symphony: stark and uncompromising

12. Epstein's portrait head of RVW
('the eighteenth-century admiral')

13. RVW in his study

14. Ralph and Ursula Vaughan Williams

survived. The orchestra involved seems to have been a medium-sized one of single wind, three brass (1 horn, 1 cornet, and 1 trombone), percussion, and strings. It is clear from the numbering of some of the pieces that have survived even fragmentarily that these were no mere perfunctory commissions. They involved a considerable amount of work: the two surviving pieces from *Henry V* are numbered 20 and 21 respectively, the latter being intended for Scene 7 of Act III, which implies that there may well have been at least half a dozen other items. For productions involving dramatists other than Shakespeare, he arranged three familiar pieces (all dating from the eighteenth century) for Shaw's *The Devil's Disciple* and composed music for Maeterlinck's *The Death of Tintagiles* and *The Blue Bird*—some of the pieces for the latter being quite substantial. The music for the water's dance, for example, extends to 102 bars, and what may be called RVW's response to Brünnhilde's Magic Fire Music, played when the fire springs out of the chimney, to fifty-five.

What is notable about the Shakespeare pieces in particular is the manner in which Vaughan Williams exploited both his own folk-song discoveries and those of others. In the *Richard II* music, for example, seven of the ten more important pieces are arrangements of traditional tunes. He uses among others 'Greensleeves', 'The Springtime of the Year', which he also arranged as one of the *Five English Folk Songs* for mixed chorus that same year, 'The Bold Princess Royal', quoted in *A Sea Symphony*, 'I'll go and 'list for a Sailor', and the Playford Dance Tune 'Jamaica'. 'Princess Royal' turns up again in *Henry IV*, for Prince Hal (in *Richard II* he had used it for Bolingbroke), where he also and appropriately uses 'Lady in the Dark' for Doll Tearsheet.

His next substantial work for the non-operatic stage was the ballet *Old King Cole*, which dates from 1923. This was commissioned by the Cambridge Branch of the English Folk Dance Society and it seems by all accounts that despite the lack of rehearsal and the fact that Vaughan Williams rather over-estimated the competence of the orchestra available, it was received with enthusiasm. Any critics of the thickness of the scoring should bear in mind that the work was first performed out of doors and that in a letter to Boris Ord, who was to conduct the performances, Vaughan Williams specifically stated[2] that he would 'score it for ordinary orch[estra] fairly thick and let it take its chance out of doors'. A feature of the score is the use, unexpected in this context but familiar from others, of a wordless chorus singing a brisk tune in unison.

The scenario of *Old King Cole* fills out the pipe, bowl, and fiddlers three of the nursery rhyme, with some speculative material on their historical origin. The King's daughter, who really existed and married the Roman Emperor Constantine, becoming the mother of Constantine the Great, brings a pipe home from her travels abroad. She arranges a

[2] Kennedy, *Works* 2, p. 163.

competition between the three fiddlers which constitutes the central episode of the ballet. Nearly all the music is of folk origin, the tunes themselves are vigorous and catchy and the harmonizations are mainly in the by now familiar impressionistic idiom, with passages in consecutive fifths. This may be why Edward Dent[3] detected influences of Stravinsky's *Rite of Spring* in the work; certainly a perusal of the score betrays very little sign of Stravinsky's metrical angularities. What seems more likely is that inaccuracies in the parts led to inaccuracies in the playing, inadvertently spiced up the harmonies and misled Dent, who, however blinkered he might be to the merits of some composers, was usually perceptive about RVW.

On Christmas Night, his next sizeable work for the stage, is adapted from Dickens's *A Christmas Carol*, and Vaughan Williams used the opportunity to weave a number of Christmas carol tunes into the musical texture. As with all his dance scores, the music is intended to support a different style of dancing from that of conventional ballet. This particular ballet was devised by Adolf Bolm, who had been with the original Diaghilev company; and it was to his choreography that the work was produced in Chicago in 1926. But it was not performed as a ballet in England until nine years later, when it was re-choreographed for the English Folk Dance Society and produced at Cecil Sharp House on 29 December 1935. Musically a folk-song rhapsody on an extended scale, it introduces a whole series of folk-songs and dances, such as 'Jamaica', 'Hunsdon House', 'Putney Ferry', 'The Triumph', 'Tink a Tink', and 'Sir Roger de Coverley'; and carols, some of which, such as 'A Virgin most Pure', 'On Christmas Night', and 'As Joseph was a-Walking', may be sung at the discretion of the producer and conductor.

In August 1937 RVW wrote to the producer of the EFDS version, Frederic Wilkinson, suggesting amendments to the work that would free it from any dependence on the Scrooge/Cratchit story—Marley's ghost had already been cut from the original plot—and showing his realistic view of children and their elders' attitudes to them:

> Personally I like the idea of children dancing Hunsdon House—something prim to 'show how nicely the children can dance' (of course it did not get a chance with those lumpy children)—I don't believe we need always represent children as being rowdy—and they have a chance of being rowdy immediately before and after . . . [4]

It is also amusing to note from the same letter that while Vaughan Williams was prepared to accept the sentimentality of a prayer scene featuring 'The White Paternoster', he didn't think he could stomach Tiny Tim and suggested jettisoning the Scrooge/Marley plot altogether. A compromise was decided on; and like many compromises, it did not work; a pity, for the freshness of the tunes and the imaginative zest with

---

[3] Kennedy, *Works* 2, p. 178.   [4] Kennedy, *Works* 1, pp. 512–13.

which Vaughan Williams employs them are attractive features of a neglected score. 'The First Nowell', for example, is used as a kind of motto-theme. 'Tink a Tink' is dignified into a dance to accompany the procession of characters associated with the Christmas festival. 'Jamaica' and 'Hunsdon House' are both treated in two-part counterpoint. 'On Christmas Night' and 'The First Nowell' are interwoven contrapuntally. The orchestral backing to 'The Seeds of Love' played on the piano by a young girl—Scrooge's former sweetheart—is enchanting and neatly symbolizes the wedded domestic bliss she now enjoys and he does not.

By far the greatest of Vaughan Williams's music for the ballet theatre is the Masque for Dancing, *Job*. Here, the technique developed in *Pastoral Symphony* and in works like *Sancta Civitas* and *Flos Campi* is put to enormously effective theatrical use. Any performance of this work involves a combination of the work of four major artists: the composer, the choreographer, William Blake, on whose engravings the choreography is based, and the anonymous genius who wrote the Old Testament poem which inspired Blake. Moreover, unlike the romanticized, sentimental, or pathetic legends on which some ballets are based, it presents in choreographic terms a quest into the nature of man's place in the universe and his eternal spiritual destiny. It will probably never be a popular ballet, for the only virtuoso part in it is that of Satan; and it offers no display dances for any prima ballerina, but the concentrated impact of superb spectacle, magnificent music, and a profound theme make *Job* one of the most irresistible aesthetic experiences available. A concert performance can be effective; but the work's true place is in the theatre.

Blake's interpretation of the Book of Job was that God was Job's spiritual self and Satan his material self, a concept with which Vaughan Williams may have been in sympathy, but which he did not introduce into his synopsis. Moreover, that synopsis, as printed in the published full score, differs from Keynes's scenario in a number of important details. For one thing, the composer makes it quite clear what kind of dance-patterns he envisages as arising from his music. They are related to the steps of English traditional dances and the rhythms and ethos, though not necessarily the figures, of baroque, Tudor and Jacobean dance rather than to those of conventional ballet. This adds a certain statuesque formality of a rather heavier nature than is usual to the miming which must be part of the dances that is lacking in the airiness and fantasy of conventional ballet. For another, he mentions a number of other visual sources apart from Blake, such as Botticelli[5] and Rubens, to hint to the set-designer and the choreographer what kind of stage-picture his music aims at underlining. In a number of places, too, his

[5] Ibid., pp. 531–2.

149

directions offer valuable hints as to the kind of playing the conductor should endeavour to obtain from the orchestra when the work is performed as a concert suite. To give an example, the versions of Scene 3 may be compared. Keynes has simply: 'Job's sons and daughters are feasting and dancing when Satan appears and destroys them.'[6] Which Vaughan Williams expands to:

> 'Then came a great wind and smote the four corners of the house and it fell upon the young men and they are dead.' (I:19). *Minuet of the Sons of Job and Their Wives*. Enter Job's sons and their wives and dance in front of the curtain. They hold golden wine cups in their left hands which they clash at points marked in the score. The dance should be statuesque and slightly voluptuous. It should not be a minuet as far as choreography is concerned. For the clashing and the wine cups suggestions should be taken from the Morris Dance *Winster Processional*. See also Botticelli 'Marriage Feast'. The black curtain draws back and shows an interior as in Blake III. Enter Satan. The dance stops suddenly. The dancers fall dead. Tableau as in Blake III.

It is clear that Vaughan Williams had in mind here exactly what his music aimed at portraying, not just in terms of Blake's symbols and grouping, but in terms of stage design and movement. As he was to do later in *The Pilgrim's Progress*, he works from a scenario that provides a scene within a scene: in this case, earth, heaven, and hell and their inhabitants are envisaged as three different aspects of the set and thus as three different, visually and spatially differentiated planes of existence; and the dynamic destructive vitality of abstractions such as plague and sudden death in Scene 4 is spelt out in specific detail:

> Satan stands over Job and calls up terrifying visions of plague, pestilence, famine, battle, murder and sudden death who posture before Job as in Blake XI. Each of these should be represented by a group of dancers. The dance should be wild and full of movement and the stage should finally be full. Suggestions may be taken from Rubens's 'Horrors of War' (National Gallery). The dancers headed by Satan make a ring round Job and raise their hands three times. The vision gradually disappears.[7]

In a sense, *Job* is RVW's most Wagnerian work: a *Gesamtkunstwerk* in which every element in the dance, the stage sets and story was clear in his mind when the music came to be written.

Vaughan Williams's sense of characterization in this great work shows him at the height of his powers. The main characteristic of God, whether or not Vaughan Williams saw him as Job's spiritual self, is music that is firm and tonal. Satan's music and that of his minions has a demonic energy and a kind of twisted majesty which is a perverted version of God's, just as the arrogant derision of Elgar's demons in *Gerontius* represents a twisted version of his familiar *nobilmente* vein. Satan's music is notable for odd melodic leaps, angular rhythms, the sudden juxtapo-

---

[6] Kennedy, *Works* 1, p. 530.   [7] Ibid., p. 531.

sition of unrelated chords, and violent scoring. Nowhere is his awful majesty more apparent than at the spine-chilling moment when, after being ministered to by the three comforters, Job is visited by a vision of heaven with Satan enthroned in God's place: the awe of *Sancta Civitas* refracted in sheer terror. The chilling irruption of the full organ stands out grimly and dramatically from that of the orchestra and with immensely powerful effect. The whole work is full of *coups de théâtre* of this kind. They may be points of scoring, such as the ghostly hollowness of the recapitulation of 'Satan's Dance of Triumph'. They may be points of structure, as when the accompaniment of the main theme of the 'Minuet of the Sons of Job and their Wives' appears right at the end without its theme, or when the evanescent wispy pattern of the theme of 'Job's Dream' is heard, not as a single line in canon with itself, but as a fully harmonized block of chords, but still in canon. Or they may be points of dramatic anticipation, such as in the expansive first movement, when a few wood-wind instruments foreshadow in mysterious chords what is to become the opening motif of one of Vaughan Williams's grandest tunes (Ex. 6). The same weird chords are eventually integrated into the stately dance end return at the very end of the work, just before the celestial vision of triumph fades into the mists of the introduction and ushers in the epilogue: Vaughan Williams's counterpart to the 'well done, thou good and faithful servant' valedictory coda of Elgar's Second Symphony.

Ex. 6

The opening movement sets the scene: Job, surrounded by his family, virtuous, prosperous, and happy, is observed by Satan. At Satan's request, God puts Job within his power. The contrasts between Satan's snarls and the ineffable majesty of the 'Sarabande of the Sons of God' is very striking, but not so striking as to obliterate the fact that the entire movement is built up out of a familiar pattern of developing embryo-elements, for example the phrase (Ex. 7a) and its reversal (Ex. 7b), two sharply juxtaposed chords (B flat minor and A major) to represent Satan and a rising scale passage, which assumes varying guises throughout the movement.

'Satan's Dance of Triumph' is by the composer's own account cribbed, angular theme, whirling ostinato and all, from the scherzo of

Ex. 7

Beethoven's Opus 135 (the music's association with diabolical powers may have a much less exalted source, however—that of Gounod's *Faust*, where the same whirling figure occurs in the orchestral introduction to Mephistopheles' 'Ballad of the Golden Calf'). This is a *tour de force* of destructive energy. And has the illusory fascination of arrogant pride ever been more convincingly portrayed in musical terms than in the powerful 'Trio' section, with its augmented fourth in the trumpet theme, its ponderous trombone and tuba accompaniment, and the gigantic shudder that goes through the orchestra, as if in helpless horror, at the release of so much crushing destructive power?

The sinuous tranquillity of the following dance is interrupted by thunderbolts from Satan, anticipated by scoring which can for once be rightly described as uncanny; as the dance proceeds, it is accompanied by a meandering viola counterpoint, a favourite Vaughan Williams point of scoring. The main theme of 'Job's Dream' grows, like a folk-song melody, from an initial germ (Ex. 8) and is interrupted by hideous visions, halfway in their grotesque violence between the finale of *A London Symphony* and the finale of the Fourth, before it leads to the utter desolation of the 'Dance of the Messengers' and the desolate cortège of Job's sons and daughters, with its curious reminiscence of a theme in the finale of Brahms's *German Requiem*.

Ex. 8

Lento moderato

Satan now presents the three comforters—a departure from the Biblical story. They are all sharply characterized and differentiated from one another and the rhythmic tension of their music is developed into a rich and ironic pattern as they work up their self-righteous indignation against Job. Eventually their antics freeze in the icy smoothness of a high note on the saxophone which leads back into an unctuous reprise, complete with crocodile tears on a solo cello. No wonder Job turns and curses God!

'Elihu's Dance of Youth and Beauty', with its slow-moving block chords as a solid background to the solo fiddle's fresh, eloquent rhapsodizing, leads back to the serenity of heaven, where Satan is banished and the Sons of God expel him from the Almighty's presence with a sea-shanty-like galliard whose robust heartiness betrays the debt the composer still owed to Hubert Parry. Earth, too, joins in to a theme whose opening phrase and its answer is a rhythmic transformation of a theme from *Flos Campi*; thus Job is finally restored to his former estate and in the epilogue sits musing peacefully on his story, surrounded by his family. This is a wonderful case of Wordsworthian emotion recollected in tough, unsentimental tranquillity, impinged on but not clouded by the chill reminder of the nightmare that he has passed through.

The Bridal Day, another Masque for Dancing, which dates originally from 1938/9, was intended for the English Folk Dance and Song Society and was the first work of RVW's to be devised in collaboration with Ursula Wood. It was scored for baritone soloist, speaker, dancers, mimers, and mixed chorus with an orchestra comprising piccolo, flute, piano, and string quintet. It may be regarded as a kind of English equivalent of *Les Noces*, for there are a number of interesting parallels: thematically, in that both works deal with a wedding; in terms of the intimate forces involved; and in terms of the respective composers' relationships with their national traditions as expressed in the story and the style. It is worth remembering in this context that *Les Noces* was one of a limited number of Stravinsky's works that Vaughan Williams wholeheartedly admired. The final version of *The Bridal Day*, in its guise as the choral work *Epithalamion*, bears a number of slight resemblances to Arthur Bliss's delightful pastoral 'Lie Strewn the White Flocks'.

Both *The Bridal Day* and *Epithalamion* are based on stanzas selected by Ursula Vaughan Williams from Spenser's nuptial poem *Epithalamion*. Originally, there were two vocal movements only; some time after seeing what in the opinion of those who saw it (including the composer) was a travesty of the piece on BBC Television on 5 June 1953,[8] RVW expanded it and re-cast it as a choral work; and it is in that form that it is better known nowadays. What had originated as a stage spectacle inspired by a poet's graphic verse now became a straightforward setting of the text itself. A work of considerable charm and lightness of touch, as the recording of the revised version amply demonstrates, it is a pity that it has not been professionally produced more frequently and with more insight in its original form.

Vaughan Williams came late in his career to the composition of film music; it was in fact as a result of a chance remark dropped to his considerably younger colleague Arthur Benjamin that he was asked by Muir Mathieson[9] towards the end of 1940 to provide music to the wartime film *49th Parallel*. The film was an exciting 'cops-and-robbers' adventure story, with moments of suspense and tension worthy of Alfred Hitchcock, involving the survivors of the crew of a sunken German submarine washed up on the Canadian coast and trying to reach safety in

---

[8] Kennedy, *Works* 2, p. 327.   [9] *National Music*, p. 160.

the then neutral United States. The script deliberately spread the plot right across the huge country, providing more than a hint of Canada's vastness and diversity as well as a touching cross-section of the cosmopolitan nature of Canadian society: it included scenes set in French Canada, among the North American Indians, and in the German-speaking pacifist Hutterite community. This gave the composer the opportunity not only to write effective descriptive and atmospheric music well suited to his personal idiom but to employ folk-song material from cultures other than his own. He approached the task with zest. Two items in particular became more widely known outside of their cinematic context: the processional, Parryesque theme of the title-music, which became the stirring unison song 'The New Commonwealth', with words by Harold Child, the librettist of *Hugh the Drover*; and the scene-painting 'The Lake in the Mountains', which was arranged into a piano solo.

Eventually, RVW provided scores for eleven films. Canada was by no means the only country abroad in which the plots were set. There were also Belgium (*The Story of a Flemish Farm*, 1943), Italy (*Stricken Peninsula*, 1945), the Antarctic (*Scott of the Antarctic*, 1948) and Australia (*Bitter Springs*, 1950). Closer to home were *The People's Land* (1943), *The Loves of Joanna Godden* (1947), *Dim Little Island* (1949), *The England of Elizabeth* (1955), and *The Vision of William Blake* (1958). A projected film on Joan of Arc to which RVW was to compose the music never materialized; but the music that he had sketched out was not wasted; it found its way into the finale of the Second String Quartet. Hence the superscription 'Greetings from Joan to Jean'. The same quartet uses a theme from *49th Parallel* in the scherzo.

Coastal Command, The People's Land, Stricken Peninsula, Dim Little Island, The England of Elizabeth, and *The Vision of William Blake* were in the nature of documentary films. The music is good, workaday stuff (though opinions among the film folk differed about *Coastal Command*; Ernest Irving was not over-impressed, but the camera-crew[10] were); and Vaughan Williams took the opportunity to use Italian folk-themes in *The Stricken Peninsula*, which dealt with the rehabilitation of Southern Italy after its liberation by the allied Fifth and Eighth Armies. The music to *Dim Little Island*, also based on folk-tunes, was apparently so unmemorable that the composer himself denied ever having written it; that to *The England of Elizabeth* backed the visual images of ceremony, buildings, paintings, and artefacts that provided useful propaganda for the tourist trade at a time when much effusive material was being churned out drawing specious parallels between the age of the First Elizabeth with that of the Second. Muir Mathieson adapted some of the music into a three-movement suite, character studies in music of an

---

[10] Lewis Foreman, sleeve-note to the Marco Polo recording (8.223665); Douglas, p. 9.

explorer (Drake), a poet (Shakespeare) and the Virgin Queen herself. The music to the Blake film consisted mainly of eight of what were to become the ten Blake songs for voice and oboe. The rest was taken from *Job*. *The Story of a Flemish Farm* is based on a genuine historical event that happened during the invasion of Belgium in 1940; and there are hints in the score, such as in the music entitled 'Dawn in the Barn; and 'The Dead Man's Kit', of the atmosphere of the close of the Sixth Symphony. Oddly enough, the two musical items intended for the film that RVW actually used in that work were never included in the film score. (The film-crew nicknamed them 'Two hot sausages' and 'Miserable Starkey'.)

Of the other feature films, *The Loves of Joanna Godden* called amongst other items for music to illustrate the impact on a farming community of foot-and-mouth disease—a challenge that the composer took on with relish, though the sombre and highly atmospheric result does not figure in the recording of music from the film made in 1948. Another of the sequences in the original score is called 'Ram montage'—one wonders whether any thoughts of 'The Ram Opera' of RVW's childhood surfaced in his mind as he composed it! The music to *Bitter Springs* was actually either composed by Ernest Irving or developed by him from themes provided by RVW: ' . . . what marvels you have done with my silly little tune', he wrote in a letter to Irving in July 1950.[11]

One score, however, a good deal of which *did* find its way into a more ambitious work—a symphony—was that to *Scott of the Antarctic*. The film score itself was awarded first prize at the Prague Film Festival in 1949; and Hans Keller, writing an appreciative but in points of detail highly critical account of the music *qua* film music for the Fifth edition of *Grove* in October 1951 put his finger on an aspect of the score that had clearly occurred to the composer as well:

> How seriously Vaughan Williams takes his own responsibility [as a film composer] is shown by what is to date . . . his latest film music, *i.e.* that to 'Scott of the Antarctic', a noble and, in parts, grandiose piece which at the same time poses urgent formal problems. In view of the exceptional value of several separate sections, it is surprising to find that the score disappoints as a whole, not because it does not make one, but rather because it makes too much of one. (Vol. 3, p. 99)

Those who criticize the *Sinfonia Antartica* for its 'episodic' nature because it is derived from a film score would do well to bear the last sentence in mind. Keller, a perceptive and immensely intelligent musician and a great admirer in particular of Schoenberg and of Britten, was not particularly sympathetic to Vaughan Williams's music, though he respected him greatly as a man and referred to him more than once as

---

[11] Kennedy, *Works* 1, p. 590.

a 'towering figure'. Nor was he one for pulling punches in his critical writings. So the fact that he refers to the 'exceptional value of several separate sections' is worth remembering. Which sections Vaughan Williams himself considered worth developing will be seen when we come to consider his symphonies.

13

Operas

As we have seen, some of RVW's earliest attempts at composition were intended to accompany the plays 'performed' in the toy theatre he had as a boy at Leith Hill Place. Titles of some of these have been preserved: *The Ram Opera*, for example, and *The Galoshes of Happienes* (sic), found in a musical exercise book dating from the year 1882. No music has survived suggesting that the nine-year-old was a budding Mozart, however.

His earliest adolescent experiences of opera included Bizet's *Carmen* ('I went to scoff,' he said, 'but remained to worship') and, above all, Wagner's *Die Walküre* which he saw for the first time as an 18-year-old in Munich. When, two years later, in London, in June 1892, he heard a visiting company from the Hamburg Opera under Gustav Mahler perform *Tristan und Isolde*, it was a revelation. Wagner remained a lifelong love in an age when some English musicians tended at times to react against or even denigrate his immense artistic achievement for various reasons, a mistake that Vaughan Williams never made.

When, later in the 1890s, he came to study with Stanford, he found himself working with a teacher who adored opera. Stanford had conducted the English premières of Cornelius's *Barber of Baghdad*, of Schumann's *Genoveva*, and of Delibes' *Le Roi l'a dit* earlier in the 1890s. He greatly admired both Verdi and Wagner: he was an early visitor to the Bayreuth Festival and was present at the first performance of *Falstaff*; and he completed no fewer than eleven operas of his own, seven of which actually reached the stage. It is sufficient commentary on the conditions under which native opera was professionally staged in Britain in the late nineteenth century that Stanford's first two operas were produced (in German) in Germany before he managed to obtain a hearing for any of them at home. When he eventually did, his opera *Shamus O'Brien*, a deliberate attempt to create a specifically Irish music-drama, first performed in March 1896, had a successful run of over 100 performances. After its initial success, it sank into the oblivion to which the lack of a permanent well-funded national opera company and of a supporting network of provincial repertory opera theatres inevitably condemned it. Sullivan had shown that genuinely musicianly—even at times 'learned'—light operatic pieces were a viable product. (The word 'product' is used advisedly, for mounting works on the musical stage in Victorian London was essentially a commercial venture.) Even his 'grand opera' *Ivanhoe*, however, had folded after an even longer initial run than that of *Shamus O'Brien*—160 performances—when Carte put it on at his new English Opera House. Had conditions been more favourable to the establishment of a well-financed, multi-centre operatic tradition in this country, perhaps some of Stanford's operas, such as *Much Ado about Nothing* or *The Travelling Companion* and a number of now forgotten works by such composers as MacCunn (for example *Jeanie Deans*), Ethel Smyth, and others might have formed the basis of a viable English operatic repertory. As it was, a good half-century passed before Britten's *Peter Grimes* finally convinced people that stageworthy British opera was more than just a pious hope. A school might even have arisen of competent English operatic librettists.

By the time Vaughan Williams actually did come to compose his first full-length opera, he had, as we have seen, already had considerable experience in writing for the stage as well as for the concert platform. A significant pointer to the future came in 1906, when he composed music for a performance of a dramatized version of Bunyan's *Pilgrim's Progress* at Reigate Priory; and by 1910, he felt ready to try his hand at an opera, regardless of whether it might ever reach the stage.

The origin of his first opera, *Hugh the Drover*, was ostensibly a desire to set a prize-fight to music; and the boxing match in the first act of *Hugh* is evidence of the fact. But he also wanted to compose a modern but musically more substantial equivalent of the tuneful ballad operas of the eighteenth century of which *The Beggar's Opera* had been the first in England and the Savoy operettas of Gilbert and Sullivan direct descendants. He also wished the music to carry the action rather than simply arising out of the situations developed in a spoken plot, as in the traditional ballad opera or the Gilbert and Sullivan type operetta.

The libretto of *Hugh the Drover* was by Harold Child, a leader-writer on the staff of *The Times*; and it is clear from the correspondence between him and Vaughan Williams that the composer had very definite ideas, however diffidently he usually expressed them, about the shape the drama should take and the relationship between libretto and music. 'The duty of the words,' Vaughan Williams had written in 1902, 'is to say just as much as the music has left unsaid and no more.'[1] From about August 1910 over a period of years, he chivvied and gently bullied Child into shaping and re-shaping his text to ensure just this.[2] There was evidently at one stage some friction between them, but the piece was virtually finished just before the outbreak of war in August 1914.

---

[1] *Heirs and Rebels*, p. 34.   [2] See UVW, pp. 400–22, Appendix I.

Set in the small town of Cotsall in the West Midlands of England during the Napoleonic Wars, *Hugh the Drover* deals basically with the time-honoured theme of love in the face of parental opposition. Mary, the daughter of the town Constable, is betrothed at her father's behest to John the town Butcher, but falls in love at first sight at a country fair with the mysterious Hugh, a drover who roams the country rounding up horses for the army. All Hugh can offer her—shades of *Songs of Travel!*—is a roving life of probable hardship, but at least she will be free, rather than having to endure caged comfort with the uncouth John. A prize fight is set up with a prize of £20 for any man who can beat John. Hugh sees his chance, stakes £50 on the result, and challenges John to add Mary's hand in marriage to the bet. Hugh wins; but John instantly accuses him of being a French spy; how else can he have come by as large a sum as £50? The crowd turns against Hugh; he is arrested and put in the stocks.

Act II takes place the next day, May Day. Mary steals the key to the stocks from her father and is about to release Hugh so that they can elope together but they are interrupted by the May revellers. She gets into the stocks beside him. Finding that his daughter is missing, the Constable arouses the townspeople. The lovers are discovered. Mary refuses to abandon Hugh and her father disowns her. A troop of soldiers arrives to take the 'spy' away. The Sergeant in charge of the detachment recognizes Hugh as a man who once saved his life; and instead of arresting Hugh, the soldiers conscript John. Mary hesitates to go off with Hugh, but he wins her over; and the lovers bid the towns-folk farewell and go off together.

The basic situation bears a superficial resemblance to that which Britten exploited so successfully in *Peter Grimes*: the 'outsider' who does not conform to solid small-town values and is thus readily suspected of criminal activities, so that he must fight for his reputation and his love. But there the parallel ends. Grimes, deservedly or not, loses; Hugh wins. The gritty insecurity of Britten's anti-hero would be out of place in this sturdy, romanticized rural community, for *Hugh* is a conscious, indeed, slightly self-conscious attempt to write a kind of English equivalent of a work like Smetana's *Bartered Bride*, with its recognizable but rather idealized Czech village milieu. Slater's and Britten's involvement with their central character both as an individual and as victim of a smug and self-righteous society, is much more personal and intense than Child's and Vaughan Williams's with theirs. Moreover, the ever-present background of the restless North Sea to which both Grimes and his adversaries owe their livelihood, is lacking. *Hugh the Drover*'s cosy rural background is, one feels, sanitized and prettified. Once glance at a Moreland rustic landscape or a Rowlandson water-colour would surely have told both composer and librettist that life in the Cotswolds during the Napoleonic Wars was by no means such an idyll as they project, even when there was a colourful and bustling holiday fair in the offing. The impulse to compose *Hugh*, in fact, seems to have arisen primarily out of an almost pre-Raphaelite aesthetic urge, rather than a genuine and realistic human dramatic interest in the characters involved in the action. This may be why, for all its robust tunefulness and defiantly 'English' idiom, it does not quite succeed as an opera. Its real spiritual forebear is Gilbert and Sullivan's Tudor pastiche of *The Yeomen of the Guard* rather than any realistic vision of Napoleonic rural England.

It is difficult to apportion the blame for its shortcomings between Vaughan Williams and his librettist. There is much fine music in the score: Hugh's stirring ballad 'Horse Hoofs' in Act I—*Songs of Travel* raised to the nth degree of full-blooded theatrical urgency—and the love music are certainly finely characterized and both Hugh's and Mary's first entries are good theatre. The fussy little motif (unconsciously derived perhaps from Elgar's *Cockaigne*) used to characterize Mary's father is also dramatically apt; the roles of the Showman and Aunt Jane, too, can be fleshed out by sensitive actor-singers. The main failure is the presentation of the 'villain', John. He is a bore as well as a boor; and for one of the lynch-pins of the action to be so wooden and colourless is a major flaw. This may have been one of the reasons why, in 1933, Vaughan Williams composed an additional scene to the opera to preface the beginning of Act II. *Hugh* had been found to be a little short for a full evening in the theatre; and it was felt that more music and more action was needed. The new scene aims mainly at filling out John's character, adding a vein of sarcastic irony and giving him the chance of a confrontation with Mary's father as the latter expresses his doubts about the strength of their case against Hugh. John points out that he has not properly explained where he got the £50. Mary dutifully offers to marry John if Hugh is released, which naturally distresses Hugh; John, however, is suspicious about Mary's motives, remains adamant and the ruse fails. Mary and Aunt Jane bewail the failure of their plan and leave Hugh alone in the stocks.

The composer was understandably dissatisfied with this scene: it holds back the action and the style is that of the Vaughan Williams of the thirties, being both melodically and harmonically more sophisticated and, oddly enough in view of works like *Sancta Civitas*, the Piano Concerto, and *Job*, less robust than that of the main part of the opera. When revising *Hugh* late in his career, Vaughan Williams jettisoned this scene; and it is not included in either of the currently (1995) available recordings.

It must also be admitted that although the two main figures are acceptable as romantic symbols of true love and the desire to challenge the unknown, they are not really three-dimensional creatures. Dramatically, the work also suffers from Vaughan Williams' inexperience in welding the constituent parts of the action into a coherent, progressive whole, an example of this being the prize-fight and its build-up to the finale of the first act. This never really quite 'jells' as an entity, though the tension in the individual sections is skilfully built up. Vaughan Williams's criticism of Delius can be applied here to his own music: it is 'addition, not multiplication'.[3] All the same, the work is easy on the ear, has a splendid fresh-air vitality and shows a strong, distinct and personal sense of the theatre, which was to be more fully realized in *Sir John in Love* and especially in *Riders to the Sea*. The musical construction is straightforward, the scoring spicy and effective, and the musical idiom solid and bracing, serious without being earnest, recognizably individual, strikingly blending an almost Pucciniesque soaring melodic line with the contours of English folk-song and basing its harmonic procedures on the modal implications of the tunes.

His second opera *per se*, *The Shepherds of the Delectable Mountains*, (1922) is a one-acter adapted from an episode in Bunyan's *Pilgrim's Progress* and incorporated many years later into the full-length opera he composed on Bunyan's book. In the meantime, *Hugh the Drover* reached the professional stage, being produced by the British National Opera Company at His Majesty's Theatre, London, on 14 July 1924 after a successful short run by a largely student cast under S. P. Waddington at the Royal College of Music.

At that time, it seemed that the BNOC, formed in 1922 from members of a defunct company of Sir Thomas Beecham's, might develop into a genuine home for professional British opera. Before it finally folded in 1931, conductors such as John Barbirolli, Adrian Boult, and Malcolm Sargent as well as a whole host of singers gained useful experience in the theatre with the company; and had the financial climate been more favourable, Vaughan Williams was by no means the only composer whose works might permanently have entered its enterprising repertory. The BNOC produced, for example, works by Holst and Ethel Smyth, to say nothing of Wagner's *Parsifal*, Humperdinck's *Hänsel und Gretel* and Debussy's *Pelléas*, none of them exactly sure-fire box-office draws, for all their undeniable musical and dramatic merits.

The success that *Hugh the Drover* achieved, despite the under-rehearsal endemic in so many English professional musical enterprises of that era, stimulated Vaughan Williams to tackle other and more ambitious operatic ventures. The first of these to achieve public performance (on 21 March 1929 at the Royal College of Music) was *Sir John in Love*, a Falstaff opera based on Shakespeare's *The Merry Wives of Windsor*, the text arranged by the composer. The main reason why this delightfully lyrical and strongly characterized piece has not become more popular is probably the sheer number of singers required. It certainly stands up well to the comparison it inevitably courts with Verdi's great masterpiece on the Falstaff story and is more stageworthy as a music-drama

---

[3] Kennedy, *Works* 2, p. 378.

than Nicolai's *Die Lustigen Weiber von Windsor*, Vaughan Williams's own favourite opera on the subject.

Sir John in Love represents a considerable advance on *Hugh the Drover*. The plot is more interesting, the lyrics, drawn mainly from sources contemporary with Shakespeare's original text, such as Jonson, Fletcher, and Campion, are of a far higher quality and the music is infinitely more supple, varied, and dramatically apt. There is all the robustness of *Hugh* but far less self-conscious open-air heartiness and far more mellow wit and rich emotion. The characterization is much more succinct; and the characters themselves—even those who are ridiculed, such as Dr Caius, (does he foreshadow Rutterkin in *Five Tudor Portraits*, perhaps?)— have more substance to them. They are, in fact, genuinely, not self-consciously English, (or French, remembering Caius's lyric sentiment as expressed in his 'Vray dieu d'amours, comfortez moy') in a way that those in the ballad opera could not be. They are flesh and blood, colourful, and occasionally grotesque whereas those in *Hugh* are merely cardboard and at best picturesque. Fenton and Anne Page give the impression that they have at least some idea of the practical side of life as well as of the glamour of an open-air existence. Anne loves Fenton not because he offers a means of romantic escape from the boring prospect of bondage to a witless or an uncouth husband with £300 a year, but because he is a genuine virile human being.

The plot of *Sir John* follows Shakespeare pretty closely; but Vaughan Williams's skilful use both of lyrics from outside the original play and of melodies such as 'John, come kiss me now' allows him to develop aspects of Falstaff's character not evident in *The Merry Wives of Windsor* without borrowing, as Boito did, from the *Henry IV* plays. The result is a gentler, more tender, more bourgeois Falstaff: not really a 'knight, gentleman and soldier', but a self-indulgent yeoman squire, almost a kind of irresponsible Hans Sachs, less given to moralizing and philosophizing, but with a similar eye for human weakness and ear for a good tune. His amorous intriguing arises out of harmless mischief rather than true lechery. Even so, it still provokes Ford into bursts of rage set to music that raises fleeting premonitions of the violent opening of the Fourth Symphony.

Vaughan Williams's music is not usually notable either for its swiftness of movement or its lightness of texture. *Sir John in Love* is an object-lesson in rhythmic suppleness and deft orchestration. The seventeen-bar prelude, with its interplay of 3/4 and 6/8, sets a cracking pace from the start; and the main threads of the action—comedy and romance—are immediately presented helter-skelter, so much so, indeed, that the criticism might be raised of too much going on all at once. Shallow and Evans (musical Welsh accent and all, in the contours of his lilting recitative) bemoan Falstaff's cavalier treatment of the decrepit old Justice; and Slender is hard at work on a sonnet to Anne Page. Without more ado, first Page and then Falstaff himself appear; and not long after-wards, the Merry Wives and Anne Page herself. It is clear from the musi-cal context that this Windsor is a lively hotbed of fun, cross-purposes and scheming: husband against wife, lovers against parents and, even-tually, everyone against the fat knight; but the action centres on indi-viduals, rather than on the community of which they are a part. Extended as opposed to short ensembles are limited in scope; and the chorus is there to provide local colour and to enrich the musical texture rather than to contribute as an integral part of the plot.

Romance and knockabout comedy are skilfully interwoven, both in the dramatic situations and in the music that underlines and exploits them. Thus in Act I, the noisy abuse of the sextet with Falstaff, Nym, Pistol, and the others gives place to Anne Page's appearance with Mrs Page and Mrs Ford. The music immediately takes on a more lyrical hue yet maintains its momentum, as it now underlines Anne's search for true love. Romance merges into comedy again when Slender tries to fill the bill for her, only to deepen into melancholy when she considers what her parents have in store for her: the preposterous French doctor. The music at Fenton's first appearance also deftly expresses both her anxiety that her parents will not agree to him as a suitor and the lovers' passionate joy at finding true love. Page gives Fenton short shrift; and the comedy is resumed with the appearance of Caius, blustering and puffing and threatening violence to all and sundry, especially Evans. The farcical nature of his rage is only too apparent; but when he decides to woo Anne Page, he is portrayed in a much more engaging light with his 'Vray dieu d'amours'. Even so, his newly-displayed sensitivity is pale compared with Fenton's robust passion.

The stage is now set for Falstaff's attempted conquest of Mistress Ford. The fat knight's conscienceless drinking companions suddenly develop a moral code when he commissions them to deliver his identi-cal love letters to Mesdames Ford and Page and decide to reveal his plot to Ford, a step neatly underlined by the canonic writing in the orches-tra. Indeed, the orchestral writing hereabouts is particularly witty and full of character: Falstaff's exit to the tune of 'John, come kiss me now' is so majestic that one is tempted to think that it is a 'Parrydy'. The rest of the act is dominated by Ford's jealous rage, sweetened by the lyrical writing associated with the two wives.

The swift movement of the plot is maintained throughout the remain-ing three acts: there is none of the dramatic marking time that mars the plots of other fine operas in the repertory; the sheer pace and variety of the music carry the action along irresistibly. In Act II, for example, the sweetness of the ladies' music is never allowed to cloy into sugariness. Mistress Page's reaction to Falstaff's preposterous letter combines flirta-tious musical-comedy amusement with a genuine anger and resolve to teach the old rascal a lesson, projected in terms that would not be musically out of place in *Job*. Yet throughout the letter scene, both the idiom and the scoring remain light but piquant. The climax both of this scene and of the fruitless hunt for the renegade, hidden in the clothes-basket, is built up with much greater skill than that to the prize-fight in *Hugh*; and Ford's jealous anger is neatly contrasted with and juxtaposed to Caius's self-important angry posturing and Falstaff's self-confident strutting. The slapstick of the third and fourth acts is handled with a deft musical conjuror's sleight-of-hand, delicacy, wit, and good, solid, roast-beef humour pointing up rage, frustration, and passion, all resolved in the lyrical splendour of 'See the Chariot at Hand' and the final robust dance of rejoicing and reconciliation. The scene where the unfortunate Evans confuses Psalm 137 with Marlowe's 'Passionate Shepherd' is one particularly good example of many that could be cited: the way Vaughan Williams depicts the emotional conflict between apprehension and love in the poor confused man's mind is witty, subtle, and dramatically effective.

But what impresses most of all about *Sir John in Love* is surely the way Vaughan Williams integrates the diversity of its warm, all-embracing delight in and forgiveness of human weaknesses and foibles into a lively musical design with a sure symphonic and dramatic touch. The former is shown by the way in which the Big Tune, 'See the Chariot at Hand', is cunningly prepared for as early as Act I; by the integration into the score as reminders, if not quite as leitmotifs, of folk-songs and folk-song allusions, affecting the listener on two levels at once; and by the composer's ability to write tunes that are totally congruent with a robust folk-song idiom, yet of his own invention. The latter is shown by his imaginative interplay of swiftly-moving recitative, sweetened by out-breaks of lyricism and spiced with a pointed rhythmic drive that unerr-ingly differentiates character and situation; and by a new-found ease of swift and telling dramatic movement. The opera as a whole strikes a splendid balance between the folky and the sophisticated, the lyrical and the dramatic, the intense and the light-hearted.

Sir John in Love was followed by what is probably the composer's operatic masterpiece: his setting of J. M. Synge's one-act tragedy *Riders to the Sea*. Work on this began in the 1920s and although the piece was completed by 1932, it was not performed until 30 November 1937. Its simplicity and terseness have caused it to become a problem opera; its quality and stageworthiness are indisputable, but because it lasts a mere thirty-five minutes and is difficult to provide with a complementary work on the right scale to fill the rest of the evening, it has been unjustly neglected. Vaughan Williams himself seriously considered setting Synge's comedy *The Tinker's Wedding* as the other half of a double bill, but unfortunately the project never got further than the sketch stage.

Riders to the Sea might almost be described as a chamber opera in enhanced plainsong. For all its eerily austere and restrained mode of expression, it deals with the same situation as the *Sinfonia Antartica*—a man (or in this case, woman) versus Nature. The sea—Nature the destroyer—is the offstage villain. It is the unremitting, mindless antagonist which also forms the all-pervading background to the claustrophobic and severely classical action. The sea provides the livelihood of the old woman Maurya and her family; but the conclusion is not all that far from a Job-like: 'the sea giveth, the sea taketh away; blessed be the name of the sea.' Maurya loses all her six sons to it; but it does not deprive her of her dignity as a human being, of her capacity to love, only of the concrete objects of her love. Whereas in *A Sea Symphony*, the sea is itself a symbol of the innermost self that man can and must discover and explore, here it is the six sons who are the tokens of Maurya's spiritual strength in her struggle with it. She suffers all the damage to those tokens that the sea can possibly inflict; and when it has stripped her of all of them, she realizes the dignity and strength of her own spirit, which it cannot destroy. Once again, the sea is an instrument of self-realization.

The action of Synge's drama, then, which Vaughan Williams sets virtually word for word, essentially takes place within the soul of Maurya and, to a lesser extent, of her two daughters Nora and Cathleen. They realize with horror that their brother Michael has been claimed a victim by the sea, a fact that imposes on them the duty of informing their mother of the tragedy. The intimate scale of the work is one reason for its tremendous power: great arching, passionate melodic lines and diminished seventh chords blasted out on every appropriate and many an inappropriate occasion by a huge orchestra would defeat their own ends in this concise and simple tragedy. The manner in which the melodic line expands to a climactic high G and then arches downwards to the words 'God rest his soul' when the women discover that their brother is dead is one example of many that could be quoted to demonstrate Vaughan Williams's combination of restraint and dramatic sense (Ex. 9).

The scoring is spare and chillingly austere: single wind with a second flute (the only clarinet is a bass one), two horns, one trumpet, strings,

Ex. 9

and percussion, which includes a sea-machine. The wordless female chorus forms an unnerving background as the climax of the drama approaches, leading to Maurya's great solo Adagio lament beginning 'They are all gone now', which in its sober grandeur ranks alongside 'When I am laid in earth' as one of the supreme tragic utterances of English opera.

The comic opera *The Poisoned Kiss*, first performed on 12 May 1936 at the new Arts Theatre in Cambridge, suffers from an irredeemably arch libretto by Cecil Sharp's sister, Evelyn. Like Harold Child, Miss Sharp was an experienced journalist and critic; the libretto shows that she had a good ear for strongly rhythmic though somewhat doggerel-style patter-verse. Unfortunately, her genuine sense of mild topical satire had almost to be shoehorned into a coy and whimsical Victorian mock fairy-tale. Unlike Vaughan Williams's other operas and in keeping with its somewhat farcical subject matter, *The Poisoned Kiss* has spoken not sung dialogue.

The Poisoned Kiss is entitled a 'Romantic Extravaganza'. For 'extravaganza' read 'farce': witness the fact that all the characters are named after flowers or herbs. It is based on a short story by Richard Garnett, whose sly, donnish wit is difficult to translate into terms of effective theatrical dialogue, let alone something acceptable to the general operatic public. The thread of this particular story is extremely artificial: the motivating characters, the baddie Dipsacus, the wicked magician and father of the heroine, Tormentilla, and his counterpart the Empress Persicaria, mother of the hero, have recourse to spells and magic to achieve their ends; and a willing suspension of disbelief is even more essential than is usually the case in the operatic theatre. It may, however, quite legitimately be argued that the use of spells and magic is no more absurd and improbable here than Wagner's use of them in *The Ring*, and that in a light stage piece of this kind, absurdities of this kind are perfectly acceptable. The plot is certainly less absurd than the action of many a ballet. But what of the libretto that Miss Sharp made of the story?

Once again, the surviving letters from Vaughan Williams to his librettist show him as perfectly capable of acting the Verdiesque gentle bully, but this time rather less diffident in expressing his ideas than he was with Harold Child. In one of these, he puts his finger on the problem that they had set themselves when planning the opera, a problem that they never really solved satisfactorily. This problem was simply whether they were to create a musical comedy, in which the action was carried on in the spoken dialogue and the music merely underlined the situation at a given juncture of the plot, or whether the work was to be a genuine opera, where the music also carried the action forward. This is surely one reason why the work has never had a proper professional performance; and one can well understand why operatic managements have fought shy of putting it on. The absence of extended and well-developed finales to any of the three acts, such as Gilbert's skilfully contrived first act finales in *Iolanthe*, *Patience*, or *The Gondoliers*, seems to indicate that they had decided on creating a musical comedy. One says *seems*, because there are in fact a number of ensembles that definitely carry forward and intensify the dramatic action, music which indicates, moreover, the quality of Vaughan Williams's stagecraft.

The plot of *The Poisoned Kiss* is not complex as such pieces go. Tormentilla has been brought up by her father on poisonous plants so that her first kiss will poison the man on whom she implants it. He wants to contrive for reasons of revenge for unrequited love many years before that that man shall be Amaryllus, the son of the Empress Persicaria. Persicaria had once loved him but married another of her own station; and Dipsacus has had a chip on his shoulder ever since. Needless to say, the two young people meet and fall in love without either knowing who the other is; the poisoned kiss is exchanged and it looks as if Dipsacus's plan has succeeded. But Persicaria has discovered his plot and has nourished Amaryllus on antidotes. He recovers physically but not emotionally; both parents have to permit their offspring to marry; they let bygones be bygones and marry too; and all ends happily. Fairy-tale love has triumphed over Silly Symphony hatred.

The main characters are supported by comic servants, Gallanthus and Angelica, who are presumably intended to act as a kind of Papageno and Papagena to the Tamino and Pamina of Amaryllus and Tormentilla. The Empress has a retinue of three bogus mediums and Dipsacus of three incompetent hobgoblins—again the parallel with *The Magic Flute* is inescapable. Miss Sharp took the incidental opportunity to poke fun at sensational journalism and public credulity in a rather flat-footed undergraduate-revue manner when she had the hobgoblins disguise themselves as tabloid journalists. Commentators have drawn attention to the note of deliberate bathos, sounded throughout the piece. A great opportunity was missed here: deflating the sentimental pretensions of the highfalutin has been a feature of comic opera from time immemorial. True, in *The Poisoned Kiss*, Angelica and Gallanthus show a healthy disrespect from time to time for their mistress and master respectively, but the bathetic element in the dialogue is all too often rather patronizingly deflected from mocking the high and mighty in favour of simply engaging in banal exchanges. No amount of revision, cutting or trimming seems capable of salvaging *The Poisoned Kiss* as a viable stage piece.

The question remains: was it worth the while of a composer of Vaughan Williams's calibre to compose music to such a plot? He evidently thought it was, for *The Poisoned Kiss* contains music that is tuneful, dramatically apt, and lighter in touch than is usually the case with Vaughan Williams. Yet *The Poisoned Kiss* is, by the composer's own admission, one of the few works that he shrank from showing to Holst:

an attitude that speaks volumes both of Holst's musical seriousness and of Vaughan Williams's knowledge of his friend. But even when he is at his best—as is often the case—Vaughan Williams seems to find it difficult to drop into genuine musical burlesque or parody, save perhaps of himself (see, for example, Dipsacus's Act I ballad: 'The sun it shone in Golden Town'). The mock 'Wolf's Glen' opening scene and the sporadic sunrise that follows it, with its crude send-up of end-of-term school production stage effects, or the Tango for the three mediums in Act III are further cases in point. Such music is wasted on the juvenile antics of the plot and the fatuous stage directions. The lighter lyrical material varies in quality: tunes such as Persicaria's 'Love breaks all rules' from Act III and Amaryllus's Act II serenade, 'Dear love, behold' are just right for their dramatic context. The spritely Act II duet between Angelica and Gallanthus 'It does not appear', with its juxtapositions of 6/8, 2/4, and 9/8 is both catchy and ingenious. Other items in similar vein just miss the mark, possibly because Vaughan Williams was trying too hard not to be obvious.

It has already been pointed out that Vaughan Williams was not given the kind of opportunity that Sullivan so enthusiastically exploited in such movements as the finale to the first act of *Iolanthe*, where the whole dramatic build-up is rhythmically brilliantly varied and the changes in tempo and metre are impeccably paced. He none the less rises to the occasion with some finely contrived ensembles, such as that arising out of the episode in Act I when Tormentilla's pet cobra is brought back to consciousness after Amaryllus, thinking to save her from its deadly poison, attempts unsuccessfully to kill it. The whole of this passage has pace and vigour, a clear texture, and a cleverly placed climax on a modulation into the major; the change from major back into the minor when the reptile actually revives is a delightfully ironic touch; and the madrigalian counterpoint of the piece works gently into a combination of Tormentilla's lilting lullaby for her pet, Angelica's and Gallanthus's patter, and Amaryllus's love-song. The passionate and finely built-up love duet in Act II between Tormentilla and Amaryllus, too, manages (surely subconsciously) to erupt into one of his characteristic 'Alleluia' phrases at its climax (Ex. 10).

Even granted that the work should not be taken too seriously, it still suffers from want of true characterization, especially in the field of the supporting roles. Alongside such characters as Gilbert's three absurd aristocratic primitives Arac, Guron and, Scynthius from *Princess Ida*, so

Ex. 10

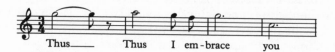

Thus___   Thus   I em-brace   you

ably brought to life by Sullivan's ponderous mock-Handelian music, Lob, Hob, and Gob are merely puerile: 'We are warriors three' is succinct musical characterization; 'Here we come, galumphing along' is mere word setting, and setting of pretty banal words into the bargain. To take another example, both words and music contribute far more satisfactorily to the illumination of what is basically the same situation—the confession of a fickle young man who ought not to be taken too seriously—in Edwin's first solo song from *Trial by Jury* than they do in Amaryllus's 'It's true I'm inclined to be fickle'. *The Poisoned Kiss* often, in fact, gives the overall impression more of an ambitious out-of-season Christmas pantomime entertainment, rather than a genuine comic or ballad opera, and is perhaps best thought of as such.

The Second World War and after saw Vaughan Williams exploiting new fields as well as continuing to cultivate old ones. Apart from his many film scores, elements from at least two of which found their way into symphonic compositions, at the age of seventy, he produced his luminous and visionary Fifth Symphony, incorporating elements from his unfinished operatic version of *The Pilgrim's Progress*.

He did finish it, in time for the Festival of Britain in 1951; and he was working on a further operatic project, with a libretto by his wife Ursula based on an amalgam of two English folk-ballads, when he died. He called *The Pilgrim's Progress* a 'Morality', which indicates that he felt it was not an orthodox opera and should not be staged as such, but in a special and stylized manner. *The Pilgrim's Progress* was first performed at the Royal Opera House, Covent Garden, on 26 April 1951. The subject matter and the absence of any conventional operatic love and intrigue interest failed to impress the audience; and Vaughan Williams seems to have been one of the few who was pleased with what at all events seems to have been a dull, gimmicky production—by the normally reliable and imaginative Nevil Coghill. The American critic Cecil Smith,[4] writing in *Opera*, was scathing about this, describing the lighting as uniformly atrocious and claiming that Coghill taught Arnold Matters, as Pilgrim, 'the gestures of a village vicar or perhaps of a provincial Elijah'. Most of the critics wrote some kind of variation on the theme that the work had been too long in gestation for it to be as effective on stage as the symphony that Vaughan Williams had fashioned from part of it was in the concert-hall. Even those who usually wrote sympathetically of RVW's works, such as Richard Capell, in the *Daily Telegraph*, claimed that it was 'trammelled by the stage', when a more appropriate comment would probably have been 'trammelled by this production'. Herbert Murrill, in *Music & Letters*, claimed that it could be played in a cathedral or before some great architectural facade. Rutland Boughton even wrote to [Sir] David Willcocks at Worcester

---

[4] Kennedy, *Works* 2, p. 314.

cathedral to see if it might be produced there by the Covent Garden cast; Edward Dent,[5] however, by no means inexperienced in opera translation and production, appreciated not just the quality of the music but its aptness to the spectacle and the story: 'It is an opera,' he wrote, 'and its only place is the theatre.' He was right. *The Pilgrim's Progress* contains some of Vaughan Williams's finest stage music, with such telling theatrical situations as the exhilarating arming of Pilgrim for his journey, the confrontation with Apollyon, spine-chillingly declaiming his part on a sinister mechanical monotone, the Hogarthian ribaldry and mockery of the Vanity Fair scene, leading to the merciless condemnation of Pilgrim to death, the laid-back musical-comedy self-satisfaction of the By-Ends couple—here, surely, if evidence is needed, is an example of what *The Poisoned Kiss* might have been like if the libretto had been much less arch—and the radiant visionary quality of the central figure's apotheosis at the end.

This great work has usually been damned with faint praise for its loftiness of aim and criticized for its clumsiness of realization. The clumsiness is more, one suspects, in the eye and the ear of the critic (and the producer) laden with preconceptions as to what is and what is not appropriate musical stagecraft than it is in the work itself. It is odd that, in an age when Wagner's great music-dramas have regularly been superbly and imaginatively staged with productions concentrating on lighting and stylized action effects, nobody in the English professional opera-theatre has applied the same techniques to Vaughan Williams's majestic vision. Some kind of abstract treatment of this kind is surely more appropriate to the work than a kind of wooden, fake-religious, semi-realistic staging. Amateur productions under the aegis of the right kind of professional, such as Dennis Arundell's memorable ones at Cambridge in 1954 and the stunningly effective one by Joseph Ward at the Royal Northern College of Music in 1992—mercifully and vividly available on CD[6]—have underlined the quality of the music and its dramatic appositeness.

The Pilgrim's Progress covers a wider and deeper emotional range than that of any of Vaughan Williams's other operas. He selected his episodes from Bunyan with care. The scenes are arranged so that each particular element is followed by something that contrasts with it in texture and tempo, yet builds on what has gone before. The action describes a kind of emotional sine-curve, through despair, spiritual enlightenment, resolve, solemn statuesque conflict, hectic, flashy, gaudy spectacle, and trivial, witty light comedy to the ineffable serenity of the Delectable Mountains and the closing transfiguration, all framed within the over-riding reminder that this is a dream vision undergone by the prisoner Bunyan in his cell. The manner is as old as Monteverdi (and if

---

[5] Kennedy, *Works* 2, p. 314.   [6] RNCM PP1.

a modern audience can accept and respond to *Orfeo* and *Il ritorno d'Ulisse* as genuine music-dramas, which they are, it can surely respond without too much adjustment to *Pilgrim*).

The exposition of the opera proceeds with a broad, stately momentum; and the sporadic use of fragments of the noble Puritan hymn-tune 'York', symbolic of the Pilgrim's true home, as a kind of leitmotif, points up the underlying course of the action. The impetus of the music arches upward as Pilgrim's fortunes plunge downward. It gathers momentum in the splendid scene, with its soaring, almost Verdian choral entries, in which Pilgrim is prepared and armed for his journey. The build-up of momentum continues through the Apollyon scene, reaches its zenith of frenzied activity in Vanity Fair (if the Fifth Symphony lifts the serene moments from the opera, then Vanity Fair surely borrows its feverish, frenetic drive from the scherzo of the Sixth), touches sublime serenity and broadens out to the noble close.

Every facet of Vaughan Williams's genius save perhaps his gift for soaring erotic melody finds its way into this score. Music formerly used in one context takes on a new significance when quoted in another. The allusions to the Fifth Symphony, for example, skilfully juxtaposed as a background to the stage action at the House Beautiful, seem exactly in place: this is no more a dilution of the music's original content than is the trumpet fanfare heralding the Governor's arrival in *Fidelio* compared with its effect in the Overture Leonora No. 2. The Siegfried-like challenge, based on the opening of the tune of Pilgrim's great hymn, that he throws down before Apollyon is matched by the giant's Fafner-like response. The mordant irony that is such a feature of works like the Fourth Symphony or *Five Tudor Portraits* finds a suitable context in the bustle of Vanity Fair, with its impressionistic episodes (characters stepping forward, singing their piece and withdrawing into the general mêlée) and insistent, nagging rhythms. There is, however, no sense of real evil or menace in this scene until the advent of Lord Hategood, least of all in the ladies selling their dubious charms, even though it is permeated with a little rhythmic figure that will later beat the words 'Beelzebub' and 'Away with him'. The chilling, sinister striding figure in octaves that announces Hategood's arrival changes the atmosphere completely; it has the same impact as the very similar device that launches and is developed in Iago's horrifying nihilistic credo in *Otello*; and when he pronounces sentence in his gabbled pseudo-plainchant, it is just as effective a distortion of the 'real thing' as Satan's 'Gloria in excelsis Deo' *fff* on the muted brass is at the end of his Dance of Triumph in *Job*. The relentless tread of the macabre funeral march after Pilgrim is sentenced to death, almost a parody of the noble funeral march in *Dona Nobis Pacem*, is—*pace* Vaughan Williams's own comment on the composer—truly Mahlerian in its ironic intensity. Equally ironic, though less intense, is the way in which the advent of the By-Ends' pseudo-sophisticated banality, with its piquant bassoon interjections, breaks into the rapt atmosphere created by the Woodcutter's lad's simple and utterly captivating song.

The jaunty, flaccid, thirties-style portrayal of the By-Ends couple (the scoring becoming brassier and more assertive as Mr By-Ends becomes more vexed when Pilgrim punctures his self-esteem, just like the tantrum thrown by Job's comforters) and the lucid, laconic scoring of the Delectable Mountains episode—as if the Flower Maidens from *Parsifal* had been purged of their seductive languor and raised to the nth degree of sublimity—are etched in with a master hand. Occasionally one feels that the composer resorts somewhat facilely to wandering, intertwining string lines accompanying some of the biblical passages, apparently at variance with the (literally) God-forsaken despair of the text, or to blaring brass formulas and thumping percussion effects to ram home his points in the more 'resolute' passages; but then one is suddenly reminded of the underlying onward flow of this majestic river of music by some thematic reminiscence of past action (as in the remainder of Vanity Fair at 'He trusted in God' or when the orchestra adds its comment to 'Show me thy way, O Lord') and this or that apparently obtrusive or irrelevant detail falls naturally into place. The portrayal in the orchestra of Pilgrim's gradual return to self-awareness through prayer and meditation on scripture after the shock of his sojourn in gaol is exactly right in terms of Bunyan's narrative: it is as if the landscape of *Pastoral Symphony* is seen by night, so to speak, instead of by the light of the fading sun. Even Apollyon's arrogantly monotonous Dalek-like recitative, if properly handled, can strike the chill and stir the resolve that Bunyan and Vaughan Williams intended to arouse through the presence of an unnamed evil force that had to be confronted and destroyed.

When this great work is stigmatized as 'undramatic', what is really meant is that it is not theatrical in the conventional sense. Vaughan Williams himself reminded Edward Dent when responding to his comments on the original production: ' . . . you must remember that the Opera is to be acted almost like a ritual and not in the ordinary dramatic sense.' It *is* a morality: but it is one where the symbols are given human shape and human attributes, set to music that may aspire towards the heavenly but is certainly rooted in the human. If the more serene passages, particularly those involving prayers and psalm quotations, are performed as if they were a sequence of 'pi' Anglican anthems in the approved Victorian manner; and if the doleful creatures and Vanity Fair are projected (as the demons in *Gerontius* so often are) with all the sense of cosmic evil of a 'ya-boo-sucks' prep-school verbal insults contest, then of course it will lack dramatic impact. The music goes much deeper than this. Time and again, Vaughan Williams underlines and enhances the effect of Bunyan's tale with music of graphic power and richness. There are appropriate tensions in the score at suitable points in the plot; and they are balanced by points of repose that transcend the mere dramatic marking time or padding out of the action such as are found even in a masterpiece such as *Don Giovanni*. The framework sets the action within the similitude of a dream; and the manner in which scene succeeds scene is indeed dream-like. In an age when Michael Tippett's operas are coming into their own, it is perhaps time for the English professional stage to take another look at *The Pilgrim's Progress*. There is many a less significant music-drama that has attracted more attention.

14

Orchestral music

Vaughan Williams came late and cautiously to orchestral composition. Disregarding student works (among which we should surely include the lost Serenade described by Stanford in 1894 as 'a most remarkable and poetical piece of work'), his first orchestral work of any consequence was the Serenade for small orchestra of 1897. This was performed by the Bournemouth Municipal Orchestra under Dan Godfrey on 4 April 1901 and comprises four movements; its maiden performance seems to have been virtually its only one, although it has been recorded in the USA, and it has remained unpublished. The most extended movement is the jolly Scherzo in a lilting jig rhythm, which extends to 205 bars. Vaughan Williams composed two slow movements for the work, one an Intermezzo and Trio, the other a Romance.

The Serenade was followed in 1900 by a *Bucolic Suite* for a larger orchestra, this time including trombones. This, too, was first performed at Bournemouth, on 10 March 1902 and a number of times subsequently. It is on an altogether larger and more ambitious scale than the Serenade; and a number of the themes have a distinctly folky cut to them, particularly the two main themes of the third movement, an Intermezzo in a modal E minor. Vaughan Williams's sense of scoring throughout this work is arresting: effects such as the strings playing *col legno* and some grateful writing for the harp are particularly noteworthy. It is in the main an undemanding and jaunty piece with thoughtful episodes, but the excursions into unexpected keys (F sharp major contrasted with a modal D minor in the first movement and C minor contrasted with A major in the finale) show the composer's interest in third-related keys, familiar from some of his songs of this period. An *Heroic Elegy and Triumphal Epilogue* from the same year, conducted by Stanford at the RCM on 5 March 1901, was thought for many years to have been lost, but the score is now at Cornell University. It turns out to be a work of considerable significance in RVW's early development. Vaillancourt[1] speaks of it as 'abound[ing] with structural surprises, employ[ing] a sophisticated brand of thematic manipulations, and display[ing] more

[1] See Michael Vaillancourt, 'Coming of age: the earliest orchestral music of Ralph Vaughan Williams', in *VWS*, pp. 23–46.

varied and colourful orchestral writing than any of its predecessors' and shows how in certain respects it displays parallels with Mahler, whose Third Symphony RVW may have heard in Berlin in March 1897. He provides examples of the manner in which Vaughan Williams transforms the main theme of his *Elegy* which are by no means incompatible with the techniques used by Liszt and Wagner (more likely the latter, one would imagine, in the light of RVW's lifelong dislike of Liszt's music). Now that the work has re-surfaced, it would be fascinating to hear it performed. As well as Vaillancourt's careful analysis of the work, the programme note for a performance in Leeds in 1905 indicates that once more Vaughan Williams was experimenting with new ways of clothing his ideas orchestrally: the main theme was apparently allotted to the trombone 'accompanied by a persistent syncopated figure on the strings' which was to play a considerable role later in the movement and turned up on the drum in the coda. Stanford liked this work, telling John Ireland that it was much better than anything he (Ireland) could write; and Parry's reaction to it was to remark to Frank Pownall, the Registrar of the RCM, that there was no shadow of doubt about Vaughan Williams's talent. It would seem that whatever his teachers told him to his face, they paid Vaughan Williams plenty of compliments behind his back.

In 1903, we find a change of direction in the titles at any rate that RVW allotted to his orchestral works. Names of landscapes begin to take precedence over more formal or abstract titles, which can surely be taken as an indication that he was trying to convey in orchestral terms the mood evoked by a particular kind of English location and was searching for the right kind of musical form to express what he felt. It is worth pointing out that this attempt to express his feelings for a specifically English kind of mood or atmosphere slightly pre-dated his first forays into the field to collect folk-songs. The first sign of this is a project for four *Impressions for Orchestra* under the general title *In the New Forest* that he embarked on in that year. Two of these, 'Burley Heath' and 'The Solent', were substantially complete and the latter actually reached performance, or at any rate a run-through, under Henry Wood, on 19 June 1903. The main theme of 'The Solent' was re-used in the film music for *The England of Elizabeth* in 1955 and in the Ninth Symphony. (Its outline also distinctly foreshadows that of the Parryesque phrase 'And on its limitless heaving breast the ships' from *A Sea Symphony*.) A Symphonic Rhapsody with a motto from Christina Rossetti indicating that the work was some kind of romantic night-piece, performed at Bournemouth on 7 March 1904, was later scrapped.

The first orchestral work by Vaughan Williams that has survived to be performed today is the 'Symphonic Impression' *In the Fen Country*, completed on 10 April 1904 and subsequently revised at least three times, the last of them as late as 1935. Beecham conducted the first performance at Queen's Hall on 22 February 1909. *In the Fen Country* is a curious, often attractive, yet somewhat uncertain amalgam of Vaughan Williams's 'pre-Raphaelite' style with his newly-emerging folk-song-based melodic idiom. As a piece of orchestral landscape evocation, the work is excitingly original if it is rather uneven in quality, for there is no denying the stylistic inconsistency between the contours of his folk-song-like themes and their post-Wagnerian harmonic support. Nor has he satisfactorily reconciled the harmonic and rhythmic implications of his thematic material and the demands of traditional form. The result is an uneasy and unintegrated pattern of meandering downward-gliding chromaticisms, unstable tonality and some rather aimless imitative writing. The orchestral texture is sometimes clear and imaginative and sometimes densely linear. Yet the first faltering steps have been taken towards his mature style.

Much the same might be said of the first of the three *Norfolk Rhapsodies*, which was first performed under Henry Wood at Queen's Hall on 23 August 1906. If Benjamin Britten did not know this work, then it is striking indeed that two of our greatest composers should have independently hit on the idea of portraying the East Anglian seascape in such similar musical terms: the evocative opening, with its harp, its insistent background rhythmic tapping, its remote high strings, its mournful viola solo and its clarinet arpeggios, foreshadows in a number of details of scoring the wonderful 'Dawn' interlude and the Passacaglia from *Peter Grimes*. Unfortunately, from then onwards, the two works part company. It would be unfair to say that the *Norfolk Rhapsody* flatters only to deceive, for it is no worse that the generality of folky rhapsodies that Elgar stigmatized in one of his professorial lectures at Birmingham as the kind of thing that English composers ought *not* to be writing. Unfortunately, it is not all that better than most of them, either, relying as it so frequently does on successive imitative entries, on Parryesque (or Elgarian) sequences built up from fragments of the themes and on chromatically descending inner parts to generate onward movement, emotional warmth, and harmonic tension. Yet both the opening and its recall at the end, with the gentle tapping rhythm again quietly persistent, are hauntingly poetic and finely calculated. It is perhaps as well that Vaughan Williams withheld the other two *Norfolk Rhapsodies*, for this must in the composer's own opinion have been the best of the three. What they do all show is the sturdy quality of the tunes he had collected in the county and the warmth and imaginative affection with which he treats them.

The Second *Norfolk Rhapsody*, in D minor, was performed at Cardiff on 27 September 1907 and first heard in London nearly five years later, in April 1912. It was based on three of the tunes that Vaughan Williams collected at King's Lynn in January 1905. The first of these, 'Young Henry the Poacher', is the fine tune that Vaughan Williams adapted to fit G. K. Chesterton's hymn 'O God of Earth and Altar' in *The English Hymnal* (No. 562). Both it and 'The Saucy Bold Robber' are rather press-ganged into service as material for a somewhat livelier movement than anyone knowing the stately hymn would think appropriate. (The original words of the tune related to the fate of the convicts transported to Van Diemen's Land, which argues that the tempo in the Hymnal—Vaughan Williams suggests 'In moderate time, dignified'—is more appropriate to it than the one suggested in the Rhapsody.) 'The Saucy Bold Robber', indeed, is actually used as the material for a small-scale scherzo section; and it is interesting that in his treatment of these tunes, and in particular of 'Young Henry', Vaughan Williams had already hit upon his characteristic manner of what might be called organically evolving a tune out of its salient melodic phrase. He also uses the variant diminished version of the tune as a kind of commentary on the tune itself when it recurs after the scherzo-section based on 'The Saucy Bold Robber'. The other tune, 'Spurn Point', forms the material both for what might be called the second subject of the Rhapsody and its coda-cum-epilogue, which, already characteristically, fades away into nothingness.

The Third Rhapsody, first performed at Cardiff in September 1907 in the same concert as the Second, makes much more 'military' use of the four tunes employed than the other two. As one of the tunes is the stirring 'Ward the Pirate',[2] a fine, sturdy almost Handelian melody originally alluded to in the early version of the First Rhapsody, it was natural for the composer to use it both as the 'Trio' of the ABA form that underlies this work and as the climax of the piece, *à la* Elgar in the *Pomp and Circumstance* Marches, before he whips up another of his tunes, 'The Lincolnshire Farmer', into a presto coda. Something more characteristic of the composer's fully-formed melodic style, however, can perhaps be traced in another tune from this Rhapsody, 'John Raeburn', with its characteristic AGAD figure.[3]

It had apparently at one time been Vaughan Williams's intention to use these three Rhapsodies as a *Norfolk Symphony*, but as neither No. 2 nor No. 3 seems ever to have been performed after 1914, it is understandable that any reference to 'Ward the Pirate' in the first and best of them should have been cut out. They may not be strikingly original, but they are competently, at times imaginatively, at times rather stolidly scored; the quiet poetic endings of the first two foreshadow the composer's mature idiom; and for all their structural debt to Stanford and other 'national' composers of orchestral rhapsodies such as Dvořák, they

---

[2] This splendid tune has a marked kinship with Sullivan's avowedly Handelian setting of the words 'For he is an Englishman . . . ' in *HMS Pinafore*, though it lacks the little mock-baroque flourish at the end. Is this coincidence or does it indicate a common ancestry? What is of particular interest is the conscious pride in the 'Englishness' of the sentiments of the words and the robust style of the music in both cases.

[3] Details from the original programme notes. See also Vaillancourt, in *VWS*.

represent the first examples of an English composer working up tunes that he had himself collected from native folk-singers—something virtually unheard-of in early twentieth-century England.

The first of Vaughan Williams's mature orchestral works to gain a foothold in the repertory was a *jeu d'esprit* developed out of the music that he composed in 1909 for a Cambridge production of Aristophanes' *The Wasps*. Since this music was originally designed for performance with the play, it is perhaps best dealt with alongside Vaughan Williams's other compositions for the stage. But his next orchestral work was deservedly to prove one of the greatest and most durable of all. The *Fantasia on a Theme by Thomas Tallis*, for string quartet, small string orchestra, and large string orchestra, is likely to figure prominently in almost any anthology CD of Vaughan Williams's works; deservedly so, for its craftsmanship, depth, and unobtrusive originality mark it out as something quite out of the ordinary. Beecham once quipped that the reason why none of Vaughan Williams's other works had quite achieved the same degree of popularity was that RVW had not used a theme by Tallis in any of them. Like so many other examples of Beecham's wit, this has to be taken not just with a pinch of salt but with a whole sackful. Tallis's noble theme does indeed make an immediate appeal; but though that is a significant factor, it is only a very minor part of the story. The more one closely listens to the Fantasia, the more one is captivated by the ingenuity and inevitability of its structure and its scoring. Here is something that resonates with the whole history of England's musical traditions, sacred and secular, yet something forever fresh and original. Its originality consists neither in its melodic structure nor in its freedom of rhythm, and certainly not in its use of unconventional harmony, but in the cast of mind that underlies it, which uses perfectly ordinary devices—extremely loud chords followed by ghostly soft ones, for example, or the use of pizzicato cellos and basses under a high held note in the violins—in a most un-ordinary way. It is a quietly self-confident mind that combines the rapt, *almost* religious fervour of a Bruckner with the stern sense of purpose and controlled will-power of a Beethoven. There is no sense of struggle or conflict (and hence no dramatic sonata-form layout: the structure is multi-motif based but entirely monothematic). There is instead a concentrated discussion of different aspects of one idea. The subsidiary ideas that blossom from the various rhythmic, melodic, harmonic, and emotive aspects of Tallis's theme flow together into a stately flood of sound whose course is inevitable and whose climax overwhelming.[4]

---

[4] For a thoroughgoing analysis of this work, see Anthony Pople, 'Vaughan Williams, Tallis and the Phantasy Principle', in *VWS*, pp. 47–80. Pople goes into considerable detail about the relationship between the original version of this work and its revised form(s). In the original version, the thematic interrelationships were to some extent more easily traceable, though the work itself was more diffuse.

The very opening, with its characteristic spread of string tone in nine parts over five octaves, immediately generates an evocative, almost visual atmosphere. It is as if shafts of sunlight were penetrating the cool shadowy nave of some great cathedral. The prefiguring of the basic rhythm of Tallis's theme (a rhythm that recurs no fewer than eight times in the theme itself) is countered by a variant of the second significant rhythmic feature of the tune: its gentle syncopations; and the third of its main rhythms is hinted at in the violins before the tune itself is actually heard in full, richly and sonorously on the G string of the second violins, violas, and first cellos, with a shimmering halo of harmony in the divided firsts. Vaughan Williams shows that his lessons with Ravel were already paying a dividend in matching clean, beautifully spaced orchestral sound to what had for some time been a feature of his idiom. When the tune is counterstated *appassionato*, high up in the firsts, with a much fuller but still transparent texture, the majestic intensity of Tallis's theme becomes fully evident. What follows searchingly explores all the emotional potential of the theme, sharply juxtaposing reflective, serene, powerful, passionate, and mysterious moods by turns, simply by examining its salient melodic, rhythmic and harmonic features and ambiguities and allowing them to interact with one another so as to generate new material.

The reflective episode for the solo quartet, for example, a colloquy in an English cloister, led off (of course!) by the viola, offers each of the soloists a slightly different melodic and rhythmic variant of the 6/8 phrase of the tune; the subsequent frequent changes of metre add an onward surge to the generally measured progress of the music's harmonic rhythms; and the supreme climax, with the rich orchestral chords in seven parts spread over five octaves, is based on a rhythm derived from the fifth phrase of Tallis's tune. It is extended to embrace a more urgent rhythmic form of its original continuation *in retrograde*, and developed in sequence until the massive web of rhythm and melody gradually ebbs away into a repeated monotone E major chord in the rhythm of the key phrase of the tune but without any melodic pattern. The second orchestra's harmonies switch boldly from C minor to E flat, via B minor to D minor, and thence to B flat minor and a harmonic sideslip into F minor. The first orchestra hints at the opening of the work (in C minor where it was originally in D minor and quietly resolving onto a chord of G major where at the beginning it had resolved on to an open fifth) and the solo violin enters with Tallis's melody, all passion spent, embellished with a beautiful flowing counter-theme on the solo viola.

The other extended work for string orchestra, the *Partita* (originally a double trio), is also laid out for two contrasting and unequal bodies. Neither of the two orchestras has second violins: it is strange that the composer left this aspect of the work untouched when arranging it for orchestra. In its present guise, the work almost sounds as if Vaughan Williams had been studying either Bartók or Tippett, or both. It would be interesting to hear a reconstructed version of the original form to see (or rather hear) if it, too, gave the same impression. Certainly, there is a restless, dynamic energy and intricacy of detail about some of the writing that makes passages in the work sound more as if it were by Tippett than Vaughan Williams. (Michael Kennedy[5] aptly comments that it sounds as if RVW had been having tea with Stravinsky.) It is a work of half-lights, quirky and teeming with closely-integrated thematic cross-references, not entirely successful texturally and difficult to bring off in performance, particularly with a big orchestra, if the conductor does not aim for razor-sharp accuracy of ensemble or goes too much for weight of tone rather than intensity of rhythm. Perhaps the *Partita*, originally intended as a chamber work, should not be performed by too large an ensemble.

There could hardly be a greater contrast with the Tallis Fantasia. Though the work has its reflective passages, its rhythms are much more dance-like and considerably more impulsive than in the Fantasia. As usual, elements of the unexpected are found here, too; but this time in irregular and quirky phrasing, rhythms, unexpected thematic contours, and sharply contrasting moods. For the most part light, genial, and earthy, the work also displays Vaughan Williams's willingness to experiment with a new kind of popular idiom—that of the dance orchestras of the thirties—and a sly humour that foreshadows the scherzo movements of the last two symphonies. Yet it somehow fails as an entity. It is an explosive musical cocktail that lacks the priming fuse to let it off with its proper impact. Vaughan Williams may perhaps have realized this; he certainly revised, re-cast, and re-wrote enough of it.

The first movement, Andante tranquillo, starts out sounding like a cross between a kind of forlana and a slow gigue, the two contrasting gently bouncing rhythms linked by a typically Vaughan Williams series of imitative entries on the solo instruments. The forlana-like rhythm gradually generates more intensity and ends up at the movement's big climax with a drive and a power not unlike that of the first movement of Beethoven's Seventh Symphony, itself 'the apotheosis of rhythm' as Wagner put it.

The whirring, Holstian scherzo-ostinato that follows—'Brook Green' upgraded to provide a challenge for virtuoso professionals—is cunningly economical in its use of material, the main theme being an augmented version of the ostinato pattern. Again as the texture thickens the music generates a fussy energy that never seems quite to come off in performance; and the thematic reference to the first movement seems somewhat contrived.

[5] Kennedy, *Works* 2, p. 358.

The third movement is an Intermezzo bearing the sub-title 'Homage to Henry Hall'. The BBC Dance Orchestra of the 1930s (which once had the distinction of being conducted by Sir Adrian Boult in 'Tiger Rag', while its own conductor, Henry Hall, directed the BBC Symphony Orchestra in the overture to *The Magic Flute*) was noted for its gentle rhythmic bounce and lilt; and it seems that these are the characteristics that Vaughan Williams was aiming to bring out rather than any direct reference to either of the orchestra's signature tunes. The main theme of this movement, played over a syncopated pizzicato accompaniment in the second orchestra, is a further rhythmic transformation of the theme of the ostinato movement. Once more there is a retrospective reference to the first movement, this time in the shape of a slightly Elgarian phrase from one of its main themes. Rhythmically, this movement is the most interesting and successful of the four, with three layers of rhythm interacting with one another and keeping the movement moving onwards as the texture thickens.

The 'Hoyda!' howl that opens the finale, as if Rutterkin had become one of the doleful creatures in *The Pilgrim's Progress*, is also based on the ostinato theme. Howes likens this movement to an Elizabethan fantasia 'but without the quasi-fugal texture which that early form of instrumental chamber music borrowed from the madrigal'. Maybe; but the vigour and energy of the music are of a totally different order, stemming from the age of the motor-car and the steam train. Again, there are problems with ensemble and texture and a curious instability—even inconsistency—of mood. The sudden, almost unmotivated outbursts of hectic movement indicate that this is neither a 'fun' movement nor a rapt visionary one. As a summing-up it does not quite succeed, despite further back-references to the previous three movements and despite the quiet, reflective ending.

English composers in general and Vaughan Williams and Britten in particular have always enjoyed the challenge of writing effectively for amateurs; and while the *Concerto grosso* for strings, commissioned for its twenty-first anniversary in 1950 by the Rural Music Schools Association, may not be in the same league as *Noye's Fludde*, it is disproof of the claim that Vaughan Williams was a clumsy amateur himself. Here is music playable by amateurs of varying levels of accomplishment which can still sound well when performed by a professional orchestra. As befits the occasion for which it was composed, it is a jolly piece, full of vigour and broad, simple humour. The forces used are: a concertino group of skilled players; a tutti comprising those who can play in the third position and manage simple double stops; and less experienced players (including those 'who prefer to use only open strings'). There are five movements; and the formal layout is not unlike that of the Tchaikovsky serenade, with a reprise at the very end of the opening music. The most attractive music is to be found in the central

Sarabande, which is flanked by two witty movements of a scherzo-like nature, a Burlesca ostinata which takes its cue from the rather more sophisticated movement of this category in the *Partita* and a Scherzo. The opening Intrada forms a fine swaggering introduction and the main theme of the march finale is curiously similar in outline to one of the themes in the finale of Elgar's Second Symphony.

Of the smaller works for orchestra, two based on folk-material deserve special mention. They are the *Suite, English Folk Songs* originally for military band and later transcribed by RVW's pupil Gordon Jacob for orchestra and for brass band, which is straightforward attractive listening, and the *Five Variants of 'Dives and Lazarus'*, a cross between a folk-song arrangement and an original composition. It is a meditation on folk-material that is more shapely and more 'learned' than a rhapsody, reaching up, like the Tallis Fantasia to a big, firm climax, dying away again to a remote, hushed conclusion, serene but not in this instance sublime. Each variant gives a different section of the orchestra (strings and harp) a chance to enjoy itself with a variant of the tune that RVW had known all his life; and in all of them he demonstrated how well he loved the haunting theme.

The Running Set is an ingenious and successful arrangement of folk dances for 'medium' orchestra (i.e. double wind and brass but no trombones or tuba). The dance itself is of British origin, and at the time of the work's composition (1934), it was still danced in parts of the USA, but the 'proper tune, if it ever had one', as RVW put it, had been lost. Vaughan Williams weaves four traditional British (not just English) dance tunes, 'Barrack Hill', 'The Blackthorn Stick', 'Irish Reel' and 'Cock o' the North', into a continuous movement.

The other work that merits mention here was originally composed for brass band. It is a set of variations composed for the 1957 National Brass Band Championship and later scored for orchestra, once again by Gordon Jacob, in which form it was first given some sixteen months after the composer's death. An interesting feature of the re-scored version is the manner in which Dr Jacob, a master orchestrator if ever there was one, produces a genuine 'late Vaughan Williams' sound from the orchestra. In the original version, there is no 'writing down' to the working-class musicians. Moreover, the graceful—and virile—waltz, the gentle flowing Arabesque, the splendidly ceremonious (and, despite its heading, extremely English) Alla polacca and brooding Adagio show that only a year before his death, the veteran composer was still enjoying the skilled practice of his craft in a medium that he had hardly explored before. Here once again is 'democratic' music of a kind of which Hubert Parry would surely have approved: straightforward, sturdy, practical, and immediately attractive. It forms a fitting coda to the lengthy catalogue of RVW's orchestral output.

15

Symphonies (1–3)

Early in his career, Vaughan Williams had shown no particular interest in writing symphonies. He did not wait quite as long as Brahms to complete his first essay in the form: Brahms was forty-three when he allowed the C minor Symphony to come before the public; but by the time he was fifty-three he had completed all his four symphonies. Vaughan Williams eventually completed nine; the first was performed on his thirty-eighth birthday, the fourth when he was sixty-two and the last four came out in the last decade of his long life. His symphonies therefore span some forty-five years or so of his creative career.

The first of them began life unambitiously as a set of Songs of the Sea, intended, no doubt, to be more sophisticated in mood and structure than the famous set composed by his teacher Stanford, but certainly not envisaged as a symphony in the formal sense of the term. Many composers, indeed, from the heyday of the Wagnerian music-drama and the Lisztian tone-poem onwards, thought that the symphony was dead—a rather premature obituary for a form that was to be successfully exploited by Mahler, Sibelius, Nielsen, Stravinsky, Shostakovich, Tippett, Maxwell Davies, and others, including of course Vaughan Williams himself.

The two principal contributory factors to this view are likely to have been respect for the sheer weight of Beethoven's achievement, which intimidated even Brahms, and the fact that Wagnerian and Lisztian innovations in form and harmony had undermined traditional approaches to what was regarded as the core of symphonic writing: structural development through tonal shifts and thematic interaction. After the kaleidoscopic tonal ambiguities of the Preludes to *Tristan* and *Parsifal* and the vast symphonically conceived dramatic structures of *The Ring*, it was difficult to see much point in going through the motions, as it were, in a form whose potential had apparently been so exhaustively explored. Moreover, in those countries where the awakening of a national consciousness in the arts was part of a general reaction against foreign rule or of a strong desire to awaken a national self-awareness, a more specifically dramatic and narrative musical form seemed to communicate better with the potential audience than a purely abstract musical design.

An opera, a patriotic cantata, or a tone-poem, either based on a national legend or evocative of a national landscape, seemed a more natural way of arousing national feelings than a purely abstract musical design, even though that design might conceal some kind of personal or popular programme. Yet distinguished composers continued to write symphonies, perhaps because the symphony was still felt to offer the supreme emotional and intellectual challenge to the serious composer, as Elgar claimed in one of his professorial lectures at Birmingham even before he himself had completed one.

Vaughan Williams's own teachers, Parry and Stanford, dutifully contributed to the British symphonic stock, if not in the long run to the regular repertory, Parry with five symphonies and Stanford with seven. The considerable merits of some of these works may be judged from modern CDs. Parry's symphonies are notable for breadth and vitality, solid craftsmanship, a seriousness of aim, and a ruggedly personal thematic cut; Stanford's for a graceful and more immediately memorable but also more derivative melodic gift (drawing largely on Brahms and Dvořák). Of the two, Stanford is generally the more resourceful orchestrator (though the Scherzo of Parry's Fifth Symphony contains some unexpectedly fresh and delicate scoring) and Parry the more ambitious formal innovator. But neither managed to break free of the dominant Germanic tradition, as represented at its contemporary best by the solid, sober, and occasionally lacklustre work of Brahms.

Both Parry and Stanford did, however, attempt to express a 'national' outlook within the Brahmsian tradition. Parry's attractive, though somewhat stolidly scored Third Symphony is subtitled 'The English' and Stanford's lively but facile Third 'The Irish'. Yet neither seemed able, or perhaps willing, to do more than decorate what were essentially teutonically-orientated structural patterns with themes of a slightly 'national' calibre. The first great symphony to bear the unmistakably individual stamp of a major English musical personality was of course Elgar's in A flat, which may be said without exaggeration to have taken the musical world by storm in 1908, achieving a hundred performances, by no means all of them in the United Kingdom, in the first year or so of its existence. Here was definitely a new symphonic voice: eclectic, serious, combining structural resourcefulness, a wistful depth of feeling, and a sometimes rather showy rhetoric with a virtuoso command of the orchestra and a distinctive musical personality. As Vaughan Williams aptly said of him:

> It falls to the lot of very few composers, and to them not often, to achieve [a] bond of unity with their countrymen. Elgar has achieved this more often than most, and be it noted, not when he is being deliberately 'popular,' . . . but at those moments when he seems to have retired into the solitude of his own sanctuary.[1]

[1] *National Music*, p. 252.

—a verdict reached quite independently and expressed in very similar terms by the distinguished Viennese-born musician Mosco Carner. Such moments surely occur in the slow movement of the A flat Symphony, especially in the deeply moving coda and in various episodes in the two middle movements of the E flat.

In his detailed and valuable study of the Vaughan Williams symphonies, the late Hugh Ottaway grouped them into three symphonic triptychs each of three works.[2] Obviously, the composer cannot have consciously set out to compose nine symphonies that conveniently fall into three groups of compatible works, yet Ottaway's categorization is extremely perceptive. But care must be taken not to think of the first three symphonies as immature or prentice works. Even *A Sea Symphony* for all its signs of being not entirely free from the influence of Parry and Elgar (the latter being vouched for by the composer himself), provides many striking examples of what were already recognizable Vaughan Williams stylistic fingerprints. Hubert Parry acknowledged its scale and grandeur—and its individuality—when he commented that it was 'big stuff, with some impertinences'. It is of course the 'impertinences' that are the aspects of the work most typical of the composer. But equally typical are the work's scale, its essential seriousness, its vigour, its grandeur, and its quest for self-realization as a musical personality, evidenced both in the texts that Vaughan Williams chose to set and the manner in which he set them. The first three symphonies represent various stages in the composer's first mature phase, whatever shortcomings they may possess and however different the sound-worlds they inhabit may be from those of his later symphonies.

What became *A Sea Symphony* gestated slowly over seven years, the title changing a number of times as the music took shape. But the idea underlying the work must always have been basically the same: the sea as a symbol. The final design perceived it as a vast natural force both separating and uniting the continents, deep, majestic, and ostensibly limitless, the arena for human endeavour and achievement and the symbol of man's never-ending spiritual quest to reach out for, explore and understand the unknown, both within himself and in the universe at large. Such a basic scheme was, as Parry said, 'big stuff' of the kind to which Parry himself was extremely sympathetic. It is hardly surprising, then, that this massive work bears traces both of Parry's spirit of noble endeavour and of Elgar's spiritual grandiloquence. Vaughan Williams himself wrote of being haunted when he wrote it by the phrase associated with the words 'Thou art calling me' in *The Dream of Gerontius*. Yet it is significant that it is of two Englishmen that one thinks when considering the background influences, though it is also mildly amusing to reflect that the Elgarisms do not always derive from such an exalted

[2] Hugh Ottaway, *Vaughan Williams Symphonies* (Ariel Music, BBC Books, 1972) (hereafter Ottaway). All quotations are from the 1987 reprint.

source as *Gerontius*: one of the most majestic phrases in the scherzo, to the words 'The wake of the sea-ship after she passes', with its little triplet flourish in the orchestra, is melodically, though not rhythmically, identical with one in the first of Elgar's *Bavarian Dances* (Ex. 11a). Elgar's fresh, cheerful, innocuous tune has been transformed into a processional theme of immense power and breadth. Vaughan Williams shows himself to be *plus royaliste que le roi même*, in fact!

Ex. 11

a)

Elgar, Bavarian Dance No.1 (**Allegro giocoso**)

b)

RVW *A Sea Symphony*

A Sea Symphony was first performed at Leeds, under the composer's direction, on his thirty-eighth birthday, 12 October 1910. It takes up where Vaughan Williams's earlier Whitman setting, *Toward the Unknown Region*, leaves off. Whereas the earlier work proceeded from a mysterious, almost hesitant beginning to a bold and confident ending, *A Sea Symphony*, fully characteristic if not yet quite fully mature, proclaims its scale and comprehensiveness from its very first bar, and the thrilling opening provides a real Vaughan Williams gesture. The sudden leap from the B flat minor chord to that of D major sweeps a cosmic curtain majestically aside and: 'Behold the sea itself!' Then the waves surge back on the tide of a truly characteristic Vaughan Williams theme with a prominent rhetorical triplet, so that a powerful and stately momentum has at once been established, backed by glowing and opulent choral writing and graphically illustrative scoring. Both this theme and the upward-surging theme in the basses to the words 'See where their white sails' recur with telling effect in the finale.

The change of mood and movement at 'Today a rude brief recitative' and the solemnity of the baritone's proud, Parryesque and virtually pentatonic 'And out of these a chant for the sailors of all nations' might seem to undermine the structural integrity of the movement. In fact, they do not; and the little modal phrase associated with the word 'recitative' is to play a considerable and evocative structural part in other movements besides the first. Ottaway sums up the form of this first movement cogently: 'The form that emerges may be usefully described as panoramic . . . but the tensions, the connections and the propelling current are strong enough to give an authentic first movement feeling.'[3] Climaxes are led up to, placed, and withdrawn from with a sure structural hand, rhetoric (as in the soprano's solo, 'Flaunt out, O sea, your separate flags of nations' at the beginning of the development) balanced with lyric expansiveness and a presage of what is to come in later works occurs when the opening is heard as a distant echo, to die away in the reflective remoteness of the ending.

The slow movement, 'On the Beach at Night Alone', broadens the scope of the work immeasurably. The same combination of chords as opened the work, this time transposed up a tone, now forms the foundation of a musical texture carrying a solemn meditation on man's place in the vast, inscrutable cosmos. What served as a symbol of man's exultation in the sea's presence as the background to human endeavour and pride now becomes a symbol of something far transcending man's heroic, yet in the long run puny efforts. The Holstian second theme, which swells up to an overwhelming climax for the voices alone at the words:

> This vast similitude spans them
> And always has spanned
> And shall forever span them
> And shall compactly hold and enclose them

punctuated with a forceful comment from the orchestra, in octaves, derived from the 'brief recitative' phrase in the first movement, has something of the inexorability of 'Saturn, the Bringer of Old Age', (which had not yet of course been written). Here, however, the inexorable procession is that of the stars in their courses, not the advent of mortality.

The scherzo is much more overtly pictorial and its brilliantly impressionistic scoring in flecks of orchestral colour rather than threads of orchestral line, its tritone chords and its sporadic excursions into wholetone scales link it firmly with what was going on across the Channel. The structure, though, is rock solid; and Vaughan Williams's Englishness, however, is amply demonstrated by the Parryesque grandeur of the broad processional melody characterizing the 'great ship'.

Ottaway finds the finale shapeless, but he grasps its point succinctly, finding the clue to it in the lines:

> Reckless, O Soul, exploring, I with thee, and thou with me,
> For we are bound where mariner has not yet dared to go,
> And we will risk the ship, ourselves and all.

---

[3] Hugh Ottaway, *Vaughan Williams Symphonies*, p. 16.

It is not so much the undigested juxtaposition of styles in this movement that occasionally causes even the sympathetic listener's interest to lapse, (one of the themes even has a faint whiff of Mahler's Sixth Symphony, which Vaughan Williams cannot possibly have known). The problem lies rather in the composer's attempt to do justice to the plethora of ideas and images in the text, which prevents him from achieving the tautness amidst expansive variety so evident in the first three movements. Yet the ebb and flow of its changing tempos can be made to sound convincing by a conductor with a sense of rhythmic rather than purely harmonic structure and Ottaway's term 'panoramic' is applicable in an even more telling sense here than in the first movement. With an awesome detachment, this gigantic sonic panorama first encompasses the loneliness of the vast but insignificant earth, 'swimming in space'. Then the music gradually gains momentum, launched by three typically-juxtaposed chords: G minor, G flat major with added sixth, and G major (all in their second inversion) as Adam and Eve descend from the gardens of Asia and the listener descends gradually to earth with them, first through primeval time and then through terrestrial space, as the sea breaks in with its powerful surge again at the soloists' impassioned and operatic 'O can we wait no longer'. But the full stature of the work is revealed only in the final pages. After a huge climax on the words 'Steer for the deep waters only', somewhat like the valedictory paean at the end of Part I of *Gerontius*, the aspiring vision vanishes and a new, mysterious vista opens out beyond with a breathtaking leap from D major, *fff*, to E flat, pianissimo, 'Molto adagio e molto tranquillo'. Here, in fact, is the first of Vaughan Williams's great symphonic epilogues: not looking back nostalgically over what has gone before, but a quiet *Verklärung*, glancing forward toward, even if not quite into, a new unknown region. The work as a whole nailed Vaughan Williams's colours firmly to the symphonic mast, just as Mahler's *Das Klagende Lied* had his, also in a multiple-movement choral symphony.

With the Tallis Fantasia and *A Sea Symphony*, Vaughan Williams had successfully emerged from the chrysallis stage as a composer. From now on, his symphonic works were to show how well he had absorbed, not just shown his awareness of, both the liberating influence of folk-song and that of impressionism, and to constitute the backbone of his prolific output as a composer.

A London Symphony, first performed at Queen's Hall on 27 March 1914, was one of the composer's favourite works. It is easy to hear why. Firstly, it is packed with attractive thematic ideas—so many, in fact, that one is reminded of Sullivan's good-natured grumble in seeing an exercise by Ethel Smyth: 'An artist is supposed to make a penny do the work of a shilling and here you go chucking sovereigns away for nothing.' Secondly, the scoring is brilliantly effective: the lessons with Ravel had been well and truly assimilated. And finally, the work's structural procedures, while clearly based on traditional form, show a freedom and conviction in handling it that is totally new in English music, the two Elgar symphonies notwithstanding.

Here, for the first time, Vaughan Williams fully faced the problems inherent in adapting 'folk-like' material to the demands of symphonic form. His attempted solution was to break away from purely tonality-based structural procedures in favour of harmonic relationships based on the pentatonic and modal contours of his themes and to apply what he had gained from the harmonic techniques of Debussyan impressionism, especially the use of strings of parallel common chords. It is perhaps worth remembering when alluding to impressionism that from 1870 onwards, London (and particularly the Thames at Westminster) became a favourite subject for Claude Monet: he produced some ninety paintings of London scenes. *A London Symphony*, especially its opening, its slow movement, and its close, to say nothing of its scherzo and the beginning of the recapitulation of its first movement, is in effect a vivid translation into musical terms of a Monet exhibition with London as its theme.

Vaughan Williams was a Londoner by inclination and by residence if not by birth. He came from a family of Londoners; but neither the fact that he himself was born in a west-country vicarage nor the fact that his father was born in London has the remotest bearing on the success or failure of *A London Symphony* as a symphonic design. Such failings as it may possess are due to the composer's imagination, not to his pedigree. And as with *A Sea Symphony*, the shortcomings relate mainly to the shape of the finale. Some time after its first successful performance, the composer made extensive cuts in this movement, deleting what he called a 'Methody' tune[4] and generally tightening up its structure. He further revised the work at various stages later in his career, mainly in matters of detail connected with the scoring. Its diffuseness, when considered from the conventional viewpoint, may possibly derive from the fact that it was originally intended as a kind of tone-poem and that material which started out with a programmatic or at any rate illustrative intent did not quite fit together well when the programme was suppressed. Consider it, however, not as a Brahmsian or even a Mahlerian symphonic essay, but as an attempt to create something recognizably symphonic in terms of impressionist scoring and harmonic procedures, and most of the difficulties evaporate.

The work begins with a phrase based on a rising fourth, which works its way upwards into a shadowy tune over the chimes of Big Ben, eventually dissolving into a kind of trill, as if the sun were rising out of the most over the gently flowing Thames; and after a quick crescendo, the 'Allegro risoluto' breaks in to a theme that applies Debussy's exploitation of consecutive triads in a manner much more ruthless and with

---

[4] Communication to the author from the late Sir Adrian Boult.

the intervals between them considerably more chromatic than Debussy himself was usually inclined to adopt. The sheer exuberance with which the short, pithy motifs follow one another, building up into themes and then into large musical paragraphs, also shows a calculatedly impressionistic approach to first-movement form. The basic pattern of a sonata movement is there, but the functions of each theme do not conform to conventional usage. There is no firm statement of tonality, followed by a decisive move towards establishing a new key, for example, such as even Elgar found it expedient to adopt particularly in the second of his symphonies. Vaughan Williams had already provided a warning of what was to be his attitude to standard harmonic procedures in his introduction, where the interplay of the parts at one stage gives rise to a dominant seventh chord that is not resolved in the conventional manner: the parts simply continue on their melodic way regardless of the traditional harmonic implications of their movement. The chord is used impressionistically in its own right, not as a cadential or modulatory pivot.

The themes themselves are fragmentary and evocative, like fleeting snapshot images of lively London street activity. One may sound like an impatient cabby; another like a group of sailors singing a shanty; yet another like a street-urchin whistling, but common to them all is a sense of bustle and vigour and an unrelenting momentum. This exposition does not get bogged down in lyrical wallowing at the appearance of the 'second subject': the music relaxes in mood, but it does not lose its onward drive and have to undergo artificial respiration through some starkly aggressive rhythmic gesture to set it on its course again. It is in the development section that the lyric potential of the themes is fully revealed. The 'shanty' (if it may be called so) becomes a new, airy, lyrical theme on the flute, interwoven with reminiscences of the music of the introduction; and a theme merely hinted at in the exposition expands into a self-contained episode. The core of the movement, in fact, is not the bustle of London's streets and docklands, but the quiet of its squares and parks, or of the city viewed from afar. The pace slackens and the mood becomes intimate and reflective, yet the underlying onward course of the music never falters, so that Vaughan Williams finds it perfectly logical to recapitulate in hushed, poetic tones what had originally sounded brash, harsh, and even intimidating in his exposition. The grand climax at the end is reinforced in the recapitulation by combining the clinching theme with itself in augmentation (a possible respectful nod in the direction of Brahms's *German Requiem*, where this procedure is used more than once, though it should not be forgotten that Henry Purcell was also fond of this technique).

The slow movement (said to have been inspired in part by Bloomsbury Square on a November afternoon) opens in a thoroughly characteristic manner with string chords into which is projected a cor anglais solo marked 'misterioso'. The clothes may belong to Antonin Dvořák, but the mood is unmistakably that of Ralph Vaughan Williams. The cor anglais tune, later taken up by the strings and followed by a highly emotive episode where fragments of theme arise out of a throbbing string background, is not a folk-song, but it is first cousin to several: 'I will give my love an apple', for example. Perhaps the most beautiful section of all in this arrestingly beautiful movement is the intimate and poetic coda, where the main theme and the lavender-seller's cry, first heard on an unaccompanied solo viola, that has been used as a contrast to it are recalled in quick succession before the movement finally fades as if in the autumn twilight.

In the Scherzo, fragments of theme continually loom out of a shimmering orchestral haze: the scoring shows a high degree of imagination, for the haze is the result of a deliberate choice of soft instrumental timbres. Moreover, the careful spacing and the volatile figuration ensures that it is never thick or lumpy. In all respects, this is possibly the most impressionistic orchestral movement that Vaughan Williams had composed yet. It is entitled 'Nocturne', but there is nothing of the limpid elegance of a Chopin night-piece here. All is bustle and perky vitality: there is a profusion of themes, unified by thematic cross-references. Some of them consist of a head and a tail which are interchanged with the heads and tails of other themes; the basic quick quaver rhythm is allowed to expand from 6/8 to 9/8 and back again, and one theme is stretched out in augmentation and treated in imitation in forceful semi-fugato as a first trio section. There is no relaxation of the onward surge until the second trio, a brilliantly imaginative evocation of cockney street-musicians with mouth-organ and barrel-organ. The condensed final recapitulation and the poignantly reflective coda hint at a sadness beneath the surface of the cheery nocturnal glitter.

The impassioned wail that opens the finale leads to a solemn processional march. Vaughan Williams's use of march rhythms is highly personal and characteristic, just as Elgar's, Mahler's, or Britten's is. This one is sombre in mood and is repeated with different scoring as if for emphasis; and it leads into a hectic Allegro not unlike the dance of Death, Famine, and Pestilence in *Job* but without the macabre element so prominent in that movement. The style here is strangely at odds with the sureness of touch shown so far throughout the symphony. There is a not wholly convincing blend of chromatic filling-out with modal and pentatonic melodic ideas when the music finally builds up to a grandiose Brucknerian climax after the processional march has been recapitulated. But as in *A Sea Symphony*, it is the quiet epilogue (with a further reference to the Westminster chimes) that has the last word. This time, the chimes recede across the ebbing Thames tide instead of building up to a huge awakening of the great city: 'all that mighty heart is lying still'. Vaughan Williams told Michael Kennedy[5] that the ending arose out of

[5] Kennedy, *Works* 2, p. 139.

a reading of the end of H. G. Wells's *Tono Bungay*: 'The river passes, London passes, England passes.' The England of 1914 did indeed pass; and Vaughan Williams's next symphony was to show how its passing affected him.

Until the composer revealed that the idea of *Pastoral Symphony*, first performed under Adrian Boult at Queen's Hall on 26 January 1922, had come to him when on military service in Northern France, it was always assumed to be quintessentially English. Constant Lambert, for example, who recognized its quality while remaining unsympathetic to its moods and style, remarked:

> . . . it is clearly difficult to appreciate either the mood or the form of the *Pastoral Symphony* without being temperamentally attuned to the cool greys and greens, the quietly luxuriant detail, the unemphatic undulation of the English scene. Beautiful as this work is, one feels that it is too direct a transcription of a local mood and that the material has not undergone that process of mental digestion, as it were, which can make the particular into a symbol of the whole . . . [6]

Yet he was also aware that Vaughan Williams had achieved something in a different league from that aspired to by the nationalist composers of the nineteenth century:

> Unlike so many composers, notably Brahms, with whom the creation of musical material and its subsequent treatment appear to be two separate mental processes, Vaughan Williams nearly always evolves his form from the implications of the melody and rarely submits his themes to a Procrustean development . . . The form of the *Pastoral Symphony* follows logically enough from the material, but hardly achieves either the contrast or sense of progression that is usually associated with symphonic form, and is the essential feature of classical symphonic writing.[7]

It is strange that it did not occur to so perceptive, widely-read, and brilliantly witty a musician that it is precisely the classical dramatic symphonic 'contrast or sense of progression' that Vaughan Williams was eschewing here in favour of a quietly revolutionary attitude to form, harmony, and symphonic ethos. The composer is not projecting either a human or an abstract conflict, as much as the almost imperceptible changes in a landscape that was in fact the dispassionate backcloth to the most cataclysmic human conflict known up till that time.

Pastoral Symphony is the least frequently performed of all Vaughan Williams's symphonies; and the reasons are surely those that caused Lambert to criticize it as a musical entity. It does seem at first hearing to lack contrast, but this is an illusion caused by the gentle pace of change within the work. Contrast is there; a sense of progression is

---

[6] Constant Lambert, *Music Ho! A Study of Music in Decline* (Faber & Faber, 1934) (hereafter Lambert), pp. 108–9. All quotations are from the Penguin Books edition of 1948.
[7] Lambert, loc. cit.

there; and the work is genuinely symphonic in the sense that certain more popular 'fabricated' post-Romantic symphonies are not. Any listener wishing to prove that there is a sense of progression need only track the work on a CD player, putting the scherzo first, the first movement immediately afterwards, the finale third and the slow movement last—and hear what havoc he wreaks with Vaughan Williams's finely-balanced design. Ottaway writes of its mood as being detached and utterly absorbed (which runs counter to Lambert's comment that the material has not undergone a process of mental digestion: it has). The gently elegiac mood of particularly the second movement has a rapt yet eerie remoteness, that looks back to parts of *On Wenlock Edge* and forward to the Vaughan Williams of the post-1945 years.

It is not an easy work to come to terms with. Scored for a large orchestra, it neither glitters nor wells up in sumptuous sound. But even a first impression is one of haunting power and immense subtlety. Vaughan Williams applies his musical impressionism consistently and in his own way, even submitting the block-consecutive-chord technique of Debussy to contrapuntal treatment. The scoring is masterly throughout, though never spectacular. The first dozen bars or so are typical, with their frequent and almost imperceptible changes of tone-colour and wonderfully thought-out instrumental combinations—the change from bassoon to clarinet as the bass-line to the flutes in bar 3, or the little splash of harp colour when the solo fiddle enters, for example. And it is interesting that the full orchestra, for all its size, is not employed until five bars after letter E in the third movement.

In much twentieth-century music, composers are self-consciously at pains to rub in the dissonance of their work through the rhythm, the scoring, and the dynamics. Vaughan Williams himself was certainly no exception to this, as his later symphonies amply demonstrate. The use of dissonance either to create momentary tension or to arouse expectancy is one of the oldest devices in Western music. Here, dissonance is used quietly, unostentatiously, almost absent-mindedly. The dissonances slip into and out of the texture, as if taking one another for granted. An example of this is the A in the horn solo at the beginning of the second movement against the A flat in the F minor chord held by the strings. Others could be cited. Yet conversely, some of the most striking dissonant effects in the work are caused by chains of unrelated consonant triads. Vaughan Williams's use of the triad in *Pastoral Symphony* is the direct antithesis of classical academic procedure. Each note of a given theme, as Tovey pointed out half a century ago, is often loaded with its own triad; and the interplay of the lines of triads creates a kaleidoscope not just of interwoven themes, but of interwoven lines of block chords. A vertical 'slice' through the harmony at many points produces some remarkable dissonant combinations, yet neither the dissonances nor the consonances play any part in a dramatic tonal scheme.

193

Instead, the themes unfold from one another in a kind of purposeful drift, changing function and relationship as they do so. An example of this occurs at the very beginning, with the change in the flowing opening chords from flutes to clarinets. Later on in the movement (at about letter Q) these chords form the bass of the harmony for the first time. No theme, no phrase even, has a predominant function: each in turn makes its appearance and then slips quietly in among its neighbours. There is no rhetoric, but simply contemplation; and in 1922, a meditative first movement in a symphony for large orchestra was something quite new.

The genesis of one particular episode in the slow movement is a wartime experience of Vaughan Williams's: a bugler practising and hitting the seventh partial instead of the octave. This is the most arresting feature of the movement, heard first in an unmeasured phrase for the natural trumpet and at the end of the movement for the natural horn. The first time it occurs, the trumpet is marked *pp*, the accompaniment on the strings is an E flat major triad and the music swells up into a passionate outburst on the full orchestra (except for the trombones and percussion, who are not used in this movement). It is as if some huge cosmic force were trying in rage and frustration to unleash its power. The trumpet's final B flat is taken over by the first violins as an inverted pedal against which the rest of the orchestra hurls itself for two bars before the strings resolve from an F minor added sixth chord on to a chord of E flat minor, while the outburst itself dies away to a whimper on the wood-wind. The second time the passage occurs, it is barred, not freely declaimed, and constitutes one melodic strand with a counterpoint on the clarinet, a variant of the movement's main theme, which flows independently round it against a background of slowly-descending common chords on the strings in a whole-tone scale: F, E flat, D flat, C flat. This dies away, leaving the horn exposed on a high C natural—a typical 'fourth symphony' dissonance, only we do not notice it as such—which dissolves into a flowing chordal passage of minor triads on the violins that dies away to nothing. Ottaway[8] comments: 'At the close the violins (*ppp*) rise high above the stave—towards what? Certainly not blessedness.' It is possible that human figures flit across the landscape in the third movement, but more likely that the cosmic remoteness of the earlier movements has simply shaped itself into a more urgent rhythmic pattern. If this is a dance, it is surely a dance of the elements rather than the ballet of oufs and fairies from which it apparently evolved. There is no sense here of Beethovenian peasants making merry, nor even of their English cousins. The rhythmic pattern of the very first bar, with its triplet quavers on the first beat slowed down by the imitation of the theme in straight quavers a quaver later, creates an unexpected tension

[8] Ottaway, p. 27.

that is maintained at the 'poco animato' section a few bars later, with the brass playing in a straight 3/4 against the 9/8 of the strings. Only the bright-toned trumpet tune in what corresponds to the trio section seems to have something human about it; certainly the will-o'-the-wisp flute theme—hardly more than an ostinato with delicately scored accompaniment—and the Arielesque coda, the logical outcome of the other themes of the movement, inhabit a landscape that is remote from normal humanity.

The remoteness is enhanced, paradoxically enough, when the wordless soprano voice is heard at the beginning of the finale—another unbarred melismatic phrase, supported only by a drum-roll on A. This may be compared with, though it bears little resemblance to, the opening of the Sibelius E minor Symphony, in which a clarinet performs much the same role. But the Sibelius is plaintive and forms a reservoir of thematic material for a good deal of the main part of the first movement; it also recurs in intensified form in the finale. Vaughan Williams's solo, it is true, is also thematic in that it recurs in the main course of the movement, forms the basis of the most impassioned climax in the finale—unsupported by any harmony save a momentary flash of B flat major in the trumpets and first trombone (against a modal E minor)—and recurs, simplified, slightly altered in rhythmic shape and with its opening phrase omitted, at the very end of the piece, under the clear blue sky (Tovey's phrase) of a high A on the violins. Michael Kennedy sums up well the effect of this strange incursion of a disembodied human voice into the scene: 'The result is unbearably poignant, like a lament for the flowers of the forest cut down in the 1914–18 war; yet the grief is somehow transcended and becomes more cosmic than personal without losing intensity.'[9] The strings outline what is shortly to become the first theme of the main movement, but it is a false start. They stretch upwards to a very high C right at the end of the fingerboard and their tentative gropings take shape as a theme not unlike the big tune from Holst's 'Jupiter', but more solemn and far less exuberant. Here indeed is what Elgar in a different context referred to a 'stately sorrow'—and, interestingly enough, the tempo indication and the metronome marking are close to that of the finale of the Elgar E flat Symphony. In fact, the movement, with its consolatory second theme, almost sounds at times as if Hubert Parry rather than Vaughan Williams had been taking lessons with Ravel: the stately onward tidal surge of the music is something quite different from, but certainly not out of keeping with the preceding three movements. The surface of the landscape has been ruffled (there are moments when the music reminds one of birds calling to their mates before a storm), yet there is no rhetoric about the turbulence; the disturbance is episodic, not dramatic. The work finally fades away in the

[9] Kennedy, *Works* 2, p. 171.

calm, not of a struggle brought to a successful or satisfying conclusion, but in a remote ending where the glimmering landscape simply fades upon the sight 'And all the air a solemn stillness holds'. The opening of Vaughan Williams's next symphony was to form the completest contrast imaginable to this poignantly elegiac ending.

16

Symphonies (4–6)

Like the first three of his symphonies, Vaughan Williams's Fourth, Fifth, and Sixth may also be considered as a group. He himself did not consciously design them so, nor did he himself number them; he simply designated them by a key signature. It is customary and convenient, however, to refer to them by number rather than key. The sheer power, concentration, cogency of argument and stylistic unity of all three, together with the fact that one of them contains material that was composed for and later worked into *The Pilgrim's Progress* has led to each of them being related to extra-musical factors. Sir Adrian Boult, who conducted the first performance of both the Fourth and the Sixth, said of the former: 'He foresaw the whole thing', by which he meant the rise of totalitarian ideologies and the outbreak of the Second World War. Vaughan Williams dismissed this idea in a letter to his friend R. G. Longman in December 1937: 'I wrote it not as a definite picture of anything external—e.g. the state of Europe—but simply because it occurred to me like this . . . '[1] Likewise, Frank Howes unhesitatingly related the Sixth to war in general and the possible consequences of a nuclear war in particular—and was sharply and publicly rebuked by Vaughan Williams for so doing. The composer himself always forcefully rejected any such 'interpretations' of his music; he thought it must stand or fall on its merits as a musical design.

One respects this viewpoint, yet it totally begs the question as to *why* 'it occurred . . . like this' to the composer, even if all three of these symphonies most emphatically do stand rather than fall on their structural merits. William Walton, who had attended rehearsals of the F minor, told Arthur Benjamin on the way to the Queen's Hall that they were going to hear the greatest symphony since Beethoven; and Deryck Cooke's powerfully argued analysis of the E minor in *The Language of Music* shows it to be as taut a musical structure as the great Mozart G minor, to which he applies the same rigorous method of analysis.

Sensitive analytical commentators such as Cooke, Michael Kennedy, and Hugh Ottaway have pointed out that no composer writing music

---

[1] Kennedy, *Works* 2, p. 247.

with such a powerful emotive charge can evade the non-musical issues that his music raises through its sheer quality and intensity; and the fact remains that after listening to any of these three masterpieces, the sympathetic listener is aware first and foremost of the emotional experience—bombardment would possibly be a better term when referring to the F minor and E minor symphonies—to which he or she has been subjected. This is so whether, as Ursula Vaughan Williams has suggested, the former resembles a Rembrandt portrait done in middle age (Elizabeth Trevelyan wrote to the composer after hearing the work saying that she found a most exciting contrast between his 'poisonous temper' in the Scherzo and the 'lovable opening' of the Trio), or whether, as the composer himself told Michael Kennedy,[2] one could get nearest in words to the substance of the last movement of the E minor by bearing in mind Shakespeare's lines from *The Tempest*: 'We are such stuff / As dreams are made on, and our little life / Is rounded with a sleep.' It is worth noting, too, that in his essay on Beethoven's Ninth Symphony, Vaughan Williams could not avoid using similes when trying to explain the effect of certain passages on the listener, even though similes were as far as he was prepared to go:

> Now the secret is out, D minor is the key, and like a bare mountain-side suddenly seen bleak and grey through a rift in the fog, the principal theme appears, a great unison arpeggio, gloomy in its stark nakedness . . . [3]

or

> But we shall meet that little phrase again when its full tragic importance will be seen. Even so Anna Karenina met the little Moujik of her dream and he said the seemingly meaningless word at the tragic climax of her story[4]

and

> What is the meaning of this stupendous passage? It stands apart, alone and unexplained, like Stonehenge on the Wiltshire Downs. Its isolation is in no way affected by the technical fact that it is built up on the opening bar of the theme.[5]

It should be clear from these quotations alone that the emotive charge of a sequence of black dots on paper did affect and matter to Vaughan Williams, though he himself was careful—and right—not to relate that emotive charge to specific events, either in his own work or in that of other composers.

None of these three symphonies was the result of a direct commission, so it is arguable that the composer was subject to some kind of intense internal pressure that helped shape them, whether or not that pressure was brought on by a reaction to external events. Ottaway, Kennedy, and

[2] Kennedy, *Works* 2, p. 302.   [3] *National Music*, p. 93.   [4] Ibid., p. 98.
[5] Ibid., p. 110.

Cooke are surely right when they argue or infer that any composer setting down music of such power and depth can rightly claim, like Mahler, that he was not composing, he was *being composed*.

The F minor Symphony simmered for some years in the composer's mind before it was completed and performed on 10 April 1935. Both work and composer were greeted with applause that one newspaper described as 'almost without parallel at Queen's Hall'; and the work was quite rightly seen as a new departure. New, but not unprecedented: works such as *Sancta Civitas*, the Piano Concerto, and above all *Job* should have alerted critics to the broadening and deepening of Vaughan Williams's idiom that had steadily taken place during the decade and more that separated the new symphony from its predecessor. Here a Brucknerian weight and majesty were allied to a Brahmsian dourness and a Beethovenian intensity and drive—all blended with an English no-nonsense bluntness and directness.

The F minor was the first of Vaughan Williams's symphonies not to have a descriptive title attached to it. It was the first not to contain any expressive solo violin passages. It was the first not to end with a reflective pianissimo epilogue. Coming as it did after the *Pastoral*, and after the longest gap in time between any two of his symphonies, its brusqueness was all the more of a shock. Yet on closer inspection there are points of similarity which indicate that both works are recognizably from the same hand.

The points of contrast are obvious enough. Whereas in the *Pastoral* every move is measured and deliberate, in the Fourth, the giant strides are swift and relentless. The *Pastoral* ruminates calmly and in remote, at times impassive mystery. Nothing every seems to 'happen' in the conventional sense. The Fourth impatiently hurls all obstacles out of the way. Things 'happen' all the time; and even when the music sinks into an exhausted calm, there is still tension not far below the surface. The rhythms of the *Pastoral* flow gently; those of the Fourth either pour forth in a volcanic stream or cavort in an ungainly caper. The orchestral texture of the *Pastoral* is gently and unobtrusively subtle. That of the Fourth is for the most part harsh to the point of brutality, sometimes tinged with an element of the grotesque. Yet as in the *Pastoral*, the composer more than once achieves that brooding, elevated remoteness that is so unmistakably his own. It is, by the way, an illuminating comment on the way attitudes to scoring were changing in the later 1930s that two young musicians later to be renowned for their own undoubted command of the orchestra, Benjamin Britten and Lennox Berkeley, studied the score and found plenty to mock in what they considered its clumsiness. This is remarkable in that perhaps of all Vaughan Williams's symphonies, the Fourth is the one in which he demonstrates the greatest economy of means, in both his exploitation of musical material and his scoring.

The layout of the orchestra shows a development in Vaughan Williams's musical outlook. For the first time in one of his symphonies, there are no harps. Neither is there a part for celesta or glockenspiel. The woodwind are often used in blocks as well as in expressive solo lines winding in and out of the texture. The scoring of much of this symphony, in fact, gives the impression that the woodwind are there only on sufferance, so much of the punch and power of the music comes from the volcanic brass and the blazing intensity of the string writing. In reality, the woodwind have a most important role to play, particularly in the two middle movements. Yet such solos as there are, particularly in the slow movement, have an air of desolation rather than serenity, or, in the third movement, or sardonic humour and perky snook-cocking, even when marked 'cantabile', rather than what had become fixed in people's minds as characteristic Vaughan Williamsy contemplation. This kind of scoring is not the result of incompetence, but because 'it occurred to [him] like this'. The Fourth is scored as it is because the tone and texture of the musical argument demand the type of rugged sound that Vaughan Williams's orchestra here produces. Moreover, it was one of the last works to which Vaughan Williams and Holst were able to devote a series of 'field days' together; and it is hardly likely that they did not discuss at some stage the most effective orchestral garb in which to clothe such a torrent of powerful ideas.

On a first hearing, it might seem that the Fourth is almost a reaction against the *Pastoral*. In fact it is nothing of the kind. The harmonic texture of the *Pastoral* is often so unobtrusively dissonant that were the dissonances to be rubbed in by rescoring any passage in the manner of the Fourth, playing it fortissimo, intensifying the sharpness of the rhythm, and accelerating the tempo (a singularly philistine procedure) the resultant effect would be not far off that produced by the Fourth. They are manifestly from the same hand; and it is a sign of the composer's Protean personality that they sound so utterly different and create such a different impact. The manner in which the themes evolve from one another—in the *Pastoral* from modal and pentatonic melodic lines; and in the Fourth from the two terse and craggy germinal motifs that underlie every significant theme in the work—is very similar. In the *Pastoral* the evolution is similar to the gentle unfolding of a plant; in the Fourth, it sounds more like a chain reaction giving off new material with almost frightening rapidity under enormous pressure. If anyone doubts the sheer intensity of this music, the composer's own recording of it, far harder driven and more massive in its effect than that of any professional conductor, should soon put matters right.

The pregnant germinal mottoes (one is almost tempted to call them micro tone-rows, because of their significance in the work's structure) have nothing to do with folk-song. One is based on the three notes E, F, and G flat in the order F, E, G flat, F. The other consists of two rising fourths and a minor third: F, B flat, E flat, and again G flat. The first motif itself is generated by the grinding semitonal clash of the opening— C against D flat. In other words, the tremendous opening is actually on the dominant of the main key, which is properly achieved only at the counter-statement of the opening. As early as the fourth bar, the tele-scoping of the original rhythm in the bass to two equal dotted minims instead of a five-plus-one combination of tied dotted minim and minim plus one crotchet begins to wind up the tension. In fact a rhythmic analysis of the first twenty bars or so of this movement (from the begin-ning to the counterstatement in the tonic at bars 19/20) lays bare a resourcefulness that is concealed by the composer's refusal to re-bar the metre every time there is a change of rhythmic emphasis. Syncopations, rhythmic foreshortenings and expansions, cross-rhythmed hemiola (with a distinct feel of 'Satan's Dance of Triumph' about it), and abrupt changes of harmonic direction all contribute to a seething turmoil of conflicting rhythms within a steady onward metrical thrust.

It is part of the 'ethos' of the Symphony that these clashes should result in a kind of rhythmic traffic jam; and at the Meno mosso section, the 6/4 metre gives way to one of 3/2 and the impassioned second main theme (a torrid extension and expansion of elements of both the motto motifs) emerges, with its Tchaikovskian scoring of a string cantabile in octaves against a background of throbbing wind and brass chords also derived from the basic material. It may be scored in a Tchaikovskian manner, but apart from its intensity of emotion, it doesn't sound remotely like Tchaikovsky. The way in which it evolves by varying its melodic curve and its rhythmic outline phrase by phrase is very charac-teristic. What is new is the way that the music erupts from one phrase to the next, the bass line see-sawing back and forth in asymmetrical rhythm: B flat, D flat, B flat, A flat. The long-limbed melody descends into the bass and eventually collapses back on to its own first three notes, which form an ostinato background to a very grim theme as near horizontal in shape as a theme can be, a bitter blossom from the stem of the first motto motif, nagging away in an attempt to break away from the F sharp on which it starts. It is punctuated from time to time by a motif on the brass derived from the first three notes of the lyrical theme. There is hardly a moment's respite from this flood of musical lava until the beginning of the working-out section, as the 'official analyst', a favourite butt of Vaughan Williams's scorn, might have called it. The tension, however, remains high, as the strings start up a mysterious tremolo based on the motif which chases its own tail. Gradually a gal-lumphing 6/4 rhythm takes over until it dominates the dialogue between violins and upper wind and brass on the one hand and the lower instru-ments and percussion on the other. Then the pent-up fourths of the other basic motif lead back to the reprise. The impact of the storm is doubled by the formal treatment: the lyrical theme is forced into canon with itself. The great surprise, however, is left until the very end, when the 'grim' theme re-appears, quietly whispered. Ottaway[6] points this up as a Vaughan Williams epilogue passage; and so it is, but the calm is of exhaustion after an intense struggle, not a vision of the field of conflict seen *sub specie aeternitatis*.

The slow movement turns its back on violence; but for all that, there is no balm in Gilead. It begins with more piled-up fourths, out of which a figure is generated that turns out to be an important constituent in the movement's main theme. It is immediately used in augmentation in the bass line as a kind of ostinato phrase and becomes one of the backbone features of the movement: a terrible reminder of the potential for brutality as well as resolution behind the power and confidence of the striding *Sine Nomine* type bass. The mournful tune that rises bleakly in loneliness above it in the first violins is notable for its persistent A and B naturals, while the bass studiously avoids either A or B, flat or natural, otherwise keeping firmly to a kind of D flat major—or at any rate a tetrachord C, D flat, E flat, F. Only when the seconds and the violas are about to take up the main theme does the 'scale' expand, and then only to a transposition of the ostinato into a kind of F major. The course of the movement is dominated by a relentless tension between the almost martial forcefulness and weight of the bass and the weary pathos of the melodic themes above it that culminates in yet another pile-up of fourths on the heavy brass, against which a phrase taken from the second main theme of the movement batters in the strings. Such moments of repose as there are are relegated to cadence themes, imitative passages, or the gradual dissolution of the music towards the end of the movement, held together only by the first of the two motto motifs on the muted heavy brass, in a menacing whisper and as a group of *sostenuto* chords. The final flute solo is inconclusive—even the composer hesitated for a very long time after the work was published before finally deciding that it should end on an E instead of the original F.

The resolution—on to a D—comes with the opening of the Scherzo, which bursts like a bomb on the startled listener. The upward explosion of fourths, one upon another, builds up a theme that is oddly similar in shape, though certainly not in mood, to the ghostly, attenuated 'Mannheim rocket' of the third movement of Beethoven's Fifth, but which is plainly a variant of the second of the basic mottoes. In no time this 'Leith Hill rocket' has thrust its way through two-and-a-half octaves before its irresistible force meets an immovable object in the shape of the other basic motto, which immediately works itself into an ostinato against which the Scherzo-theme in varying guises hurls itself almost as if in desperation. Finding itself blocked, it kicks out in a jerky rhythmic figure containing a re-ordered version of all four notes of the first basic

[6] Ottaway, p. 32.

motto whose rhythm is to become important later; and a new theme asserts itself, a distant cousin of one of the themes in *Till Eulenspiegel* (hardly a work likely to have appealed over-much to Vaughan Williams), but soon developing a will of its own, complete with syncopated downward fourths and fifths and suspensions that now hold the rhythm back and now thrust it forward. The bucolic trio, an angular fugato (again the parallel with Beethoven's Fifth is noteworthy) on yet another theme with prominent fourths in it, does bring some relaxation. As the theme lurches upward through the orchestra, its grotesqueness subsides into a comic caper on the flute and piccolo, with the violins and oboes providing a background that starts out as a descending scale but soon reverts to sequences of descending fourths. The lead-back into the Scherzo is abrupt and startling; and at the end of the movement, the jerky rhythmic figure mutters in the background while the strings—as in the parallel passage in Beethoven's Fifth—tentatively whisper an outline of the motto based on fourths. There is a quick crescendo based on the other basic motto and the finale is upon us: a strident march, whose main theme, according to the composer, is a reincarnation of the lyrical cadence-theme from the second movement.

All the main themes in the finale are cousins to one or other of the motto-motifs: a prominent feature of each is either a dropping semitone or a leap of a fourth. The 'second subject' sounds like a bad-tempered folk-song—Frank Howes[7] likens it to the kind of song that a simple-minded pirate might whistle—and later on in the movement, its rhythm modified, it sounds suspiciously like a parody of a phrase from the soldier-song 'Mademoiselle from Armentières'. Some of the themes of the finale would seem to have been after-thoughts, for in a letter to Holst at the time of the composition of the work, Vaughan Williams mentions replacing the 'made-up' tunes with 'real' ones. The pace is still hectic, though the mood is possibly more relaxed, in a savage sort of way, than that of the other movements.

The climax of the main part of the movement, however, is once again a quiet passage—what ought to be the expected visionary coda, reaching out towards some new unknown region. Here, however, it is savagely dismissed. The tension is stepped up in the recapitulation and reaches its peak in the electrifying epilogue, which begins as a fugato on the semitonal motto motif and throws in both the main themes of the finale as counter-subjects for good measure, casting a new and even more lurid light on them. When the tension has become almost intolerable, the final *coup de grâce* is delivered by a completely unexpected reference to the opening of the first movement. The listener has just time to realize that all that has gone before can be directly related to that cataclysm, when the music simply stops abruptly on an open fifth. One

---

[7] Frank Howes, *The Music of Ralph Vaughan Williams* (OUP, 1954), p. 39.

of the tightest musical arguments in the history of the art has come full circle. 'There! That's all I have to say about that', Vaughan Williams seems to say, 'Take it or leave it.'

Just over eight years separated the first performance of the F minor Symphony from the D major; and again the stark contrast between the two seems to smack of a deliberate reaction against the earlier work. Actually, it is once more nothing of the kind. Kennedy calls this the 'symphony of the celestial city'; and the term is apt, particularly as the composer admitted at the time of its first performance that it contains material from the then unfinished opera *The Pilgrim's Progress*.[8] Once again, the scoring fits the material superbly: gone is the stridency and harshness of the F minor; there is instead a luminous fullness about it, even when only a few instruments are being used, that marks it off from the *Pastoral*, to which it bears no superficial resemblance. Once again the orchestra is pared: no harps, no percussion save the timpani, only two horns, and no tuba.

The very opening is one of Vaughan Williams's most striking examples of giving a new meaning to an old device. The octave Cs on the cellos and basses (see Ex. 12a) with which the work opens sound like a dominant seventh, when the horns enter in D major (Ex. 12b) and are answered by the violins with a pentatonic theme in G (Ex. 12c). But is it? Ottaway (to whose excellent BBC Music Guide monograph the reader is referred for a fuller, more technical analysis) argues convincingly that the key centre is in fact D, first a Mixolydian major and then a Dorian minor. The ending of the work as a whole is unequivocally in D; and though there is no sense of Mahlerian or Nielsenian progressive tonality, the music is a kind of harmonic pilgrimage from distant, slightly hazy modal glory to glowing tonal certainty. The music seems, as Scott Goddard remarked soon after the work first came out, to have been going on underground beforehand, and the flat seventh is part of the tonality—or rather the modality—of the movement. The key centre is D, not G. The movement seems to be proceeding in the most leisurely manner possible, yet in fact by the end of the sixth bar, the three main constituents of the thematic material of the whole of the first section of the movement have already been aired and by the eighth, the intrusion of an F natural in the clarinet part has changed the mode—and the mood. This first section of the movement actually sub-divides still further. A section in a definite E major introduces a new theme, part of whose outline derives from the cellos' and basses' opening phrase and which is to crown the climax of the movement. It is, in fact, the translation into symphonic terms of the triumphant Alleluia from *Sine Nomine*.

[8] Parts of this symphony were tried out in Vaughan Williams's contribution to the music for military band and chorus for the pageant *England's Pleasant Land*, performed at Westcott, Surrey, in July 1938.

Ex. 12

The central part of the movement is heralded by an ambiguous semi-tonal switch that turns out to be an important three-note thematic frag-ment (Ex. 12d). It is projected in the wind against the theme that has developed in the strings out of the cello and bass opening. The transi-tion is not just a modification of tempo and key; it grows organically out of the thematic material. In *The Pilgrim's Progress* an identical phrase is associated with words like 'Beelzebub' and 'Away with him' in the Vanity Fair scene of Act III; and it may be assumed that some sym-bolism of a similar kind is intended here—akin, perhaps, to the mysteri-ous 'malign influence on a summer night' that plays so graphic a part in the first and third movements of Elgar's Second Symphony (itself described by its composer as 'the passionate *pilgrimage* of a soul'). An interesting point of orchestration is that at the very climax of the move-ment, where the strings are playing *fff* in octaves for all they are worth, the double basses leave off at the very apex of the phrase, only to rejoin the rest when the dynamic level is reduced. This climax is modal, not tonal, being cast in the Phrygian mode based on the note A; and it leads back into the opening music, with its Mixolydian mode based on D: a masterly blend of tonal and modal patterns, putting old devices ('dom-inant preparation') into a new and arresting context. The original music returns, mounting to a final climax first in B flat major and then in G on the *Sine Nomine* theme, after which the music gradually subsides into the half-light from which it emerged at the beginning of the movement, this time with the violas holding the D a tone above the C of the cellos. The music finishes there, but it does not end.

The Scherzo could hardly be more different from that of the Fourth Symphony, yet like its predecessor, it opens with a chain of rising fourths. This time, however, the device is used in a much more delicate manner than it was in the Fourth; and the hemiola cross-rhythms glide across rather than hurtle against one another. The first change from uni-son or octaves into full harmony does not come until the twenty-second bar of the music, when the parts move in two-part canon for a few bars, with the second violins filling in the harmonies. Out of their harmonic infill, the woodwind develop a tune in irregular phrases that gradually becomes more assertive, even breaking into a staccato falling pattern faintly reminiscent of the Scherzo of the F minor Symphony. The themes are fluid and fragmentary, often implied rather than fully stated, for they follow one another in rapid succession; and both the feather-light scoring and the masterly treatment of the material are a tribute by Vaughan Williams the sturdy hobnail-booted Englishman to Vaughan Williams the impressionist pupil of Ravel. The 'trio', if it can be called such, consists of a kind of fragmentary chorale in the brass, interspersed with champings in the strings; and there is a bipartite coda, in which a little phrase of one of the Scherzo themes is altered and expanded into a theme in its own right, rather in the manner of the coda of the parallel movements in Brahms's Second or Dvořák's Eighth symphonies, before the original metre and themes are resumed and the movement vanishes into the mist like a will-o'-the-wisp.

The third movement, Romanza, is one of those supreme movements that give the listener the sense that time has been suspended and that seem to hover in space without any reference to its passage. Their serenity and profound clarity mark out their composers as belonging to the few transcendentally great masters of all time. If ever a movement deserved the term 'heavenly', this music surely does. Yet the serenity is not the wishful thinking of escapism: the underlying tensions still erupt from time to time; and they erupt logically from the course of the music.

As in *A London Symphony*, there is an introductory phrase of long, slow chords, this time spread over an immense span in the strings, divided into no fewer than sixteen parts, against which is projected a tune on the cor anglais. The combination of an expressive melody and a simple yet subtle background of carefully juxtaposed triads (C major, A major, G minor, A major), the spaciousness and depth of the texture, the immensely quiet dynamic—each constituent adds something to the total effect of this outstandingly beautiful opening. But it is not just the serene hush of the opening that strikes the listener. There is the unobtrusive introduction and extension of significant material from the first two movements (violas, bars 12–14) which will play an important part in a later stage of the movement. There are the subtle changes of rhythm in the continuation of the theme after it is counterstated in rich unison on the strings. There is the way in which the opening harmonic pattern is transformed into a thematic, or at any rate motivic episode. There is the assured manner in which the music unfolds and the mood changes, working up to an eloquent, almost anguished climax before returning to the serene and luminous mood of the opening, with the cor anglais backed by shimmering string tremolos, only to break out in an intensified version of the anguished cry. And finally, there is the simple masterstroke whereby the final thematic word is left, on a muted horn, with the second strain of the theme, not the first. This is not the place to speak of the function of the material of this movement in *The Pilgrim's*

Progress, for here they are worked out in an abstract symphonic design. The sheer mastery of the movement as it stands is enough.

The Passacaglia finale is unequivocally in D major; yet its barring and the relationship between the ground bass and the equally important counter-melody that is immediately heard against it are both unorthodox. The theme itself is seven bars long, sometimes with overlaps between statements of the theme, so that it is foreshortened to six; and the counter-melody quite happily moves at one stage in consecutive sevenths with it. The stately onward movement of the Passacaglia gradually gathers momentum until it breaks out into the jubilation of the central section, where the Passacaglia theme is transformed into a great, almost Brucknerian paean of exultation. This section later develops at some length the first phrase of the original bass as a jaunty theme in its own right in the woodwind. But the blaze of glory vanishes and the new theme derived from the bass, now in the minor and four in a bar, gradually begins to show its kinship with the falling bass line of the opening of the first movement. The music moves through a kaleidoscope of keys and rhythmic metamorphoses, much being made of a familiar Vaughan Williams triplet figure, until with awesome yet surprising inevitability and fortissimo, a variant of the very opening of the work appears, combining the main motifs of the opening of the prelude and of the finale, and managing to sound like both a triumph and a warning. What had been remote and indeterminate is now projected with all the consuming power of a Turneresque sunrise; and it is this material that dominates the remainder of the movement as the vision gradually fades and the work moves to its tranquil close.

The fifth is not only one of Vaughan Williams's greatest and most economically-laid-out achievements, it was also thought by many when it appeared to be his final word in terms of the symphony. But in April 1948 the BBC Symphony Orchestra under Adrian Boult premièred its successor. It was immediately taken up all over the Western world and achieved almost as many performances as had Elgar's First after its debut. Here, the violence of the Fourth Symphony and the visionary quality of the Fifth are wedded, resulting in one of the most disquieting works in the entire symphonic repertory. The conductor Andrew Davis, listening to a playback of the slow movement when recording the work, was simply reduced to shaking his head and commenting 'Horrible, horrible!', not in criticism of the playing, the recording, or of the musical craftsmanship, but of the intense nihilism and brutality of the score.[9] It is as if the composer had arrived in the Unknown Region and found it an uninhabited and meaningless desert.

Whether or not any extra-musical stimulus, such as a warning about the consequences of atomic warfare, or an inner personal crisis of some

[9] See p. 4 of Christopher Palmer's sleeve-note to the Teldec recording by Davis and the BBC Symphony Orchestra in their 'British Line' series (903173127-2).

kind led to the creation of this horrendous masterpiece, the work is far from meaningless in terms of tonal, rhythmic, and thematic structure. Indeed, it coheres with an extraordinary and relentless consistency that was brilliantly demonstrated by Deryck Cooke in his masterly essay on the piece in *The Language of Music*.

In the Fourth Symphony, Vaughan Williams worked from what were in effect two micro-tone-rows that conditioned the shape of the themes and the harmonic procedures that he was going to adopt. Here, as Cooke points out, he works from four of the basic items of his musical vocabulary: the opposition of major and minor thirds, the interval of the augmented fourth, a figure that starts on the tonic, rises a third and falls back again, and another figure that falls back from the supertonic on to the tonic. These are given life and drive by various rhythmic devices, such as a nagging, insistent figure of two semiquavers and a quaver that plays an important part in three of the four movements and a combination of restless rhythmic instability and grinding relentlessness that is concealed rather than revealed by Vaughan Williams's refusal to change the barring every time the rhythm changes across or within the bar line. Had he done so, his score would have resembled more than a little one of the more aggressive dances in *Le Sacre du Printemps*.

The certainty of touch that Vaughan Williams shows in his first movement is demonstrated nowhere with greater sureness than in the way in which the whole structure leads up to the noble transformation of the 'second subject' material at the very end of the movement. This theme has been heard in various guises after the initial stampede from the angular opening challenge. A sudden abrupt change of metre leads to a curious fragmentary figure over an 'oom-pah' bass (see Ex. 13a). This is temporarily filled out by the violins into a sort of jolting melody (Ex. 13b) and then tried over in a smoother, more lyrical and more extended form (Ex. 13c) in a kind of B minor. It is heard again shortly afterwards, complete with Scotch snap, blared out on the trumpets and heavy brass. Pushed into the background for a while by the recapitulation of the principal theme, in stretto and without its opening flourish, it finally re-emerges in the shape that it has been seeking all through the movement: in the tonic major and with an effortless lyrical strength. This is one of those moments of sudden revelation which are as difficult to describe as they are thrilling to experience. It is as if the listener has been climbing a vast mountain slope towards a distant and intermittently visible peak, when suddenly the clouds lift and the summit is revealed in all its power and grandeur. The theme is repeated, finally lifting itself up almost casually into the opening flourish of the movement before it collapses onto a valedictory growl from the cellos and basses.

The second movement is a kind of cortège; its nearest relative in English music is perhaps Britten's chilling setting of the Lyke-Wake dirge in the *Serenade*—also composed in the midst of the war, in 1943. There

Ex. 13

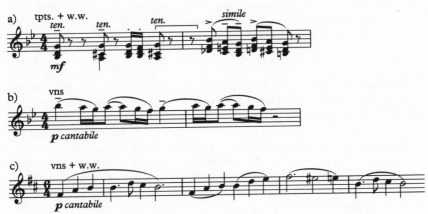

is the same obsessive insistence on a rigid rhythmic drive, the same macabre mood, the same sense of the menace of death in the air. But metrically as opposed to rhythmically, Vaughan Williams's main theme cannot make up its mind where its main stress should fall, nor can it decide whether C flat or C natural is the correct inflection of the key of B flat minor. The leap of an augmented fourth from the tonic of the first movement to that of the second (all the movements are connected to one another) is the first of a series of shocks which this movement is to inflict on the listener. As in the first movement, the steady unyielding barring is misleading. The continual cross-rhythms give the movement the effect of an insecure 3/4 rather than the nominal 4/4. The prominent rhythmic kick of the main theme fluctuates between an opening on its quaver and one on its semiquavers. But the most prominent feature of the movement, and the one that those who heard the first performance can still remember after nearly half a century, is the passage in which the trumpets and drums insistently repeat the latter version of this rhythm. If the Romanza of the Fifth sublimated time into timeless time, this batters time mercilessly into a feeling of brutal everlasting recurrence. If the close of the work has any sense of our little life being rounded with a sleep, this movement surely depicts a sleep of which it is true to consider: ' . . . what dreams may come / When we have shuffled off this mortal coil, / Must give us pause.' It is a nightmare mental landscape, portrayed with an intensity that shows how far Vaughan Williams's concept of symphonic logic and his sense of aesthetic aptness had travelled from his early days. There is one particularly arresting passage, surely (unconsciously?) cribbed from Beethoven. In his essay on the Ninth Symphony, Vaughan Williams draws attention to a remarkable passage in the coda of the first movement with these words:

> But the light soon dies away. The theme is taken up by the strings in four octaves in the minor, first softly, then louder and louder, while the wind continues a little semiquaver figure. As the strings get louder the wind figure gets drowned, but as they die down again it is found that the wind is still persistently playing its part—a wonderfully poetical conception which is, I am sure, intentional.[10]

Here, he himself does something very similar. The strings, which have been playing an eerie, swirling figure in octaves, related to the main theme but without its little rhythmic kick, are swamped behind the relentless trumpet and drum figure composed of that kick itself. The trumpet fades a little; and we find with a sense of shock that the strings are actually recapitulating the main theme and that the trumpets' figure now fits into its place as part of that theme. The sense of menace is sustained until the very end, when the movement leads, with a wail from the cor anglais, into the Scherzo.

The key relationship between the first movement and the Moderato was that of two keys an augmented fourth apart. The augmented fourth now becomes the main feature of the third movement's main theme. The theme is constructed simply by piling up this interval and alternating it with that of a semitone. Thus the augmented fourths shoot off into erratic motion as soon as they are heard. The scoring is coarse and congested: there is neither the delicacy of the fifth nor the wit of the fourth. The musical activity is hectic, almost hysterical; and there is an atmosphere of somewhat swaggering brutality, even a trace of trivial vulgarity about the music. None of this hectic activity leads anywhere—the Devil indeed finds work for idle hands to do and the motto *Lasciate ogni speranza, voi ch' entrate* could justifiably be placed over this movement. Even the contrasting section that corresponds roughly to the trio is dominated by what Cooke aptly characterizes as a 'mindless drooling' by the saxophone of the emptiest type of 1940s jazz-based dance music; and when this theme is squared up and delivered in augmentation by the full orchestra, the effect is shattering: as mocking and truculent as the theme at the end of the first movement was noble and dignified. Yet it fits its context with a terrifying and inexorable musical logic.

So, too, does the amazing finale, the longest movement in the work, the unexpected, and as Cooke demonstrates, the inevitable solution to the problems posed by the first three movements. Pianissimo throughout, yet never peaceful, attenuated in texture, yet keeping the large orchestra quite busy, well supplied with full chords, yet giving every impression of being starved of them, this movement is an astonishing *tour de force*: a fugal texture without a fugue theme, the projection of a limitless waste of the wreckage of musical fragments all thematically, harmonically, or rhythmically related to what has gone before. And it

---

[10] *National Music*, p. 100.

ends with a Vaughan Williams mannerism placed in a context which gives it remarkable freshness. The juxtaposed chords of E minor and E flat major are sighed over and over again by the strings after all pretence at thematic treatment has been abandoned. As Cooke[11] puts it: is the G the minor third of E or the major third of E flat? The vigorous challenge flung down at the beginning (Is A flat the major third of E or the minor third of F?) was worked out in the first movement and the decision made on balance that the confident major assertion was right. Here, the question is left unanswered. Perhaps some kind of answer is to be found in the final symphonic triptych.

[11] *The Language of Music*, p. 269.

17

Symphonies (7–9)

'After such knowledge, what forgiveness?' Deryck Cooke's allusion,[1] through Eliot's 'Gerontion', to Vaughan Williams's Sixth Symphony, is chillingly apt. It is not surprising that Hugh Ottaway finds a change of direction in the final three symphonies. In his view, the symbolic figure behind them is no longer Bunyan's Pilgrim, but Captain Scott—the explorer into 'Unknown Regions' who deliberately courted suffering and death for the sake of the quest itself. Yet surely, if Ottaway[2] is right, Scott himself is a symbol for another figure: Prometheus, who challenges and defies whatever arbitrary powers control human destiny. Why otherwise should Vaughan Williams have chosen to preface his next symphony, much of its material taken from music that he had composed for a film on the subject of Scott of the Antarctic, with a quotation from Shelley's *Prometheus Unbound*,[3] the very poem whose setting by Hubert Parry is often considered as the first symptom of the regeneration of English music after a hundred years and more of pale imitation of foreign models?:

> To suffer woes which Hope thinks infinite,
> To forgive wrongs darker than death or night,
> To defy Power which seems omnipotent,
> Neither to change, nor falter, nor repent:
> This . . . is to be
> Good, great and joyous, beautiful and free,
> This is alone Life, Joy, Empire and Victory.

Vaughan Williams must surely have thought of Prometheus as well as Scott, and of Parry as well as Shelley, when he headed his new symphony with that text. In a sense, then, the *Sinfonia Antartica*, through the link with Shelley, is an indirect tribute to Parry and his musical values, as well as to Scott.

The *Antartica*, first performed by the Hallé Orchestra under John Barbirolli on 14 January 1953, is thus in more senses than one Vaughan Williams's 'Eroica'. It calls for the largest orchestra that he had so far employed in a symphony, including piano, a wind machine, gongs,

---

[1] *The Language of Music*, p. 265.   [2] Ottaway, p. 46.   [3] Lines 570 ff.

organ, glockenspiel, celesta, xylophone, and vibraphone; and once more he employs the human voice instrumentally—wordless, as in the *Pastoral*, but this time with the solo voice backed by a female chorus.

Parallels have often and rightly been drawn between the 'ethos' of this symphony (or at any rate of the film music on which it is based) and that of *Riders to the Sea*. In both cases Nature is an amoral, destructive force and man (or woman) triumphs morally over it, even when it has destroyed those human companions that are the tokens of the force of love or comradeship. But there is a difference. In *Riders to the Sea*, Maurya is passive; she does not throw down a conscious challenge to the Sea. She accepts it as a fact of life and submits to its power, for it is the source of and background to her family's livelihood as well as the blind destructive element that claims all her sons as victims. In the film (and, by implication in the symphony, else why preface each movement with a poetic quotation?) Scott deliberately persists in his challenge, even when he knows he will perish in the attempt. In a sense, the *Antartica* is *A Sea Symphony* viewed from the other side of the Unknown Region: aspiration frustrated, yet the spirit emancipated; human voices that stand for impersonal forces—the voice parts have deserted to the enemy, so to speak; man in heroic combat with Nature rather than Nature as incidental to human aspiration. Yet man rises superior to the destructive power that she can unleash against him and thereby displays his own moral strength. Vaughan Williams must have seen something like this in the saga of Captain Scott, as Shelley and Parry had seen it in the legend of Prometheus. The questions that have to be investigated are: how well did he symbolize and realize these factors in purely musical terms without reference to any latent programme?; did this particular technical challenge affect the rest of his symphonic output; and if so, how?

Whether or not the *Antartica* is an epic or heroic work, it has none of the brusque swiftness of movement with which Beethoven begins the 'Eroica'. The first movement may—wrongly in my view—be regarded simply as scene-painting. Michael Kennedy criticizes the main theme for being magnificent and aspiring, but not a tune which lends itself to development. He is right, but it is equally true that the tune itself does evolve and expand from its initial germinal phrase: in other words, it develops out of itself. Ottaway sees the movement as setting out the two contending forces: Man and Nature. He, too, is right. Using the functions of the various themes in the film as a pointer, that is what they stand for. But considered merely as 'dots on paper', the movement also holds together remarkably well.

In his book on Vaughan Williams's symphonies, Schwartz observes that Vaughan Williams often juxtaposes major and minor triads in passages of great dramatic import and that they seem to have a highly expressive meaning for him. The opening of the *Antartica* bears this out. Each note of the main theme is loaded, *Pastoral Symphony*-wise, with its own chord; but the chord alternates from bar to bar, major to minor: E flat minor, G major, A flat minor, G major, B flat minor, D major, E flat minor (Ex. 14). (To say that this movement is 'in' a specific key is stretching a point, to say the least). The choice of harmonies is not, however, arbitrary. The sequential treatment of the opening phrase pivots on the G major chord and treats its B natural enharmonically as the C flat of the subdominant A flat minor chord of the next bar. When the phrase is repeated a third higher, it is this G major chord that becomes its point of departure; and the D major, dominant chord towards which the harmony moves is reached through a favourite Vaughan Williams juxtaposition of the type familiar from the end of the Sixth Symphony. This time, however, the chords are all in their root position. The pace of rhythmic, harmonic, and melodic movement alike is extremely deliberate: there may be a parallel with the opening of another Seventh Symphony, that of Sibelius. The hectic vitality of the Fourth and the Sixth Symphonies has frozen into a ponderous and at times menacing gait, with pauses for breath, as it were, as each phrase hauls itself up out of the debris of the previous one.

Ex. 14

The scoring of this movement, too, is heavy and chunky. This must surely be deliberate and not the result of miscalculation, for when the 'atmospheric' music depicting the ice-scape appears, it is impressionistic writing of a very imaginative order indeed. The 'icy' sound has a translucent purity, with the disembodied female voices in the manner of Holst's 'Neptune' rather than Debussy's *Sirènes*, weaving over repeated chords an undulating sound-pattern whose descending augmented fourth outline resembles that of a theme in the second movement of the Sixth. Once more, Vaughan Williams is paying tribute to Holst—and possibly, in the turmoil of bells and brass before the end, even to his teacher Ravel's orchestration of Mussorgsky's *Pictures at an Exhibition*. But what he makes of these elements is all his own, especially when the opening music returns in chilling unease combined with a counter-theme that seems to have strayed from 'Job's Dream'. Is it a vision seen by the young Scott, or is it a dream, dreamt by the veteran composer? Michael Kennedy likens the opening of Britten's *War Requiem* to the dragging of a heavy artillery piece through the Flanders mud.[4] The outer movements of the *Antartica* evoke a picture of the dogged dragging of a heavily-laden sledge through impenetrable snow and fog. The harmonies move as they might in a typical lyrical or reflective Vaughan Williams slow movement; but the mood is quite different.

The *Antartica* is in five movements, not the usual four of Vaughan Williams's other symphonies. It is wrong to think of the second and fourth movements as lightweight intermezzi, but they do act as foils to the 'heavier' first, third, and fifth. Not long before composing this work, Vaughan Williams had written his *Fantasia on the Old 104th*, concentrating on the splendid and dignified tune that carries a hymn paraphrase of the psalm whose words he quotes as a motto to this second movement, again a return visit to territory familiar from the *Sea Symphony*, but with what a difference!

> There go the ships
> and there is that Leviathan
> whom thou has made to take his pastime therein[5]

The purely illustrative aspect of this movement, with its foggy, Debussyesque opening, its great wallowing theme (again with a prominent descending augmented fourth), which in the film symbolized the majestic whales that awed the explorers, and the trumpet theme that stood for the waddling penguins which so amused them, makes it all too easy to overlook the way in which the main theme emerges from the 'foggy' chords on the horns at the beginning. It also conceals the fact that the penguin theme—a misty reminiscence perhaps of the aria 'Könnten Tränen meiner Wangen' from the *St Matthew Passion*—is cunningly based on two interlocked descending tonally ambivalent tritone arpeggios: originally intended, perhaps, to illustrate their oddly secure yet ungainly gait amidst the slippery ice-floes? The form of the movement is concise: the recapitulation is an allusion to, rather than a repeat of, the main material. There is no full-scale reprise of the opening section, simply a coda based on it. Vaughan Williams adopted this procedure again in the Scherzo of the Eighth symphony. The cadence at the end is indeterminate, the implied tritone of the penguin tune merging with a chord of G flat major. From the implications of this chord arise both theme and harmony of the opening of the next movement.

This third movement, Landscape, is the core of the work: another of those movements where time seems to stand still, but in a totally different sense from the serenity of the Romanza in the Fifth Symphony. Here, the timelessness is of time frozen into immobility, not time sublimated by a release from a sense of flux. At the beginning, Vaughan Williams uses impressionistically a device similar to that which Britten uses structurally in the first movement of his last quartet. The movement opens

---

[4] *Britten* (London, 1981; rev. edn 1993), p. 209.   [5] Psalm 104, v. 26.

with a long-phrased theme on the horn, muted. It is immediately answered by the flutes with two syncopated chords that start a major third apart and close in slow contrary motion to a dissonant clash a tone apart—a skeletal retrograde, *without the tonic note*, of the final cadence of the E minor Symphony. The first time this is heard, the horn has landed on a B flat and resolves on to an A, creating an harmonic impasse; the second time, immediately afterwards, it has landed on a G flat (= F sharp) and continues on its way to extend the theme, finally landing on an E-flat/D cadence. So yet another example of Vaughan Williams's by now familiar use of an organically self-developing melodic cell is blocked by this little thematic icicle. Ottaway finds the continuation of the theme contrived. I am not so sure. The clash to come is here foreshadowed between an unyielding, inflexible death force, however remote as yet, and a life force that seeks to defeat it. The next episode is a canon where the thematic elements consist entirely of tritones and seconds: the very elements out of which the original theme 'unfroze' as it were at the beginning of the movement. The 'motionless torrents, silent cataracts' from the Coleridge quotation that heads the movement are vividly portrayed both in the substance of the music and in the scoring.

Vaughan Williams's choice of the organ in his orchestral music as a symbol of evil, or at any rate of a negative force triumphant, familiar from *Job*, was put to equally effective use here. The organ's irruption sounds like a distorted quotation from the *Dies irae*. Against it, the rest of the orchestra hurls all its 'mobile' sound resources in vain and in a magnificent display of tonal contrast. There is no way round *this* massive obstacle.

It is at least arguable that Landscape is the real climax of this work and that the two subsequent movements are a kind of extended 'humanistic' epilogue: 'the show must go on', as it were. Love, courage, and resolution must still persist in spite of Nature's implacable hostility. Certainly, the warm, lyrical fourth movement, Intermezzo, is the nearest that Vaughan Williams allows himself to revert in this symphony to his 'folky' style. Yet even here there is an undercurrent of unease, as the music shifts from one mood to another and the inflections of the theme vary from major- to minor-key resonances. One of the thematic flashbacks is to the opening theme of the first movement and shows its underlying kinship with that of the intermezzo itself; another is derived from the music originally associated with the departure of Oates in the film and it casts its shadow across a soundscape that is considerably less sombre than that of the other movements.

The finale, Epilogue, is the tragic outcome of its predecessors. The challenge is joined, after an extraordinary tremolo for virtually the entire orchestra, including the piano, to the music of a resolute march based on a variant of the opening theme from the first movement. From time to time its dogged course is disrupted by a ponderous triplet figure (which in the film represented the blizzard that destroyed the Scott expedition). Eventually, it merges with the atmospheric music of the Prelude and finally dissolves into its original shape as the opening theme of that movement. From then onwards, Nature the destroyer, portrayed by the wordless voices and the wind-machine, dominates the score until the music dies away to an E flat and then finally into silence.

This work is every bit as symphonic as its predecessors. What is new is not so much an abandonment of symphonic structural techniques as a paring of the connective tissue to the absolute minimum. This procedure was to become ever more evident in the last two symphonies.

The Eighth, first performed by the Hallé Orchestra under 'glorious John' Barbirolli on 2 May 1956, is the lightest and shortest of the nine. Yet its wit and good humour are controlled by an intellect as keen as ever: this is the most Haydnesque of Vaughan Williams's symphonies in more senses than one. The composer dubbed the first movement 'Seven Variations in Search of a Theme'; and the whimsical reference to Pirandello's famous play goes a good deal more than skin deep. Pirandello was exploring the difference between the real inner nature of human character and the outer manifestations by which it is assessed from the viewpoint of a sceptic who can never be sure that there is any such real inner nature. Vaughan Williams is exploring the inner nature of a theme that is never heard and quite probably never existed as a coherent musical entity. He thus subjects a number of motto-phrases to variation treatment as if they were constituent parts of that non-existent theme. It is as if Britten had built *The Young Person's Guide* out of an upward arpeggio, an up-and-down-the-scale flourish and a downward arpeggio rather than presenting us with Purcell's vigorous theme first.

This process is in fact a further development of that which Vaughan Williams adopted in the first movement of the Sixth Symphony, though his actual musical starting point in this highly original design may well have been the *Five Variants of 'Dives and Lazarus'*, where each variant is just as valid a version of the possible *Urgestalt* of the theme as any other. Another possible point of departure may have been Vincent d'Indy's Istar Variations, where the variations are heard first and culminate in a statement of the theme itself, stripped of all embellishment, just as the goddess Ishtar strips off her garments one by one before she goes in naked to meet her lover. And this impressionistic submitting of what are to all intents and purposes Wagnerian germinal motifs to Brahmsian variation treatment neatly gets the best of both worlds. Structural sleight-of-hand and the imaginative insight born of long experience go hand in hand.

This movement constitutes one of the most successful examples of Vaughan Williams's ability to combine old and new. The scoring and the manner in which the variations are built up blends traditional technique with a formal and orchestral impressionism of the most sophisticated order. The way in which the thematic fragments encompass a wide emotional range, grow organically to the final climax of the movement and dissolve into the material of the opening takes more than one leaf out of Sibelius's structural book. Colin Mason, reviewing the first performance for the *Manchester Guardian*, shrewdly pointed out the 'modal variety and flexibility of the melodic lines', commenting that they were 'easy and graceful in motion, less tied to his usual distinctive but rather lumpish modal formulas than any he has ever written, and show[ing] him at 83 still extending his musical range . . . ' and saying that this was 'the most sophisticated, civilized and universal music he [had] ever written'.

Not all the variations are light-hearted. The contrasting nature of the melodic fragments on which they are based ensures this, although all of them show enough similarity of shape in their various guises to prove that the Colonel's Lady and Judy O'Grady are sisters under the skin. The first motif is based on juxtaposed rising fourths. The second sways gently, while the more opulent third descends stepwise down a rather un-diatonic scale. The frequent contrasts—even occasional clashes—of rhythm, tempo, mood, and scoring all show a remarkable ingenuity. The new orchestral sound is most obviously, though by no means entirely, due to the addition of tuned percussion instruments to what remains basically a genuine Vaughan Williams orchestra. And the movement ends, like a snake biting its own tail, with a reference to the deliciously cool-sounding opening bars. As in the Fourth Symphony, the wheel has come full circle, but the voyage has been exhilarating fun, not a terrifying exposure to rage and violence.

The tiny Scherzo, for wind instruments only, resembles a kind of untemperance meeting. A witty, Prokofiev-like march, cocky, mischievous, and slightly raucous, it sounds as if the players are more than a little 'under the influence', especially in the sly, mock-lugubrious trio section, with its faint echoes of the first movement of the *Partita for Double String Orchestra*. Michael Kennedy says it all when he states that the penguins from the Antarctic seem, at any rate until the folk-song inflections of some of the material reveal the real composer, to have taken a course with Hindemith.[6] The skilful layout of the instruments merits mention: the spacing is such that the texture is full without any trace of thickness, and the crispness of the sound that Vaughan Williams evokes through his use of the brighter wind and brass instruments is also noteworthy. Formally, the movement follows the pattern set in the parallel movement of the *Antartica*, in that the recapitulation of the main music is telescoped into a short stretto, with the themes piled on top of one another. Again, the Fourth Symphony comes to mind: this time, the

---

[6] Kennedy, *Works* 2, p. 366.

climax of the epilogue to the finale; but here the effect is completely different, leading to the witty coda in which the movement bursts like a tiny balloon being popped.

The Cavatina which follows, for strings alone, is not so obviously original, but closer inspection reveals that in writing for the section of Barbirolli's Hallé that was most celebrated and most envied, Vaughan Williams surreptitiously struck out in some new directions. The most obvious of these is what might be called a sin of omission: sonorous block chords are almost entirely lacking. What is arresting is that Vaughan Williams can still find new ways of exploiting contrasts of tonality. The eloquent surface serenity of the music is troubled by these key-conflicts, so that the final serene coda is well-earned rather than simply posited as there by right.

The final Toccata 'commandeers all the available instruments which can make definite notes'; and in a letter to Michael Kennedy not long after the first performance, Vaughan Williams shows that he was still not quite sure whether he had overdone the use of the percussion: ' . . . I am thinning down the percussion a bit—if John [Barbirolli] will allow me to—because it may be the Hittites [i.e. the percussion] who obscure the tunes and a few bars less of phones and spiels won't do any harm.'[7] (It will be noted that the jocular old agnostic remembered his Old Testament well enough!) The composer himself referred to the opening of the movement as 'sinister', which indicates that he was trying to convey something more than the rumbustious good-humoured mood of celebration that permeates the movement as a whole. This is no visionary epilogue; and it makes no attempt to sum up what has gone before, merely to round it all off. Ottaway calls it 'generously vulgar', and it is slightly ironic that it should bear the same tempo heading, 'Moderato [e] Maestoso', the same metronome marking, and be cast in the same basic metre as the dignified finale of Elgar's E flat Symphony. A rondo of sorts, it is basically a more mature development of the same kind of hearty, exuberant romping vein that he had tapped over forty years previously in pieces like 'Let all the world in every corner sing'. Yet the mood darkens in the middle of the movement, where there is a distinct reminder of Pilgrim's 'What shall I do to be saved?' But all ends well, perhaps with a sidelong brassy glance at the finale of *The Firebird*, one of Vaughan Williams's favourite Stravinsky works.

The Ninth Symphony was composed in 1956–7, mostly in London, but partly in Majorca and at Ashmansworth, the home of the Finzis in Newbury. It was first performed by the Royal Philharmonic Orchestra under Malcolm Sargent, on 2 April 1958. Once again, Vaughan Williams shows his interest in new kinds of sonority: this score includes a flügel-horn—'this beautiful and neglected instrument', as the composer called

7 Ibid., p. 385.

it in his typically whimsical programme note for the first performance[8]—
and three saxophones, 'not expected, except possibly in one place in the
scherzo, to behave like demented cats, but . . . allowed to be their own
romantic selves'.

The point of departure for this work seems to have been a fascination
with Salisbury Plain and a life-long love of Thomas Hardy's *Tess of the
d'Urbervilles*. The composer hints at a suppressed programme, particularly in reference to the second movement, but 'it got lost on the journey—so now, oh no, we never mention it—and the music must be left
to speak for itself—whatever that may mean': something of an admission from one who always claimed that he was just putting down black
dots on paper.

Speak for itself the music certainly does. In this work, all connective
tissue is cut with a ruthlessness reminiscent of the brusque Fourth
Symphony, even though the gait of the music is recognizably and understandably slower and the build up of the paragraphs more deliberate.
This terseness of approach impressed even unsympathetic critics of
Vaughan Williams's later works such as Peter J. Pirie, though others
damned the work with faint praise.[9] It does not give up its secrets easily. There is a (deliberately?) unresolved dichotomy between the grim,
unsettled mood that pervades much of the music and an idyllic calm that
is just as typical of it, but often simply juxtaposed with it without any
sense of transition or resolution of the tension between them: the music
is simply wrenched back and forth from one mood to the other. The
scoring, too, shows this dichotomy. Sometimes it is not just rich and full,
but thick and heavy. At other times it shows delicacy and imagination
of a high order.

The gait of the first movement (originally Allegro moderato, later
altered to Moderato maestoso, the same indication as that of the finale
of the Eighth) is slow, but the move from mood to mood is swift. There
is a surprise right at the very beginning. The broad spread string chords
seem to presage a serene wind or viola solo. What happens is that a baleful passage for brass emerges almost truculently from the texture. Being
wise after the event, one can relate this music fancifully to the stark,
awesome Salisbury Plain landscape, just as *Pastoral Symphony* is a rec-
ollection of a Corot-like evening landscape in war-torn Northern France.
Perhaps, too, the Hardy connection is there: this music fits well the dour
but sturdy stoic pessimism of the great novelist's outlook. This mood is
brusquely contrasted, via a Neapolitan cadence, with the gentler mood
of the 'second subject': an upward-arching theme on the clarinets (ori-
ginating in a reference to the innocent Tess herself, perhaps?). It starts
out momentarily as if it is to be a diminished variant of the main theme,
but takes in both a leap of a minor sixth and a downward-drooping

[8] Kennedy, *Works* 1, p. 635.   [9] *Music and Musicians* (September 1971).

chromatic triplet surely related to the insistent triplets that have previously battered against the onward movement of the main theme. It is to this theme that the composer devotes most of his attention, the main theme recurring almost as a kind of afterthought at the very end of the movement. The interplay of the themes is constantly changing; and the handling of key-contrasts masterly.

The second movement, Andante sostenuto, injects an element of the macabre into the soundscape. The first movement had originally been entitled 'Wessex Prelude'—in itself surely an indication of a connection with Hardy; and the macabre atmosphere of the second took its departure from the pervading sense in the novel of the blind, brooding hostility of the forces controlling human destiny towards the fragile and basically blameless Tess.[10] Whether or not the music at it emerged bears any resemblance to Tess, her fate in the novel exemplifies for Hardy the inscrutability—hostility even—of the cosmos towards innocent human aspirations; and that is perhaps what the 'black dots on [the] paper' may—consciously or unconsciously—be intended to convey. The whole question of interrelationships and cross-references between the design of RVW's works and various extra-musical stimuli, particularly literary ones, is a fascinating one, as the headings to the movements in the *Sinfonia Antartica* and works like *Flos Campi* indicate. The beautiful unaccompanied flügelhorn solo, with its curious half-modal, half-tonal scale based on the juxtaposition of a major and a minor tetrachord, is immediately and curtly countered with a spooky march that wanly reflects, as if through a distorting mirror, the martial vigour of the fourth movement of *Flos Campi*. The flower of *this* field, it seems, was originally the ghostly drummer of Salisbury Plain; and there could be no more telling reminder of the ambivalence of the attraction of this part of the Wiltshire landscape than these two themes. But the landscape and the drummer are transmuted into symbols of something more universal here: of an almost mocking unease. The 'ghostly drummer' makes his presence ever more strongly felt as the movement progresses, culminating in a fortissimo statement towards the end of the movement on the full orchestra, yet he cannot undermine the security of the flügelhorn theme, which always recurs at the same pitch whatever accompaniment the composer provides it with. The other main element in this movement involves a complete change of metre to 3/4 and what the composer himself calls a 'romantic' episode. Ottaway[11] says that this episode is notable for its detachment from the rest of the movement, yet in thematic outline, though not in rhythm, the music derives at least in part

---

[10] See Oliver Neighbour, 'The place of the Eighth among Vaughan Williams's symphonies', in *VWS*, pp. 213–33, especially pp. 225–6. Neighbour acknowledges his debt, as I do mine, to Frogley's 'Vaughan Williams and Thomas Hardy', in *Music & Letters*, Vol. lxviii (1987), pp. 42–59.

[11] Ottaway, p. 63.

from the basic melodic elements of the 'ghostly drummer' theme. Is it fanciful to think in terms of *Pastoral Symphony* revisited when the flügelhorn theme is supported by a clarinet counter-subject at the end of the movement, just as the natural horn cadenza is in the earlier work? And is it therefore quite irrelevant to remind ourselves that part of Vaughan Williams's First World War service was spent on Salisbury Plain?

The uneasy repose that ensues is quickly dispelled by the highly effective Scherzo, which is by Vanity Fair out of 'Satan's Dance of Triumph', with a touch of Holst's 'Uranus' and the music that characterizes Dr Caius in *Sir John in Love* somewhere in its mongrel pedigree. Spritely rhythms conflict with heavily moving harmonies; the dashing orchestration particularly features the saxophones, the xylophone, and the celesta in combination; and there is an angular, slightly tipsy-sounding fugato. Vaughan Williams also indulges in his 'Elinor Rumming' vein for the last time: roguishly playful and acidly witty, especially when in the fugato the saxophones play a lachrymose chorale against a glittering accompaniment to the protesting woodwind. This movement has an easier sense of flow than its fellows: the changes of mood are less abrupt. Yet the sense of a ghostly non-human presence is still there; and it is no joke when Vaughan Williams resorts to the same device as in the third movement of the Sixth Symphony of playing a previously spritely theme (this time the main theme of the movement) in a kind of tipsy, truculent augmentation. He reserves the most telling stroke of all for the very end, when the movement, like the Scherzo of the Eighth, dissolves into nothingness, this time via the sharp side-drum rhythm with which the movement began.

If the close of the slow movement is slightly reminiscent of *Pastoral Symphony*, the opening of the finale recalls the opening of that of the Sixth. But it does not inhabit the same dead, nihilistic world. It may well in fact refer at least in part to the composer's experience of Salisbury Cathedral, particularly an occasion in 1938 when, after a day's walking on the Wiltshire Downs and a (doubtless hearty) dinner, RVW entered the cathedral and listened to the cathedral organist, Walter Alcock, play Bach in the dark, deserted building.[12] Thus the bleakness of much of the earlier music is mitigated by the human warmth and a sense that the finest constructions of man, though eventually destined to 'leave not a wrack behind' are none the less worth the technical skill and spiritual aspiration that go towards their creation. There is bleakness here, but there is also contrasting warmth. Vaughan Williams himself pointed out that the movement was really two movements in one; and he makes no real effort to reconcile their contrasting moods, not even at the very end, where the gigantic climax is interrupted by soft saxophones, a most

[12] UVW, pp. 222–3.

poetic touch. There is no epilogue. Perhaps Thomas Hardy could supply any that might be needed:

'Justice' was done, and the President of the Immortals, in Aeschylean phrase, had ended his sport with Tess. And the d'Urberville knights and dames slept on in their tombs unknowing. The two speechless gazers bent themselves down to the earth, as if in prayer, and remained thus a long time, absolutely motionless: the [black] flag continued to wave silently. As soon as they had strength they arose, joined hands again, and went on.[13]

Thus ends Vaughan Williams's symphonic testament. The voyage into the uncharted seas of sound had taken him a very long way indeed.

[13] *Tess of the Durbervilles*, chapter 59.

18

Concertos and other concertante works

Vaughan Williams never trusted display for its own sake, so when he allotted an important part to a solo instrument in a concert work, it came naturally to him to emphasize its expressive qualities rather than the sheer power or brilliance of the soloist. Only one of his concertos bears any relation to the great showpiece concertos of the Romantic and post-Romantic eras. This is not to say that the soloist in the others has an easy time of it: indeed, even so intimate a work as *The Lark Ascending* taxes the technique as well as the sensitivity of the soloist; and the solo part in his piano concerto proved so demanding that the piano part was revised and divided up between two soloists, in which form it was at one time probably better known. But in all Vaughan Williams's concertos, the soloist is allowed to enjoy the limelight without hogging the stage. The relationship between soloist and accompaniment more often that not resembles that in a Bach or Vivaldi concerto rather than in a symphonic concerto such as those of Brahms or a glittering virtuoso display piece by Liszt or Saint-Saëns. The possible exception is the piano concerto, where Bartók (who admired the work) may also be one of the models.

If we include *Flos Campi* and the *Fantasia on the 'Old 104th'*, there are nine works of this kind involving soloists: four full-scale concertos, all but one on a restricted scale, a suite, two short rhapsodic works, and the two works involving a prominent solo instrumental part and a chorus as well as the orchestra. At the time of his death, Vaughan Williams was working up some sketches for a cello concerto, but they were left in such a fragmentary state that any attempt to complete the work would involve 'tinkering' with it in the same way as would an attempt to reconstruct Elgar's Third Symphony.

Even though his concertos so designated are few in number, Vaughan Williams was prepared to be unorthodox in his choice of solo instruments. One of them is for tuba and orchestra; and one of the shorter works is the delightful Romance for Harmonica and Orchestra, written for and commissioned by the virtuoso Larry Adler. Two of the works featuring a concertante soloist are for the viola, Vaughan Williams's favourite instrument.

His earliest effort at pitting soloist against orchestra was a Fantasia for piano and orchestra in a single movement 514 bars long, divided into six sections in differing tempos and ending not with a brilliant bravura display but with a thoughtful Andante sostenuto. It was begun in October 1896 and must have been worked at sporadically over the years, for he completed it on 9 February 1902 and revised it twice in 1904. It does not appear to have been performed and remains unpublished. Michael Kennedy dismisses it as Brahmsian. Vaillancourt[1] finds in it outward similarities with the Franck *Symphonic Variations* but also points out that it owes little to typical nineteenth-century concerto form other than the highly rhetorical solo introduction, commending RVW's 'rigorous and exhaustive' development of his material. It would seem that he had not forgotten the work when he composed his *Fantasia on the 'Old 104th'*, judging by the way he used his material there (see below, p. 233).

The Lark Ascending, composed just before the First World War and revised after it, is a favourite Vaughan Williams work that is almost sure to turn up on any anthology CD of his orchestral music. No wonder. One of Vaughan Williams's most attractive and convincing pastoral soundscapes, it makes an immediate appeal. It also, incidentally, provides an interesting if tenuous personal link with Elgar, for its dedicatee, Marie Hall, was at one time a violin pupil of his. *The Lark Ascending* is prefaced by lines from Meredith's poem and though the solo part is undoubtedly intended to imitate a lark's song and fluttering, upward-aspiring flight, the song of this lark has little or nothing to do with the kind of birdsong that Messiaen exploits so skilfully. Its aim is to evoke an atmosphere and a number of contrasting moods rather than telling any kind of story or exploring the musical implications of a bird's song; the work is simply and solidly constructed in an ABA form prefaced by and closing with a free outpouring by the soloist that is in fact thematic as well as rhapsodic; and though the lark is always in the centre of the picture, the background to its flight changes slowly and subtly throughout.

Careful inspection of the work's thematic outlines reveals that the harmonically hazy opening in the orchestra and the rhapsodic outpouring which immediately introduces the lark (i.e. the violin soloist) generate the musical material of the entire piece. The manner in which the violinist's phrases gradually and organically expand from the initial melisma over the orchestra's softly hummed sustained chord is a splendid early example of what was to become a hallmark of Vaughan Williams's style and formal procedure, providing yet another example of Holst's comment that the effect of the *real* RVW's music was like that of listening to very lovely lyric poetry. Yet this is not mere musical

---

[1] See VWS, p. 31.

doodling. The falling major third that recurs so frequently in the cadenza-like first solo gradually takes shape as the embryo of the main theme and finally emerges as a significant feature of that theme itself.

The gentle lilt of the accompaniment, derived from the short introductory bars, shows with what unobtrusive skill Vaughan Williams had learned to apply the ambiguities of impressionist harmonies: one can imagine the gentle tune harmonized in any number of different and rather boring ways, but Vaughan Williams anchors it to his opening phrase in a kind of ruminative ostinato, which in its turn expands (with an allusion in the first cello part to the basic outline of the main theme) after four bars. When the theme returns in the recapitulation, the harmonization is fuller and less static and the melody itself is further coloured by a G flat/G natural false relation. The delicately varied colours and textures of the orchestral part and the effective use of the solo instrument's different registers and technical resources are all the more telling because they are so unobtrusive. The effect is almost as if the lark were flying over the gentle Cotswold woods and fields among which the composer revised it before its first public performance. In the central 2/4 section, the lark almost seems to be taking what is literally a gentle bird's-eye view of human activity, both sedate and more lively, with just a hint of the power behind all the serenity. Man is reduced to his true proportions as an integral part of the natural world.

The neo-classical Violin Concerto is dedicated to the Hungarian violinist Jelly d'Arányi; and it is not being fanciful to hear a slight tinge of central European gypsy-music in one or two passages (notably, for example, in the double-stopped passage in thirds and sixths just after letter O in the first movement). For all its apparently limited scale and restricted orchestral resources (strings only, but divided far more frequently than any baroque composer would ever have envisaged doing), this work should not be dismissed as a mere miniature. It has substance as well as style; and its relaxed, playful charm fuses the thoughtfulness of the Tallis Fantasia, the fresh, open-air vigour of *Hugh the Drover*, from which it actually borrows a theme for its finale, and something of the mystery of *Pastoral Symphony* into a succinct summary of Vaughan Williams's stylistic development up till the time of its composition in 1924/5. It was first performed at the Aeolian Hall on 6 November 1925 by the dedicatee and the London Chamber Orchestra conducted by Anthony Bernard.

Vaughan Williams's approach to neo-classicism did not involve any kind of *outré* spicing up of baroque melodic and rhythmic formulas, designs, and textures by adding clusters of incongruous and irrelevant notes, falsifying the harmonies, or jazzing up baroque motor-rhythms. The manner of the work may be mildly reminiscent of Bach or Vivaldi, but the moods, the formal procedures, and the cut of the themes are all characteristic of Vaughan Williams and of nobody else. The opening theme, for example, may well have taken its point of departure from that of Bach's fiddle concerto in A minor; and like a baroque opening ritornello, this one, too, contains all the thematic elements that go to make up the movement. But Vaughan Williams substitutes for baroque formal techniques a rhythmic metamorphosis of his themes belonging to a rather later age and harmonic procedures involving modal outlines and progressions of open perfect fifths that either antedate the baroque era by a couple of centuries or post-date it by almost as much. The result is not, as might well have been the case, a stylistic mish-mash, but a spritely and tautly-constructed movement that uses all manner of devices naturally and with perfect timing within the basic and unyielding momentum of the movement. Thus the main theme of the 3/4 section is a rhythmic transformation of the second strain of the principal theme of the movement as a whole, a theme which also turns up in its original rhythm but in diminished form as a counterpoint to its new guise.

The slow movement also develops from a Bach-like pattern, but the layout and the texture are far lusher than anything in any Bach concerto; the sound retains a kind of soft luminosity and never becomes thick. (There is hardly a bar in which one section or other of the orchestra is not divided, and at one point the divisions extend into chords of nine separate parts.) Bach's slow movements of this kind often start out with a very simple and strongly rhythmic tune over which, as a harmonic background pattern, the soloist weaves arabesques forming the melodic and emotional core of the piece. Vaughan Williams does not just divide the melodic interest between his solo violin and a solo cello: the theme is later taken up by the orchestral violins. When, after a second and less elaborate theme has been heard, the first theme returns and the relationship between the parts is exactly inverted. The solo violin plays a high pianissimo inverted pedal note, the orchestral violins and the solo cello playing the main theme in consecutive full chords, almost as if it had strayed from *Pastoral Symphony*, and the quasi-ostinato which was originally heard on the violins is in the tutti cellos and basses.

Vaughan Williams's 'organic' technique of presenting his themes is used to good effect in the finale. Every time the main theme recurs, it has a slightly different outline. The jig-like momentum of the movement is highlighted both by the cantabile counter-melody on the violas, more like *Pastoral Symphony*'s scherzo than anything out of *Hugh the Drover*, from which the main theme comes, and by the frequent changes of macro-rhythm in the phrase-lengths. There is thus a rhythmic tension beneath its apparently jovial and unruffled surface, a feature already evident in some of Vaughan Williams's earlier works (for example the Tallis Fantasia) and one that was to become ever more prominent and fruitfully exploited later on. The Violin Concerto may not be a seminal work, but it does stand at a stylistic crossroads from which the composer was free and able to progress in a number of different directions.

One of those directions is exemplified in his next work featuring a solo instrument: *Flos Campi*. This preceded the Violin Concerto to its first performance by some three weeks; and it puzzled not just the critics, but even Gustav Holst.[2] The composer did not clarify matters over-much by prefixing a motto in Latin from the *Song of Solomon* to each of the six movements. This misled many early commentators into classing it either with his 'religious' works, with his choral works, or with both, especially as the forces involved include a wordless chorus. The voices, however, are treated as part of the instrumental colouring; and though the chorus part is prominent, it projects, reflects, and stands over and against the ravishing concertante part for the solo viola. The work is a superb love-poem, expressing both physical and spiritual longing, as anyone must surely appreciate who takes the trouble to consider the meaning and the context of the motto quotations; and it is expressed with an intensity that may well have sounded distinctly un-English to the work's first listeners. The notorious reaction—'What's an English public schoolboy doing writing this kind of stuff?'—of one of RVW's colleagues on examining some of the music composed by the young Benjamin Britten might well be applied to RVW himself here. He can hardly have imagined that *Flos Campi* would be frequently performed: however effectively they are used (which they certainly are) the resources for which it calls are so unusual as to indicate that he must have written it out of some urgent inner impulse. He might almost have deliberately designed it for infrequent performance.

Flos Campi sounds in fact remarkably like Vaughan Williams's *Tristan und Isolde*, even if the passion it expresses is projected with an economy of means that is poles apart from Wagner: and searing, full-blooded passion is surely what it demands in performance. The passion is not so febrile, nor does the composer need to rationalize it with reams of fustian sub-Novalis philosophizing—the headings to each movement suffice to provide a clue to its interpretation—, but of its intensity there can be no doubt. Vaughan Williams's harsh, bright orchestral and vocal palette overwhelms the listener by its sheer intensity as well as by the work's sumptuous tonal complexity and ambivalent harmony. This music has nothing whatever to do with buttercups and daisies, as the composer himself caustically observed in a programme note to an early performance. This is no rustic rapture: the folk-song element has been so thoroughly assimilated into his style that he can now afford to experiment in bitonality (or rather bi-modality) and rhythmic freedom in the approved manner of the age in which the work was written.

If the Latin headings to the six movements are to be taken seriously, as they surely should be, then the emotional curve of the work moves in the second movement from the poignant longing of the opening to the

<hr/>

[2] *Heirs and Rebels*, p. 62.

stirring of nature in spring and therefore the awakening of energy and desire. Such a reading is confirmed by the heading to the third movement, in which the beloved has sought her lover and not found him. (The sense of desolation in this section may possibly also be tinged with feelings of loss and loneliness caused by the death of so many companions in the Great War.) A depiction of the virile and masculine aspect of the lover as a man of war follows, with the viola performing a sinuous, voluptuous, and alluring yet essentially masculine dance in counterpoint against it, which leads into the most intense and passionate movement of the six, simply aching and pulsing with ardent longing. The rapturous fulfilment and the retrospective epilogue that follow round the work off to perfection. The true measure of *Flos Campi* is revealed by this finale, which unfolds gently, almost imperceptibly and in an unambiguous D major, like a Japanese flower opening out in water, not surging onward to a fortissimo climax, and finding time to look back before it dies away in remote peace, neither in nostalgia nor in regret, but in quiet, reflective satisfaction, to the opening of the work from which everything else has evolved. The emotional scheme behind the work is thus perfectly consistent and explicable in purely human terms; and the level to which Vaughan Williams had developed his technique of evolving a long melodic span out of an initial short phrase is notable throughout.

Flos Campi is thus a glance into yet another unknown region, this time not into deep waters or towards some remote symbolic Heavenly City, but inwards into the passionate—at times highly erotically charged—depths of the human psyche. It is at the same time rich and fervent, yet remote and strange. The viola writing is effective and expressive (and so it should be: the viola was Vaughan Williams's own favourite instrument and his choice of it here to bear the solo part is yet another pointer to the highly personal nature of the work's message). The scoring throughout is beautifully judged, the wordless voices in particular adding a purely human and partly mystical ardour to the music rather than projecting any philosophic or impersonal timelessness, as they do in some other of his works.

Vaughan Williams wrote another and neglected work featuring a solo viola: the *Suite for Viola and Small Orchestra* dedicated to Lionel Tertis and first performed by him at Queen's Hall on 12 November 1934. Ostensibly, this may be a small-scale work, but it is in fact quite a substantial one. Its scale is misleading in that none of its movements is complex, so that it is easy to underestimate its quality. It really comprises three suites in one, the eight short movements being divided into three groups: three 'Christmas' pieces, two 'character' pieces and three dance movements. This arrangement of movements invites a wide variety of mood, of rhythm, and of texture. The small orchestra is used with restraint and imagination, not all the instruments (even the violins) being used in every movement. The music itself is easy to listen to, but it requires a real virtuoso soloist; and the work as a whole may be said to stand in the same relation to Vaughan Williams's more substantial compositions as Beethoven's Bagatelles or Bach's two part inventions do to his. That is to say, its apparent small scale indicates the concentration of a great mind relaxing rather than the triviality of a small mind turning out elegant trifles. Indeed, the 'Carol' movement, with its haunting tune and its simple yet subtle treatment (particularly in its fourth verse) is Vaughan Williams at his most eloquent and moving.

Vaughan Williams never claimed to be a pianist of any standing, yet his Piano Concerto, the first two movements of which were composed in 1926 and the finale in 1930, is not only effective, but contains a solo part so demanding that the composer (wrongly, in the present writer's view) was persuaded to re-arrange it for two pianos. In the revised version the soloists obscure the theme by clattering away through and above the orchestral texture; and sporadically throughout the work Vaughan Williams thickens the piano part with ruthless zeal. Sometimes, he uses the extra keyboard to introduce antiphonal effects between the soloists, sometimes to embellish the original texture, sometimes to harden the outline of the melodic or harmonic framework, but in performance, it sounds all too often only as if he has simply thickened it. Occasionally, it is true, but not very often, he actually does thin out the piano texture. Admittedly, in the original version, the demands on the soloist's stamina are heavy; but the same sense of desperate effort as that experienced when a good quartet rather than a string orchestra performs the *Grosse Fuge* is surely worth the sacrifices involved. If the single soloist has too hard a time of it, the duo version gives too hard a ride to the orchestra.

The Piano Concerto was first performed by the dedicatee, Harriet Cohen, with the BBC Symphony Orchestra under Adrian Boult on 1 February 1933. It was apparently received with some dismay and even with hissing; and after the first performance, the work underwent considerable revision. This[3] included the excision of a quotation from the Third Symphony of Arnold Bax, Miss Cohen's long-time friend and lover, inserted 'according to my promise', as the composer wrote in the original programme-note, and to be played 'quite slow and very far off like a dream', as he put it in a letter to Miss Cohen. The reference, as Vaughan Williams pointed out, was understood by Bax, Miss Cohen, and himself, but not by the uninstructed listener, yet even though it was later cut out, the quotation itself must have had some relevance to the content of the concerto itself. It is some indication of the nature and quality of the work that when Bela Bartók heard Miss Cohen play it under Hermann Scherchen at Strasbourg in 1933, he was much

[3] Kennedy, *Works* 2, p. 236.

impressed by it; and it is a strange commentary on the work—or on the attitude of British audiences to concertos standing outside the conventional repertory—that it has been played more frequently abroad than in the UK.

Nothing could be less like a folk-song than the almost brutally assertive first theme of the opening Toccata. In 7/8 time, it simply takes the interval of a tone and repeats it again and again, each time a fourth further up. Meanwhile, the soloist is busy preaching on the text of a chain of fourths in contrary motion, implied in both the left and right hands of the solo part. Folk-song or no, this thematic layout is typical of the composer: the interval of the fourth, piled up remorselessly, became a fingerprint of his style in the 1930s; and the choice of such a main theme for this Toccata gives the lie to those detractors who would dismiss the composer as a folky homespun. Having discharged his stream of disguised fourths and whole tones, Vaughan Williams expands his theme at the fifth bar by introducing a new motif which immediately contracts into a *grupetto* of quavers. The metre changes abruptly to 3/4 and the mood to one of tough, rollicking, and good-natured fun, disturbed from time to time by the irruption of the opening music, which then actually contrives to combine with the secondary material it has so rudely interrupted.

The jaunty music, however, is calmed into some kind of serenity in the second movement Romanza, one of those movements completely typical of the composer in that all the feverish activity of the first movement is forgotten in a delicate and poignant meditation. Michael Kennedy[4] aptly points out that the piano writing here (and the orchestration, too, for that matter) is Ravelian or Fauré-esque in its transparent delicacy. The composer himself did not draw attention to any thematic connection between the second theme of the first movement and the two main themes of the Romanza, so perhaps it is fanciful to think that there is one. But, to apply a phrase from Vaughan Williams himself: 'It *looks* like it; and it *sounds* like it . . . ' For that matter, there is an outline kinship between the same theme and one of the themes of the first movement of the Fourth Symphony: Vaughan Williams's mind was clearly much preoccupied with such rhythmic and melodic issues at this time.

The mood of reflective calm is curtly shattered by the trombones, who announce the theme of the fugal finale. Vaughan Williams's piano writing in this work is coloured by his contact with Busoni's transcriptions of Bach; but the cut of this theme is oddly like a distorted version of a theme from the minuet of Mozart's 'Jupiter' symphony. The fugue develops considerable momentum—so much so that, paradoxically, it grinds to a halt in a kind of contrapuntal traffic pile-up, relieved by a

[4] Ibid., p. 263.

massive cadenza for the soloist that leads first to the lilting 'alla tedesca' and finally to the deep peace of the ending. Nowadays, however, pianists tend to use the new ending that RVW composed for the two-piano version.

There are so few well-known English piano concertos—even Britten's fine essay in the form is usually (and wrongly) regarded as something of a failure—that it is a great pity that this one is not better known. The solo part is on a much more massive scale than in Vaughan Williams's other concertos and the work's sporadic thicknesses and squareness of gait are more than offset by its power, its intensity, its sense of fun and above all by the beautiful slow movement.

The predominantly genial little three-movement Oboe Concerto composed for Leon Goossens was a product of the war years and was first performed in Liverpool on 30 September 1944. It is a gentler work than either the Violin or the Piano Concerto; much of it is cast in a kind of *mezza-voce* murmur. The orchestra—strings only—is kept firmly on the leash: for the most part it tends to nod sagely in agreement every time the soloist says anything particularly wise. This happy give-and-take makes for a work full of felicitous touches of scoring, poetry, and unexpected extensions or foreshortenings of what sound at first hearing like square, straightforward themes. There is even a slight reminiscence—in mood as well as in style—of the finale of *Flos Campi* when the strings in the last movement have a majestic waltz tune (another 'alla tedesca' element that perhaps had to be played down when the concerto was first performed) rising against a descending counterpoint from the soloist. The reminiscence is strengthened when the soloist's theme is taken up in imitation by the orchestra. There is no genuine slow movement: the second movement is a minuet with the tang of the open air rather than the scent of the ballroom about it; and its return is neatly contrived by allowing the trio section to dissolve into a tripping series of quavers that develop into a counterpoint to the theme of the minuet itself. After the pastoral first movement and the spritely little minuet, the finale introduces virtuosity for the first time in the work. The coda is retrospective, recalling themes from the earlier movements, but leads into no unknown regions.

The little Romance in D flat for Harmonica, nine-part strings and piano was for many years a Saturday-night prom favourite. It was commissioned by and composed for Larry Adler, whose artistry and technical skill made a complete orchestra in itself of the humble mouth organ, an instrument that Vaughan Williams had encountered at first hand through his friend Harry Steggles during the First World War and to which he had already paid tribute in the second trio of *A London Symphony*'s Scherzo. It was first performed at New York Town Hall on 3 May 1952, its première in England being conducted by Hugo Rignold at Liverpool some six weeks later. Based on two main subjects and in two gently contrasting sections, it combines the unusual (one of the cadenzas is made the justification for what amounts to a confrontation between soloist and orchestra) and the unspectacular. Vaughan Williams's consecutive-triad writing suited the harmonica admirably; and his pastoral vein is given a further airing. The Romance may not be more than another chip from the master-carpenter's work-bench, but its dedicatee liked it. And Vaughan Williams did his homework, as usual: his widow Ursula wrote of its composition:

> he asked Larry Adler for full details. 'Write down everything it [the harmonica] can do, and everything it can't do,' he said. This Larry did, and the sheet of foolscap with all the possibilities was propped up on his study desk for weeks while he worked all the can-dos into his tune.[5]

The *Fantasia on the 'Old 104th' Psalm Tune*, for piano solo, chorus, and orchestra was composed for the Gloucester Festival of 1950, with Michael Mullinar as the soloist. It consists of a set of variations on the famous melody attributed to Thomas Ravenscroft and associated with the words 'Disposer supreme and Judge of the Earth' in *The English Hymnal*. This is not the text that Vaughan Williams chooses here; he takes instead the version of the Psalm by Sternhold and Hopkins, which pre-dates the text of *The English Hymnal* version (a translation from the French) by almost 300 years. As in Dohnányi's *Variations on a Nursery Song*, the theme is foreshadowed in a portentous introduction before the piano states it in full, working it up in massive chords and bravura display-passages until the seven variations (two for the piano alone) get under way. But whereas the rhetorical posturing of Dohnányi's introduction is a splendid spoof, the bubble of pretentiousness being wittily burst when the naïve little nursery-rhyme is stated by the piano, here, the theme is not intended to be a let-down, and it does seem rather as if Vaughan Williams is painting the lily by embellishing it so much and so soon.

The *Fantasia* is a curious work. For once, Vaughan Williams seems to be most uncharacteristically showing off: if ever a work of his reminded the listener of the grandiose tub-thumping of a Lisztian sub-concerto such as the *Hungarian Fantasia*, it is surely this one, a comment which, one fears, the composer would hardly have appreciated. It is not likely to get many performances because it is laid out for such unusual forces. Dare one suggest that despite Vaughan Williams's affection and respect both for the tune and for the soloist and despite the ingenuity of some of the variations (notably the fugato fourth variation, with piano and voices in sturdy counterpoint), it does not really deserve many?

The Tuba Concerto composed for Philip Catelinet, the tuba player of the London Symphony Orchestra, as part of the orchestra's Golden Jubilee celebrations in 1954, is likewise a slightly perverse work. For

[5] UVW, p. 324.

once in a way, the 'Teddy-bears' picnic' humour of one of the themes seems laboured and the jokes fall flat; yet that is not the whole story, for the work has its serious side as well. But even there, the inspiration is not vintage Vaughan Williams; and the haunting main tune and expressive lyricism of the Romance do not make up for the rather pedestrian dullness of the outer movements: even the final Rondo alla tedesca—at times more a kind of ponderous corranto, with its flowing triplet passages, rather than a waltz or landler,—lacks the spice and verve that the veteran composer was able to conjure up in other late works. (Michael Kennedy[6] suggests that Vaughan Williams may have had the caperings of Falstaff and the fairies in mind for this movement.)

The disappointing quality of much of this last concerto is sad, for the technical difficulties of writing an effective concerto for an instrument whose compass lies even lower than that of the cello or the bassoon were a stimulating challenge to the composer; and the layout of the work is evidence that he enjoyed tackling them. He also arranged the slow movement for cello.

It is a pity that he did not live to finish his cello concerto. His only concertante work for that instrument, the *Fantasia on Sussex Folk-Tunes*, was composed for Casals in 1928/9 and performed by him on 13 March 1930 with the Royal Philharmonic Society's orchestra under John Barbirolli, his fellow-cellist and great admirer of both soloist and composer. It has been recorded, but published only in an arrangement for cello and piano, yet it shows that RVW managed to highlight the solo instrument without thinning out the orchestra excessively. Two of the five folk-songs used were collected by Vaughan Williams himself; and the technique that he employed in the *Fantasia on Christmas Carols* of linking them by a kind of musical punning on their more prominent melodic features is here managed with considerably more sophistication.

Neither he nor Casals was happy with the very pleasant end-product.[7] His own highly uncharacteristic reaction to the performance was merely a peremptory 'Thank-you' to the soloist, who had spent a year preparing the work for performance and who was justifiably puzzled. As Vaughan Williams had been awarded the Society's gold medal at the concert, he may have felt embarrassed that the work of his featured on this occasion was not one of his best. It is also possible that he had been irritated by the great cellist's approach to it, though he admired him both as a man and as an artist. The unfinished concerto was intended for Casals (as an *amende honorable*?) and he did in fact pay a graceful tribute both to Casals and to their hero J. S. Bach with the arrangement for cello and strings of 'Schmücke dich, O liebe Seele' composed for Casals's eightieth birthday in 1956. Both the *Fantasia* and the sketches

---

[6] Kennedy, *Works* 2, p. 362.
[7] H. L. Kirk, *Pablo Casals: A Biography* (London, 1974), p. 365.

for the concerto, which Michael Kennedy[8] conjectures date from about 1942/3, show that the challenge of matching Elgar's valedictory master-piece would certainly have stimulated his invention; and there is little evidence either from the sketches or from his other late works that his last essay in concerto form would have been as elegiac and heartbroken as that of his great predecessor. It looks as if it would have been in three movements, the two outside ones in moderate tempo and framing what promised to be an attractive Lento. But then, with Vaughan Williams, nothing was ever predictable; and the sketches are surely best left untouched.

[8] Kennedy, *Works* 1, p. 643.

19

Chamber music

Vaughan Williams's first composition with any claims to ambition was a Piano Trio in G, performed under typically unorthodox circumstances (another boy sharing the violin part) in the Great Hall at Charterhouse on 5 August 1888, some two months before the composer's sixteenth birthday. His own comment on the piece was characteristically terse: 'All I remember about it is that the principal theme was distinctly reminiscent of César Franck, a composer whose name I did not even know in those days, and whom I have since learned to dislike cordially.'[1] Clearly he did not consider the work worth preserving; yet it made enough of an impression on at least one adult member of the audience, as we have seen, to persuade him to encourage the fledgling composer to continue his efforts.

As an RCM student, Vaughan Williams was predictably required to compose chamber works as exercises in technique. These included another Piano Trio, completed in June 1895. Yet it is strange that, having gained his Cambridge Mus.Bac. and finished his second stint at the Royal College, he did not compose more chamber music. In view of his love of stringed instruments, this is especially regrettable, particularly when we remember the regular meetings of the 'Cowley Street Wobblers', an enthusiastic quartet comprising himself and his wife, Nicholas Gatty, and Holst. His sole early venture in this medium seems in fact to have been a String Quartet in C minor, completed in 1898 and performed at the Oxford and Cambridge Music Club on 30 June 1904.

This had been preceded to performance by a Quintet in D for clarinet, horn, violin, cello, and piano. performed at the small hall of Queen's Hall on 5 June 1901. The clarinettist was G. A. Clinton, who had organized the series of concerts at which the work was played; and the horn player was the famous Adolph Borsdorf, later to become a founder member of the London Symphony Orchestra. Neither of these pieces was published, though Michael Kennedy notes more than a hint of folk-song in the second movement of the Quartet and a madrigalian flavour about the third. The quintet, despite its unusual layout and a

[1] *National Music*, p. 179.

finale nearly as long in terms of bars (418) as the other three movements put together (488), shows little sign of inventive originality.

A three-movement Quintet in C minor for a more orthodox combination (piano, violin, viola, cello, and double bass), taking the 'Trout' Quintet, perhaps as a point of departure, (Schubert was one of RVW's youthful enthusiasms), was completed on 27 October 1903, revised in August 1904, and further revised in September 1905. Apart from the Brahmsian opening movement, which is on an expansive scale (384 bars), this is a more characteristic work altogether, so much so that Vaughan Williams lifted and slightly adapted the theme from the finale, which has a nice flexibility of rhythm and metre, for the Violin Sonata that he composed in 1954. A *Ballade and Scherzo* for 'Mozart-type' string quintet (two violas rather than two cellos) written in 1904, with the Scherzo based on a folk-song that Vaughan Williams himself had collected in Sussex that year, shows him wrestling with the problem of how to fit folk material into an acceptable formal pattern. The song melody occurs only in snatches throughout most of the Scherzo's 174 bars, being heard in its entirety only at the end of the movement. This formal experiment is similar to those engaged on at this time by Sibelius, who was likewise drawn to new solutions of the problem of reconciling unusual thematic material with the demands of more traditional forms. There is no suggestion that Vaughan Williams was in any way using Sibelius as a model, but simply that both composers were feeling their way towards new forms because the logical development of their musical ideas did not fit the old ones.

The first of his published chamber works came out after he had completed his studies with Ravel. On their first appearance, commentators were eager to spot French influences in them, subconsciously fearing, perhaps, that, like Pelham Humfrey two centuries previously, Vaughan Williams might have returned from France 'an absolute monsieur'. The first of them to achieve performance was the G minor String Quartet, played by the Schwiller Quartet at a meeting of the Society of British Composers on 8 November 1909; exactly a week later both the quartet and the song-cycle *On Wenlock Edge* were performed at the Aeolian Hall. Gervase Elwes was the solo singer and the Schwiller Quartet was joined in *On Wenlock Edge* by the pianist Frederick Kiddle.

While *On Wenlock Edge* is comparatively well known, the G minor String Quartet (which was not published until 1923) is unjustly neglected. It is strange to think that this spirited and civilized little work was criticized on its first appearance for being 'difficult to assimilate' and as 'an extreme development of modernism, so much so that not even the advanced taste of an audience of British composers could find everything in [it] acceptable'.[2] Vaughan Williams himself remarked that a

---

[2] Kennedy, *Works 2*, p. 115.

colleague claimed that the Quartet sounded as if he had been having tea with Debussy. Certainly it does show traces of impressionism in the harmonic treatment, the textures, and some of the colouristic effects, but far less so than the song-cycle. The strongest influence in the outline of the themes is surely that of English folk-song.

It is typical of Vaughan Williams at any stage in his career that a work that opens so ingenuously in an ambiguous modal G minor should have its first full chord in F major. It marks out at once the composer's approach to harmonic procedures in this work. The flattened seventh is given prominence by being allowed its own common chord—evidence of an unacademic approach to harmonic logic that the composer might (or might not) have derived from his studies with Ravel. The first movement is cast in a fairly orthodox sonata form, allowing the viola a chance to display its capacity for slightly melancholy lyricism. Both the main themes have modal contours; and the music in general is characteristic enough to absorb a curious little passage, both in the exposition and the recapitulation, that foreshadows a similar one in Elgar's E minor Quartet of a decade later. The development is quietly resourceful, exploiting mainly the melodic rather than the harmonic implications of the themes, building up to a neatly-proportioned climax; and at the end of the coda, after a very brief nod in the direction of the great Tallis Fantasia that was brewing in the composer's mind at this time, the first fiddle part drifts upwards reflectively until it is hovering nearly three octaves above the top note of the quite unexpected progression of common chords—E major, F major, G major—that closes the movement.

The second movement, Minuet and Trio, opens as if Joseph Haydn had set up as caller at an English country dance, with its robust rhythmic opening in octaves and its persistent flattened sevenths. The little rhythmic tag that characterizes the main theme is found all over the texture and the theme itself tends to land up on unexpected notes. The Trio is based on a modal Anglo-Saxon first cousin to the tune of the minuet from Bizet's *l'Arlésienne*, though its continuation seems never quite sure whether it ought to present itself in a modal, a whole-tone, or a chromatic guise.

The Romance is a simple ternary design based on a flowing theme in a 5/4 metre and the Dorian mode. Its most striking effects are achieved, as so often with Vaughan Williams, by the simplest means: the resourceful and unorthodox use of the common chord. Though there are hints of the 'visionary' Vaughan Williams, notably in the contrasting central section of the movement, with its prominent triplets in thirds, the movement functions on the whole as a gentle contrast to the minuet rather than as a still, sad core to the work. Once more at the end, the first fiddle part rises reflectively aloft into the heights.

If Vaughan Williams had been having tea with anyone when thinking up the frolicsome and hearty Rondo Capriccioso the host was surely Holst rather than Debussy. It is based on a folk-dance jig tune resembling the finale theme of Schubert's *Death and the Maiden*, but with none of the tension and insistent urgency of that movement. As so often, Vaughan Williams makes skilful use of the contrast between 6/8 and 3/4. His treatment of the material is once more resourceful without being sensationally original, despite some interesting string colour effects; and he has some fun with a second episode that tries to inject a lyrical tone into the discussion, only to be ruled out of court by the jig theme. This tune gets its own back towards the end of the movement, though; and there is also an angular fugato that develops out of the 3/4 episode. The movement allows the players to show off their bowing technique and allows both them and the composer to let their hair down.

Those who look for Bartókian intensity, technical innovations, or brow-furrowing intellectual problems will be disappointed with the G minor Quartet. Though passages in it are un- or other-worldly, they are far outweighed by those that are either purely reflective or else downright rumbustious. It is in the line of descent of the kind of music composed by Haydn for reasonably well-equipped amateur players: grateful to play, challenging, but nowhere mercilessly demanding and neither trivial on the one hand nor solemnly profound on the other.

There could hardly be a greater contrast between two works than that between this sunny quartet and *On Wenlock Edge*. Once more there is a fusion of folk-music in the melodic line and full-bloodied impressionism in the accompaniment; but in the song-cycle, the impressionism is much more obvious: bleak, frozen chords, frenzied atmospheric tremolos, flickers, and flourishes both in the string lines and in the piano part create a much more vivid texture, time-bound and timeless at one and the same time, than anything found in the quartet. Housman's laconic, elegantly ironic melody is underlined in dramatic, even epic terms rather than purely lyrical: what would nowadays be called the subtext of the poems is brought to the surface, a fact of which early commentators were clearly aware and of which some strongly disapproved as being in some way unfaithful to the spirit of the poet. Such disapproval begs the whole question of why a composer should bother to set a poet's verse at all. It also gives the poet scant credit for possessing a wider range of sub-textual moods than the critic suspected.

The work acts on several planes at once. The vocal line is firm but free, while the essentially drawing-room combination of piano and string quartet is used to evoke an atmosphere that is both outdoor and pictorial and at the same time symbolic of the inner turmoil and pessimistic despair in the singer's soul. The illustrative writing is so graphic that it elicited the sour and obtuse comment 'mere pictorial melodrama' from Ernest Newman. This is nonsense. There is nothing sham or overdrawn about this music, though at times, the expression—*pace* the composer himself—is almost Mahlerian in its intensity and in its combination of inner numbness and outer agitation.

239

The gale so vividly portrayed in the first movement, 'On Wenlock Edge', stands in Housman's poem both for present inner storms and those of the long-distant past; it too, and the singer, will be things of the past before very long. Vaughan Williams keeps his initial bass line relatively high, so that it may enter with all the more telling effect underlining the voice an octave below. The three elements of the accompanimental texture: swaying tremolo triplets, surging arpeggios, and stormy trills, echoing the singer's inner torment on another plane, as it were, are lit up from time to time by a distant flicker of lightning from the violin or the piano. (Unless the pianist observes carefully Vaughan Williams's *ppp* marking at such moments, the whole effect is spoiled.) Such striking musical imagery must indeed have taken the work's first hearers by surprise.

'From Far, from Eve and Morning', the second song, sketches in by the simplest means the sense of the mysterious, eternal sky—Vaughan Williams simply writes a succession of common chords in the piano part. When the strings enter alone to support the simple but highly expressive vocal line in the second verse, which transfers the interest from scene-setting to personal reaction, the contrast is spell-binding. The strings are used to telling effect, too, in the next song, 'Is my team ploughing?'. The full impact of the gaunt, thin voice from beyond the grave is cunningly projected by omitting the cello and muting the other strings, which gives the texture a ghostly insubstantial sound. Perhaps the chromaticisms in the answering verses are somewhat out of keeping, but this is a spine-chilling setting of a poem whose juxtaposition of pathos and irony is a real challenge to the composer.

'Oh, When I was in Love with You' is almost folk-song-like in its simplicity, though even here there is subtlety of colour, as when the violin echoes the viola at the end *an octave lower*. Impressionism returns with a vengeance in 'Bredon Hill', not only in the masterly versatility with which Vaughan Williams portrays the different sounds and evokes the symbolic mood associations of the bells, but also in the atmospheric dissonant chord progressions that depict the lazy calm of summer and in the chill high pianissimo of the widely-spaced strings (again, minus the cello) portraying the desolate winter landscape. And when the final calm of death is achieved in 'Clun', the music has strayed into a realm that transcends Housman's mood completely and foreshadows the peace that passeth all understanding of so many of Vaughan Williams's later works. One cannot explain the strange fascination of this kaleidoscopic work by pointing out 'how it's done' any more than one can explain away the violence and vehemence of the F minor Symphony by a bar-by-bar analysis of the structure. The total effect of the music is far more than simply the sum of its not particularly original components (many of which can certainly be found in Debussy and Ravel); and though it may not be as convincing a work as the *Fantasia on a Theme by Thomas*

Tallis, which received its first performance not so much later, it is perhaps a more protean one, especially in its form as arranged for tenor and orchestra.

Vaughan Williams's *Phantasy Quintet* is on the Mozartian pattern, with two violas, rather than the Schubertian, with two cellos. In 1905, William W. Cobbett had established a prize for chamber music; the works submitted were expected to be cast in one movement that formed a coherent whole, in the manner of the Tudor and Jacobean viol fantasias. Generations of English composers have profited from Cobbett's initiative, just as generations of commentators on chamber music and chamber musicians on the look-out for worthwhile but offbeat works to perform have benefited from the massive survey of chamber music universally known simply as 'Cobbett' that he compiled. Though the *Phantasy Quintet* was not a Cobbett prize entry, it was written at Cobbett's request and is dedicated jointly to him and to four of those who took part in its first public performance: the London String Quartet. It is short enough to form a curtain-raiser to one of the more familiar recital pieces, yet substantial enough to stand alongside them. The first performance was at the Aeolian Hall on 23 March 1914 as part of one of F. B. Ellis's chamber music concert series.

This work is a delight. It can easily be underrated, for it abounds in mood-changes, at times abrupt to the point of caprice. The thoughtful unaccompanied viola opening, 'Lento ma non troppo', is on a pentatonic theme (Frank Howes[3] claims it is in a pentatonic F, but the presence of an E flat in it contradicts that; and the first entry of the violins with their F major chord comes as a distinct shock) but the background harmonies when they emerge are treated in the familiar and by now completely assimilated impressionist manner, with progressions of consecutive triads, major and minor chords being juxtaposed in a striking manner. One of these progressions, in fact, extends a rhetorical juxtaposition of two common chords familiar from the Tallis Fantasia into a typically Vaughan Williams 'organically emergent' theme. The contrasting textures, rich but never thick, and clear yet never thin, are often arresting. A typical case is the beginning. The manner in which the thematic leads converge into block chords following a free inversion in the first violin part of the viola's upward-arching theme shows a highly sensitive feeling for the colour contrasts available in the medium Vaughan Williams had chosen.

The second section, Prestissimo, in 7/4 time is both spritely and substantial, light in mood but solid in texture. The ostinato bass, with its alternation of four running crotchet beats and three dancing ones (crotchet, two quavers, crotchet) has very soon to reconcile its own rhythm with a conflicting one of $2+3+2$ on a theme derived from the

---

[3] *The Music of Ralph Vaughan Williams*, p. 216.

viola's motto from the very beginning of the work. The tensions are not
violent and the movement does not lead to anything approaching a musical punch-up. Instead, it subsides into a gentle saraband, in which the
absence of cello tone lends a delicate radiance to the sound. The outline
of the ostinato motif is allowed to expand into a flowing, lyrical theme
in its own right.

Instead of summing up the contrasting moods of the preceding sections, the final Burlesca introduces new elements of its own. It starts off
with what sounds as if it is to be a stealthy, skittish, and slightly sardonic cousin to the 'March Past of the Kitchen Utensils' from the music
for *The Wasps*, but becomes in fact a fantasia within the fantasia, based
this time on the new ostinato theme. For all its being an excellent example of the wit that was to come to full flower nearly half a century later
in the second movement of the Eighth Symphony, and for all its coun-
try-dance capering, it also has passionate and reflective moments, with
the main theme being played in diminution and with its rhythm altered
to take on a lyrical hue as the harmonies freeze and the violin line melts
into a rhapsodic cadenza and a reference back to the opening, as if to
show how far the music has travelled in so short a time-span.

This work shows in a striking manner how many varied moods—
ruminative, grotesque, ethereal, and hyper-active, sardonic, rumbustious, and passionate, can be extracted from a simple basic theme in a
remarkably short time-span. Perhaps Vaughan Williams does not
develop some of them as much as he might; but then the work's concentration would have been undermined. ('The trouble about **** is that
he will go on so': the reader may choose any suitable Romantic or post-
Romantic composer's name to fit the asterisks.) The trouble about the
Phantasy Quintet is that perhaps it *doesn't* 'go on so' quite enough, especially in the last section, where the frequent and drastic changes of mood
seem sometimes not to be integrated into a satisfactory overall design.

At least two of the three settings for voice and string trio to words
attributed to Chaucer, published under the title *Merciless Beauty*, are of
considerable interest. Unusually for Vaughan Williams, it is the viola
that is omitted from the string quartet texture rather than one of the
violins. These three rondels were composed in about 1921 and while the
first of them is somewhat square and rigid in the rhythm of its word-
settings, the second and third have a much more expressive and flexible
vocal line. Michael Kennedy[4] writes of their wild-flower freshness, an
apt comment, for the atmosphere is much more aloof and delicate than
the intensity and power so characteristic of *On Wenlock Edge*. It is a
mood in keeping with the scornful disdain so evident in the poems. He
also comments that they show how completely Vaughan Williams had
absorbed folk-music into his personal idiom. One might add that the

---

[4] Kennedy, *Works* 2, p. 178.

third of them, 'Since I from love' has the effect of a 1920s version of some Elizabethan consort song, too.

In 1926, Vaughan Williams composed *Six Studies in English Folk Song* for cello and piano for the cellist May Mukle. These slight but attractive pieces are not literal transcriptions of folk-melodies, but are based on well-known tunes, freely treated and ornamented, whose identity can be easily traced. Perhaps the most attractive of them is the first, a setting of 'Lovely on the Water', in which the tune emerges naturally from the accompaniment. Also of interest is the fourth: 'She borrowed some of her mother's gold', where the arpeggio piano accompaniment rocks gently back and forth, occasionally acting as a kind of emergent descant for the cello. The last of the set, 'As I Walked over London Bridge', ('Geordie') with its air of innocent jollity, its varied accompanimental texture, and its surprise ending, is so terse that one regrets the composer did not treat the tune more expansively. But then perhaps the succinct wit of the setting would have been lost.

The four-movement *Suite for Pipes*, composed in 1939 for the Pipers' Guild, is affable and easy on the ear; and the three movements of *Household Music: Three Preludes on Welsh Hymn Tunes*, designed for domestic music-making in the Second World War for those who, like Vaughan Williams during World War I, might find themselves with musical friends but no established repertory because the combination of instruments available did not fit an orthodox ensemble, are fun to play and pleasant to listen to. The setting of the solemn tune 'St Denio' ('Immortal, invisible God only wise') as a spritely scherzo—restoring it from its august hymn-book gravity to its original mood and tempo—and the eight resourceful variations on 'Aberystwyth' ('Jesu, lover of my soul') are particularly enjoyable.

One wonders what the violist Jean Stewart's feelings were besides delight, pride, and gratitude at so handsome a birthday present as the A minor Quartet when she and her colleagues in the Menges Quartet first played it through. RVW had sent her two of the movements in time for her birthday in the spring of 1943 with a note to the effect that the Scherzo had so far failed to materialize. It did later in the year; and it proved to be as terse as the movements already delivered. The Menges gracefully returned the birthday compliment by giving the first public performance at the National Gallery on Vaughan Williams's seventy-second birthday on 12 October 1944, following the tradition he had established when premièring Holst's works with the Bach Choir of performing it twice at the same concert, sandwiching a Haydn quartet in between the two performances.

Yet this concentrated and—once more—underrated masterpiece is a strange birthday-offering. Its final hard-won serenity is the outcome of a dour and relentless struggle; and it shows little evidence of the conventional high spirits normally associated with birthday gifts. But then

Vaughan Williams was no rigid follower of convention. Janus-like, recalling *Riders to the Sea* and even *Wenlock Edge* at times, doffing its cap at the Fifth Symphony and foreshadowing the chilly ambivalence of the end of the Sixth, it naturally gives the viola a rich share of the musical pickings. There is little or nothing in the string writing that goes beyond what the impressionists had already done and there are no outrageous calculated harmonic or rhythmic effects. Like Bartók's Sixth or one of Shostakovich's mature quartets, its originality lies in the unusual use of conventional devices—particularly, as so often with Vaughan Williams, in the manner in which he juxtaposes common chords.

The first movement, Prelude, is surely a much closer companion in mood (and even at times in thematic outline and texture) to *On Wenlock Edge* than the G minor Quartet composed over a generation previously. But here there is the added mastery of over thirty years' further exploration and development of a fully-formed highly personal idiom. The mood is much tighter-lipped and almost obsessively concentrated, the music swiftly and restlessly expanding from the viola's opening flourish—as though some English Smetana was picturing the stormwind on Wenlock Edge blowing through his hair. Where the opening movement of the G minor Quartet unwinds in a leisurely fashion, this one drives onwards headlong, the partners almost nagging away at one another rather than conducting a civilized Senior Common Room discussion, and generating a mood of extreme and unremitting intensity.

A Prelude, the violist dedicatee must have thought as she played it through, to what? Certainly not to any real respite, for the ensuing Romance is as different as could be from that of the First Quartet: a weird, partly contrapuntal, partly chordal meditation on a cool, rather aloof theme that unwinds waywardly, changing its shape as each instrument takes it up, each casting its own individual light on its bleak—Kennedy's apt word[5]—inner landscape. The instruments are asked to play without vibrato; and the resultant viol-like sound evokes no archaic stately Tudor solemnity, but rather an austere, remote, disembodied world. There is little here of the rapt contemplation of a work like the Tallis Fantasia. The music seems to have strayed into yet another unknown region where the stars twinkle pitilessly out of the musical equivalent of outer space. The hymn-like double-stopped chords (Ex. 15), so cunningly spaced so that there is no hint of thickness or romantic warmth, add a touch of humanity to the scene; but it is the 'still, sad music' of humanity that they seem to project, not the flow of fulfilment that the title Romance almost automatically conjured up in Vaughan Williams. This Romance is poles apart from that of the Fifth Symphony, yet it is palpably from the same hand. Again, one wonders if any sense of puzzlement tempered Jean Stewart's delight at receiving the piece.

[5] Sleeve-note to the EMI recording by The Music Group of London, p. 6.

Ex. 15

In the Scherzo, lifted in part from the music to *49th Parallel*, the viola is allowed to stand out from the other instruments by being unmuted against their muted tremolando effects. The effect is striking: the soft yet tension-laden background creates an astonishing combination of speed, power, and lightness: not the elfin lightness of a Mendelssohn scherzo (or even that of the coda to the scherzo of VW's own *Pastoral Symphony*), but one with a kind of Shostakovichian ambivalence, with its shadowy echoes of the Fifth Symphony's 'First Nowell' tune that derive from the viola's opening phrase. There is no real trio section, only fourteen contrasting bars that reawaken flickering visions of the first movement's turmoil, but this time driven almost violently home in martial, fortissimo double stops; and the telescoped recapitulation leads via a short coda into the epilogue, where the first hint of human warmth and serenity begins to relieve and resolve the tensions and ambiguities and casts a glow over the half-light embers of the rest of the music. This movement was apparently taken from the music to a projected but never completed film about Joan of Arc, hence the sub-title: Greetings from Joan to Jean. It is a noble, gently ruminative meditation of the utmost simplicity and fluency; and it rounds off this enigmatic mid-twentieth-century counterpart of the great Beethoven F minor Quartet in a consummation that is as effective and as inevitable, yet as unexpected as the ending of that work.

The Violin Sonata of 1954, first performed on the composer's eighty-second birthday by Frederick Grinke (the dedicatee) and Michael Mullinar, is a substantial work that reserves most of its surprises for the finale. The opening Fantasia is an attractive lyrical movement whose theme, like so many of Vaughan Williams's themes, develops from its context: two fragments of phrase into which a third fragment is inserted. Its solemn, brooding atmosphere is undermined, indeed in the central section dominated, by a rhythm similar to that of the opening of the *Partita*; and it is only at the end that comparative calm is regained.

The Scherzo—sounding almost as if Bartók and Shostakovich were capering about on Leith Hill—is a real spitfire of a movement, with innumerable displaced accents, insistent to the point of obsessiveness on its basic rhythm and keeping the pianist busy all the time. The finale,

Tema con Variationi, as long as the two preceding movements put together, opens with a texture and therefore an atmosphere that is possibly unique in violin sonatas. The violin plays *inside* the top two lines of the piano part, which itself is laid out in double octaves with a gap between the left and right hands that sometimes reaches three octaves. The first variation threads the theme (taken from the 1903 Piano Quintet) with rich embroidery in the piano part. The second announces it in two modes at once in fairly strict imitation at an interval of four bars: each time, one version starts on F sharp and the other on D. The third is rather in the vein of 'Famous Men'; the fourth creates a mysterious atmosphere by cunning technical means: the composer inverts the theme in the violin part and it is played against itself augmented and the right way up in the accompaniment. With the fifth variation, in a kind of major, but with a flattened sixth and seventh degree of the scale, we return to familiar RVW territory: warm, serene, and lyrical—what Holst would have called the *real* RVW. The final variation brings us back to earth again with lively syncopations in the piano part, while the coda recalls the accompanying gestures of the *Fantasia*, squared up into a solid 4/4.

Vaughan Williams's published chamber music all dates from his years of maturity. It is a pity indeed that more of it is not better known.

20

Epilogue

If we disregard his one completed and performed schoolboy composition, Ralph Vaughan Williams's long career as a composer covered some sixty-five years. At the time of his birth, *The Ring* was only half-completed, the only Gilbert and Sullivan collaboration had resulted in an apparent one-off, performed today only as a reconstructed curiosity, none of the four Brahms symphonies had seen the light of day, the Royal College of Music did not exist, and if people attended a promenade concert, they really did promenade during the music. During RVW's lifetime Western European music changed out of almost all recognition, as anyone can hear for themselves by simply juxtaposing the openings of Brahms's Fourth Symphony, written when RVW was a lad of thirteen, and of Pierre Boulez's *Pli selon Pli*, work on which was begun in the year before Vaughan Williams died. Both of these works are regarded as masterpieces of their age, yet on a superficial hearing there is virtually no point of contact between them.

The status of music and of musicians in England also underwent profound, perhaps radical changes. The public for music of all kinds expanded enormously. State and municipal support for music became the (often grudging) norm rather than the unheard-of ideal. Orchestral playing, both professional and amateur, improved immensely and with it, the number of permanent orchestras with a stable personnel and the chance for a young composer of hearing a new composition performed. Operatic life improved as well. Permanent native opera companies may not abound even now; but they do exist. At least one of RVW's younger contemporaries was acknowledged both at home and abroad as a composer whose next opera was eagerly awaited, whatever its subject and wherever it might be staged, instead of his having to plough almost a lone furrow in quiet desperation as Vaughan Williams's own teacher Stanford had done. Large-scale amateur choirs still existed, performing that democratic and English music so dear to Hubert Parry's heart, but their repertory had broadened to take in music whose technical difficulties might well have frightened off their predecessors two generations previously. The harvest of folk-songs had been largely gathered in and absorbed into the musical bloodstream of thousands of children exposed to the work of such pioneers as Sharp and Vaughan Williams himself.

Nobody as open-minded as RVW could have failed to respond to all these developments. Yet nobody as strong-minded and possessing such integrity as he did would simply have accepted all of it without hesitation. From the emergence of the *real* RVW at the turn of the twentieth century to the day of his death, there is a steady consistency and concern about lasting musical values and their expression. These can be studied both in his private and public writings about music and in the ethos of those influences that most strongly marked his own output.

As he grew older, he often liked to project himself as an old fogey, yet even when doing so he generally showed his essential broad-mindedness. As the acknowledged doyen of folk-song composers, for example, he wrote in 1943 of Britten's first collection of folk-song arrangements:

> Are we old fogeys of the Folk Song movement getting into a rut? If so, it is very good for us to be pulled out by such fiery young steeds as Benjamin Britten . . . We see one side of a folk song, they see the other.
>
> They probably think our point of view hopelessly dull and stodgy, but that is no excuse for us to label them self-conscious or deliberately freakish.
>
> Personally I am delighted to see these rockettings come to a sound *terra firma* from which I believe all flights of fancy must take off—beautiful, spontaneous melody which belongs essentially to us.
>
> The tune's the thing with which we'll catch the conscience of the composer. Do these settings spring from a love of the tune? Then, whatever our personal reaction may be we must respect them.[1]

The implications of this comment are clear. Vaughan Williams may not have responded personally to Britten's arrangements: he may even have thought them self-conscious or freakish, but he did recognize that they sprang from a love of the tune. They were therefore to be welcomed. This contrasts strongly with his comment to Christopher Finzi on Stravinsky's arrangement of Bach's 'Vom Himmel Hoch': 'If he dislikes Bach as much as that, I don't know why he bothers to orchestrate him.'[2]

In the forthright expression of his opinions he spared no one, not even those friends whom he admired and to whom he owed much, as he would have been the first to acknowledge. Nor did he indulge in any false modesty, let alone self-pity, when he felt that a performance had failed to do justice to one of his 'tunes' as he habitually called them. Writing to Sir Adrian Boult, for instance, in November 1941 about a performance of *England, my England*, he was trenchant in his criticisms:

> . . . I cannot pretend that I was not rather dismayed by the performance—As a matter of fact the 1st verse was the best—the controllers toned down the orchestra so much that it did not matter—But it was fatal in the 2nd and 3rd

[1] Quoted by Donald Mitchell in the sleeve-note to Benjamin Britten, *The Folk Songs* (Collins Classics, 70392).

[2] *RCM Magazine*, p. 53.

verses where the descant and harmonies swamped the tune—& the whole thing was sung without conviction as if they [i.e. the BBC's professional Chorus] did not know it (which according to your account they do not)—Do you not think that the B.B.C. with all its tradition would have done better to cut it out altogether rather than give an unrehearsed performance? I was particularly sorry because the tune is rather a ewe lamb of mine & I feel that if it had got a proper send off it might hit the nail on the head—But I felt on Sunday night that it had been strangled at birth.[3]

He could be equally brusque when dealing with a technical point. Some years later, in June 1948, Boult wrote to him asking whether he could clarify when vibrato should or should not be used in performing the *Partita*. Vaughan Williams curtly replied:

Dear Adrian
Thank you so much for your letter about 'Vibrato'. I have decided to put nothing into the score. If people cannot play it right by light of nature I feel that no amount of explanations will make them do it.

Yrs, RVW[4]

Yet when unsure of the cause for something that did not satisfy him, he was the soul of diffidence. Writing to thank and congratulate Boult about a broadcast later that same month of the Sixth Symphony, he asked:

. . . in the Scherzo the side drum sounded over the wireless to be still muffled as it is in the slow movement. Do you think the player did not tighten his snares, or whatever he does, to get that very sharp high sound which I want? I wonder if you could ask him next time you see him what the proper direction should be to get that effect, and if there is still time I will have it put into the score . . . [5]

This attention to detail in essential matters relating to his music should surely dispel any dismissal of his approach to his craft as 'amateurish'. At the age of seventy-two he could still worry about details in works as early in his output as *A Sea Symphony*, commenting to Boult in February 1945 on a problem passage in the finale:

'O Soul thou pleasest me' is more difficult—we have tried de-muting the 4th horn—now it sticks out too much. Would you try a *single cello* muted *and pp added* to the 4th horn? I believe that would solve it—but it must *not* be played like a solo with lots of vibrato etc.[6]

If dissatisfied with the shape or scoring of a work, he would revise it over and over again. All the symphonies underwent revision on points of detail after—sometimes long after—they were published. Even a comparatively unimportant early work like *In the Fen Country*, first performed in April 1904, was revised in 1905, 1907, and 1935. His

---

[3] Boult, p. 138.   [4] Ibid., p. 151.   [5] Ibid., p. 152.   [6] Ibid., p. 146.

craftsmanship may not always have been flawless; but he was always practical in his approach. Hence the innumerable arrangements of and modifications to those of his works that he felt good enough to offer to a wider audience than that for which they were originally intended: *Hugh the Drover* adapted to form *A Cotswold Romance*, the re-casting of seven songs from *The Pilgrim's Progress* for voice and piano, the extraction of the 'plums' from *Sir John in Love* for the cantata *In Windsor Forest*, the considerable number of different arrangements of folk-songs or songs like 'Linden Lea', and so on.

The obvious starting-point for any consideration of Vaughan Williams's musical language is of course English folk-song. There is no need to labour the point about his deep love of English (and other) folk-music, or his sympathy for those of his contemporaries whose own genius was released by the discovery of their native heritage (not necessarily that of folk-music *per se*), such as Sibelius, Bartók, Kodály, and Janáček. It would seem from reactions at various times in his life that he also enjoyed much of their music.

It is certainly true that Vaughan Williams's absorption of the essence of English folk-song is evident from any of what may be called his 'post-pre-Raphaelite' compositions. But in his Mary Flexner lectures, he was careful to point out both the pros and the cons of using folk-song as the basis for a compositional style; and he cast an interesting light on its appeal to him:

> In the days when Elgar formed his style, English folk-song was not 'in the air' but was consciously revived and made popular only about thirty years ago [i.e. in about 1904]. Now what does this revival mean to the composer? It means that several of us found here in its simplest form the musical idiom which we were unconsciously cultivating ourselves, It gave a point to our imagination . . . the knowledge of our folk-songs did not so much discover for us something new, but uncovered for us something which had been hidden by foreign matter.[7]

Folk-song was, in other words, a short cut to musical self-knowledge: 'what we were unconsciously cultivating ourselves.' It was not a model to be copied from the outside. This is why Vaughan Williams developed an idiom which may have based its inflections and methods on those of folk-song but which also expanded the whole technique beyond the bounds of the folk-song itself and into the realm of symphonic style.

One of the features of English folk-song that most affected Vaughan Williams was its modality. Most Western scales are based on two identical or similar tetrachords. The modern C major scale, for example, has intervals of three consecutive tones and one semitone (from C to F), the pattern being repeated from G to C. The Aeolian mode, common in English folk-music (and in the music of Benjamin Britten) runs TSTT,

---

[7] *National Music*, p. 41.

TSTT. But some of the modes are not symmetrically constructed. The Mixolydian scale, for example, runs TTST, TSTT. Vaughan Williams often exploited differing tetrachords from different modes. This gives his themes a flexibility that at first hearing sounds as if the modal inflections have been chromaticized, but on closer investigation shows that he has cunningly combined two modal tetrachords to produce a scale of which he can then exploit the melodic and harmonic implications. Sometimes, he uses different tetrachords in an ascending scale from those in the descending version. This may or may not have been a conscious process. It was certainly a very characteristic one.

It is a noticeable feature of quite a few English folk-song melodies that they are built up, not on the square repetition of balanced phrases, but by the fitting together of contrasting but related musical motifs: 'I will give my love an apple', which Vaughan Williams himself arranged, is a case in point. There are a number of key elements which are blended together to form a tune; and one complete phrase is repeated almost note for note to form the second and fourth lines of the tune. For the key motifs see Ex. 16a, b, and c; the complete phrase is (d), and the whole tune is shown in Ex. 17. The great sweeping melody which comes at the end of the first movement of the Sixth Symphony, for example, might be described as an enhanced folk melody. How it arises out of its context, however, is equally important and has been considered elsewhere (p. 208); what is of present interest is the elements from which the theme is constructed. It, too, is built up from a number of motifs welded together by balance and variation. The tune itself could not be a folk-song: its mood is too sophisticated and its flow just a little too irregular; but it is a development from the same root as 'I will give my love an apple'; and that root is an English root (Ex. 18).

Ex. 16

Ex. 17

Ex. 18

In his earlier works, Vaughan Williams made much use of material that was so like some of the folk-songs he had collected that critics and listeners were hard put to it to tell the difference. His first approach was to adapt the technique of quoting snatches of a theme at varying intervals in imitation, as in works such as *In the Fen Country* and the *Fantasia on Christmas Carols*. To begin with, this served him well, but he was not satisfied; and it seems to have taken him some time to hit on the best way of giving some kind of onward movement and formal cohesion to his musical designs. More than once he quotes with a sense of rueful admission of its truth Constant Lambert's malicious but regrettably accurate observation that 'the only thing you can do with a folksong when you have played it once is to play it again, and play it rather louder'.[8] After a few early essays, many of which had landed up on his very considerable scrap-heap of rejected compositions, he no longer cultivated the mosaic-like rhapsody nor fitted his themes into the Procrustean bed of sonata form. Instead, he developed his own forms and harmonic procedures from his melodic idiom.

This involved working out a new way of what might be called paragraphing his larger-scale compositions. Where the harmonic progression of a phrase is constructed according to accepted conventions, the phrase-lengths and the modulatory scheme can in the hands of an unimaginative composer become totally predictable. A certain freedom is gained when the themes are built on scales outside those conventions; and the balancing and contrasting of the phrases can take account of the shape of the melody rather than the implications of the harmony underlying it. Vaughan Williams's essay on Beethoven's Ninth Symphony shows his awareness of this problem and his sensitivity to Beethoven's solution to it in that work. In his own music, he worked out his own ways of dealing with it. There is thus a world of difference between his use of modal material, which is fundamental not only to his melodic idiom but to his

[8] Lambert, p. 117.

large-scale forms, and that of a composer who treats modality or folk-song-like inflections as a purely local colour or evocative effect. It is the difference between the swallow that incorporates material into the structure of its nest and the magpie that merely decorates it with garish objects. Naturally, the forms that he developed bear some resemblance to sonata form, simply because sonata form, too, is a sophisticated extension of older, balanced, and purely melodic forms. The difference between the two is the difference between the tonal, melodic, and rhythmic structure of modal English folk-song and the tonal conventions of post-baroque harmonic theory.

It is not often realized how original Vaughan Williams was in the matter of devising new forms, simply because his respect for tradition made them appear as mere deviations from old ones (and thus as evidence of shortcomings in his technical ability). This process of grafting new shoots onto old stocks can be seen at work in the Tallis Fantasia; it is also at work in *Pastoral Symphony*; and above all in the remarkable opening movement of the Sixth which, for all its pretence at being a sonata movement, is in fact a series of variations culminating in a theme instead of branching out from one. This technique is developed further in the first movement of the Eighth, where the variations are 'in search of a theme' that itself is never stated, as the composer put it. (Even so, he roguishly covered his tracks by indicating that the movement could in fact be analysed on sonata lines.)

The sense of forward movement and development in large-scale classical structures depended to a considerable extent on two important factors: the tension between rhythmic vitality and lyric appeal of the themes used and their tonal and harmonic implications. Too often in his very earliest works, Vaughan Williams tried to combine the structural procedures that he had absorbed as a student with the rather different harmonic implications of the folk-songs which now so strongly affected his style. Once he had worked out how to exploit the modal contours of his themes and the harmonic implications of the modal scales in which they were often cast, he began to develop new and original formal procedures of his own.

His first step was to develop a way of generating development by evolution rather than by harmonic conflict, thematic interaction, and mood-contrast, which was the essence of traditional sonata form. Here again, he took a leaf out of the book of English folk-song. Certain English folk-songs, such as 'It's a rosebud in June', show a tendency to expand from an initial phrase by varying its length, the shape of its intervals, and its rhythm. In 'It's a rosebud in June', the little phrase shown in Ex. 19a becomes Ex. 19b and c, so that the whole tune seems to evolve out of the first phrase. There are any number of examples of this in Vaughan Williams's own themes: the theme quoted in Ex. 18 from the Sixth Symphony is one of them. So is Ex. 20a from the *Sinfonia Antartica* and Ex. 20b from *Flos Campi*.

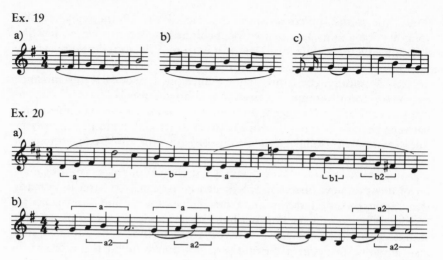

Ex. 19

Ex. 20

That he regarded this as a legitimate way of developing symphonic material is shown by a passage in his long essay on Beethoven's Ninth Symphony, where he points out that when Beethoven wishes to develop the thematic fragment, Ex. 21a, he turns it into Ex. 21b, which is exactly what Vaughan Williams himself does in the Tallis Fantasia, where he takes the upward minor third at the beginning of the theme and expands it (taking his cue from Tallis himself) first into a perfect fifth (Ex. 22a) and then to an octave (Ex. 22b) before submitting it to a further process of melodic expansion which is really only that of 'It's a rosebud in June' on a much larger and more consciously applied scale.

Ex. 21

Ex. 22

Having discarded the tonal basis of orthodox sonata form, Vaughan Williams had to seek new and more appropriate ways of organizing his material. His studies of French impressionist music gave him some hints as to how to set about doing this. Clearly, it simply would not suffice to submit modal themes to tonal treatment or to cobble them together in an attempt to generate rhythmic or harmonic tension between different folk-like themes. By the time he composed *A London Symphony*, he was already some way on the path to a solution by applying what might be called the technique of organic evolution to them. In that case, his attempted solution, especially in the first movement, was to base his first subject group on a series of very short and contrasting motifs rather than genuine themes, leaving the more obvious melodic themes to the second subject material. The harmonies were already becoming incidental to the melodic material rather than determining the course and structure of the movement.

When it came to *Pastoral Symphony*, he took this approach a considerable step further. He combined the Debussyian method of using chords as sensations in themselves with the more traditional one of using in counterpoint thematic lines with different rhythmic characteristics to create the necessary tensions in the music that needed resolution. In the latter symphonies, the harmonic movement varies enormously in scope, but it is always self-consistent. In the Fourth, it centres on the semitonal clash at the beginning and the chain reaction of fourths that follows it. In the Fifth, as Hugh Ottaway made clear, it is based on a highly imaginative interaction of modal and tonal elements; and in the Sixth, it depends to a large extent on the ambiguities inherent in two harmonic propositions: the tonal ambiguity of the interval of the augmented fourth and the ambiguous nature of the same note: G sharp when it is considered as the major third of the scale of E, or its enharmonic A flat, considered as the minor third of F minor.

Most symphonies of any genuine significance seem to fall into one of two categories. The first of these may, for want of a better term, be called *convergent*. In a 'convergent' symphony, the movements are consistent with one another, offering variety within a schematic unity, but there is no feeling that a conflict stated at the beginning of the first movement is not totally resolved until the close of the finale. A Kellerian functional analysis may well bring to the surface thematic interrelationships that lie hidden beneath the apparent differences, but as Hans Keller himself was at pains to point out, the unity that such an analysis reveals is and should be felt before it can be demonstrated and rationalized; and that unity is not necessarily underlined by the work's onward progress from movement to movement.

The second type of symphony may perhaps more justifiably be called *linear*. In a 'linear' symphony, such, for example, as Beethoven's Fifth, the underlying idea of the work seems to be such that the emotional charge that the various movements carry unites them so strongly that the music moves onward through time with a formal and emotional *inevitability*. Each movement is not merely *compatible* with its predecessors; it is felt to be the *consequence* of them. Thus, a 'linear' symphony seems to progress almost relentlessly from the opening bars of the first movement to the final cadence of the last.

Vaughan Williams's symphonies have been misunderstood and underrated because not all of them are undoubtedly 'linear'. His three 'middle' symphonies, the F minor, the D major, and the Sixth in E minor, move almost inexorably from their opening to their closing bars.[9] The F minor, indeed, like the Brahms Clarinet Quintet, alludes quite unexpectedly, yet inevitably, to its actual opening at the very end. This is no backward glance in nostalgia (or even in anger). There is simply a reminder that all the material in the work grew—exploded would perhaps be a better word—out of the very opening. In Vaughan Williams's earlier symphonies and in at least two of the later ones (the Eighth and the Ninth) this sense is not as strong.

In the first movement of the Eighth Symphony, Vaughan Williams follows a very similar procedure to that adopted by Britten in *The Young Person's Guide to the Orchestra* of highlighting now this aspect of Purcell's superb tune and now another one in each variation. There is, however, an important innovatory difference. The motifs Vaughan Williams deals with are not part of a full-blown melody as such, but simply scraps of music in their own right. (In this context, we should remember that Vaughan Williams's Eighth Symphony was composed ten years after *The Young Person's Guide*. If Vaughan Williams was 'cribbing', he was cribbing a technique rather than actual musical substance.)

If the Eighth were a 'linear' symphony, we might expect the 'theme' of which the fragments of music were in search to turn up somewhere in the finale as a grand clinching climax of the work as a whole, as Purcell's theme arises majestically out of Britten's fugue at the end of *The Young Person's Guide*. Nothing of the kind happens. The first movement remains an unresolved question, the music evaporating mysteriously into the opening phrase. There follows the quirky, cocky scherzo-movement for wind instruments alone, the slow movement and the exuberant finale. Thematically, they have nothing obviously in common with one another; the finale is in a sense the crowning (and certainly the noisiest) movement of the work, but it does not, as does that of the Sixth Symphony, for example, grow musically out of the previous three. Anyone expecting a 'linear' construction is bound to be disappointed if not baffled.

A work like the *Fantasia on a Theme by Thomas Tallis* creates its own way of coming to terms with time by developing a kind of rhythmic flux that eschews regularity of phrasing and of metre in the gentlest and most contemplative manner, in fact 'updating' the 'Medieval' or 'primitive' attitude to time. The Sixth Symphony does the same thing, but in a much more abrupt and aggressive way, wrenching our sense of pulse

---

[9] The same is certainly true of a work like *Flos Campi*, which moves with a steady inevitability from its bi-modal opening to the radiant D major of its close.

into unexpected directions or putting it under continual stress: witness
the first two movements, which are barred in regular common, 12/8 or
6/4 metres but which in performance give an impression far removed
from the predictable regularities of the metres in which they are
couched. The same may be said of the 'swing-music' saxophone solo of
the third movement. And in the second movement,[10] the rhythmic and
metrical tension between the main theme and its accompanying rhythm
is a structural element not only in this movement, but throughout the
first three.

These tensions operate throughout the work, as Deryck Cooke so brilliantly showed in *The Language of Music*, towards the finale, the
inevitable outcome of the three previous movements, in which all the
most vital elements of the first three movements are assimilated into a
texture that is in itself utterly drained of any sense of purpose or onward
movement.[11] In other words, an essentially 'linear' work has in some
remarkable way found its musically logical outcome in a pattern that is
as remote from linearity as it is possible to be.

If the great *Et vitam venturi saeculi* fugue from Beethoven's Mass in D
or the opening of Part II of *Gerontius* do not convey in some way or
other that the flux of time has ceased to operate, then once again, the
performers have missed the metaphysical bus. In the right kind of performance, Vaughan Williams's music repeatedly conveys this impression. Sometimes, the sense of the timeless is what the German baroque
poets would have called 'Time without time'—*Zeit ohne Zeit*. In at least
one case, that of the massive central movement of the *Sinfonia Antartica*,
it is more a case of *Zeit ohne Ende*: the appalling prospect of endless
duration in a situation of complete numb hopelessness.[12]

When the composer flippantly referred to his *Pastoral Symphony* as
being 'in four movements, all of them slow' he was perhaps drawing
attention to the highly individual way in which this work relates the listener to the sense of time—or of timelessness. The sense of 'timelessness'
in Vaughan Williams is one of the salient characteristics of certain of his
works; and in *Pastoral Symphony*, he seems to express it most consistently. Considered in 'linear' terms, the *Pastoral* might almost be
described as an 'anti'-symphony rather than as a symphony as the term
is generally understood. Perhaps this is why it has taken so much time
to make as much headway as works like the *London* or the Sixth. The
listener may subconsciously be trying to impose a 'linear' pattern on a

---

[10] See Lionel Pike, 'Rhythm in the symphonies: a preliminary investigation', in *VWS*, pp.
166–86.
[11] And, as Pike points out, the finale 'almost completely eschews triple elements', op.
cit., p. 178.
[12] Perhaps the endless repetitions of the trumpet-and-drum figure in the second movement of the Sixth Symphony convey a similar impression through a markedly different
means.

work which is not only 'convergent' but which also treats time not so much as something with which one has, as a sentient human being, to come to terms but as something which is irrelevant if not completely meaningless.

This is so even though, or perhaps even because, the movements are cast in formal patterns that can be related to orthodox sonata forms. One has a right to expect a sonata-pattern movement to be 'linear'. The *Pastoral*'s first movement has a number of recognizable sonata-form characteristics; but it does not create a 'linear' impression. The music does not drive onwards through time. It is almost as if the composer had chosen to view time in an eastern rather than a western manner.[13] The music *seems* to meander. In actual fact it does nothing of the kind. The pattern is balanced and satisfying; the themes evolve from the basic cells heard right at the start; and the course of the music is perfectly logical in terms of melodic, rhythmic, and—oddly enough—harmonic movement as well as conveying a mood that is quite unique in any sonata structure known to the present writer. This is a musical design poles apart from the calculated sonic solid geometry of the outright serialists; but it is just as inevitable.[14]

Yet the *Pastoral* is one of those works where the sequence of the movements matters a great deal. Anyone who doubts this should listen to it in its entirety with the CD-player arranged so that the movements are played in the wrong order: 3, 1, 4, 2, for example, or 4, 2, 1, 3. It is not just a matter of being used to the published sequence; it is a matter of the way in which each contributes to the overall design. This is a further indication of the fact that the work does not meander, but has a powerful inner coherence. Tovey is worth quoting here:

> Across this landscape of saturated colours there float the sounds of melodies older than any folk-song. These melodies are harmonized on the plan first reduced to formula by Debussy: whatever chord the melody begins with is treated as a mere sensation, and the chord follows the melody up and down the scale, instead of dissolving into threads of independent melodic line. But Vaughan Williams adds to this principle another, which is that two or even three melodic threads may run simultaneously, each loaded with its own chord, utterly regardless of how their chords collide. . . . As applied to classical coun-

---

[13] The composer seems to have sensed this when he told Adrian Boult to play it rather faster than Boult thought to be the correct tempo. The next time the work came up for performance, Boult says RVW told him to take it more slowly, claiming that having heard it performed and having conducted it himself, he had found that it wasn't as boring as he had feared.

[14] It is a great pity that Deryck Cooke had neither the time nor the space to analyse the *Pastoral* as thoroughly as he did the Sixth. Ottaway's perceptive essay on the work necessarily relates to RVW's other symphonies rather than looking at it on its own terms. Tovey's essay was designed as a programme-note and could not go into the analytical detail needed.

terpoint this principle is as old as Bach; but the systematic application of it to the anti-contrapuntal method of Debussy is new.[15]

The music may not be 'about' anything, any more than the Fourth or the Sixth are 'about' anything, yet the order in which the black dots are put down on paper matters exceedingly. The inner logic is felt rather than analytically perceived. Can it be analytically demonstrated? Does indeed it have to be?

What that inner logic comprises depends on a number of factors. A Kellerian functional analysis would relate the themes to a melodic *Urkeim*, a cell of a few notes involving a melodic curve, basic intervals, the harmonies implied by these elements and (possibly) certain relevant rhythmic factors. Deryck Cooke's analysis of Vaughan Williams's Sixth Symphony shows how effectively this suits music built up in the way that Vaughan Williams chooses to employ in that work. Hugh Ottaway shows in his penetrating account of mode and key relationships in the Fifth how another similar but not quite identical approach may also yield interesting results. To adopt this approach to the *Pastoral* is not quite as simple. But the work is far from being the rhapsodic dream as which it is sometimes dismissed.

To begin with, the melodic outlines of many of the themes of the work are plainly very similar anyway; and for a second point, Vaughan Williams's use of harmony in *Pastoral Symphony* is certainly influenced by the way chords are used by French impressionists. This is hardly surprising in view of his studies with one of the two major figures of the movement, Maurice Ravel. The most interesting harmonic feature of the *Pastoral*, though, is the fact that the overwhelming majority of the chords RVW uses are common chords. It is the manner in which he uses them that constitutes a major factor in the work's originality. These Debussyesque chains of common chords—chords moreover that also form part of a polyphonic network—make all thought of relating modal procedures in Ottaway's manner rather problematic. (Many of the themes in *Pastoral Symphony* are pentatonic rather than modal anyway.)

First of all, they move for the most part extremely slowly. And Vaughan Williams's use of impressionist methods of treating chords as sensations in their own right enables him to project blocks of chords against one another that move in differing harmonic rhythms. A very simple case of this can be found almost at the very start of the piece (two bars before letter A). The solo violin is imitated by the oboe a tone lower playing a theme that could be harmonized in a number of ways, with a harmonic rhythm that could change by the beat, by the half-bar or by the bar. The accompanying texture, however, is provided by the four horns, playing a second inversion of the chord of A flat with an added

---

[15] *Essays in Musical Analysis*, vol. on *Symphonies and other orchestral works* (OUP, new edn., 1981), pp. 524–5.

seventh. This resolves on to a chord of F major. Meanwhile, the lower strings, tremolando, are playing descending consecutive triads: A flat major (3 beats), G flat major (1 beat), and then a variant of the theme just heard on the violin and the oboe, but harmonized in consecutive block chords and starting on that of E flat major in the second inversion. Against this is played a fleck of arpeggio on the harp, an amalgam of the arpeggios of A flat major and of a gapped pentatonic scale based first on G, then on F, resolving onto a bitonal chord fusing those of E flat and C minor. The interesting thing here is that none of these chords is unconventional; what is unconventional is the fact that the progressions move at different speeds. Such a procedure is quite incompatible with conventional harmonic development; and Vaughan Williams shows, in each of his four movements, that he is aware of the fact when he recapitulates his themes.

So what sort of structural principles does he adopt in this work? They are those of organic growth of the themes from a germinal cell: motif becomes phrase; phrase becomes theme; theme is, as Tovey put it, 'loaded' with its chain of consecutive chords; the chords themselves are used as pure sensations, so that they can also be treated as lines of block harmony clashing with one another as they move contrapuntally against one another; and the themes themselves grow new heads and tails as the movement passes through time. In certain cases (notably the opening music of the third movement) there is also the pull of two rhythms one against the other while the thematic outline is basically similar. These different techniques are used with a subtle skill that creates a remarkable formal unity and generate the necessary tension that can promote genuine symphonic development in a new, unobtrusive, and extremely subtle way. A symptom of this in *Pastoral Symphony*, especially its first movement, is the almost continual change of metre; and even when the metre is constant, the phrasing of the themes crosses the bar-lines. This adds to the effect of a drift through time without any real insistent rhythm: the tension generated is a kind of floating one rather than anything harshly or even overtly confrontational.

The *Pastoral*, then, is not a 'linear' symphony. The Fifth, however, which bears a superficial resemblance to it, may certainly be considered as one.[16] Ottaway shows how skilfully Vaughan Williams uses harmonic techniques to build up his structure; but the main indication of the 'linear' nature of the work is the thematic cross-reference between the finale and the first movement. This is one of the main differences between the Fifth and the *Pastoral*. The other is that the whole mood of the Fifth— its 'permanent moral character', to use Thomas Hardy's telling phrase— is utterly different. Here, the serenity may not be unclouded; but it is

[16] See also Arnold Whittall's essay 'Symphony in D major: models and mutations', in *VWS*, pp. 187–212 for a cogent appraisal of the Fifth's structure and significance in Vaughan Williams's output.

nowhere near as shot through with loneliness and melancholy as the surface calm of the *Pastoral* seems to be.

A comparison between the two E minor symphonies, numbers Six and Nine, shows that while one is definitely 'linear', because all four movements are required to be played without a break, the other has many points in common with its predecessor, but moves much more deliberately and juxtaposes moods and themes much more brusquely. Common to both these works are the key, the mood of the opening of the finale, the eloquent use of the saxophone, and the martial nature of some of the themes (notably in the second movement). But the way in which the composer switches abruptly from one theme to another is a feature of his late style that seems to have developed (in his symphonies at any rate) from the *Antartica* onwards. It is present to some degree in the first movement of the Sixth, but not nearly to the same extent as in the Ninth. Nowhere in the Sixth is there such an abrupt juxtaposition of totally different material as with the opening serene flügelhorn solo and the ghostly march that immediately succeeds it. Moreover, the manner in which Vaughan Williams manipulates his two themes—one impinged on rather than genuinely affected by the other, the other occupying more and more of the musical foreground, as it were—is a new and original formal procedure. This seems to indicate that resigned though the mood of the work seems often to be, the alert mind behind it was still capable of springing formal surprises on his listeners at the age of eighty-five.

The Ninth moves through time almost in a series of jerks rather than in a linear flow. This may at first glance seem a failure on Vaughan Williams's part. On closer inspection, it seems much more likely to be the result of the attempt at a (surely unconscious) new solution to the ever-present musical problem of organizing the listener's sense of the passage of time. The composer is in effect applying to an entire symphonic design the fascinating formal procedure he had developed in the first movement of the Eighth Symphony. Much of the Ninth sounds like 'the mixture as before'. Yet though the basic substance of the musical material is not new, the manner of organizing it certainly is.

The more obvious features of Vaughan Williams's style can be briefly mentioned. There is no need to harp yet again on the pentatonic or modal aspect of most of his themes. But onto this, he grafted a number of features of his own that he 'cribbed' from contemporary developments. The first and most obvious is the experimenting with piled-up intervals, stable in themselves, that undermined the tonal stability of a given passage and in particular with the perfect fourth. The interval of a fourth is a common feature of the opening phrase of many English folk-songs; and its implications seem to have fascinated Vaughan Williams (possibly via Debussy, from whom he may also have derived his predilection for strings of consecutive chords) from the time of *A London Symphony* onwards. This seems to have culminated in the works of what may facetiously be called his 'Fourth' period, such as the Piano Concerto, *Job*, and the Fourth and Fifth Symphonies. Yet it is important to note that this was as usual an extension of his style, bringing into focus what had previously been incidental. It was not a passing fancy.

Secondly, there is his experimenting, already touched on above, with juxtaposed tetrachords from different scales or modes. This was particularly noticeable in works like the *Sinfonia Antartica* and the Ninth Symphony. Instead of casting his themes and their treatment within the confines of a given tonal or modal system, he would add what seem at first hearing to be extraneous chromatic inflections onto modal themes. But when these inflections are examined more closely, they are found to be those of artificial scales built up on a double tetrachord from two different modes. It was the implications of this procedure in the Ninth Symphony in particular that led logically to his exploitation of Neapolitan harmonic relationships in the first and fourth movements of that work.

A feature of Elizabethan and baroque music that is often, rightly or wrongly, considered as peculiarly English is the false relation of the third and sixth degrees of the scale. Using his knowledge of the modal scales in which many English folk-tunes are cast, Vaughan Williams exploited this characteristic, not merely because it was English, but because he found it endlessly fascinating and deeply expressive. At its simplest, it is to be found in the alternating major and minor inflections of the saxophone solo in *Job*, fitting like the proverbial glove the 'wily hypocrisy' of Job's comforters. (The same association of the saxophone with this melodic and harmonic quirk can be found in the Scherzo of his last symphony.) But false relations can be found exploited as one of the salient structural and expressive features of the last five symphonies. The skilful treatment of the Dorian, Phrygian, and Mixolydian modes in the first movement of the Fifth, for example; the way in the Sixth and the *Antartica* in which these features are blended with his imaginative use of more conventional tonalities; and the manner in which the same features are probed even further in the Ninth show that his mind was alert to the very end. Each of his symphonies takes us a stage further in his quiet evolution of new modes of expression within the context of the already known.

Yet even when he was not investigating the harmonic potential (and particularly the harmonic ambiguities) of modal/tonal relationships, he could startle. He is a master of the original use of the musical commonplace. He once wrote that Sibelius could make the chord of C major sound stranger than the maddest polytonalities of the maddest central Europeans. The same could certainly be said of him. On a first hearing of *Pastoral Symphony*, for example, a progression at the beginning of the slow movement sounds strange and other-worldly. Inspected more closely, it turns out to be a succession of major and minor triads cunningly juxtaposed so as to give an air of remoteness to the very simple melodic line (Ex. 23). In the Sixth Symphony, a harsh and overbearing passage on the brass, which sounds more cruel and unsettling than any sequence of crude dissonances, turns out to be simply the same device as the other, used for a different end (Ex. 24). This mastery over the rhetorical or dramatic function of the common chord was a feature of Vaughan Williams's music from his very earliest days. It is already to be found in the *Songs of Travel*, for example.

Ex. 23

Ex. 24

Successions of triads grew to be a mannerism, yet it was a mannerism often used in an inspired way. The openings of the *Sinfonia Antartica* and of the Ninth Symphony show that he was aware of this to the very end of his life. It affects both the παθωσ and the εθωσ of his work: the immediate emotional impact of a passage and the overall structure and mood of a movement as a whole. Chords are often treated purely as sensations in the approved impressionist manner; but more frequently, their occurrence in a given context depends less on the relationship of the bass notes to one another than of the tensions between the notes and intervals of the melodic line. The harmony works from the top downwards, not from the bottom upwards. The theme may be heard several octaves deep, with the supporting harmonic texture moving along *inside* the melodic parts, giving the sound a firmness, a weight, and a fullness that are utterly characteristic. Where the intervals are wide and not 'pure', the harmony becomes bitter and dissonant; where they are even and diatonic, it is placid and gentle. But in either case, it is always logical; and the logic depends on the shape of the melodic line. The result at its best is an amazing monolithic unity of melody, form, texture, rhythm, and harmonic movement; and it is this impressionistic and empirical use of harmony and texture that gives his music its unique combination of solidity and what one can only describe as cosmic vastness.

There are certain melodic formulae that seem to occur at key points in many of his works. An obvious one is the drooping triplet that returns again and again to its apogee (Ex. 25a). Another is the formula set out in Ex. 25b, and two others what might be called the 'Sine Nomine' motifs (Ex. 25c and d) (though these in fact both predate the great hymn tune). Yet another is the restless, striding (usually descending) bass in even crotchets.

Ex. 25

Rhythmically, Vaughan Williams's music is at least as flexible as that of most of his continental contemporaries and a good deal more subtle than he is often given credit for being. If, in fact, his music were barred with a change of metre every time the movement of the rhythm across the bar-line demanded it, the barring of a work like the Sixth Symphony would look almost as complex as that of, say, *The Rite of Spring.* Vaughan Williams preferred to keep to the original metre where possible and indicate by the phrase-marking how flexibly the rhythm had to be treated (Ex. 26).

Ex. 26

which sounds like:

This characteristic is found at least as early as the Tallis Fantasia, where the music flows into apparently meandering irregular rhythmic patterns instead of jolting brusquely along in them. It may be said to relate both to ancient and to modern sources: the metrical freedom of folk-song, plainsong, and the Tudor composers on the one hand and the metrical procedures of, for example, *Job* or RVW's Fourth Symphony on the other. All of these fall quite outside the often commonplace and

264

predictable micro- and macro-rhythmic patterns prevalent in the Austro-German academic tradition which had dominated English music for so long.[17] And although sometimes, as in the setting of 'Let all the world in every corner sing', in the Benedicite, and even in 'The Tunning of Elinor Rumming', RVW's basic rhythm, too, settles down into a solid and rather hearty metrical rut, there are also also many more occasions, (as in the *Partita for Double String Orchestra* and the Scherzo of the Eighth Symphony) where the music is propelled onwards by the interplay of rhythms.[18] The opening of 'Elinor Rumming', for example, is driven onwards by the interplay of the rhythm of the curt, spiky orchestral gesture that introduces the movement and the natural and more fluent movement of the chorus's racy theme, which derives from Skelton's own phrase-rhythms, metres, and paragraphing. More often, Vaughan Williams resorts to grinding two rhythmic patterns against one another, as in 'Satan's Dance of Triumph', or, more gently, to running an ostinato across the bar-line while keeping the melodic line flexible, but within the confines of the basic metre, as in the 'Evening Hymn' from the *Four Hymns*.

Most of these features are touchstones of resourcefulness and originality that have nothing to do with RVW being English or developing his idiom out of English folk-music; and it is one of the reasons why, as their autobiographies and critical writings testify, musicians like Cecil Gray and Arnold Bax, who abhorred folk-song composers as such, were ready to admit Vaughan Williams's greatness. 'Nationalism' was merely one component of the yeast that brought on the fermentation of his genius. The musical wine that resulted may not be to all tastes, but it *is* wine, not just grape-juice and water.

Cecil Gray remarked in his autobiography, *Musical Chairs*, that Vaughan Williams once told him: 'You never attempt anything which you know you cannot do.' The corollary of this remark sums up Vaughan Williams's own attitude to composition admirably. He spent much of his career doing just that: meeting challenges that people believed he could not meet. This was a feature of his outlook from his very earliest days: in his *Musical Autobiography*[19] he points out that S. P. Waddington told him that he tried to run before he could walk. It is not surprising, therefore, that he produced a number—a remarkably

---

[17] For a provocative account of the way this tradition affected the English Renaissance in General and Vaughan Williams as a contributor to it, see Robert Stradling and Meirion Hughes, *The English Musical Renaissance 1860–1940* (London and New York, 1993). Stradling and Hughes acknowledge neither the non-pastoral, and thus non-'cow-pat', aspects of RVW's style and output, nor his undoubted debt to impressionism, but many of the general points they make, both about him and about others, are shrewd and often witty.

[18] For a stimulating discussion of this aspect of RVW's style, see, with reference to the Eighth Symphony in particular, Lionel Pike, 'Rhythm in the Symphonies: a preliminary investigation', in *VWS*, pp. 166–86.

[19] *National Music*, p. 192.

small number—of musical failures and a rather more considerable number of flawed masterpieces. Once he had developed the tools of his craft, he used them to create works that even he himself could scarcely have visualized as a young man. He rebuilt his music from its sturdy melodic and rhythmic foundations upwards; and thus he always had a point of reference from which he could take his musical bearings.

His musical integrity was of a peculiar kind, consistent with his personal integrity. On the one hand there are anecdotes like that told of him as a student at Cambridge: when the local Musical Society intended to perform Beethoven's Fifth Symphony at an orchestral concert, he found that they could not afford a double-bassoon for the finale and were going to dispense with the instrument. Vaughan Williams set about on his own initiative collecting the money, so that a player could be hired, rather than allowing a performance that weakened the force of Beethoven's music. On the other, we remember that he was quite capable of giving a performance of Bach's *St Matthew Passion* with modified instrumentation, provided that all the strands of the texture were there, tone-colour being in this case a secondary consideration. Similarly, in his own scores there is nearly always provision for performance with forces smaller than or different from those he originally envisaged. In a certain sense, it is a mistaken respect for his wishes that insists that those works are only performed when the full—sometimes very large—orchestra is assembled that the composer calls for, simply because the 'cueing' is there to allow the works in question to be performed by a smaller combination than the ideal forces. Even the formidable impact of the organ in the Landscape movement of the *Sinfonia Antartica* can if necessary be replaced (though far less effectively) by a blast from the full orchestra.

His scoring and his sense of orchestral texture are often intensely ingenious. There is no 'typically RVW sound'; instead, there are several differing but typical Vaughan Williams textures. Much of the instrumentation of the Fourth Symphony, for example, looks and sounds harsh to the point of rawness, yet it is also notable for the unobtrusive ingenuity of colour and texture throughout. The spacing of the stringed instruments at the opening of the slow movement, after the wood-wind introduction, has a unique air of uneasy remoteness, yet it is difficult to point to anything spectacularly original about it. Virtuoso scoring he generally eschewed, yet there are passages in many of his works from the Tallis Fantasia onwards that show a remarkable ear for orchestral balance and blend. Those who dismiss his scoring as clumsy would do well to listen carefully to 'Jane Scroop's Lament', to parts of *Job*, such as the cavernous sounds of the recapitulation of 'Satan's Dance of Triumph', to *Riders to the Sea*, to the first and second movements of his Fifth and Eighth Symphonies, or to the Scherzo of the *London*. Here, every effect is calculated to a nicety. Even when the texture is lighter than air, as it is in the coda of the third movement of the *Pastoral Symphony*, there is deliberately no glitter about it.

What is usually more remarkable is his sense of the colour-effect of acoustic spacing rather than that of orchestral timbre. The vast spread of some of his string chords, as in *Tallis*, contrasts most vividly with the close-textured richness of the slow movement of the Violin Concerto, yet each is unmistakably his own. His eloquent, ruminative use of solo instruments, whether wind or strings (in the latter case the viola in particular—acting as a fairy godfather to the Cinderella of the orchestra long before its ardent propagandists made their mark), is another hallmark of his style. The pitch at which both solo and accompanying lines intermingle is always neatly calculated. Sometimes his fondness for reinforcing the main melodic line leads to thickness—but far more rarely than his detractors claim, for the gain in colour, weight, and atmosphere usually offsets the loss in clarity.

His originality, his willingness to try almost anything (except perhaps dodecaphonic and serial techniques), his elephant's child's 'satiable curtiosity': all these factors contribute to give his music the unity, variety, symmetry, development, and continuity which he asserted in *National Music* were the principles of great art. But underlying them was a vision that soared to greater heights than that of almost any other musician of his time. Hans Keller, not one of RVW's greatest admirers, though he referred to him more than once as a 'towering figure', once stigmatized the modern generation of composers for failing to face what he called the metaphysical problem. Vaughan Williams was one of the few who did. His art was rooted in the earthy and its roots were solid. But from those roots it sent forth shoots that often left the earthy far behind. And that was the result of his character, not of his technique.

Appendix A

Calendar

Year	Age	Life	Contemporary musicians and events
1872		Ralph Vaughan Williams born, 12 Oct. at Down Ampney, Gloucestershire, son of the Revd Arthur Vaughan Williams (1834–75) vicar of Down Ampney, and Margaret (née Wedgwood) (1842–1937).	Scriabin born, 6 Jan.; Bantock 4; Bizet 34; Brahms 39; Bruckner 48; Davies (Walford) 3; Debussy 10; Delius 10; Dvořák 31; Elgar 15; German 10; Liszt 61; Mahler 27; Parry 25; Stanford 20; Strauss (R.) 8; Verdi 59; Wagner 59. First performance in Italy of Verdi's *Aida*, Milan, 7 Feb. Foundation stone of Bayreuth Festspielhaus laid, 22 May. First performance of Bizet's *Djamileh*, Paris, 22 May.
1873	1		Reger born, 19 Mar.; Rachmaninoff born, 1 Apr.; Bruch's *Odysseus* performed, 2 Feb.; Tchaikovsky's Second Symphony, Moscow, 7 Feb.; Verdi's String Quartet, 1 Apr.; Liszt's *Christus*, Weimar, 29 May; Bruckner's Second Symphony, Vienna, 26 Oct.; Brahms, *St Antoni Chorale* Variations, Vienna, 2 Nov.
1874	2		Suk born, 4 Jan.; Schoenberg born, 13 Sept.; Holst born, 21 Sept.; Cornelius (50), dies, 26 Oct. *Boris Godunov* performed, St Petersburg, 8 Feb.; Verdi's *Requiem*, Milan, 22 May.
1875	3	Ralph's father (40) dies, 9 Feb. Ralph's mother, brother, and	Bennett (58) dies, 1 Feb.; Ravel born, 7 Mar.; Bizet (36) dies,

Vaughan Williams

Year	Age	Life	Contemporary musicians and events
		sister move to Leith Hill Place, Surrey.	3 June; Coleridge-Taylor born, 15 Aug. *Carmen* produced, Paris, 3 Mar.; Gilbert and Sullivan: *Trial by Jury*, 25 Mar.; Tchaikovsky's First Piano Concerto performed, Boston, 25 Oct.
1876	4		Wolf-Ferrari born, 12 Jan.; Wesley (65) dies, 19 Apr.; Falla born, 23 Nov.; Goetz (35) dies, 3 Dec. Grieg's *Peer Gynt* performed, Oslo, 28 Feb.; First *Ring* cycle at Bayreuth, 13–17 Aug.; Brahms's First Symphony performed, Karlsruhe, 6 Nov.
1877	5		Dohnányi born, 27 July; Quilter born, 1 Nov.
1878	6	First composition, 'The Robin's Nest'. Begins music lessons with his aunt Sophy Wedgwood.	Boughton born, 23 Jan.; Palmgren born, 16 Feb.; Schreker born, 23 Mar.; Holbrook born, 6 July. *HMS Pinafore* (Gilbert and Sullivan) produced, 25 May.
1879	7	Begins to learn the violin.	Jensen (42) dies, 23 Jan; Bridge born, 26 Feb.; Ireland born, 6 July; Respighi born, 9 July; Cyril Scott born, 27 Sept.; Karg-Elert born, 21 Nov.
1880	8	Takes a correspondence course in musical theory and passes.	Medtner born, 5 Jan.; Bloch born, 24 July; Pizzetti born, 20 Sept.; Offenbach (61) dies, 4 Oct. *Prometheus Unbound* (Parry) performed at Gloucester, 11 Sept.
1881	9		Bartók born, 25 Mar.; Mussorgsky (42) dies, 28 Mar.; Miaskovsky born, 20 Apr.; Enescu born, 19 Aug. *Patience* (Gilbert and Sullivan) produced, 23 Apr.
1882	10	First visit abroad, to France.	Stravinsky born, 17 June; Kodály born, 16 Dec. *Parsifal* produced, 26 July.

Year	Age	Life	Contemporary musicians and events
1883	11	Goes to Field House School at Rottingdean.	Wagner (69) dies, 13 Feb.; Casella born, 25 July; Berners born, 18 Sept.; Bax born, 6 Nov.; Webern born, 3 Dec.
1884	12	During his schooldays, attends concerts and is particularly impressed by his first exposure to the music of Wagner. Also performs Raff's *Cavatina* at a school concert.	Smetana (60) dies, 12 May; van Dieren born, 27 Dec. Dvořák (43) comes to England to conduct his Sixth Symphony and *Stabat Mater*.
1885	13		Berg born, 7 Feb.; Hiller (73) dies, 10 May; Butterworth born, 12 July; Wellesz born, 21 Oct. *The Mikado* (Gilbert and Sullivan) produced, 14 Mar.
1886	14		Ponchielli (51) dies, 16 Jan.; Liszt (74) dies, 10 May. Bach's B minor Mass and Sullivan's *Golden Legend* performed to great acclaim at Leeds Festival, 13–16 Oct.
1887	15	Enters Charterhouse School, where he plays the violin and later the viola in the orchestra.	Borodin (53) dies, 27 Feb.; Villa-Lobos born, 5 Mar.; Toch born, 7 Dec.; Atterberg born, 12 Dec.
1888	16	Gives a joint concert at school of compositions by himself and his friend H. Vivian Hamilton.	Alkan (74) dies, 29 Mar.; Boulanger born, 16 Sept. *Otello* (Verdi) produced, Milan, 5 Feb. *Blest Pair of Sirens* (Parry) performed, 17 May.
1889	17		Adrian Boult born, 8 Apr.
1890	18	Visits Munich and hears *Die Walküre*. Enters the Royal College of Music, where he studies harmony with F. E. Gladstone, composition with Parry and organ with Parratt.	Myra Hess born, 25 Feb.; Ibert born, 15 Aug.; Gurney born, 28 Aug.; Frank Martin born, 15 Sept.; Franck (67) dies, 8 Nov.; Martinů born, 8 Dec.; Gade (73) dies, 21 Dec.
1891	19		Delibes (54) dies, 16 Jan.; Prokofiev born, 23 Apr.; Cole Porter born, 9 June; Bliss born, 2 Aug. *Ivanhoe* (Sullivan) runs for 160 nights at the new Royal English Opera House.

Vaughan Williams

Year	Age	Life	Contemporary musicians and events
1892	20	Enters Trinity College, Cambridge, where he reads History and works for his Mus. Bac. under Charles Wood. Studies organ under Alan Gray. Meets Hugh P. Allen (organ scholar of Christ's College). Mahler (32) comes to London and conducts *Tristan und Isolde*, which greatly impresses RVW.	Kilpinen born, 4 Feb.; Honegger born, 10 Mar.; Eva Turner born, 10 Mar.; Lalo (69) dies, 22 Apr.; Milhaud born, 4 Sept.; Howells born, 17 Oct.
1893	21	Early compositions performed at the University Music Club. Attends Jubilee concert of University Musical Society after presentation of honorary doctorates to Bruch, Boito, Saint-Saëns, and Tchaikovsky.	Goossens born, 26 May; Gounod (75) dies, 18 Oct.; Tchaikovsky (53) dies, 6 Nov. Verdi's *Falstaff* produced, Milan, 9 Feb. Bournemouth Municipal Orchestra founded.
1894	22	Takes Mus. Bac. degree at Cambridge.	Piston born, 20 Jan.; Lekeu (24) dies, 21 Jan.; Chabrier (53) dies, 13 Sept.; Warlock born, 30 Oct.; Moeran born, 31 Dec. Debussy's *Prélude à l'après-midi d'un faun* performed, Paris, 23 Dec.
1895	23	Takes BA at Cambridge. Resumes his studies at the RCM, studying composition with Stanford and taking part in Purcell's *Dido and Aeneas*. Takes post as organist at St Barnabas Church, S. Lambeth.	Orff born, 10 July; Hindemith born, 16 Nov. Queen's Hall promenade concerts founded, conducted by Henry J. Wood.
1896	24	Visits Bayreuth.	Ambroise Thomas (84) dies, 12 Feb.; Bruckner (72) dies, 11 Oct.; Sessions born, 28 Dec. *Shamus O'Brien* (Stanford) runs for over 100 performances, London.
1897	25	Marries Adeline Fisher, 9 Oct. Studies with Max Bruch in Berlin, where he hears a great variety of music.	Brahms (63) dies, 3 Apr.; Korngold born, 29 May.
1898	26	Settles in London at 16 North Street, Westminster, later moving to 5 Cowley St. Writes a substantial number of mainly vocal works.	Rieti born, 28 Jan.; Roy Harris born, 12 Feb.; Gershwin born, 25 Sept. Folk Song Society founded.

Year	Age	Life	Contemporary musicians and events
1899	27	Moves to 10 Barton Street. Continues work on a number of ambitious works, none of which reach performance until much later.	Poulenc born, 7 Jan.; Auric born, 15 Feb.; Johann Strauss II (73) dies, 3 June; Chausson (44) dies, 10 June; Barbirolli born, 2 Dec. Enigma Variations performed, 19 June.
1900	28	Meets Cecil Sharp. Writes *Bucolic Suite* for orchestra. Attends disastrous first performance of Elgar's *Dream of Gerontius* in Birmingham, 3 Oct.	Antheil born, 9 July; Copland born, 14 Nov.; Sullivan (58) dies, 22 Nov.; Bush born, 22 Dec.
1901	29	Takes Mus. Doc. at Cambridge. First published composition, the song 'Linden Lea'.	Verdi (87) dies, 27 Jan.; Stainer (60) dies, 31 Mar.; Rubbra born, 23 May; Finzi born, 14 July; Rheinberger (62) dies, 25 Nov.
1902	30	*Bucolic Suite* performed at Bournemouth. Begins to give University Extension Lectures and to write articles for *The Vocalist*.	Walton born, 29 Mar. Debussy's *Pelléas et Mélisande* produced, Paris, 30 Apr.
1903	31	Begins collecting folk-songs. Writes articles on Fugue and Conducting for Grove's *Dictionary*. Composes *Willow Wood* and a number of other vocal works.	Blacher born, 3 Jan.; Wolf (42) dies, 22 Feb.; Lennox Berkeley born, 12 May; Khachaturian born, 6 June. *The Apostles* (Elgar) performed, Birmingham, 14 Oct.
1904	32	Begins work as music editor of *The English Hymnal*. Composes *In the Fen Country*, *The House of Life*, and *Songs of Travel*. Goes on a wide range of folk-song collecting expeditions.	Addinsell born, 13 Jan.; Dallapiccola born, 3 Feb.; Skalkottas born, 21 Mar.; Dvořák (61) dies, 1 May; Petrassi born, 16 July. Mahler's Fifth Symphony performed, Cologne, 18 Oct. London Symphony Orchestra founded.
1905	33	Composes *Toward the Unknown Region* and begins work on *A Sea Symphony*. Edits Purcell's *Welcome Songs* (Part I) for the Purcell Society. Continues folk-song collecting, an expedition to Norfolk in Jan. being particularly fruitful. First Leith Hill Festival, 10 May. Moves to 13 Cheyne Walk, Chelsea, 1 Nov.	Tippett born, 2 Jan.; Rawsthorne born, 2 May; Seiber born, 4 May; Lambert born, 23 Aug. Strauss's *Salome* produced, Dresden, 9 Dec.

Vaughan Williams

Year	Age	Life	Contemporary musicians and events
1906	34	*English Hymnal* published. Composes three *Norfolk Rhapsodies* using tunes he had collected himself.	Frankel born, 31 Jan.; Arensky (44) dies, 25 Feb.; Lutyens born, 9 July; Shostakovich born, 25 Sept.
1907	35	*Toward the Unknown Region* performed at Leeds Festival. Goes to Paris to study with Ravel.	Maconchy born, 19 Mar.; Grieg (64) dies, 4 Sept.
1908	36	Composes String Quartet in G minor. Begins work on *On Wenlock Edge*.	MacDowell (46) dies, Jan.; Rimsky-Korsakov dies, 21 June; Ferguson born, 21 Oct.; Messiaen born, 10 Dec. Elgar's First Symphony performed, Manchester, 3 Dec.
1909	37	*On Wenlock Edge* performed, 15 Nov.; music for *The Wasps* performed at Cambridge, 26 Nov.	Albéniz (48) dies, 18 May; Martucci (53) dies, 1 June. Strauss's *Elektra* staged, Dresden, 25 Jan.
1910	38	*Fantasia on a Theme by Thomas Tallis* performed at Gloucester, 6 Sept. *A Sea Symphony* performed at Leeds, 12 Oct. Edits second volume of Purcell's *Welcome Songs*.	Barber born, 9 Mar.; Balakirev (71) dies, 29 May. Stravinsky's *Firebird* performed, Paris, 25 June.
1911	39	*Five Mystical Songs* performed, Worcester, 14 Sept. Begins work on opera *Hugh the Drover*.	Mahler (50) dies, 18 May; Menotti born, 7 July. Strauss's *Der Rosenkavalier* staged, Dresden, 26 Jan.
1912	40	Composes *Phantasy Quintet*. *Fantasia on Christmas Carols* performed, Hereford, 12 Sept.	Massenet (70) dies, 13 Aug.; Coleridge-Taylor (37) dies, 1 Sept. Schoenberg's *Pierrot Lunaire* performed, Berlin, 16 Oct.
1913	41		Britten born, 22 Nov. Stravinsky's *Rite of Spring* staged, Paris, 29 May.
1914	42	*A London Symphony* performed, 27 Mar. Various works composed, but not performed, as RVW enlists as a Private in the RAMC after war breaks out on 4 Aug.	
1915	43	Posted to Dorking with 2/4 London Field Ambulance. Unit moves to Watford in April, and in May to Audley End Park,	Goldmark (84) dies, 2 Jan; Scriabin (43) dies, 27 Apr.; Taneiev (58) dies, 19 June.

274

Year	Age	Life	Contemporary musicians and events
		where RVW enjoys making music with family on whom he is billeted.	
1916	44	Posted to Sutton Veny, Wilts. and then to France, 22 June, where his unit is heavily involved in Battle of Somme. Later in the year, it is transferred to Salonika.	Babbit born, 10 May; Granados (48) dies in torpedoed ship, 24 Mar.; MacCunn (48) dies, 2 Aug.; Butterworth (31) killed in action, 5 Aug. *For the Fallen* (Elgar) performed, London, 3 May.
1917	45	The Carnegie Trust arranges for the publication of *A London Symphony*. RVW transfers to and is commissioned in the Royal Garrison Artillery.	Russian Revolution
1918	46	Serves in France in RGA, and becomes Director of Music, First Army, BEF.	Debussy (55) dies, 25 Mar.; Boito (76) dies, 10 June; Parry (70) dies, 7 Oct. *The Planets* (Holst) performed under Adrian Boult, London, 29 Sept.
1919	47	Appointed professor of composition at the Royal College of Music. Awarded honorary Mus.D. at Oxford.	Leoncavallo (61) dies, 9 Aug. Cello Concerto (Elgar) performed, 27 Oct.
1920	48	Revised version of *A London Symphony* performed, 4 May.	Fricker born, 5 Sept.; Bruch (82) dies , 2 Oct. *Hymn of Jesus* (Holst) performed, London 25 Mar. *Mr Broučeks Adventures* (Janaček) stayed, Prague, 23 Apr.
1921	49	Appointed conductor of the Bach Choir. *The Lark Ascending* performed in London, 14 June.	Robert Simpson born, 2 Mar.; Humperdinck (67) dies, 27 Sept.; Malcolm Arnold born, 21 Oct.; Saint-Saëns (86) dies, 16 Dec.
1922	50	*Pastoral Symphony* performed, London, 26 Jan. *The Shepherds of the Delectable Mountains* performed, RCM, 11 July. Visits USA to conduct *Pastoral Symphony* at Norfolk (Conn.). Mass in G minor performed, performed, Birmingham, 6 Dec.	Xenakis born, 1 May; Pedrell (81) dies, 19 Aug.
1923	51	*Old King Cole* performed at Cambridge, 5 June.	Ligeti born, 28 May; Ned Rorem born, 23 Oct.

Vaughan Williams

Year	Age	Life	Contemporary musicians and events
			Les Noces (Stravinsky) performed, Paris, 13 May. *Facade* (Walton) performed, London, 12 June. *Dance Suite* (Bartók) performed, Budapest, 19 June.
1924	52	*Hugh the Drover* staged at the RCM, 4 July and by the British National Opera Company under Malcolm Sargent, 14 July.	Stanford (71) dies, 29 Mar.; Busoni (58) dies, 27 July; Fauré (79) dies, 4 Nov.; Puccini (65) dies, 29 Nov. Schoenberg's *Erwartung* performed, Prague, 6 June and his *Serenade*, Donaueschingen, 20 July. *The Cunning Little Vixen* (Janáček) staged, Brno, 6 Nov.
1925	53	*Flos Campi* performed, London, 19 Oct.; Violin Concerto performed, London, 6 Nov. *Songs of Praise* published, of which RVW is musical editor.	Boulez born, 25 Mar.; Satie (59) dies, 1 July; Berio born, 24 Oct. *Wozzek* (Berg) staged, Berlin, 14 Dec.
1926	54	*On Christmas Night* staged in Chicago, 26 Dec. *Sancta Civitas* performed in Oxford, 7 May.	Henze born, 1 July; Charles Wood (60) dies, 12 July. *The Miraculous Mandarin* (Bartók) performed, Cologne, 27 Nov.
1927	55	Composes *Along the Field*, for voice and violin. First performed, London, 24 Oct.	*Oedipus Rex* (Stravinsky) performed, Paris, 30 May. Janáček's *Glagolitic Mass* performed, Brno, 11 Sept.
1928	56	Resigns conductorship of Bach Choir. Moves from London to Dorking. Co-editor, with Martin Shaw, of the music of *The Oxford Book of Carols*. His Te Deum in G is performed at the enthronement of Cosmo Gordon Lang as Archbishop of Canterbury.	Musgrave born, 27 May; Janáček (74) dies, 12 Aug; Stockhausen born, 22 Aug. Webern's String Trio performed, Siena, 12 Sept.
1929	57	*Sir John in Love* staged at the RCM, 21 Mar. Composes three works for performance at the Silver Jubilee of the Leith Hill Festival in 1930 and completes *Fantasia on Sussex Folk Tunes* for Casals.	Previn born, 6 Apr. Walton's Viola Concerto performed, London, 3 Oct.

Year	Age	Life	Contemporary musicians and events
1930	58	Concert performance of *Job* at the Norwich Festival, 23 Oct.	Warlock (36) dies, 17 Dec. *Symphony of Psalms* (Stravinsky) performed, Brussels, 13 Dec. BBC Symphony Orchestra makes its public debut under Adrian Boult, 22 Oct.
1931	59	*Job* staged at the Cambridge Theatre, London, 5 July.	Carl Nielsen (66) dies, 2 Oct.; Williamson born, 3 Oct.; d'Indy (80) dies, 2 Dec. *Belshazzar's Feast* (Walton) performed at Leeds, 8 Oct.
1932	60	Magnificat performed at Worcester Festival, 8 Sept. Lectures on *National Music* at Bryn Mawr College (Penn.). Elected President of the English Folk Dance and Song Society.	Hugh Wood born, 27 June; Alexander Goehr born, 10 Aug.
1933	61	Piano Concerto performed in London, 1 Feb.	Duparc (85) dies, 13 Feb. Hitler comes to power in Germany.
1934	62	Suite for Viola performed in London, 12 Nov.	Elgar (76) dies, 23 Feb.; Holst (59) and Schreker (55) die, 21 Mar.; Delius (72) dies, 10 June; Birtwistle born, 15 July; Maxwell Davies born, 8 Sept.; Schnittke born, 24 Nov.; Sekles (62) dies, 15 Dec. *A Boy was Born* (Britten) performed, 23 Feb.
1935	63	F minor Symphony (No. 4) performed under Boult, at BBC Symphony Concert, 10 Apr.	Dukas (69) dies, 18 May; Suk (61) dies, 29 May; Maw born, 5 Nov.; Berg (50) dies, 24 Dec. Walton's First Symphony performed, London, 6 Nov.
1936	64	*The Poisoned Kiss* performed, Cambridge, 12 May. *Five Tudor Portraits* performed, Norwich, 25 Sept. *Dona Nobis Pacem* performed, Huddersfield, 2 Oct.	Glazounov (70) dies, 21 Mar.; Richard Rodney Bennett born, 29 Mar.; Respighi (56) dies, 18 Apr.; van Dieren (51) dies, 24 Apr.; Edward German (74) dies, 11 Nov. *Our Hunting Fathers* (Britten) performed, Norwich, 25 Sept.
1937	65	*Festival Te Deum* performed at George VI's Coronation Service in Westminster Abbey, 12 May. *Riders to the Sea* staged at the RCM, 30 Nov.	Gershwin (38) dies, 11 July; Crosse born, 1 Dec.; Ravel (62) dies, 28 Dec. *Variations on a Theme of Frank Bridge* (Britten)

Year	Age	Life	Contemporary musicians and events
			performed, Salzburg, 27 Aug. *Carmina Burana* (Orff) performed, Frankfurt, 8 June. Shostakovich, Symphony No. 5, Leningrad, 21 Nov.
1938	66	*Serenade to Music* performed in London, 5 Oct.	Britten's Piano Concerto performed, London, 18 Aug. Hindemith's *Mathis der Maler* staged, Zürich, 28 May.
1939	67	*Five Variants of 'Dives and Lazarus'* performed, New York, 1 Nov.	Bartók's Second Violin Concerto performed, Amsterdam, 23 Mar. Second World War begins, 3 Sept.
1940	68	First film score: *49th Parallel*. Composes *Household Music* for impromptu groups of musicians in wartime. *Six Choral Songs to be sung in Time of War* performed, broadcast 20 Dec.	*Les Illuminations* (Britten) performed, London, 30 Jan. *Dies Natalis* (Finzi) performed, 26 Jan. Concerto for Double String Orchestra (Tippett) performed, London, 21 Apr. Bartók's Divertimento performed, Basel, 11 June.
1941	69		Frank Bridge (61) dies, 10 Jan.; H. Walford Davies (71) dies, 11 Mar. *Sinfonia da Requiem* (Britten) performed, New York, 29 Mar.
1942	70	Music for the film *Coastal Command* and incidental music for BBC adaptation of *The Pilgrim's Progress* composed.	Zemlinsky (69) dies, 16 Mar. Shostakovich, Symphony No. 7 ('Leningrad') performed, Kuibishev, 5 Mar. *Capriccio* (Richard Strauss) staged, Munich, 28 Oct.
1943	71	Symphony in D (No. 5) performed under the composer, London, 25 June. Music for the films *The People's Land* and *The Story of a Flemish Farm* composed.	Rachmaninoff (69) dies, 28 Mar.; Holloway born, 19 Oct. *Serenade for Tenor, Horn and Strings* (Britten) performed, 15 Oct.
1944	72	Oboe Concerto performed, Liverpool, 30 Sept. Second String Quartet ('For Jean on Her Birthday') performed, London, 12 Oct.	Tavener born, 28 Jan.; Graener (72) dies, 14 Nov. *A Child of Our Time* (Tippett) performed, London, 19 Mar. *Concerto for Orchestra* (Bartók) performed, Boston, 1 Dec.
1945	73	*Thanksgiving for Victory*	Mascagni (81) dies, 2 Aug.;

Year	Age	Life	Contemporary musicians and events
		broadcast, 13 May. Music for the film *Stricken Peninsula* composed.	Webern (61) dies, 15 Sept.; Bartók (64) dies, 26 Sept.; Rutter born, 24 Oct. *Peter Grimes* (Britten) staged, London, 7 June.
1946	74	Introduction and Fugue for two pianos composed. Arranges Concerto for two pianos from his Piano Concerto. It is performed in London, 22 Nov.	Bantock (78) dies, 16 Oct.; Falla (69) dies, 14 Nov. Symphony in Three Movements (Stravinsky) performed, New York, 24 Jan. *The Rape of Lucretia* (Britten) staged, Glyndebourne, 12 July. *The Young Person's Guide to the Orchestra* (Britten) performed, Liverpool, 15 Oct.
1947	75	*The Souls of the Righteous* performed in Westminster Abbey. Music for the film *The Loves of Joanna Godden* composed. *The Voice out of the Whirlwind* performed, London, 22 Nov.	Casella (63) dies, 5 Mar. *Albert Herring* (Britten) performed, Glyndebourne, 20 June.
1948	76	*Partita for Double String Orchestra* (arranged from Double String Trio, performed 21 Jan. 1939) broadcast, 20 Mar. Symphony in E minor (No. 6) performed under Boult, 21 Apr. Music to the film *Scott of the Antarctic* composed; the film first screened publicly at the Odeon Theatre, Leicester Square, 30 Dec.	Wolf-Ferrari (72) dies, 21 Jan.; Michael Berkeley born, 29 May; McEwen (80) dies, 14 June. First Aldeburgh Festival opens, 6 June.
1949	77		Pfitzner (80) dies, 22 May; Novák (78) dies, 18 July; R. Strauss (85) dies, 8 Sept.; Skalkottas (45) dies, 19 Sept.
1950	78	*Folk Songs of the Four Seasons* performed, London, 15 June. *Fantasia on the 'Old 104th' Psalm Tune* performed, Gloucester, 6 Sept. *Concerto Grosso* for Strings, performed, London, 18 Nov.	Miaskovsky (69) dies, 9 Aug.; Moeran (55) dies, 1 Dec. Richard Strauss, *Four Last Songs* performed, London, 22 May. *Zweite Kantate* (Webern) performed, Brussels, 23 June.
1951	79	*The Pilgrim's Progress* staged at Covent Garden, 26 Apr. *The Sons of Light* performed, London, 6 May. Begins work on *Sinfonia*	Schoenberg (76) dies, 13 July; Lambert (45) dies, 21 Aug.; Medtner (71) dies, 13 Nov. *The Rake's Progress*

Year	Age	Life	Contemporary musicians and events
		Antartica (based on material from the music for *Scott of the Antarctic*. Adeline Vaughan Williams dies, 10 May.	(Stravinsky) staged in Venice, 11 Sept. *Billy Budd* (Britten) staged at Covent Garden, 1 Dec.
1952	80	*Romance* for Harmonica and orchestra performed, New York, 3 May. *An Oxford Elegy* performed, Oxford, 19 June.	Accession of Elizabeth II, 6 Feb.
1953	81	*Sinfonia Antartica* performed under Barbirolli at Manchester, 14 Jan. Marries Ursula Wood, 7 Feb., and moves to London.	Prokofiev (61) dies, 4 Mar.; Quilter (75) dies, 21 Sept.; Bax (69) dies, 3 Oct.
1954	82	Tuba Concerto performed in London, 13 June. *Hodie* performed, Worcester, 8 Sept. Visiting professor at Cornell University, where he lectures on *The Making of Music*. Also lectures at Toronto, Universities of Michigan, Indiana, California, and Yale. Conducts *A London Symphony* in Buffalo. Violin Sonata broadcast, 12 Oct.	Schoenberg's *Moses und Aaron* performed, Hamburg, 12 Mar. *The Turn of the Screw* (Britten) staged in Venice, 14 Sept. *Troilus and Cressida* (Walton) staged at Covent Garden, 3 Dec. Boulez composes first version of *Le Marteau sans maître*.
1955	83	Is invited to write a work for the Salvation Army Staff Band and responds with *Prelude on Three Welsh Hymn Tunes*, broadcast on 12 Mar.	Enescu (73) dies, 4 May; Honegger (63) dies, 28 Nov. *The Midsummer Marriage* (Tippett) staged at Covent Garden, 27 Jan.
1956	84	Symphony in D minor (No. 8) performed under Barbirolli, Manchester, 2 May. *A Vision of Aeroplanes* performed, London, 4 June.	Charpentier (95) dies, 18 Feb.; Finzi (55) dies, 27 Sept. Stravinsky's *Canticum Sacrum* performed, Venice, 13 Sept.
1957	85	*Epithalamion* performed, London, 30 Sept. Variations for brass band, performed as Test Piece at National Brass Band Championship of Great Britain, London, 26 Oct.	Sibelius (91) dies, 20 Sept.; Korngold (60) dies, 29 Nov. *Les Carmelites* (Poulenc) performed, Milan, 26 Jan. *Moses und Aaron* (Schoenberg) staged, Zürich, 6 June.
1958	86	Symphony in E minor (No. 9) performed in London, 2 Apr. *Ten Blake Songs* performed, London, 8 Oct. Vaughan Williams dies in London, 26 Aug.	Holbrooke (80) dies, 5 Aug.; Tippett's Second Symphony performed in London, 5 Feb. *Noye's Fludde* (Britten) performed, Aldeburgh, 18 June. Stravinsky's *Threni* performed in Venice, 23 Sept.

Appendix B

List of works

This list is arranged in the following broad categories:

I   Stage works
II   Incidental music to plays, films, and radio
III Orchestral music
IV   Choral works
V   Solo songs
VI   Chamber music
VII Concertos and other music involving instrumental soloists
VIII Arrangements
IX   Miscellaneous other works, arrangements, and music edited by RVW

For full, detailed information about the genesis, performance, and publication of Vaughan Williams's output, including a list of folk-songs collected by him, the reader is referred to Michael Kennedy's *Catalogue of the Works of Ralph Vaughan Williams* (second edition, Oxford University Press, 1995). I am greatly indebted to OUP and to Michael Kennedy for permission to 'crib' from this catalogue.

I STAGE WORKS

(A) Operas

1. *The Shepherds of the Delectable Mountains*. One act. Libretto by RVW from John Bunyan. Later incorporated, save for the final section, into *The Pilgrim's Progress*. First performance: London, Royal College of Music, 11 July 1922. Publication: London, Oxford University Press, 1925.
2. *Hugh the Drover, or 'Love in the Stocks'*. Two acts. Libretto by Harold Child. First performance: London, Royal College of Music, 4 July 1924. Dedication: Sir Hugh Allen. Publication: Vocal score, London, J. Curwen & Sons Ltd, 1924. Final revision (originally published in 1959) reissued by Faber Music in 1977 with an introduction by Michael Kennedy. See also *A Cotswold Romance* (IV Choral Works (B), 31).
3. *Sir John in Love*. Four acts. Libretto adapted by RVW from Shakespeare's *Merry Wives of Windsor* and other sources. First performance: London, Royal College of Music, 21 March 1929. Dedication: S. P. Waddington. Publication: Vocal score, London, Oxford University Press, 1930. See also *In Windsor Forest* (IV Choral Works (B), 14). A Prologue, Episode, and Interlude were also composed for performance at Bristol Opera School in October/November 1933 and published in 1936 by OUP. The Prologue has been withdrawn.

4. *The Poisoned Kiss, or The Empress and the Necromancer.* Three acts. Libretto by Evelyn Sharp, later amended by the composer and Mrs Ursula Vaughan Williams. First performance: Arts Theatre, Cambridge, 12 May 1936. Publication: Vocal score, London, Oxford University Press, 1936.

5. *Riders to the Sea.* One act. J. M. Synge's play set to music. First performance: London, Royal College of Music, 30 November 1937. Publication: London, Oxford University Press, 1936.

6. *The Pilgrim's Progress.* A Morality. Prologue, four acts, and epilogue. Libretto adapted from Bunyan by RVW with interpolations from the Bible and verse by Ursula Vaughan Williams (Ursula Wood). First performance: Royal Opera House, Covent Garden, 26 April 1951. Publication: London, Oxford University Press, 1952.

(B) Ballets, pageants, and other stage spectacles

1. *Pan's Anniversary.* 'A Masque by Ben Jonson, music composed and arranged by R. Vaughan Williams. The dances arranged for orchestra from Elizabethan virginal music and English folk tunes by Gustav von Holst.' First performance: Stratford-upon-Avon, 24 April 1905. Unpublished.

2. *Music for 'The Pilgrim's Progress'.* Dramatized from Bunyan by Mrs W. Hadley and Miss E. Onless. A prelude, music for twelve episodes, and an epilogue were composed. Eight numbers survive: Prelude; The Arming of Christian and Apollyon; The Right between Christian and Apollyon; Vanity Fair; The Death of Faithful; Final Scene; Epilogue. First performance: Reigate Priory, Surrey, December 1906. Unpublished.

3. *London Pageant.* May Day Scene, thirteen items, all based on folk tunes and dances.

4. *Old King Cole.* A ballet for orchestra and chorus (ad lib). First performance: Trinity College, Cambridge (Nevile's Court), 5 June 1923. Publication: London, J. Curwen & Sons Ltd, 1924.

5. *On Christmas Night.* A masque with dancing, singing, and miming, freely adapted from Dickens's *A Christmas Carol.* First performance: Eighth Street Theatre, Chicago, Ill., 26 December 1926. Dedication: Douglas Kennedy. Publication: London, Oxford University Press, 1957, with pianoforte arrangement by Roy Douglas.

6. *Job, A Masque for Dancing.* Founded on Blake's *Illustrations of the Book of Job.* First performance (concert version): Norwich, 23 October 1930. First staged: Cambridge Theatre, London, 5 July 1931. Dedication: Adrian Boult. Publication: Full score, London, Oxford University Press, 1934; pianoforte arrangement by Vally Lasker, 1931.

7. *The Running Set.* Founded on Traditional Dance Tunes. First performance: Royal Albert Hall, London, 6 January 1934. Publication: London, Oxford University Press, 1952.

8. Music for the English Folk Dance Society Masque. Composed 1934; unpublished.

9. *Music for 'The Pageant of Abinger'* (arrangements of traditional tunes, plainsong, and familiar hymns). First performance: Old Rectory Garden, Abinger, Surrey, 14 July 1934. Unpublished save for 'O How Amiable' (see IV Choral Works (D), 5).

10. *England's Pleasant Land.* Music for a pageant by various composers, includ-

ing RVW, for mixed chorus and military band. First performance: Milton Court, Westcott, Surrey, 9 July 1938. Unpublished. Of interest in that it contains some of the music later used in the Fifth Symphony.

11. *The Bridal Day*. A Masque by Ursula Wood, founded on Spenser's *Epithalamion*. For baritone soloist, speaker, dancers, mimers, mixed chorus, flute, piano, and string quartet. First performance projected for 1939 but cancelled because of the Second World War. First public performance: 5 June 1953 on BBC TV. See also *Epithalamion* (IV Choral Works (B), 39).

12. *Solemn Music for the Masque of Charterhouse* (final scene). First performance: Founder's Court, Charterhouse School, 12 July 1950. Unpublished.

13. *The First Nowell*. A Nativity Play for soloists, mixed chorus, and small orchestra. Libretto adapted from medieval pageants by Simona Pakenham. Music composed and arranged from traditional tunes by Vaughan Williams; additions were made after his death by Roy Douglas. First performance: Theatre Royal, Drury Lane, 19 December 1958. Publication: Oxford University Press, 1959. There are 20 movements, eight of which were completed, adapted, revised, or added by Roy Douglas.

II INCIDENTAL MUSIC TO PLAYS, FILMS, AND RADIO

(A) Music to stage dramas

(NB Incidental music to juvenile plays is not included here. Michael Kennedy gives a comprehensive list in his catalogue.)

1. *The Wasps* (Aristophanes, translated H. J. Edwards). Incidental music commissioned by the Greek Play Committee, Cambridge. First performance: Cambridge, 26 November 1909. The numbers are: Overture; Act I: Introduction (Nocturne); Melodrama and Chorus (Allegro vivace); The Wasps' Serenada; Chorus (Allegro molto); Chorus (Allegro moderato); Melodrama and Chorus (Allegro); Melodrama and Chorus (Moderato); Act II: Entr'acte and Introduction; Melodrama and Chorus; March-past of the Witnesses; Parabasis; Act III: Entr'acte; Introduction; Melodrama (Moderato alla marcia); Chorus; Melodrama (Allegro); Chorus and Dance. Publication: Cambridge 1909 as vocal score with pianoforte reduction of the orchestral part.

The familiar *Aristophanic Suite* (Overture; Entr'acte; March-past of the Kitchen Utensils; Entr'acte; Ballet and Final Tableau) was first performed at Queen's Hall, London, on 23 July 1912 and published London, Schott & Co., 1914. The piano duet arrangement by Constant Lambert was published by J. Curwen & Sons, Ltd in 1926 (Curwen Inc., Philadelphia). Curwen also re-published the full score in 1933. The miniature score of the Overture was published by Boosey and Hawkes, by arrangement with Curwen, in 1943.

2. Incidental music to Greek plays (all unpublished save for one item):

    (a) *Bacchae* (Euripides, trans. Gilbert Murray). The Duet 'Where is the home for me?', for soprano, mezzo-soprano, and pianoforte, was published by Edwin Ashdown Ltd in 1922.

    (b) *Iphigenia in Tauris* (Euripides, trans. Gilbert Murray). Prelude and four choruses.

    (c) *Electra* (Euripides, trans. Gilbert Murray). Three choruses.

Michael Kennedy dates these works from 1911.

3. Incidental music to Maeterlinck's *The Death of Tintagiles*. Performed in June 1913. Unpublished.
4. Incidental music to Maeterlinck's *The Blue Bird*. Piano score only.
5. Incidental music for F. R. Benson's Shakespearean season at Stratford-upon-Avon, 1913:

> (a) *The Merry Wives of Windsor*. One page only survives, marked 'molto moderato'.
>
> (b) *King Richard II*. Thirty-two numbers, mostly fanfares and entrance-music. Three movements were composed: a March for Richard's entrance; an Agnus Dei for soprano and organ; and a Prelude to Act V. Seven of the remaining movements are arrangements of traditional tunes.
>
> (c) *King Henry IV, Part 2*. The music was almost entirely arranged from Tudor or traditional sources. There are six items.
>
> (d) *King Richard III*. Four items survive, one based on the Hampshire 'Dargason'; one adapted from the music to *King Richard II*; and one a fanfare for Richard's defeat at Bosworth.
>
> (e) *King Henry V*. Two items survive, one of them the Agincourt Song, the other for Act III, scene 7.

For this season, Vaughan Williams also arranged music for Shaw's *The Devil's Disciple*, comprising arrangements of 'The British Grenadiers', the March from *Judas Maccabaeus* and a verse of 'Yankee Doodle'. Fourteen numbers of incidental music for Shakespeare's *Twelfth Night*, mostly arrangements of 16th- or 17th-century pieces, also exist. It is not known for what occasion these were composed.

(B) Film music

1. *49th Parallel*. First shown at the Odeon Cinema, Leicester Square, 8 October 1941. A suite of nine movements: Prelude; Warning in a Dance Hall; Hudson's Bay; Nazis on the Prowl; The Hutterite Settlement; Indian Festival; The Lake in the Mountains; Nazis on the Run; Epilogue. Vaughan Williams made use of French-Canadian and German traditional melodies in the Hudson's Bay and Hutterite scenes respectively; the Prelude music was adapted for words by Harold Child in the song 'The New Commonwealth'; and 'The Lake in the Mountains' was later published as a piano solo.
2. *Coastal Command*. First shown at the Plaza Cinema, Piccadilly Circus, 16 October 1942. A suite of seven movements was arranged by Muir Mathieson, six of which were broadcast from Manchester on 17 September 1942.
3. *The People's Land*. Based mainly on folk-songs. Privately screened 17 March 1943.
4. *The Flemish Farm*. First shown at the Leicester Square Theatre, London, 12 August 1943. A suite of eight movements: The flag flutters in the wind; Night by the Sea: farewell to the flag; Dawn in the Barn: the Parting of the Lovers; In a Belgian Café; The Major goes to face his fate; The Dead Man's Kit; The Wanderings of the Flag. This was first performed under the title *The Story of a Flemish Farm* at a Henry Wood promenade concert on 31 July 1945. The composer conducted.
5. *The Stricken Peninsula*. The film was made in 1945 and trade-shown in October that year. None of the music is known to have survived.

6. *The Loves of Joanna Godden*. First shown at the New Gallery Cinema, 16 June 1947. The music comprises: Title music; Funeral; Arthur goes away; Waking Ellen; Arthur in Trap; Sheep; Farm Montage; Lamb's Foster-mother; Marriage Banns; Driving to Dungeness; Martin Drowning; Ram Montage; Ellen Arriving Home; Fairground Sequence; Fair Music; Arthur on Horseback; Night Scene; Seasons Montage; Sunrise; Ellen Riding; Foot and Mouth; Sheep Burning; End music; End titles.
7. *Scott of the Antarctic*. First shown at the Royal Film performance, the Empire Theatre, Leicester Square, 29 November 1948. Twenty-eight items were composed, six of which were not used in the film. See also *Sinfonia Antartica* (III Orchestral Works (A), 7).
8. *Dim Little Island*. First shown at the Edinburgh Film Festival, 1949. Vaughan Williams's voice was also heard on the sound-track. The music consisted of a short prelude based on two folk-songs from RVW's own collection and 'Dives and Lazarus'.
9. *Bitter Springs*. First shown at the Gaumont Cinema, Haymarket, 10 July 1950. The music was arranged and scored by Ernest Irving from thematic material supplied by RVW.
10. *The England of Elizabeth*. First shown at the Leicester Square Theatre, first week of March, 1957. The *Three Portraits* suite (Explorer; Poet; Queen), published by Oxford University Press in 1964, and the *Two Shakespeare Sketches*, published in the same year, were arranged by Muir Mathieson from the continuous music of the film. Michael Kennedy gives the full details.
11. *The Vision of William Blake*. First shown at the Academy Cinema, London, 10 October 1958. The *Ten Blake Songs* (see V Solo Songs (B), 33) were composed for this film; only eight were used: 'A Poison Tree' and 'The Piper' were excluded. The remainder of the music consisted of excerpts from *Job*.

(C) Music for radio

1. *Incidental Music for 'The Pilgrim's Progress'*, adapted for radio by Edward Sackville-West. First broadcast 5 September 1943.
2. *Incidental Music for 'Richard II'*. Thirty-four items to cover fifteen scenes. Not used. Unpublished.
3. *Incidental Music for 'The Mayor of Casterbridge'*, serialized in ten weekly episodes. The first was transmitted on 7 January 1951. The titles are: I. Casterbridge; II. Intermezzo; and III. Weyhill Fair. See also *Prelude on an Old Carol Tune* (III Orchestral Works (B) 19).

III ORCHESTRAL WORKS

(A) Symphonies

1. *A Sea Symphony*. For soprano, baritone, mixed chorus, and orchestra. Words by Walt Whitman. First performance: Leeds, 12 October 1910. Dedication: To R.L.W. [(Sir) Ralph Wedgwood]. Four movements: A Song for All Seas, All Ships; On the Beach at Night, Alone; Scherzo (The Waves) Allegro brillante; The Explorers: Grave e molto adagio. Publication: Vocal score, 1909 by Breitkopf & Härtel, London, Leipzig. Revised edition, London, Stainer & Bell Ltd 1918. Full score, revised edition, Stainer & Bell, 1924. Revised vocal score with pianoforte arrangement, Stainer & Bell, 1961.

2. *A London Symphony.* For orchestra. First performance: Queen's Hall, London, 27 March 1914. Dedication: To the memory of George Butterworth. Four movements: Lento–allegro risoluto; Lento; Scherzo (Nocturne) Allegro vivace; Finale: Andante con moto – maestoso alla marcia (quasi lento) – allegro – maestoso alla marcia – Epilogue: Andante sostenuto. Publication; Full score, London, Stainer & Bell, Ltd, 1920. This was not the original score, but the (second) revision of 1920. The composer revised the work for a new edition in 1933, which was the first to bear the title 'revised edition'. It appeared in or about 1936. The centenary edition of the score, with introduction by Michael Kennedy, dates from 1972. The work also exists arranged as a piano solo by Vally Lasker (Stainer & Bell, 1922) and as a piano duet, arranged by Archibald Jacob (Stainer & Bell, 1924). The slow movement, Lento, was published in an organ arrangement by Henry G. Ley for Stainer & Bell in 1922.

3. *Pastoral Symphony.* For full orchestra, with soprano (or tenor) voice. First performance: Queen's Hall, London, 26 January 1922. No dedication. Four movements: Molto moderato; Lento moderato; Moderato pesante; Lento. Publication: London, J. Curwen & Sons, Ltd, 1924. Miniature score, Boosey & Hawkes. Revisions of 1950/1 were incorporated in the printed score in 1954.

4. *Symphony in F minor.* For full orchestra. First performance: Queen's Hall, London, 10 April 1935. Dedication: To Arnold Bax. Four movements: Allegro; Andante moderato; Scherzo: Allegro molto; Finale con Epilogo fugato: Allegro molto. Publication: Full and miniature scores, London, Oxford University Press, 1935.

5. *Symphony in D major.* For full orchestra. First performance: Royal Albert Hall, London, 24 June 1943. To Jean Sibelius, without permission. Four movements: Preludio: Moderato; Scherzo: Presto; Romanza: Lento; Passacaglia: Moderato. Publication: Full score London, Oxford University Press, 1946. Revised full score, 1961.

6. *Symphony in E minor.* For full orchestra. First performance: Royal Albert Hall, London, 21 April 1948. Dedication: To Michael Mullinar. Four movements: Allegro; Moderato; Scherzo: Allegro vivace; Epilogue: Moderato. Publication: Full score, London, Oxford University Press, 1948. Revision, incorporating modifications to the Scherzo, 1950.

7. *Sinfonia Antartica.* For full orchestra, soprano soloist, and women's chorus. First performance: Free Trade Hall, Manchester, 14 January 1953. Dedication: To Ernest Irving. Five movements: Prelude: Andante maestoso; Scherzo: Moderato – poco animando; Landscape: Lento; Intermezzo: Andante sostenuto; Epilogue: Alla marcia moderato (ma non troppo). Publication: Full score, London, Oxford University Press, 1953.

8. *Symphony No. 8 in D minor.*[1] For full orchestra. First performance: Free Trade Hall, Manchester, 14 May 1956. Dedication: To John Barbirolli. Four movements: Fantasia (Variazioni senza Tema): Moderato – presto – andante sostenuto – allegretto – andante non troppo – allegro vivace – andante sostenuto – Tempo I ma tranquillo; Scherzo alla marcia (per stromenti a

---

[1] This is the title which Vaughan Williams himself gave the work after having it pointed out to him that the original title ('Symphony in D') might cause confusion with the symphony now known as No. 5.

fiato): Allegro alla marcia – andante – Tempo I (allegro); Cavatina (per stromenti ad arco): Lento espressivo; Toccata: Moderato maestoso. Publication: Full score, London, Oxford University Press, 1956. The second and third movements were also published separately by OUP in 1958.

9. *Symphony No. 9 in E minor*. For full orchestra. First performance, Royal Festival Hall, London, 2 April 1958. Dedication: To the Royal Philharmonic Society. Four movements: Moderato maestoso – tranquillo; Andante sostenuto – moderato tranquillo – poco animato ma pesante – moderato sostenuto – Tempi I; Scherzo: Allegro pesante; Andante tranquillo – poco animato – andante sostenuto – poco meno mosso – ancora poco animando – poco animato ma pesante – largamente. Publication: Full score, London, Oxford University Press, 1958.

(B) Other orchestral works

1. *Serenade in A minor*. For small orchestra. First performance: Winter Gardens, Bournemouth, 4 April 1901. No dedication. Four movements: Prelude: Andante sostenuto; Scherzo: Allegro; Romance: Andantino; Finale: Allegro. Unpublished.
2. *Bucolic Suite*. For orchestra. First performance: Winter Gardens, Bournemouth, 10 March 1902. No dedication. Four movements: Allegro; Andante; Intermezzo: allegretto; Finale: allegro. Unpublished.
3. *Heroic Elegy and Triumphal Epilogue*. For orchestra. First performance: Royal College of Music, London, 5 March 1901. No dedication. Unpublished.
4. *Four Impressions for Orchestra (In the New Forest)*. Two of these were completed between 1903 and 1907. *Burley Heath*, the intended first of the projected four, was left as a 169-bar fragment. *The Solent*, the second of the set, is recorded as having been performed on 19 June 1903. It is not known where. Material from it was taken up in *A Sea Symphony*, the Ninth Symphony, and the music to *The England of Elizabeth*. *Harnham Down* was first performed as the first of *Two Impressions for Orchestra* on 12 November 1907 at the Queen's Hall, London. None of them has been published.
5. *Symphonic Rhapsody*. For orchestra. First performance: Bournemouth, 7 March 1904. Inspired by verses of Christina Rossetti beginning 'Come to me in the silence of the night'. Unpublished MS destroyed.
6. *In the Fen Country*, Symphonic Impression for Orchestra. Completed 10 April 1904. First performance: Queen's Hall, London, 22 February 1909, after two revisions, in 1905 and 1907. The scoring of the work was further revised in 1935. Publication: Full score, London, Oxford University Press, 1969. Dedication: To RLW [(Sir) Ralph Wedgwood)].
7. *Norfolk Rhapsody No. 1 in E minor*. First performance: Queen's Hall, London, 23 August 1906. The work was revised between then and a further recorded performance at Bournemouth on 21 May 1914. Publication: Full score London, Oxford University Press, 1925.
8. *Norfolk Rhapsody No. 2 in D minor*. First performance: Cardiff, 27 September 1907. Unpublished.
9. *Norfolk Rhapsody No. 3 in G*. First performance: Cardiff, 27 September 1907. Unpublished MS lost.
10. *Aristophanic Suite: The Wasps*. See II Incidental Music to Plays . . . (A), 1.
11. *Fantasia on a Theme by Thomas Tallis*. For double stringed orchestra and solo

quartet. First performance: Gloucester Cathedral, 6 September 1910. Revised in 1913 and 1919. Publication: Full score, London, Goodwin & Tabb, 1921; miniature score Boosey & Hawkes, 1943. Arrangement for two pianofortes by Maurice Jacobson, London, J. Curwen & Sons, 1947.

12. *English Folk-Songs.* Suite for full orchestra. See III Orchestral Works (C), 1.

13. *Prelude and Fugue in C minor.* For orchestra. Prelude composed September 1921 and revised July 1923. Fugue composed August 1921 and revised in July 1923 and March 1930. First performance : Hereford Cathedral, 12 September 1930. Published (Oxford University Press) as parts for hire only (3.2.2.2.1; 4.3.3.1; timps, percussion, 2., organ, str.). Dedication: To Henry Ley. Also arranged for organ (published by Oxford University Press, 1930).

14. *Fantasia on 'Greensleeves'.* Adapted from *Sir John in Love* and arranged by Ralph Greaves for strings and harp with optional flute(s). First performance: Queen's Hall, London, 27 September 1934. Publication: Full score, Oxford University Press, 1934. Also arranged for pianoforte solo (OUP, 1937), pianoforte duet (OUP, 1942), two pianofortes (OUP, 1945), violin and pianoforte (OUP, 1944), cello (or viola) and pianoforte (OUP, 1947).

15. *Two Hymn-Tune Preludes.* For small orchestra. Based on 'Eventide' (W. H. Monk) and 'Dominus regit me' (J. B. Dykes). First performance: Hereford, 8 September 1936. Publication: Full score, London, Oxford University Press, 1960. Organ arrangement by Herbert Sumsion, OUP, 1938.

16. *Partita for Double String Orchestra.* See also *Double Trio* (VI Chamber Music (B), 9). First performance in this form, 20 March 1948. Publication: London, Oxford University Press, 1948. Dedication: to R. Müller-Hartmann.

17. *Five Variants of 'Dives and Lazarus'.* For strings and harp. First performance: Carnegie Hall, New York, 10 June 1939. Publication: Full score, London, Oxford University Press, 1940.

18. *Concerto Grosso.* For string orchestra (Concertino, Tutti and ad lib section including parts ' . . . for those players who prefer to use only open strings). Five movements: Intrada; Burlesca Ostinata; Sarabande; Scherzo; March and Reprise. First performance: Royal Albert Hall, London, 18 November 1950. Publication: Full score, London, Oxford University Press, 1950.

19. *Prelude on an Old Carol Tune.* Founded on incidental music written for Hardy's *The Mayor of Casterbridge.* First performance: BBC broadcast, 18 November 1952. Publication: London, Oxford University Press, 1953.

21. *Flourish for Glorious John* from RVW. First performance: Free Trade Hall, Manchester, 16 October 1957. Unpublished.

(C) Works for military or brass band

1. *English Folk Songs.* Suite for military band, transcribed in 1924 by Gordon Jacob for full orchestra and for brass band. Three movements: March: Seventeen come Sunday; Intermezzo: My Bonny Boy; March: Folk Songs from Somerset (based on 'Blow away the Morning Dew' and 'High Germany'). First performance: Kneller Hall, 4 July 1923. Publication: London, Boosey & Hawkes. Military band 1924, orchestral transcription 1942, brass band transcription, 1956.

2. *Sea Songs.* Quick march for military and brass bands. Based on 'The Princess Royal', 'Admiral Benbow', and 'Portsmouth'. First performance (probably) at Wembley in 1924 during the British Empire Exhibition. Publication: Brass and

military band versions, London, Boosey & Hawkes, 1924; RVW's own transcription for full orchestra, 1943.

3. *Concerto Grosso*. For military band (1924). Two movements: Allegro moderato and Molto adagio. Unperformed and unpublished in this form. The music of the second movement was used in the *Violin Concerto* and that of the first in *Toccata Marziale* (§ 4).

4. *Toccata Marziale*. For military band. First performance: Wembley, British Empire Exhibition, 1924. Publication: London, Paris, etc., Hawkes & Son, 1924.

5. *Henry the Fifth*. Overture for brass band. (Composed in 1933 and based on 'The Agincourt Song', 'Magali', 'Réveillez-vous, Picars', and 'The Earl of Oxford's March'.) First performance: Maurice Gusman Concert Hall, Miami, Florida, 3 October 1979. Publication: London, Boosey & Hawkes, 1981.

6. *The Golden Vanity*. March for military band. Composed in 1933; unpublished.

7. *Flourish of Trumpets for a Folk Dance Festival*. For brass band. First performance: London, International Folk Dance Festival, Royal Albert Hall, 17 July 1935. Unpublished, but recorded in 1937 on Columbia DB 1671 by the Morris Motors Band.

8. *England's Pleasant Land*. For more detail see I Stage Works (B), 10.

9. *Flourish for Wind Band*. First performance: Royal Albert Hall, London, 1 April 1939. Publication: London, Oxford University Press, 1973. This piece has also been arranged for brass band by Roy Douglas (© OUP, 1981) and adapted by him for orchestral wind, double basses, timps., and percussion (© OUP, 1972).

10. *Prelude on Three Welsh Hymn Tunes*. For brass band. Based on the tunes 'Ebenezer', 'Calfaria', and 'Hyfrydol'. First public performance: 12 March 1955 in the BBC programme *Listen to the Band*. Publication: London, Salvationist Publishing and Supplies Ltd, July 1955.

11. *Variations for Brass Band*. First performance: Royal Albert Hall, London, 26 October 1957. Publication: London, Boosey & Hawkes, 1957. Arranged for orchestra by Gordon Jacob and first performed in that form in Birmingham Town Hall, 8 January 1960.

IV CHORAL WORKS

(A) Student works

1. Three Kyries. Composed at Charterhouse, June 1889.

2. *Music, when Soft Voices Die* (Shelley). Part-song for male voices. First performance: Cambridge University Musical Club, 18 November 1893.

3. Gloria. Student exercise for Parry, RCM, Summer Term 1891.

4. Anthem: *I heard a Voice from heaven* (Revelations, 14:13) for tenor and chorus. RCM, Summer Term 1891.

5. *Super Flumina Babylonis* (Psalm 137). RCM, Spring Term 1892.

6. *Vexilla Regis*. Hymn for soprano solo, mixed 5-part chorus (SSATB), strings, and organ. Mus. Bac. Exercise. Four movements: Vexilla Regis; Impleta sunt; O Crux; Fons salutis. Composed 1894, unpublished.

7. *Peace, Come away* (Tennyson). For four voices and small orchestra. Dated 27 September 1895.

8. *Wine, Vine and Eglantine* (Tennyson). Vocal valse for SATB and piano. Dated 12–16 March 1896. Unpublished.
9. *Sonnet 71* (Shakespeare). For six voices (SSATBB). No date, but Kennedy conjectures that it was almost certainly written between October 1895 and March 1896. Unpublished.
10. *Echo's Lament of Narcissus* ('Slow, slow, fresh fount') (Jonson). Madrigal for double chorus. Date as for § 9. Unpublished.
11. *Mass.* For soloists (SATB), mixed double chorus and orchestra (1897–9). Degree exercise for Doctorate of Music at Cambridge. Five movements: Credo; Offertorium; Sanctus; Hosanna; Benedictus. No record of any performance. Unpublished.

(B) Works for chorus and orchestra

1. *The Garden of Proserpine* (Swinburne). Completed in 1899. No record of performance. Unpublished.
2. *Willow Wood* (D. G. Rossetti). Cantata for baritone or mezzo-soprano solo and orchestra. Four movements: Adagio quasi andante; Andante con moto; Adagio quasi andante; Allegro quasi andante. First performed as solo with piano accompaniment, St James's Hall, London, 12 March 1903. First performance of version with orchestra, Liverpool, 25 September 1909. Publication: Leipzig, Breitkopf & Härtel, 1909.
3. *Sound Sleep* (Christina Rossetti). For female voices (SSA) and pianoforte. First performance: Spilsby, Lincolnshire, 27 April 1903. Publication: London, Novello & Co., 1903. Orchestrated in the same year. Dedication: Mrs Massingberd.
4. *Toward the Unknown Region* (Whitman). Song for chorus (SATB) and orchestra. First performance, Leeds Town Hall, 10 October 1907. Publication: Vocal score by Breitkopf & Härtel, Leipzig and London, 1907. Full score, Stainer & Bell Ltd, London, 1924. Dedication: To F.H.M. (Florence Maitland, RVW's sister-in-law).
5. *Three Nocturnes* (Whitman). For baritone solo, semi-chorus, and orchestra. I. Come, O voluptuous sweet-breathed earth; II. By the Bivouac's fitful flame, III. Out of the rolling ocean. Nos. I and III are dated 18 August 1908. A theme used in III recurs in a modified form in *Sancta Civitas*. Substantial but incomplete. Unpublished.
6. *A Sea Symphony.* See III Orchestral Works (A), 1.
7. *Five Mystical Songs* (George Herbert). For baritone soloist, mixed chorus (SATB) ad lib, and orchestra. Easter; I got me flowers; Love bade me welcome; The Call; Antiphon. First performance: Worcester Cathedral, 14 September 1911. Publication: Vocal score, London, Stainer & Bell Ltd, 1911. 'Antiphon' is available as a four-part anthem and in an arrangement for organ (Stainer & Bell 1923) by Henry G. Ley. 'The Call' was arranged for organ by Herbert Byard (Stainer & Bell, 1946).
8. *Fantasia on Christmas Carols* (trad.). For baritone soloist, mixed chorus (SATB), and orchestra. First performance: Hereford Cathedral, 12 September 1912. Publication: Chorus edition, London, Stainer & Bell Ltd, 1912. Full score, London, Stainer & Bell Ltd, 1924. Arranged for male voices (TTBB) and pianoforte by Herbert W. Pierce (Stainer & Bell, 1925).
9. *Lord, Thou Hast Been Our Refuge.* Motet for chorus (SATB), semi-chorus

(SATB), and orchestra (Psalm 90). Publication: London, J. Curwen & Sons Ltd, 1921.

10. Fanfare: '*So he passed over . . .* '. For double chorus of women's voices (SA), trumpets, cello, double bass, and bells. Publication: London, Goodwin & Tabb, in *Fanfare*, a musical causerie, 15 November 1921, p. 70.

12. *Sancta Civitas (The Holy City)*. Oratorio for tenor and baritone soloists, mixed chorus (SATB), semi-chorus, distant chorus, and orchestra. Text from the Authorized Version of the Bible, with additions from Taverner's Bible (1539) and other sources. First performance: Sheldonian Theatre, Oxford, 7 May 1926. Publication: Vocal score, London, J. Curwen & Sons, Ltd, 1925.

13. Te Deum in G. For Decani and Cantoris (SATB men's and boys' voices) with organ or orchestra. Instrumentation by Arnold Foster. First performance: Canterbury Cathedral, 4 December 1928. Publication: London, Oxford University Press, 1928.

14. *In Windsor Forest*. Cantata for mixed chorus (SATB) and orchestra. Music adapted from the opera *Sir John in Love*. Five sections: The Conspiracy; Drinking Song; Falstaff and the Fairies; Wedding Chorus; Epilogue. First performance: Queen's Hall, London, 14 April 1931. Publication: London, Oxford University Press, 1931.

15. *Benedicite*. For soprano, mixed chorus (SATB), and orchestra. Words from 'The Song of the Three Holy Children' (the Apocrypha) and 'Hark, my soul, how everything' (John Austin). First performance: the Drill Hall, Dorking, 2 May 1930. Publication: London: Oxford University Press, 1929. Dedication: to L.H.M.C. [Leith Hill Musical Competition] Towns Division.

16. *The Hundredth Psalm*. For mixed chorus (SATB) and orchestra. Words from Psalm 100 and Doxology from *Daye's Psalter*, 1561. First performance: the Drill Hall, Dorking, 29 April 1930. Publication, London, Stainer & Bell Ltd, 1929. Dedication: To L.H.M.C. Division II.

17. *Three Choral Hymns*. For baritone (or tenor) solo, mixed chorus (SATB), and orchestra. Words by Miles Coverdale, translated from the German. Three movements: Easter Hymn; Christmas Hymn; Whitsunday Hymn. (The words of 2 and 3 were translated by Coverdale from Luther.) First performance: the Drill Hall, Dorking, 30 April 1930. Publication: London, J. Curwen & Sons, Ltd, 1930. New edition of vocal score with revised keyboard part, Faber Music, 1993. Dedication: To L.H.M.C. Division I.

18. *Three Children's Songs for A Spring Festival*. For voices in unison with string accompaniment. Words by Frances M. Farrer. Three movements: Spring; The Singers; An Invitation. First performance: the Drill Hall, Dorking, 1 May 1930. Publication: London, Oxford University Press, 1930. Dedication: To L.H.M.C. Children's Division.

19. Magnificat. For contralto solo, women's choir (SA), solo flute, and orchestra. Words adapted from the Bible.[2] First performance: Worcester Cathedral, 8 September 1932. Publication: London, Oxford University Press, 1932. Dedication: To Astra Desmond.

20. *Five Tudor Portraits* (Skelton). For contralto (or mezzo-soprano), baritone, mixed chorus (SATB), and orchestra. Five movements: The Tunning of Elinor

---

[2] The composer solemnly adjures the performers: 'This work is not designed for liturgical use!'

Rumming (Ballad); Pretty Bess (Intermezzo); Epitaph on John Jayberd of Diss (Burlesca); Jane Scroop (Her Lament for Philip Sparrow) (Romanza); Jolly Rutterkin (Scherzo). First performance: St Andrew's Hall, Norwich, 25 September 1936. Publication: London, Oxford University Press, 1935. Full score, Oxford University Press, 1971.

21. *Nothing is here for tears* (Milton). Choral song (unison or SATB) with accompaniment for pianoforte, organ or orchestra. First performance: London, BBC broadcast concert, 26 January 1936. Publication: London, Oxford University Press, 1936.

22. *Dona Nobis Pacem*. Cantata for soprano and baritone soloists, mixed chorus (SATB), and orchestra. Five sections: Agnus Dei (the Liturgy); Beat! Beat! Drums! (Whitman); Reconciliation (Whitman); Dirge for Two Veterans[3] (Whitman); The Angel of Death (John Bright) and sections from the Old and New Testaments. First performance: Huddersfield Town Hall, 2 October 1936. Publication: London, Oxford University Press, 1936.

23. *Flourish for a Coronation*. For mixed chorus (SATB) and orchestra. Three movements: Let the priest and the prophet anoint him (The Bible); O prince, desire to be honourable (Chaucer); Now gracious God he save our King (The Agincourt Song). First performance: Queen's Hall, London, 1 April 1937. Publication: Vocal score, London, Oxford University Press, 1937.

24. *Festival Te Deum in F major*. Founded on traditional themes. For mixed chorus (SATB) and organ or orchestra. First performance: Westminster Abbey (coronation service) 12 May 1937. Publication: Vocal score, London, Oxford University Press, 1937.

25. *Serenade to Music* (Shakespeare). For 16 solo voices[4] (4S, 4C, 4T, 4B) and orchestra. First performance: Queen's Hall, London, 5 October 1938. Publication: Vocal score, London, Oxford University Press, 1938. Full score, 1961.

26. *Six Choral Songs—To be Sung in Time of War* (Shelley). For unison voices with pianoforte or orchestra. A Song of Courage; A Song of Liberty; A Song of Healing; A Song of Victory; A Song of Pity; A Song of the New Age. First performance: BBC broadcast concert, 20 December 1940. Publication: Vocal score, London, Oxford University Press, 1940.

27. *The New Commonwealth* (Harold Child). For unison voices with pianoforte accompaniment or orchestra. Publication: Vocal score, London, Oxford University Press, 1943. See also IX Arrangements.

28. *England, My England* (W. E. Henley). Choral song, for baritone soloist, double choir, unison voices, and orchestra. First performance: BBC broadcast concert, 16 November 1941. Publication: Vocal score, London, Oxford University Press, 1941.

29. *Thanksgiving for Victory* (renamed *A Song of Thanksgiving* in 1952). Words from various sources including The Bible, Shakespeare, and Kipling. For soprano solo, speaker, mixed chorus (SATB), and orchestra. Recorded in London, 5 November 1944, for broadcasting on 13 May 1945. Publication: Vocal score, London, Oxford University Press, 1945.

---

[3] This section dates from 1911 and was originally part of *Two Nocturnes*.

[4] It has been thought better to include this work here, as it is often performed in the version for SATB soloists and SATB chorus.

30. *The Voice out of the Whirlwind*. Motet for mixed chorus (SATB) and orchestra or organ. Adapted from 'Galliard of the Sons of the Morning', from *Job*. First performance: Church of St Sepulchre, Holborn Viaduct, London, 22 November 1947. Publication: Vocal score, London, Oxford University Press, 1947.

31. *A Cotswold Romance*. Cantata for tenor and soprano soloists, mixed chorus (SATB), and orchestra, adapted from the opera *Hugh the Drover* by Maurice Jacobson. Ten movements: Chorus: Men of Cotsall; SATB unaccompanied: Sweet Little Linnet; Tenor and SATB: Song of the Road; Tenor, soprano and SATB: Love at First Sight; SATB with baritone solo: The Best Man in England; Tenor solo: Alone and Friendless; Tenor, Soprano and SATB: The Fight and its Sequel; Tenor solo: Hugh in the Stocks (Gaily I go to die); Soprano and SATB: Mary escapes (a) alternative version for women's voices: Here, Queen Uncrown'd; Tenor, soprano and SATB: Freedom at Last. First performance: Central Hall, Tooting Broadway, London, 10 May 1951. Publication: London, J. Curwen & Sons Ltd. © USA 1951 by RVW and Maurice Jacobson.

32. *Folk Songs of the Four Seasons*. Cantata, based on traditional folk songs, for women's voices (SSAA) and orchestra. Four movements: Prologue: To the Plough Boy; Spring; Summer; Autumn; Winter. First performance: Royal Albert Hall, London, 15 June 1950. Publication: Vocal score and voice part, London, Oxford University Press, 1950. A Suite for small orchestra was arranged from this work by Roy Douglas with the following movements: I. To the Ploughboy and May Song; II. The Green Meadow and An Acre of Land; III. The Sprig of Thyme and The Lark in the Morning; IV. The Cuckoo; V. Wassail Song and Children's Christmas Song. Publication: London, Oxford University Press, 1956.

33. *An Oxford Elegy* (Matthew Arnold). For speaker, small mixed chorus (SATB) and small orchestra. First public performance: The Queen's College, Oxford, 19 June 1952. Publication: Vocal score, London, Oxford University Press, 1952.

34. *Fantasia (Quasi Variazione) on the 'Old 104th' Psalm Tune*. See VII Concertos (A), 8.

35. *The Sons of Light* (Ursula Wood [Ursula Vaughan Williams]). Cantata for mixed chorus (SATB) and orchestra. Three movements: I. Darkness and Light; II. The Song of the Zodiac; III. The Messengers of Speech. First performance: Royal Albert Hall, London, 6 May 1951. Publication: Vocal score, London, Oxford University Press, 1951. Dedication: To Bernard Shore.[5] Sections of this work were adapted into *Sun, Moon, Stars, and Man*, a cycle of four songs for unison voices with accompaniment for strings and/or pianoforte, first performed at Birmingham Town Hall on 11 March 1955. This version was published in vocal score by OUP in 1954.

36. *The Old Hundredth Psalm Tune* ('All People that on Earth do Dwell') (W. Kethe). Arranged for mixed choir (SATB), congregation, orchestra, and organ. First performance: Westminster Abbey, 2 June 1953 at the coronation

---

[5] Shore was a distinguished viola player (former leader of the viola section in the BBC Symphony Orchestra), author, and HM Staff Inspector in Music, Ministry of Education, who commissioned the work for the Schools' Music Association of Great Britain's second national festival.

of Queen Elizabeth II. Publication: Vocal score, London, Oxford University Press, 1953.

37. *This Day* (*Hodie*). A Christmas Cantata for soprano, tenor, and baritone soloists with mixed chorus (SATB), boys' voices, organ (optional), and full orchestra. Words from various sources. Sixteen movements: Prologue; Narration; Song (Milton: soprano and women's voices); Narration; Choral; Narration; The Oxen (Thomas Hardy: baritone and orch.); Narration; Pastoral (George Herbert: baritone and orch.); Narration; Lullaby (William Ballet: soprano and women's voices); Hymn (William Drummond: tenor and orch.); Narration; The March of the Three Kings (Ursula Vaughan Williams: soprano, tenor, baritone, chorus, and orch.); Choral (v. 1 anon.; v. 2 Ursula Vaughan Williams); Epilogue (adapted from St John's Gospel, 1: 1–14 and Milton's Nativity Hymn). First performance: Worcester Cathedral, 8 September 1954. Publication: Vocal score, London, Oxford University Press, 1954. Full score, OUP, 1967. Dedication: To Herbert Howells.[6]

38. *Song for a Spring Festival* (Ursula Vaughan Williams). For mixed chorus. Written for and given to the Leith Hill Musical Festival in April 1955, by the author and composer, to be performed nowhere else. First performance: Dorking, the Dorking Halls, Leith Hill Musical Festival, 15 April 1955. Privately printed by Oxford University Press.

39. *Epithalamion.* Cantata founded on the Masque *The Bridal Day*, for baritone, mixed chorus, and small orchestra. Words chosen by Ursula Vaughan Williams from Spenser's *Epithalamion*. Eleven movements: Prologue; 'Wake now'; The Calling of the Bride; The Minstrels; Procession of the Bride; The Temple Gates; The Bellringers; The Lover's Song; The Minstrel's Song; Song of the Winged Loves; Prayer to Juno. First performance: Royal Festival Hall, London, 30 September 1957. Publication: Vocal score, London, Oxford University Press, 1957.

(C) Choral works (unaccompanied)

(NB Apart from the *Five English Folk Songs*, (below, § 9) this list does not include folk-song arrangements, which will be found under IX.)

1. *Three Elizabethan Songs*[7]. For chorus (SATB): Sweet Day (George Herbert); The Willow Song (Shakespeare); O Mistress Mine (Shakespeare). First performance (probably): Shirehampton Public Hall, 5 November 1913. Publication: London, Joseph Williams & Co. Ltd, 1913.

2. *Come away, Death.* SSATB. Publication: London, Stainer & Bell Ltd, 1909.

3. *Rise early Sun.* SATB. First (?) performance: Hooton Roberts, September 1899. Unpublished, but performed with missing tenor part reconstructed by

---

[6] The dedication continues: 'Dear Herbert, I find that in this Cantata I have inadvertently cribbed a phrase from your beautiful *Hymnus Paradisi*. Your passage seems to germane to my context that I have decided to keep it. RVW.'

[7] There has always been some confusion about the date of composition of these songs. Michael Kennedy rightly points out that 'the assurance and style of the music are far ahead of any other of his compositions of this time' (i.e. 1890–2, which must be the date of at any rate 'The Willow Song' if Vaughan Williams's contention in *A Musical Autobiography* that the last two bars of it were 'almost certainly composed by Parry' is correct). They were certainly composed much earlier than their date of publication.

Roy Douglas at Hooton Roberts as part of the Vaughan Williams Centenary Festival in 1972.

4. *Ring out your Bells* (Philip Sidney), SSATB. Publication: J. Laudy & Co., 1904–5. Dedication: To Lionel Benson Esq. & the members of the Magpie Madrigal Society (who probably gave the first performance, though it is not mentioned in their list of programmes).

5. *Rest* (Christina Rossetti), SSATB. Publication and dedication as § 4.

6. *Fain would I change that note* (anon.). Canzonet for four voices (SATB). Publication: London, Novello & Co., 1907. Also published by Novello (1927) in an arrangement for TTBB and for a trio of women's voices (SSA).

7. *Love is a Sickness* (Samuel Daniel). Ballet for four voices (SATB). Publication: London, Stainer & Bell Ltd, 1913; Leipzig, Breitkopf & Härtel, 1913.

8. *O Praise the Lord of Heaven*. Anthem for two full choirs and semi-chorus (Psalm 148). First performance: London, St Paul's Cathedral, 13 November 1913. Publication: London, Stainer & Bell Ltd, 1914.

9. *Five English Folk Songs*. Freely arranged for mixed chorus[8] (SATB). Five movements: The Dark-eyed Sailor; The Springtime of the Year; Just as the Tide was Flowing; The Lover's Ghost; Wassail Song. First performance not known. Three of the songs were performed by the Guy's Hospital Musical Society at a choral and orchestral concert on 1 May 1914. Publication: London, Stainer & Bell Ltd, 1913.

10. *O Vos Omnes* ('Is it nothing to you?'). Words from the Maundy Thursday office of Tenebrae. Motet for mixed voices (SSAATTBB) with alto solo. First performance: Westminster Cathedral, 13 April 1922. Publication: London, J. Curwen & Sons, Ltd, 1922. Dedication: To Dr R. R. Terry.

11. *Mass in G minor*. For soloists (SATB) and double chorus, unaccompanied,[9] with organ part ad lib: Kyrie; Gloria; Credo; Sanctus, Osanna I, Benedictus, Osanna II; Agnus Dei. First performance: Birmingham Town Hall, 6 December 1922. Publication: London, J. Curwen & Sons Ltd, 1922. Dedication: to Gustav Holst and his Whitsuntide Singers.

12. *The Souls of the Righteous*. Motet for treble (or soprano), tenor, baritone soloists, and mixed chorus (Treble ATB or SATB), unaccompanied. Words from *The Wisdom of Solomon*, III vv. 1–5. First performance: Westminster Abbey, 10 July 1947. Publication: London, Oxford University Press, 1947.

13. *Valiant for Truth* (Bunyan). Motet for mixed chorus (SATB) unaccompanied, or with organ or pianoforte. First performance: London, St Michael's Church, Cornhill, 29 June 1942. Publication: London, Oxford University Press, 1941.

14. *Prayer to the Father of Heaven* (Skelton). Motet for mixed chorus (SATB).

---

[8] Strictly speaking these are arrangements and should perhaps be included under that heading. Vaughan Williams's treatment of the songs, however, is so much freer than his usual manner and the songs form so self-consistent a group that it has been seen fit to include them here.

[9] The Mass was adapted to the words of the Anglican communion service by Maurice Jacobson, revised by the composer. The order of movements (*Responses to Commandments*; *Kyrie*; *Creed*; *Sanctus*; *Benedictus*; *Agnus Dei*; *Gloria in Excelsis*) follows that of the 1662 Anglican communion service, with the *Hosanna* as an appendix. This version was published in 1923 by Curwen & Sons.

First performance: Sheldonian Theatre, Oxford, 12 May 1948. Dedication: To the memory of my master Hubert Parry . . . [10]

15. *Three Shakespeare Songs.* For mixed chorus (SATB) unaccompanied. 1. Full Fathom Five; 2. The Cloud-Capp'd Towers; 3. Over Hill, Over Dale. First performance: Royal Festival Hall, London, 23 June 1951. Publication: London, Oxford University Press, 1951. Dedication: To C. Armstrong Gibbs.

16. *O Taste and See.* Words from Psalm 34, v. 8. Motet for mixed choir (S or treble solo, ATB), with an organ introduction. First performance: Westminster Abbey, 2 June 1953 at the coronation of Queen Elizabeth II. Publication: London, Oxford University Press, 1953.

17. *Silence and Music* (Ursula Wood [Ursula Vaughan Williams]). For mixed chorus (SATB). No. 4 of *A Garland for the Queen.* First performance: Royal Festival Hall, London, 1 June 1953. Publication: London, Oxford University Press, 1953. Dedication: To the Memory of Charles Villiers Stanford, and his Blue Bird.

18. *Heart's Music* (Campion). Song for mixed chorus (SATB). First performance: London, Church of St Sepulchre, Holborn Viaduct, 25 November 1954. Publication: London, Oxford University Press, 1955. Dedication: Written for Wilfrid Dykes Bower and the St Thomas's Hospital Musical Society.

19. *A Choral Flourish.* Words from Psalm 22 (AV, Psalm 33). For mixed chorus (SAT and high bar; B) with introduction for organ or two trumpets. In Latin, with English version as alternative. First performance: Royal Festival Hall, London, 3 November 1956. Publication: London, Oxford University Press, 1956. Dedication: To Alan Kirby.

(D) Works for choir or unison voices and piano or organ accompaniment

1. *Let Us Now Praise Famous Men.* Text selected from *Ecclesiasticus*, Ch. 44. Unison Song, with accompaniment for pianoforte, organ, or small orchestra. Publication: London, J. Curwen & Sons Ltd, 1923. The orchestration (2.2.2.2.; 4.3.3; timp., organ (optional), and str.) is by Arnold Foster.

2. *Darest Thou Now, O Soul* (Whitman). Unison song. Publication: J. Curwen & Sons Ltd, London and Philadelphia, 1925.

3. Magnificat and Nunc Dimittis (*The Village Service*). Set to music for the use of village choirs for mixed chorus (SATB) and organ. Publication: London, J. Curwen & Sons Ltd, 1925.

4. *The Pilgrim Pavement* (Margaret Ridgeley Partridge). Hymn for soprano solo, mixed chorus (SATB), and organ. First performance: New York, 10 February 1935. Publication: London, Oxford University Press, 1934.

5. *O How Amiable.* Words from Psalms 84 and 90. Anthem for the dedication of a church or other Festivals. For mixed chorus (SATB) and organ. Originally composed for the Abinger Pageant, 1934. Publication: London, Oxford University Press, 1940. Dedication: to F.F. [Dame Frances Farrer].

6. *Services in D minor.* For unison voices, mixed choir (SATB) and organ. Morning Service: Te Deum; Benedictus; Jubilate. Communion Service: Kyrie,

---

[10] The full dedication continues ' . . . not as an attempt palely to reflect his incomparable art, but in the hope that he would have found in this motet (to use his own words) "something characteristic" '.

Responses, Before the Gospel; After the Gospel; Creed; Sursum Corda; Sanctus; Benedictus qui venit; Agnus Dei; Gloria. Evening service: Magnificat; Nunc Dimittis. Publication: London, Oxford University Press, 1939. Dedication: Written for and dedicated to Dr C. S. Lang and his singers at Christ's Hospital.

7. *A Hymn of Freedom* (Canon G. W. Briggs). For unison voices with pianoforte or organ. Publication: London, Oxford University Press, 1939. See also § 9, *Five Wartime Hymns*.

8. *A Call to the Free Nations* (Canon G. W. Briggs). Hymn for choral or unison singing. Publication: London, Oxford University Press, 1941. See also § 9, *Five Wartime Hymns*.

9. *Five Wartime Hymns* (Canon G. W. Briggs). For unison voices with pianoforte or organ, by RVW, Martin Saw, and Ivor Atkins. §§ 7 and 8 were the first two items in this collection. Publication: London, Oxford University Press, 1942. Republished with revised words in *Songs of Faith*, (OUP, 1945).

10. *The Airmen's Hymn*. Words by the Second Earl of Lytton. Unison song with pianoforte or organ. Publication: London, Oxford University Press, 1942.

11. *Hymn for St Margaret* ('St Margaret') (Ursula Wood [Ursula Vaughan Williams]). Composed in January or February 1948, No. 748 in *Hymnal for Scotland, incorporating the English Hymnal*. Publication: London, Oxford University Press, 1950.

12. Te Deum and Benedictus. Set to well-known metrical psalm tunes for unison voices . . . or mixed voices (with occasional optional harmony) with accompaniment of organ, harmonium, or pianoforte. Publication: Vocal score, London, Oxford University Press, 1954.

V SOLO SONGS (Pianoforte accompaniment unless otherwise stated)

(A) Student and unpublished works

1. *Crossing the Bar* (Tennyson). 1892. Unpublished.

2. *Wishes*. Words by 'T', from the *Cambridge Observer* of August 1893. Unpublished.

3. *The Virgin's Cradle Song* (S. T. Coleridge). Performed at Cambridge University Musical Club, 3 November 1894. Published in *The Vocalist*, April 1905.

4. *To Daffodils* (Herrick). Dated 3 July 1895. Unpublished.

5. *Lollipops Song*; *Spinning Song*. Settings from *Rumpelstiltskin*.

6. *Spring* (Tennyson). Vocal Valse for voice and pianoforte. Dated 17 February 1896.

7. *Winter* (Tennyson). Vocal Valse for voice and pianoforte. Dated 16 March 1896.

8. *Rondel* (Swinburne). For contralto or baritone with pianoforte accompaniment. First performance probably at Bechstein Hall, London, 28 May 1906.

9. *The Willow Whistle* (M. E. Fuller). For voice and pipe. Undated, but quite likely to be contemporary with the *Suite for Pipes* (1938 or 1939). First performance: Holy Trinity Church, Hinckley, 16 October 1982.

Vaughan Williams

(B) Published works

1. *How can the tree but wither?* (Thomas, Lord Vaux). Probably composed in 1896. First known performance: 5 June 1907. Publication: London, Oxford University Press, 1934.
2. *Claribel* (Tennyson). Probably composed before 1900. First performance probably at Bechstein Hall, London, 2 December 1904. Publication: London, Boosey & Co., 1906.
3. *Linden Lea* (William Barnes). Almost certainly composed in 1901. Sub-titled 'A Dorset Folk Song'. First performance: Hooton Roberts, 4 September 1902. Publication: London, the Vocalist Co. Ltd, in *The Vocalist*, Vol. 1, No. 1, April 1902. Re-issued by Boosey & Co., 1912. Dedication: To Mrs Edmund Fisher. Michael Kennedy lists thirteen arrangements of and a Fantasia on this song, RVW's first published work.
4. *Blackmwore by the Stour* (William Barnes). 'A Dorset folk song'. First performance: Hooton Roberts, 4 September 1902. Published in *The Vocalist*, May 1902. Re-issued by Boosey & Co., 1912.
5. *Whither must I wander?* (R. L. Stevenson). First performance: St James's Hall, London, 27 November 1902. Published in *The Vocalist*, June 1902. Re-issued by Boosey & Co., 1912. Incorporated into *Songs of Travel* (see below, § 14).
6. *Boy Johnny* (Christina Rossetti). First performance: Oxford, Commemoration Week, 1902. Published in *The Vocalist*, September 1902. Dedication: To J. Campbell McInnes, Esq.
7. *If I were a Queen* (Christina Rossetti). First performance: Exeter, 16 April 1903. Published in *The Vocalist*, November 1902. §§ 6 and 7 were jointly re-published by *The Vocalist* in 1905 and by Boosey & Co. in 1914.
8. *Tears, Idle Tears* (Tennyson). First performance: St James's Hall, London, 5 February 1903. Published in *The Vocalist*, June 1903. Re-issued by Boosey & Co., 1914. Dedication: To J. Francis Harford, Esq.
9. *Silent Noon* (D. G. Rossetti). First performance: London, St James's Hall, 10 March 1903. Publication: London, Willcocks & Co., March 1904 in advance of the publication of the complete *House of Life* cycle (see below, § 13).
10. *Orpheus with his Lute* (Shakespeare). Composed 1902. First performance: Bechstein Hall, London, 2 December 1904. Publication: London, Keith Prowse & Co. Ltd, 1903. Dedication: To Miss Lucy Broadwood.
11. *When I Am Dead, my Dearest* (Christina Rossetti). First performance: Aeolian Hall, London, 28 November 1905. Publication: London, Keith Prowse & Co. Ltd, 1903.
12. *The Winter's Willow* (William Barnes). Date of first performance unknown. Published in *The Vocalist*, November 1903 and re-issued by Boosey & Co., 1914.
13. *The House of Life* (D. G. Rossetti). A cycle of six sonnets: Love-Sight; Silent Noon; Love's Minstrels; Heart's Haven; Death in Love; Love's Last Gift. First performance: Bechstein Hall, London, 2 December 1904. Publication: London, J. Willcocks & Co., 1904. Re-issued in 1933 by Edwin Ashdown Ltd.
14. *Songs of Travel* (R. L. Stevenson). The Vagabond; Let beauty awake; The Roadside Fire; Youth and Love; In Dreams; The Infinite Shining Heavens; Whither must I wander?; Bright is the ring of words; I have trod the upward and the downward slope. First performance of the first *eight* songs at the

Bechstein Hall, London, 2 December 1904. The final song was not discovered until after the composer's death; and the first complete performance of the cycle took place only on 21 May 1960. The songs were originally published in two books. Book I, containing The Vagabond, Bright is the ring of words, and The Roadside Fire was published by Boosey & Co. in 1905, followed by Let beauty Awake, Youth and Love, In Dreams and The Infinite Shining Heavens as Songs of Travel, Part II, in 1907. The complete cycle, including Whither must I wander? and I have trod the upward and the downward slope, was published by Boosey & Hawkes in 1960.

Vaughan Williams himself orchestrated the accompaniment to the songs of the original Book I in 1905; Roy Douglas orchestrated the remainder in 1961–2.

15. *Ye Little Birds* (Thomas Heywood). First performance: Aeolian Hall, London, 3 February 1905. Destroyed.

16. *A Cradle Song* (S. T. Coleridge). See V Solo Songs (A), 3. Published by *The Vocalist*, April 1905.

17. *The Splendour Falls* (Tennyson). Published in *The Vocalist*, May 1905 and re-issued by Boosey & Co. in 1914.

18. *Dreamland* (Christina Rossetti). First performance: Aeolian Hall, London, 31 October 1905. Publication: London, Boosey & Co., 1906.

19. *Buonaparty* (Thomas Hardy). Composed in 1908. Publication: Boosey & Co., London and New York, 1909.

20. *The Sky above the Roof* (Paul Verlaine, trans. Mabel Dearmer). Publication: Boosey & Co., London and New York, 1909.

21. *Is my team ploughing?* (A. E. Housman). First performance: Aeolian Hall, London, 25 January 1909. Not published in this form.

22. *Four Hymns*. For tenor voice, with accompaniment of pianoforte and viola obbligato. Lord! Come Away (Bishop Jeremy Taylor); Who is this fair one? (Isaac Watts); Come love, come Lord (Crashaw); Evening Hymn (trans. from the Greek by Robert Bridges). These songs are probably more familiar in the version with orchestral accompaniment which was how they were first performed, at Cardiff, on 26 May 1920. Publication: Boosey & Co., London and New York. Dedication: To J.S.W. [Sir Steuart Wilson].

23. *Dirge for Fidele* (Shakespeare). Song for two mezzo-sopranos, with pianoforte accompaniment. Probably composed in 1895; published London, Edwin Ashdown Ltd, 1922. Arranged for organ by Alec Rowley in 1928 and published in that year by Ashdown Ltd.

24. *It was a lover and his lass* (Shakespeare). Part-song for two voices with piano accompaniment. Publication: London, J. Curwen & Sons Ltd, 1922.

25. *Two Poems by Seumas O'Sullivan* (James Starkey): The Twilight People; A Piper. First performance: Aeolian Hall, London, 27 March 1925. Publication: London, Oxford University Press, 1925.

26. *Three Songs from Shakespeare*: Take, O take those lips away; When icicles hang by the wall; Orpheus with his lute. First performance: Aeolian Hall, London, 27 March 1925. Publication: London, Oxford University Press, 1925. The first two of these songs also appeared as unison songs in 1926 (OUP) 'Orpheus with his lute' is also available for mixed chorus (SATB) and as a unison song with string orchestra accompaniment.

27. *Four Poems by Fredegond Shove*: Motion and Stillness (dated 1922); Four

Nights; The New Ghost; The Water Mill. First performance: Aeolian Hall, London, 27 March 1925. Publication: London, Oxford University Press, 1925.

28. *Three Poems by Walt Whitman*: Nocturne; A Clear Midnight; Joy, Shipmate, Joy! Publication: London, Oxford University Press, 1925.

29. *Along the Field* (A. E. Housman). Eight songs for voice and violin. We'll to the woods no more; Along the Field; The half-moon westers low; In the Morning; The Sigh that Heaves the Grasses; Goodbye; Fancy's Knell; With rue my heart is laden. First performance; Grotrian Hall, London, 24 October 1927.[11] Publication: London, Oxford University Press, 1954.

30. *In the Spring* (William Barnes). Publication: London, Oxford University Press, 1952. Dedication: To the members of the Barnes Society.

31. *Menelaus on the Beach at Pharos* (Ursula Vaughan Williams). First performance: New York, Cornell University, 14 November 1954. Publication: See below, § 34, *Four Last Songs*. Dedication: To Keith Falkner.

32. *Hands, Eyes and Heart* (Ursula Vaughan Williams). Completed by 7 March 1955. First performance: Christchurch, New Zealand, recital broadcast by NZ Broadcasting Corporation, 21 December 1956. Publication: see below, § 34, *Four Last Songs*.

33. *Ten Blake Songs*, for voice and oboe. Composed Christmastide 1957. Infant Joy; A Poison Tree; The Piper; London (oboe tacet); The Lamb; The Shepherd (oboe tacet); Ah! Sunflower; Cruelty has a human heart; The Divine Image (oboe tacet); Eternity. Eight of these songs were used for the film *The Vision of William Blake*, produced in commemoration of the bicentenary of Blake's birth in 1957. This may be accounted their first performance. The first concert performance was by Wilfred Brown and Janet Craxton, the artists on the sound-track of the film, in a BBC broadcast on 8 October 1958. The film was first shown two days later. Publication: London, Oxford University Press, 1958. Dedication: To Wilfred Brown and Janet Craxton.

34. *Four Last Songs* (Ursula Vaughan Williams): Procris; Tired; Hands, Eyes and Heart; Menelaus. First performance of the complete group:[12] BBC Home Service, 3 August 1960. Publication: London, Oxford University Press, 1960.

35. *Three Vocalises*. For soprano voice and B flat clarinet. Prelude: Moderato; Scherzo: Allegro moderato; Quasi menuetto: Moderato. First performance: Free Trade Hall, Manchester, 8 October 1958. Publication: London, Oxford University Press, 1960. Dedication: To Margaret Ritchie.

VI CHAMBER MUSIC

(A) Student and unpublished works

1. *Pianoforte Trio in G*. Performed at Charterhouse, 5 August 1888, with the composer taking one (sic!) of the violin parts.

2. *Finale* of a String Quartet (RCM exercise, 1891).

3. Pianoforte Trio (pf., vn., vc.) in C. Completed 28 June 1895.

4. String Quartet in C minor. (1898). Four movements: Allegro; Andantino;

---

[11] At this first performance, only seven of the songs were actually performed. It is not known which was omitted. There were originally nine songs, but Vaughan Williams destroyed 'The Soldier' when he revised them for publication.

[12] The term 'group' is used advisedly; the songs were intended for two projected song cycles.

Intermezzo (Allegretto); Variazione con finale fugato. There are six variations and a fugal finale. First performance: Oxford and Cambridge Musical Club, 30 June 1904. Unpublished.

5. Quintet in D. For clarinet, horn, violin, violoncello, and pianoforte. (1898). Four movements: Allegro moderato; Intermezzo: Allegretto; Andantino; Finale: Allegro molto. First performance: Queen's Hall (small hall) London, 5 June 1901. Unpublished.

6. Quintet in C minor. For pianoforte, violin, viola, violoncello, and double bass. Three movements: Allegro con fuoco; Andante; Fantasia (quasi variazioni). Finished 27 October 1903, revised in 1904 and again in 1905. First performance: Aeolian Hall, London, 14 December 1905. Withdrawn some time after 8 June 1918; the main theme of the finale was re-used in the Violin Sonata of 1954.

7. *Ballade and Scherzo*. For string quintet (2vn., 2va., vc.). Finished 22 May 1904, revised 1 October 1906. Unpublished.

8. Two Short Pieces for string quintet: Nocturne, By the Bivouac's fitful flame; Scherzo 'founded on an English folk song', incorporated in § 7. The MS of *Ballade and Scherzo* itself has a different Scherzo, which was presumably discarded as part of the revision.

9. Two Vocal Duets. For soprano, baritone, pianoforte, and string quartet, with violin obbligato (Walt Whitman). The Last Invocation; The Love-Song of the Birds. The first of these was finished on 23 July 1904. First performance: Reading Town Hall, 24 October 1904.

(B) Published works

1. String Quartet in G minor (2vn., va., vc.). Four movements: Allegro moderato; Minuet and Trio; Romance: Andante sostenuto; Finale: Rondo capriccioso. First performance: Novello's Rooms, London, 8 November 1909. Revised 1921. First performance of revised version: Russell Street, London (Contemporary Music Centre concert), 6 March 1922. Publication: Miniature Score, London, F. B. Goodwin Ltd, 1923. Reissued by J. Curwen & Sons Ltd and by Faber Music.

2. *On Wenlock Edge* (Housman). A cycle of six songs for tenor voice with pianoforte and string quartet accompaniment. On Wenlock Edge; From Far, from Eve and Morning; Is my team ploughing?; Oh, When I was in Love with You; Bredon Hill (In Summertime on Bredon); Clun. First performance: Aeolian Hall, London, 15 November 1909. Publication: Full score London, 1911, Novello & Co. Ltd. Full score also published by Boosey & Co. Ltd, London, 1942. RVW's own orchestral version was first performed on 24 January 1924 and published by Boosey & Hawkes in 1994. The composer could not remember when it was made, but another version scored by Eric DeLamarter (1880–1953) was performed in Chicago on 1 and 2 April 1921.

3. *Phantasy Quintet* (2vn., 2va., vc). One movement in four sections: Prelude: Lento ma non troppo; Scherzo: Prestissimo; Alla Sarabanda; Burlesca: Allegro moderato. Probably composed in 1912. First performance: Aeolian Hall, London, 23 March 1914. Publication: London, Stainer & Bell Ltd, 1921. An arrangement for organ of the Alla sarabanda section, by Henry G. Ley, was published by Stainer & Bell in 1922. Dedication: To W. W. Cobbett, Esq.

4. *Suite de Ballet.* For flute and pianoforte. Composed probably in 1913. Four movements: Improvisation; Humoresque: presto; Gavotte: quasi lento; Passepied: allegro vivacissimo. First performance: 62 Cadogan Place, London, 20 March 1920. First public performance: BBC broadcast, 9 April 1962. Publication (ed. Roy Douglas): London, Oxford University Press, 1961.

5. *Merciless Beauty* (attrib. Chaucer). Three rondels for high voice and string trio (2vn., vc.): Your eyën two; So hath your beauty; Since I from love. First performance: Aeolian Hall, London, 4 October 1921. Publication: London, J. Curwen & Sons Ltd, 1922.

6. Two pieces for Violin and Pianoforte: Romance, Andantino; Pastorale, Andante con moto. Publication: London, F. & B. Goodwin Ltd, 1923. Re-issued by J. Curwen & Sons Ltd; new edition re-engraved by Faber Music, 1994. Dedication: To D.M.L. [Dorothy Longman].

7. *Six Studies in English Folk Song.* For violoncello and pianoforte. Adagio; Andante sostenuto; Larghetto; Lento; Andante tranquillo; Allegro vivace. First performance: Scala Theatre, London, 4 June 1926. Publication: London, Stainer & Bell Ltd, 1927. Dedication: to May Mukle. Arrangements for violin, viola, or clarinet; also arranged by Arnold Foster for cello and small orchestra (1957).

8. *Suite for Pipes.* Four movements: Intrada: Moderato maestoso; Minuet and Trio: Allegro moderato; Valse: Lento; Finale: Jig, Presto. First performance: Chichester, Pipers' Guild Summer School, August 1939. Publication: London, Oxford University Press, miniature score, 1947. Version for recorders, OUP, 1980. Dedication: The Pipers' Guild Quartet.

9. *Double Trio*, for string sextet (2vn., 2va., 2vc.). Four movements: Fantasia; Scherzo ostinato; Intermezzo (Homage to Henry Hall); Rondo. First performance: Wigmore Hall, London, 21 January 1939. Revised version first performed, National Gallery, London, 12 October 1942. Unpublished in this form, but further revised (with a completely new finale) and published as *Partita for Double String Orchestra* (see III Orchestral Works (B), 16).

10. *Household Music: Three Preludes on Welsh Hymn Tunes.* For string quartet or alternative instruments. Composed 1940. Crug-y-bar (Fantasia), Andante sostenuto; St Denio (Scherzo), Allegro vivace; Aberystwyth (eight variations). The first documented performance is of a version for medium orchestra, given at Bournemouth on 25 November 1940. Publication: London, Oxford University Press, 1943. The finale was arranged for organ by Herbert Byard and published by OUP in 1949.

11. String Quartet No. 2 in A minor (For Jean on her Birthday). Composed 1942–4. Four movements: Prelude: Allegro appassionato; Romance: Largo; Scherzo: Allegro; Epilogue—Greetings from Joan[13] to Jean: Andante sostenuto. First performance: National Gallery, London, 12 October 1944. Publication: Full score and parts, London, Oxford University Press, 1947.

12. *Fantasia on 'Linden Lea'* for oboe, clarinet, and bassoon. Composed 1942–3 for John Parr of Sheffield. Unpublished.

13. Sonata in A minor. For violin and pianoforte. Three movements: Fantasia: Allegro giusto; Scherzo: Allegro furioso ma non troppo; Tema con variazione:

---

[13] Of Arc: the music was adapted from that intended for a film on the French Saint that never materialized.

Andante – Allegro (six variations). First performance: BBC broadcast 12 October 1954. Publication: London, Oxford University Press, 1956. Dedication: To Frederick Grinke.

14. *Romance for Viola and Pianoforte.* Date of composition unknown. First performance: The Arts Council, 4 St James's Square, London, 19 January 1962. Publication (eds. Bernard Shore and Eric Gritton): London, Oxford University Press, 1962.

VII CONCERTOS AND OTHER WORKS INVOLVING INSTRUMENTAL SOLOISTS

(A) Student and unpublished works

1. Fantasia for pianoforte and orchestra. Begun October 1896; completed 9 February 1902. In one movement (six sections). Revised 14 October 1904. Unpublished.

(B) Published works

1. *The Lark Ascending.* Romance for violin and orchestra. Composed 1914, revised 1920. First performance: Shirehampton Public Hall, 15 December 1920. Further revised before the publication of the full score by Oxford University Press (London, 1926). The miniature score followed in 1927. Copyright in both cases is held from 1925. Dedication: To Marie Hall.

2. *Flos Campi.* Suite for solo viola, small wordless mixed chorus (SATB), and small orchestra. Six movements. The headings, originally in Latin, are here given in abbreviated form in English. I As the lily among thorns . . . ; II For lo, the winter is past . . . ; III I sought him whom my soul loveth; IV Behold his bed, which is Solomon's . . . ; V Return, return, O Shulamite! . . . ; VI Set me as a seal upon thine heart. First performance: London, Queen's Hall, 10 October 1925. Publication: London, Oxford University Press, 1928.

3. Concerto in D minor (*Concerto Accademico*). For violin and string orchestra. Composed 1924–5. Three movements: Allegro pesante; Adagio – tranquillo; Presto. First performance: Aeolian Hall, London, 6 November 1925. Publication: full score and miniature score, London, Oxford University Press, 1927. Arrangement for violin and pianoforte by Constant Lambert, © OUP, 1927. Dedication: To Jelly d'Aranyi.

4. *Fantasia on Sussex Folk Tunes.* For violoncello and orchestra. First performance: Queen's Hall, London, 13 March 1930. Unpublished. Dedication: To Pablo Casals.

5a. Concerto in C Major for Pianoforte and Orchestra. Three movements: Toccata: Allegro moderato; Romanza: Lento; Fuga chromatica, con finale alla tedesca. First two movements composed 1926, finale in 1930–1. First performance: Queen's Hall, London, 1 February 1933. Publication: London, Oxford University Press, 1936. Dedication: To Harriet Cohen.

5b. Concerto for Two Pianofortes and Orchestra. Adapted from § 5(a) by Joseph Cooper in collaboration with the composer. First performance: Royal Albert Hall, London, 22 November 1946. The main differences between the two versions in terms of musical substance (as opposed to texture) lie in the end of the finale. Principal among them are the insertion of a new solo for the two pianos, the deletion of ten bars of ritornello and the substitution of a quiet ending with the fugue subject pizzicato in the strings leading to a chord of B major (the original ending was on G).

6. Suite for Viola and Small Orchestra (2.1.2.2.; 2.2.; timp., perc., cel., hp, str.). Eight movements in three groups: Group I: Prelude; Carol; Christmas Dance; Group II: Ballad; Moto perpetuo; Group III: Musette, Polka mélancolique; Galop. First performance: Queen's Hall, London, 12 November 1934. Publication: London, Oxford University Press, with orchestral part arranged for pianoforte, 1936; full score, 1963. Dedication: To Lionel Tertis. The Galop was arranged for violin and pianoforte by Louis Persinger © 1949; the Carol and the Musette for organ by Herbert Sumsion, © OUP 1938.

7. Concerto in A minor for Oboe and Strings. Three movements: Rondo pastorale – Allegro moderato; Minuet and Musette: Allegro moderato; Finale (Scherzo) – Presto. First performance: Philharmonic Hall, Liverpool, 30 September 1944. Publication: London, Oxford University Press, 1947 (orchestral part arr. for piano by Michael Mullinar). Full score, OUP, 1967. Dedication: To Léon Goossens.

8. *Fantasia (Quasi Variazione) on the 'Old 104th' Psalm Tune.* For pianoforte solo, accompanied by mixed chorus (SATB), and orchestra. The choral text is that attributed to Sternhold and Hopkins. First performance, Gloucester Cathedral, 6 September 1950. Publication: Vocal score and pianoforte part, London, Oxford University Press, 1950.

9. Romance in D flat for harmonica, accompanied by an orchestra of strings and pianoforte. First performance: Town Hall, New York, 3 May 1952. Publication: London, Oxford University Press, 1953. Dedication: To Larry Adler.

10. Concerto in F Minor for Bass Tuba and Orchestra. Three movements: Allegro moderato; Romanza; Andante sostenuto; Finale: rondo alla tedesca. First performance: Royal Festival Hall, London, 13 June 1954. Publication: arrangement for tuba and pianoforte, London, Oxford University Press, 1955. Full score, OUP, 1979.

VIII KEYBOARD WORKS

(A) Pianoforte

Student and unpublished compositions

1. *The Robin's Nest.*[14] (1878). First public performance: BBC broadcast, 16 November 1964. Unpublished.
2. *Sonatina* in E flat. Student exercise, RCM, 1890.
3. *Theme with Variations.* Student exercise, RCM, 1891.
4. *Variations on a Ground Bass by Lully.* Student exercise, 1892.
5. *Suite for Four hands on one Pianoforte* (4 October 1893). Unpublished.
6. *Reminiscences of a Walk at Frankham* (28 August 1894). A programmatic piece[15] with titles over the various sections such as A Steamy Afternoon; Little River Hall; Anxiety on the Way Home; Grinham's Cottage appears in sight; Evening comes on. This was composed, of course, before the cinema became more than just an experimental toy, but the titles are of interest, even so. Unpublished.

---

[14] It is, I hope, not just frivolity to include this—RVW's first known composition.
[15] 'Not to be taken seriously', according to the composer.

7. *Andante Sostenuto*, for pianoforte solo. Dated 17 July 1904. Unpublished. Dedication: 'For your [i.e. his wife's] birthday'.

Published works

1. *Pezzo Ostinato*. For pianoforte. Dated 27 January 1905. Publication: London, Stainer & Bell Ltd, 1994 as No. 3 of *Birthday Gifts*.
2. *Suite of Six short pieces for Pianoforte*: Prelude; Slow Dance; Quick Dance; Slow air; Rondo; Pezzo ostinato. Publication: London, Stainer & Bell Ltd, 1921. Arranged for string orchestra as *The Charterhouse Suite*. Publication: London, Stainer & Bell Ltd, 1923.
3. *Hymn Tune Prelude on 'Song 13' by Orlando Gibbons*. Composed 1928. Publication: London, Oxford University Press, 1930. First performance: Wigmore Hall, London, 14 January 1930. Dedication: To Harriet Cohen.
4. *Six Teaching Pieces for Pianoforte*. In Three Books: Book I: Two 2-part Inventions: 1. Andante con moto; 2. Allegro moderato. Book II: 1. Valse Lente and 2. Nocturne; Book III: 1. Canon and 2. Two-part Invention. Publication: London, Oxford University Press, 1934 (Oxford Piano Series, ed. A. Forbes Milne).
5. *A Winter Piece (for Genia* [Hornstein]*), with love from Uncle Ralph*. New Year's Day, 1943. Publication: London, Stainer & Bell Ltd, 1994 as No. 2 of *Birthday Gifts*.
6. *Introduction and Fugue for Two Pianofortes*. First performance: Wigmore Hall, London, 23 March 1946. Publication: London, Oxford University Press, 1947. Dedication: To Phyllis [Sellick] and Cyril [Smith].
7. *The Lake in the Mountains*. Based on music from *49th Parallel*. Publication: London, Oxford University Press, 1947. Dedication: To Phyllis Sellick.

(B) Organ

Student and unpublished works

1. *Organ Overture* (1890).
2. *Passacaglia on B.G.C., composed for the Bride* [Barbara Gordon Clark, née Lawrence]. Composed 1933. Unpublished.
3. *A Wedding Canon (2 in 1 infinite)*. 'For Nancy [Elias, née Harvey], 30 May 1947, with love from Uncle Ralph'. Unpublished.

Published works

1. *Three Preludes*. Founded on Welsh hymn-tunes. For organ. Three movements: Bryn Calfaria; Rhosymedre (or 'Lovely'); Hyfrydol. Publication: London, Stainer & Bell Ltd, 1920. Nos. 2 and 3 were orchestrated by Arnold Foster. No. 2 (2.1.2.2.; 2.1.; str.) was published by Stainer & Bell in 1938, No. 3 (2.2.2.2.; 2.2; timp. str.) in 1951. They can also be performed by strings only. All three were arranged for two pianofortes by Leslie Russell and published by Stainer & Bell in 1939.
2. *A Wedding Tune for Ann, 27 October 1943.* [For the wedding of Ann Pain to Anthony Wilson]. Published (ed. Christopher Morris) as No. 1 of *A Vaughan Williams Organ Album*, London, 1964.
3. *Two Organ Preludes*. Founded on Welsh folk-songs: I. Romanza ('The White

Rock'); II. Toccata ('St David's Day'). Publication: London, Oxford University Press, 1956. Also published in *A Vaughan Williams Organ Album* (1964), as Nos. 5 and 3 respectively.

4. *A Vaughan Williams Organ Album.* Eight pieces: A Wedding Tune for Ann, [see § 2 above] ed. Christopher Morris; Greensleeves, arr. Stanley Roper; Toccata (St David's Day) [see § 3 above]; Carol, arr. Herbert Sumsion [from Suite for Viola; see VII Concertos (B), 6]; Romanza ('The White Rock') [see § 3 above]; Prelude ('The New Commonwealth'), arr. Christopher Morris (see IV Choral Works (B), 27); Musette, arr. Herbert Sumsion [from Suite for Viola; see VII Concertos (B), 6]; Land of Our Birth, arr. S. de B. Taylor [from A Song of Thanksgiving: see IV Choral Works (B), 29].

IX ARRANGEMENTS

1. *The Willow Song* (trad.). For voice and pianoforte. 19 February 1897. Unpublished.
2. *Adieu* (German, trans. A. Foxton Ferguson). Soprano and baritone duet with pianoforte. First performance: Exeter, 16 April 1903. Publication: London, *The Vocalist*, October 1903. Reissued by Boosey & Hawkes with 'Think of Me', as *Two Old Airs*, 1933.
3. *Think of Me* (German, trans. A. Foxton Ferguson). Soprano and baritone duet with pianoforte. First performance: Steinway Hall, London, 22 March 1904. Publication as § 3.
4. *Cousin Michael* (German, trans. A. Foxton Ferguson). Soprano and baritone duet with pianoforte. First performance: Exeter, 16 April 1903. Unpublished.
5. *Réveillez-vous, Picars* (French; English adaptation by Paul England). For voice and pianoforte. First performance: Church Room, South Street, Eastbourne, 19 October 1903. Publication: London and New York, Boosey & Co., 1907.
6. *Jean Renaud* (French, 15c.; English adaptation by Paul England). For voice and pianoforte. First performance: St James's Hall, London, 11 February 1904. Unpublished.
7. *L'amour de Moy* (French, 15c.; English version by Paul England). For voice and pianoforte. First performance, London, St James's Hall, 11 February 1904. Publication: London and New York, Boosey & Co., 1907.
8. *Folk Songs from the Eastern Counties.* Collected and set with an accompaniment for pianoforte by RVW. Dates of collection given in brackets.
   (a) From Essex: Bushes and Briars (1903); Tarry Trowsers; A Bold Young Farmer; The Lost Lady Found: As I Walked Out; The Lark in the Morning (all 1904).
   (b) From Norfolk: On Board a Ninety-Eight; The Captain's Apprentice; Ward the Pirate; The Saucy Bold Robber; The Bold Princess Royal; The Lincolnshire Farmer; The Sheffield Apprentice (all 1905).
   (c) From Cambridgeshire: Geordie; Harry the Tailor (both 1906).
   All in *Folk Songs of England*, Book II, ed. Cecil J. Sharp, London, Novello & Co., 1908.
   Bushes and Briars. Arranged for four male voices (TTBB), was published by Novello, 1908. A four-part arrangement (SATB) was published by Novello in 1924, dedicated to The English Singers.
   Tarry Trowsers (voice and pianoforte) was also published in Novello's School Songs series in 1927.

Ward the Pirate (arr. TTBB) was published by J. Curwen & Sons in 1912; for voice and pianoforte in Novello's School Songs series in 1927; and this version was included in *Folk Songs II*, Novello, 1935.

The Saucy Bold Robber was issued separately by Novello in 1936.

9. *The Jolly Ploughboy* (Sussex folk-song). Arranged for TTBB unaccompanied. Publication: London, Novello & Co. Ltd, 1908. Arranged for unison singing with pianoforte accompaniment in *Folk Songs for Schools*, Novello, 1912. This version was reprinted in *Folk Songs II*, Novello, 1935. It also appears in the Prologue to *Folk Songs of the Four Seasons*.

10. *Down among the Dead Men* (trad.). Arranged for TTBB unaccompanied. Publication: London, Joseph Williams & Co. Ltd, 1912.

11. *The Spanish Ladies* (trad.). Arranged for voice and pianoforte. Publication: London, Boosey & Co., 1912. Also arranged for unison and mixed voices in *The Motherland Song Book*, Vol. iv *Sea Songs*, selected and arr. by RVW and others (Stainer & Bell).

12. *Alister McAlpine's Lament* (Scottish air; words by Robert Allan). Arranged for mixed voices (SATB) unaccompanied. Publication: London, Novello & Co. 1912 in *The Orpheus*, a collection of glees and part songs for male voices.

13. *Folk Songs for Schools*. Arranged for unison singing with pianoforte accompaniment. The following were collected and arranged by RVW: 1. The Jolly Plough Boy; 2. The Cuckoo and the Nightingale; 4. The Female Highwayman; 5. The Carter; 7. My Boy Billy; 11. The Painful Plough. Nos. 3, Servant Man and Husbandman; 6. I will give my love an apple; 8. Down by the Riverside; 9. The Fox; and 10. Farmyard Song, were collected by H. E. D. Hammond and arranged by RVW. Publication: *Novello's School Songs*, ed. W. G. McNaught (each song also available separately).

'The Female Highwayman' appears (arr. by RVW for voice and pianoforte) as No. 25 in *Folk Songs I*, Novello & Co. Ltd, 1917. 'The Carter' appears as No. 22 in the same collection. 'I will give my love an apple' appears as No. 12, 'My Boy Billy' as No. 15, 'Down by the Riverside' as No. 8, 'The Fox' as No. 26, and 'The Painful Plough' as No. 31.

14. *Folk Songs of England*, V. *Folk Songs from Sussex*. ed. Cecil J. Sharp. Collected by W. Percy Merrick, with pianoforte accompaniments by RVW and Albert Robins. 1. Bold General Wolfe; 2. Low Down in the Broom; 3. The Thresherman and the Squire; 4. The Pretty Ploughboy; 5. O who is that that raps at my window?; 6. The Unquiet Grave (How cold the wind doth blow) (Violin accomp. ad lib.); 7. Captain Grant; 8. Farewell Lads; 9. Come all you worthy Christians; 10. The Turkish Lady; 11. The Seeds of Love; 12. The Maid of Islington; 13. Here's adieu to all judges and juries; 14. Lovely Joan; 15. The Isle of France. Publication: London, Novello & Co. Ltd, 1912. *The Unquiet Grave* also appears in an arrangement (SSA), also available separately, for unaccompanied women's voices in *Folk Songs of the Four Seasons*. Both versions published by Oxford University Press, 1950. 'Come all you worthy Christians' is in *The Oxford Book of Carols* (see below (B), 6), as No. 60 (OUP, 1928). 'The Seeds of Love' arranged for TTB with pianoforte ad lib. was published in Stainer & Bell's *Male Voice Choir* series (London, 1923). *Lovely Joan* is used by *Sir John in Love*, Act II and in *The Penguin Book of English Folk Songs*, ed. RVW and Frank Lloyd (Harmondsworth, 1959), p. 64.

15. *Ward the Pirate*. Arranged for mixed chorus (SATB) and small orchestra (2.2.2.2., timp., cym., tri., str.). Unpublished.
16. *Tarry Trowsers*. Arranged as in § 15. Unpublished.
17. *And All in the Morning* (*On Christmas Day*). Arranged as in § 15. Unpublished.
18. *The Carter*. Orchestra 2.2.2.2.; 2.2.2.; timp., perc. hp. and str. Unpublished.
19. *The Minehead Hobby-Horse* (English folk dance). Arranged for orchestra (fl., picc., 1.2.2.; 1.1.; tri., b.d.; pf., str.). Unpublished.
20. *Phil the Fluter's Dancing* (English folk dance). Arranged for flute and strings. Unpublished.
21. *Mannin Veen* ('Dear Mona'; Manx trad.). For mixed chorus (SATB) unaccompanied. Publication: London, J. Curwen & Sons Ltd, 1913.
22. *The Dark-eyed Sailor* (English folk-song).[16] Unison song with pianoforte accompaniment. Publication: London, Stainer & Bell Ltd, 1935.
23. *Just as the Tide was Flowing* (English folk-song). Unison song with pianoforte accompaniment. Publication: London, Stainer & Bell Ltd, 1919, as No. 3 in Vol. iv, *Sea Songs* of *The Motherland Song Book*.
24. *The Lover's Ghost* (English folk-song). Arranged by RVW for voice and pianoforte in *Folk Songs from Newfoundland*, Vol. ii, *Ballads*, No. 7. Publication: London, Oxford University Press, 1934.
25. *Wassail Song* (English folk-song). Arranged for unison voices with descant and orchestral accompaniment in the cantata *Folk Songs of the Four Seasons*. Publication: London, Oxford University Press, 1950. See IV Choral Works (B), 32.
26. *Selection of Collected Folk Songs*, Vol. I. Probably published in 1917 while RVW was serving in the Great War. Arranged for voice and pianoforte by Cecil J. Sharp and RVW. Eight songs arranged by RVW were included: Down by the Riverside; Farmyard Song; I will give my love an apple; My Boy Billy; The Carter; The Female Highwayman; The Fox, and The Painful Plough. Publication: by Novello & Co. Ltd.
27. *The Motherland Song Book*, published in four volumes by Stainer & Bell Ltd in 1919, included the following arrangements by RVW as well as those already mentioned above as appearing in it:
    Vol. I, No. 13: O God of Earth and Altar (words G. K. Chesterton, set to the tune 'Young Henry the Poacher', collected at King's Lynn).
    Vol. III, No. 1, The Arethusa (words by Prince Hoare; tune adapted from a traditional melody by W. Shield); No. 5, Full Fathom Five (words by Shakespeare, music by Henry Purcell); No. 6, Jack the Sailor (folk-song, arr. by RVW for TTBB male voice chorus); No. 8, We be three poor mariners (old English song, arr. for mixed voices and for three male voices (TTB) unaccompanied).
    Vol. IV, No. 1, The Golden Vanity (folk-song).
28. *Eight Traditional English Carols*. Arranged for voice and pianoforte. An unaccompanied version of each carol for mixed choir (SATB) is included: 1. And all in the Morning (On Christmas Day), collected by RVW at Castleton,

[16] *The Dark-eyed Sailor, The Springtime of the Year, Just as the Tide was Flowing, The Lover's Ghost*, and *Wassail Song* were published in 1913 as a set of *Five English Folk Songs* freely arranged for unaccompanied mixed chorus (SATB) and also separately in 1920.

Derbyshire, in 1908; 2. On Christmas Night (Monk's Gate, Sussex, 1904); 3. The Twelve Apostles (Staffordshire); 4. Down in Yon Forest (Castleton, Derbyshire, 1908); 5. May-Day Carol (Fowlmere, Cambs., 1907); 6. The Truth Sent from Above (King's Pyon, Herefordshire, 1909); 7. The Birth of the Saviour (Derbyshire) and 8. The Wassail Song (Yorkshire, unison only). Publication: London, Stainer & Bell Ltd, 1919. Nos. 2, 4, 5, and 6 also appear in *The Oxford Book of Carols*, and Nos. 2 and 6 are used in the *Fantasia on Christmas Carols* of 1912.

29. *The Turtle Dove*, arranged for male voices, with pianoforte ad lib. Solo part for tenors and baritones, chorus TBB. Publication: London, J. Curwen & Sons Ltd, 1919. Also arranged for mixed voices (SSATB), published by Curwen in 1924 and for unison voices with pianoforte accompaniment (Curwen, 1934). The 1934 version is available with orchestral accompaniment (1.0.1.0.; 2.0.; hp., str.).

30. *Our love goes out to English skies*. Patriotic Song (Harold Child), adapted from Queen Zempoalla's march in Purcell's *Indian Queen*, for unison or mixed choir (SATB). Publication: London, Stainer & Bell Ltd, 1920; also with string accompaniment, 1924.

31. *Twelve Traditional Carols from Herefordshire*. Collected, edited and arranged for voices with pianoforte accompaniment, or to be sung unaccompanied (SATB), by Mrs E. M. Leather and RVW. 1. The Holy Well; 2. The Holy Well (2nd version); 3. Christmas now is drawing near at hand; 4. Joseph and Mary (to the tune 'There is a fountain'); 5. The Angel Gabriel; 6. God rest you merry, gentlemen; 7. New Year's Carol; 8. On Christmas Day (All in the Morning); 9. Dives and Lazarus; 10. The Miraculous Harvest (or 'The Carnal and the Crane'); 11. The Saviour's Love; 12. The Seven Virgins (or 'Under the Leaves'). Publication: London, Stainer & Bell Ltd, 1920. Nos. 1, 2, 4, 9, 10, and 12 appear in *The Oxford Book of Carols*. No. 6 is one of *Nine Carols for Male Voices* (OUP, 1942).

32. *The League of Nations Song Book* (music ed. by Martin Shaw) contains two hymns arranged by RVW: 5. Pilgrim Song (Tune: Monk's Gate) and 8. Chesterton's Hymn (see § 27). Publication: London, Stainer & Bell Ltd, 1921.

33. *The Lass that Loves a Sailor* (words and music by Charles Dibdin). Edited and arranged for unison voices or SATB, with soprano solo, with pianoforte accompaniment. Publication: London, Stainer & Bell Ltd, 1921.

34. *The Mermaid* (trad.). Arranged for SATB with soprano solo, unaccompanied, or unison with pianoforte accompaniment. Publication: London, Stainer & Bell Ltd, 1921.

35. *Heart of Oak* (attrib. Garrick; melody by William Boyce). Arranged for unison singing with pianoforte accompaniment, for male voices (TTBB) unaccompanied and for SATB with soprano solo and pianoforte accompaniment. Publication: London, Stainer & Bell Ltd, 1921.

36. *The Farmer's Boy* (old English air). Arranged for male voices (TTBB) unaccompanied. Publication: London, Stainer & Bell Ltd, 1921.

37. *Loch Lomond* (Scottish air). Arranged for male voices (TTBB) with baritone solo, unaccompanied. Publication: London, Stainer & Bell Ltd, 1921. Also arranged for mixed voices (SSATB) unaccompanied. Publication: London, Stainer & Bell, 1931.

38. *A Farmer's Son So Sweet* (folk-song). Arranged for male voices (T.Bar.B.).

With pianoforte accompaniment ad lib. Words and melody from Cecil J. Sharp's *Folk Songs from Somerset*. Publication: London, Stainer & Bell Ltd, 1923. Dedication: To the English Singers. Also arranged for mixed voices (SSAT Bar.B.).

39. *Ca' the Yowes* (Burns). Scottish folk-song arranged for tenor solo and mixed chorus (SATB) unaccompanied. Publication: London, J. Curwen & Sons Ltd, 1922. Also transcribed by Herbert Pierce (© 1925) for male chorus, unaccompanied (TTBB), publication: London, J. Curwen & Sons, 1925.

40. *High Germany* (folk-song). Arranged for male voices, with pianoforte accompaniment ad lib. Solos for tenor and bass. Words and melody from Cecil J. Sharp's *Folk Songs of England* (Novello & Co. Ltd). Publication: London, Stainer & Bell Ltd, 1923.

41. *Mr Isaac's Maggot* (English traditional country dance tune). Arranged for clarinet, pianoforte, triangle, and strings. First performance: Abinger, Surrey, opening of Village Hall, January 1925. Unpublished.

42. *Old Folks at Home* (melody by Stephen Foster). Arranged for male voices (TTBB) with baritone solo. Publication: London, Stainer & Bell Ltd, 1921.

43. *The 'Giant' Fugue*. (J. S. Bach). Transcribed for strings by RVW and Arnold Foster. Publication: London, Oxford University Press, 1925.

44. *Epithalamium* (John G. Brainard), set to an old English air, slightly adapted, for Carl Stoeckel. Dated 30 October 1925. Unpublished.

45. *The Lawyer* (English folk-song, collected by George Butterworth). Arranged by RVW for unaccompanied mixed voices (SSATBB). First performance: London, 13 June 1927. Unpublished in this form.

46. *Twelve Traditional Country Dances*. Collected and described by Maud Karpeles. Pianoforte arrangements by RVW in collaboration with Maud Karpeles. Published by Novello & Co. Ltd for the English Folk Dance Society in 1931. The tunes used are: Corn Rigs; Morpeth Rant; Soldier's Joy; Roxburgh Castle; The Sylph ('Off she goes'); Haste to the Wedding; Pleasures of the Town; Steamboat; The New Rigged Ship; The Tempest; The Self, and Kitty's Rambles.

47. Choral and Choral Prelude: *Ach bleib' bei uns, Herr Jesu Christ* ('Now Cheer our Hearts this Eventide') by J. S. Bach, freely arranged for pianoforte by RVW. Publication: London, Oxford University Press, 1932.[17]

48. *An Acre of Land* (English folk-song). For male voices, (TTBB) with pianoforte accompaniment ad lib. Publication: London, Oxford University Press, 1934. Also arranged for unaccompanied mixed voices (SATB, published by OUP, 1934) and for unison voices with piano accompaniment (from the cantata *Folk Songs of the Four Seasons*: OUP, 1950).

49. *John Dory* (English folk-song from William Chappell's *Ballad Literature and Popular Music of the Olden Time*, 1879). Arranged for unaccompanied mixed voices (SATB). Publication: London, Oxford University Press, 1934.

50. *I'll never love thee more*. Words by James Graham, 1st Marquis of Montrose; tune from Playford's *Dancing Master*. Arranged for unaccompanied mixed voices (SATB). Publication: London, Oxford University Press, 1934.

[17] This was RVW's contribution to *A Bach Book for Harriet Cohen*, an anthology of transcriptions for pianoforte pieces by J. S. Bach. The other contributors were Bantock, Bax, Berners, Bliss, Bridge, Goossens, Howells, Ireland, Lambert, Walton, and W. Gillies Whittaker.

51. *The World it went well with me then* (trad., from Chappell's *Popular Music*). Arranged for male voices (TTBB) unaccompanied. Publication: London, Oxford University Press, 1934.

52. *Tobacco's but an Indian Weed* (trad., from Chappell's *Popular Music*). Arranged for male voices (TTBB) unaccompanied. Publication: London, Oxford University Press, 1934.

53. *The Ploughman* (English folk-song). Arranged for male voices (TTBB) with pianoforte accompaniment ad lib. Publication: London, Oxford University Press, 1934.

54. *Folk Songs from Newfoundland*. Collected and arranged by Maud Karpeles, with pianoforte accompaniments by RVW and others. RVW arranged: Vol. I. Ballads, 1. Sweet William's Child; 2. The Cruel Mother; 3. The Gypsy Laddie; 7. The Bloody Gardener; Songs: 8. The Maiden's Lament; 9. Proud Nancy; 10. The Morning Dew. Vol. II. Ballads: 1. The Bonny Banks of Virgie-O (The Bonny Banks o' Fordie); 2. Earl Brand; 3. Lord Akeman (Lord Bateman); 7. The Lover's Ghost; Songs: 8. She's like the swallow; 9. Young Florio; 10. The winter's gone and past; 11. The Cuckoo. Publication: London, Oxford University Press, 1934. Dedication: To Fred and Isabel Emerson of St John's.

54(a). Republished (OUP, 1968) as *Fifteen Folk Songs from Newfoundland*, collected and edited by Maud Karpeles, with pianoforte accompaniments by R. Vaughan Williams. Ballads: 1. Sweet William's Ghost; 2. The Cruel Mother; 3. The Gipsy Laddie; 4. The Bloody Gardener; 5. The Bonnie Banks of Virgie-O; 6. Earl Brand; 7. Lord Akeman; 8. The Lover's Ghost. Songs: 9. She's like the swallow; 10. The Maiden's Lament; 11. Proud Nancy; 12. The Morning Dew; 13. The winter's gone and past; 14. The Cuckoo; 15. Young Florio.

55. Folk Songs, Volume II. A Selection of thirty-three less-known folk-songs, arranged by Cecil Sharp, RVW, and others for voice and pianoforte. Compiled by Cyril Winn. Those collected and arranged by RVW are: 7. The Bold Princess Royal; 18. The Jolly Ploughboy; 32. Ward the Pirate. Publication: London, Novello & Co. Ltd, 1935.

56. *Two English Folk Songs*. Arranged for voice and violin. 1. Searching for Lambs; 2. The Lawyer. Publication: London, Oxford University Press, 1935. Dedication: To Margaret Longman.

57. *Six English Folk Songs*. Arranged for voice and pianoforte. Robin Hood and the Pedlar; The Ploughman; One man, two men; The Brewer; Rolling in the Dew; King William. Nos. 3, 4, and 6 came from the collection of H. E. D. Hammond; the others were collected by RVW himself. Publication: London, Oxford University Press, 1935.

58. *My Soul Praise the Lord* (W. Kethe, slightly adapted). Hymn arranged for chorus (SATB) and unison singing with descant, and organ (or strings and organ). Publication: London, S.P.C.K., 1935; Oxford University Press, 1947.

59. Te Deum (Dvořák). For soprano and bass, mixed chorus (SATB), and orchestra. English adaptation (for the Leith Hill Festival) by RVW. First performance: Royal Albert Hall, London, 9 January 1937. Publication: Leipzig, N. Simrock, 1937.

60. Benedictus and Agnus Dei in *Liturgical Settings of the Holy Communion* (editor J. H. Arnold). All those parts of the service that belong to the congregation are set to traditional melodies. Publication: London, Oxford University Press, 1938.

61. *All Hail the Power* (Perronet). To the tune 'Miles Lane' (W. Shrubsole), arranged for unison (congregation), mixed chorus (SATB) with organ or orchestra (2.2.2.2.1.; 4.3.3.1.; timp., perc., org.; str.). Publication: Vocal score, London, Oxford University Press, 1938. Dedication: To Ivor Atkins.

62. *Nine Carols for Male Voices* (TTBB unaccompanied). God rest you merry; As Joseph was a-walking (The Cherry Tree Carol); Mummers' Carol; The First Nowell; The Lord at First; Coventry Carol; I saw three ships (bar. solo and chorus); A Virgin most Pure; Dives and Lazarus. Publication: London, Oxford University Press, 1942.

63. *Three Gaelic Songs*. Melodies and Gaelic words published in the *Journal of the Folk Song Society* in 1911. Arranged in October 1954 for unaccompanied mixed voices (SATB). English version of the Gaelic words by Ursula Vaughan Williams. Dawn on the Hills (S'tràth chuir a'ghrian); Come let us gather cockles (An téid thu bhuain mhaoraich); Wake and rise (Mhnàthan a'ghlinne so!). Publication: 1963.

64. Diabelleries. (Variations by various composers for 11 instruments on a theme 'Oh! Where's my little basket gone?' (attrib. Alfred Scott-Gatty).) A composite work by RVW, Howard Ferguson, Alan Bush, Alan Rawsthorne, Elizabeth Lutyens, Elizabeth Maconchy, Gerald Finzi, Grace Williams, and Gordon Jacob. First performance: Arts Council, 4 St James's Square, London, 16 May 1955. Unpublished.

65. *God Bless the Master of this House* (from the 'Sussex Mummers' Carol'). Arranged for unaccompanied mixed chorus (SATB). Publication: London, Oxford University Press, 1956.

66. *Schmücke Dich, O liebe Seele* (J. S. Bach). Arranged for violoncello and strings. First performance: Friends' House, Euston Road, London, 28 December 1956 (in honour of the Casals 80th birthday fund). Unpublished.

67. *Fen and Flood* (Charles Cudworth). Cantata for male chorus (TTBar.B) and orchestra by Patrick Hadley; arranged for soprano and baritone soloists and mixed chorus (SATB) by RVW. First performance: Gonville and Caius College, Cambridge, 12 June 1955.[18] Publication: London, Oxford University Press, 1956.

68. *Nine English Folk Songs from the Southern Appalachian Mountains*. For voice and pianoforte. Publication: London, Oxford University Press, 1967. The arrangements were made by RVW in about 1938 and given to Maud Karpeles. The songs were: The Elfin Knight (or The Lovers' Tasks); Lord Randal; Lord Thomas and Fair Ellinor; Fair Margaret and Sweet William; Barbara Allen; The Daemon Lover, or The House Carpenter; The Rich Old Lady; The Tree in the Wood; and The Ten Commandments, or The Twelve Apostles. The last three were published separately by OUP in 1968.

69. Certain unpublished arrangements: The Shooting of his Dear; O Sinner Man; Locks and Bolts; Salisbury Plain (vocal score only), and melody and words only of The Maid Freed from the Gallows; Geordie; The Lady and the Dragoon; The Lowlands of Holland and The Brown Girl are to be found in British Library MS 71491, along with the melody and words (in Maud

---

[18] For this performance, the 'orchestra' comprised two pianofortes and, as the composer put it, 'odd instruments in addition which happened to be available'. The first performance with orchestra was at St Nicholas's Chapel, King's Lynn, on 27 July 1956.

Karpeles' hand) of Lord Randal, Lord Thomas and Fair Ellinor, Fair Margaret and Sweet William, Barbara Allen, and The Daemon Lover.

X MISCELLANEOUS OTHER WORKS, ARRANGEMENTS, AND MUSIC EDITED BY RVW

(A) Juvenilia, student works, and fragments

1. *Happy Day at Gunby.* Parts for violins, violoncellos, pianoforte, and organ. Student exercise, 1892. Unpublished.
2. *Five Valses for orchestra.* Condensed score. Student exercises, 1892. Unpublished.
3. *Fantasia à la valse.* Short score and arrangement for pianoforte duet. Unpublished.
4. *Dover Beach* (Matthew Arnold). Completed by April 1899. Lost.
5. Sonata for horn and pianoforte. Only slow movement, scherzo, and finale of horn part survive.
6. *Dirge* for orchestra. May have been incorporated in *Heroic Elegy and Triumphal Epilogue* (1900/1).
7. *Rhapsody.* Possibly a sketch for the *Symphonic Rhapsody.*
8. *Dramatic March.* May also have been incorporated in *Heroic Elegy and Triumphal Epilogue.*
9. Symphonic Poem (or Suite?) *Ozymandias.* Fragments survive of an intended finale, with a part for solo singer, a theme marked '1st desert tune, then pizzicato tune, then this' ('this', according to Michael Kennedy, is 'barely decipherable').
10. Sketches for *Let us now praise famous men* (not the setting known to us).
11. 'Viola piece'.
12. 'Ballet tune'.
Items §§ 4 to 12 are in a sketch-book in the British Library (57294B).
13. *Aethiopia Saluting the Colours* (Whitman). Unpublished. No date. The chief solo part is for a narrator. The words of Aethiopia are sung by a soprano, except for the last verse, when they are given to a male voice. The accompaniment includes a humming chorus.
14. *The Future* (Matthew Arnold). For solo soprano, chorus, and orchestra. Unpublished and incomplete.
15. *Fantasia on English Folk Songs: Studies for an English Ballad Opera.* For orchestra. Performed 1 September 1910 at Queen's Hall, London. In three sections: Allegro [risoluto]; Slow; scherzando. Unpublished and lost. The tunes used seem to have been from Sharp's and Lucy Broadwood's collections; and RVW wrote to Harold Child saying that he wanted the slow middle section to be 'a sort of study for what I should like my love scene [of *Hugh the Drover*, Act II] to be like . . . '.
16. First and last verses and notes for vv. 2 and 3 of a setting of Charles Wesley's 'Come, O thou traveller unknown'. Never completed.
17. Sketches for a Cello Concerto (1942–3?). Three projected movements: Rhapsody: Andante con moto; Lento; Finale: Allegro moderato. Intended for Casals.
18. *Thomas the Rhymer*, an opera in three acts. Libretto by Ursula Vaughan Williams. Completed in pianoforte and vocal score, but not revised.

19. Sketches or themes for proposed works:
Settings of Robert Graves's 'Star Talk', G. K. Chesterton's 'In Praise of Wine'; *Exsultate, jubilate,* for double choir; *London Calling,* for SATB chorus with pianoforte accompaniment; for an opera, *Belshazzar;* a string quartet, a symphony, and various other pieces listed in full by Michael Kennedy.

(B) Works edited or contributed to by Vaughan Williams

1. Henry Purcell: *Welcome Songs,* Part I. Vol. xv of the *Works of Henry Purcell.* Edited for the Purcell Society. The works included are:
    1. Welcome, Vice-gerent of the mighty King [Z. 340].
    2. Swifter, Isis, swifter flow [Z. 336].
    3. What shall be done on behalf of the man [Z. 341]
    4. The summer's absence unconcerned we bear [Z. 337]
    5. Fly, bold Rebellion [Z. 324]
    Published by Novello & Co., 1905.
2. *The English Hymnal,* with tunes. Publication: London, Oxford University Press, 1906.

    Tunes contributed anonymously by RVW:
    152, Down Ampney; 524, Randolph; 624, Salve, festa dies; 641, Sine Nomine.

    Vaughan Williams also held the copyright on the following folk-song arrangements:
    15, Forest Green, 23, Dent Dale; 186, Rodmell; 239 and 385, Sussex; 295, Danby; 299, 572, and 594, Gosterwood; 402, Monk's Gate; 525, Farnham; 562, King's Lynn; 595, East Horndon; 597, Herongate; and 607, Ingrave and 611, Rodmell.

    He also harmonized the following tunes (anonymously in the original edition): 18 and 38, St Venantius; 65, Jesu Corona; 123, Solemnis haec festivitas; 125, Rex gloriose; 129, Orientis partibus; 159, Adesto Sancta Trinitas; 165, Christe sanctorum; 181, Deus tuorum militum; 208, Diva servatrix; 242, Coelites plaudant.
2(a). Revised edition (OUP, 1933). The tunes Magda (273), King's Weston (368), White Gates (541), and Stalham (638, part iii) were added, as well as some half-a-dozen new arrangements. The revision was very thorough, but these are the main changes relevant to RVW's work as a composer.
3. *Henry Purcell: Welcome Songs,* Part II. (Purcell Society, Vol. xviii). Contains the following works:
    1. From those serene and rapturous joys [Z. 326]
    2. Why, why, are all the muses mute? [Z. 343]
    3. Ye tuneful muses [Z. 344]
    4. Sound the Trumpet [Z. 323]
    Published by Novello & Co. in 1910. No. 4 was orchestrated by RVW (2.2.2.2.; 2.2.3.; timp., tri.; str.). The score has been held in the hire library of Augener Ltd, London, since 1934. No. 3 was published in vocal score by Novello in 1933.
4. *Church Songs.* Collected by Revd S. Baring-Gould, music arranged by Revd H. Fleetwood Sheppard and RVW. RVW arranged hymns 1–9, 11–13, 15–17, 19–21, and 23–5. Publication: S.P.C.K., London, 1911.

5. *Songs of Praise.* Words edited by Revd Percy Dearmer. Vaughan Williams composed the following original tunes: 37, Magda; 41(i), Oakley; 110, *Sine Nomine;*[19] 123, (i) Cumnor; 185, Guildford; 217, Down Ampney; 406, Randolph; 443, King's Weston; 445 (i) *Salve festa dies.* Publication: London, Oxford University Press, 1925.

Separate arrangements were later published of the following tunes from *Songs of Praise*: 12, Danby ('Tis winter now': Unison voices); 37, Magda ('Saviour, again to thy dear name': SATB); 41, Oakley ('The night is come': SATB); 123, Cumnor ('Servants of God, or sons': SATB); 185, Guildford ('England arise!': Unison); 438, Hardwick ('So here hath been dawning': trad., arr. RVW for SATB), and 443, King's Weston ('At the name of Jesus': Unison); and of the following tunes by other composers arranged by RVW: 200, Eventide ('Abide with me': Descant by RVW) and 246, Crüger ('Hail to the Lord's annointed': Descant by RVW).

5(a). *Songs of Praise for Boys and Girls.* Editors as for *Songs of Praise.* Publication: London, Oxford University Press, 1929. For this version, Vaughan Williams adapted the Processional Chorus in *Parabasis* from the incidental music to *The Wasps* as a tune called 'Marathon' for the hymn 'Servants of the great adventure' (No. 95).

5(b). *Songs of Praise* (enlarged edition), OUP, 1931. A further 207 hymns were added. Three of RVW's arrangements from the first edition were dropped 226, Regina and 427, East Horndon, and 330, Londonderry. Five new tunes were included: 126, Mantegna; 302, Marathon; 319, Abinger; 432, Famous Men; and 489, White Gates.

5(c). *Songs of Praise for Children* (OUP, 1933) contains RVW's tunes: *Sine Nomine* (No. 87), White Gates (No. 113); Hardwick (No. 135), and Randolph (No. 147) and his arrangements of *Resonet in Laudibus* (No. 37); Forest Green (No. 44); Rodmell (No. 45) and Monk's Gate (No. 68).

6. *The Oxford Book of Carols.* Words edited by Revd Percy Dearmer. Music edited by RVW and Martin Shaw. Publication: London, Oxford University Press, 1928. Vaughan Williams composed the following tunes for the book: 173, The Golden Carol; 185, Wither's Rocking Hymn; 186, The Snow in the Street; 196, Blake's Cradle Song.

The following versions of collections from the *OBC* are also available:

6(a). *The Oxford Book of Carols for Schools.* Fifty carols from the *OBC* arranged for unison singing. Publication: OUP, 1956.
and

6(b). *English Traditional Carols.* Twenty-one carols from the *OBC* arranged for soprano (or treble) and alto voices in two, three, or four parts, some with descant. Publication: OUP, 1954.

7. *Hymns for Today, Missionary and Devotional.* Contains two hymn-tunes by RVW: Monk's Gate and *Sine Nomine.* Publication: London, The Psalms and Hymns Trust, 1930.

8. *Hymns for Sunday School Anniversaries* (eds. RVW, Martin Shaw, Revd Percy Dearmer, and Canon G. W. Briggs, London, OUP, 1930). Contains fourteen hymns, including 'Down Ampney' (No. 12).

[19] *Sine Nomine*, 'Down Ampney, 'Randolph', and *Salve, festa dies* first appeared in *The English Hymnal.*

Appendix C

Personalia

Adler, Larry (born 1914), self-taught American harmonica virtuoso for whom Vaughan Williams wrote the *Romance* for harmonica and strings. After his first success in a C. B. Cochran revue in 1934 he quickly gained an international reputation and has done much to interest serious composers in the possibilities of his instrument.

Allen, Hugh P. (1869–1946), organist, conductor, and educationist. A superb choir-master who was Vaughan Williams's predecessor as conductor of the Bach Choir, he became a fellow of New College in 1908 and Professor of Music at Oxford in 1918 on Party's death. The same year he was appointed director of the Royal College of Music and was responsible for appointing Vaughan Williams and Holst to the teaching staff there.

d'Aranyi, Jelly (1893–1966), Hungarian-born violinist who settled in London in 1923 after having studied at the Budapest Conservatory under Hubay. She greatly impressed Vaughan Williams by her musical gifts and gave the first performance of his Violin Concerto, as well as appearing many times as a soloist at the Leith Hill Festival.

Barbirolli, John (1899–1970), English conductor of Italian extraction who studied at the Royal Academy of Music, formed his own chamber orchestra, and was for a time conductor of the Scottish Orchestra before going to New York in 1936 to take over the Philharmonic Symphony Orchestra from Toscanini; in 1943 he returned to England to re-form and revitalize the Hallé Orchestra which he conducted until his death.

Bax, Arnold (1883–1953), British composer and friend of Vaughan Williams, who dedicated his Fourth Symphony to him. A prolific writer, he composed seven symphonies, a number of tone-poems and much chamber and keyboard music, richly Romantic and mainly lyrical in idiom.

Boult, Adrian (1889–1983), English conductor who studied under Nikisch and at Oxford. In 1924 he became conductor of the City of Birmingham Orchestra, and director of music and chief conductor of the BBC Symphony Orchestra in 1930, training it to such a pitch that it became one of the best in the world. After retiring from the BBC in 1950, he accepted the post of musical director of the London Philharmonic Orchestra.

Boughton, Rutland (1878–1960), composer and writer who was much influenced ideologically (though not necessarily musically) by Wagner on the one hand and by Christianity and by William Morris on the other. He tried to establish a kind of English equivalent of Bayreuth at Glastonbury, basing his festivals on what were intended to be a cycle of operas on the Arthurian legends. His opera

The Immortal Hour (1914) was an enormous success when staged in London in 1922 and there have been fitful revivals of interest in his music since his original venture collapsed in the late 1920s.

Broadwood, Lucy (1859–1929), the first hon. secretary of the Folk Song Society and one of the first systematic collectors of English folk-song. Together with J. A. Fuller-Maitland she was responsible for the publication, in 1893, of *English County Songs*.

Butterworth, George S. K. (1885–1916), composer, critic, and folk-song collector. Vaughan Williams made his acquaintance after he had gone down from Oxford, where he had been president of the University Music Club. A sensitive and gifted musician who, like Vaughan Williams, felt that English folk-song fertilized his own idiom. It was on his suggestion that Vaughan Williams wrote *A London Symphony*, and he provided programme notes for its first performance.

Child, Harold (1869–1945), author and journalist who became secretary to the Royal Society of Painters, Etchers and Engravers in 1902, Assistant editor of the *Academy* in 1905, and dramatic critic of the *Observer* in 1912. He was the librettist of Vaughan Williams's ballad opera *Hugh the Drover* and also wrote the words of the song 'The New Commonwealth'.

Cobbett, Walter W. (1847–1937), amateur violinist, musical patron, and lexicographer, who instituted and endowed prizes for chamber music and its performance at the Royal College of Music and elsewhere. A great lover of chamber music and of string instruments, he also collected and constructed violins. Vaughan Williams won one of the Cobbett prizes with his *Phantasy Quintet*, the fantasy being a form that Cobbett particularly admired. He was also responsible for the encyclopaedic *Survey of Chamber Music* which bears his name.

Cohen, Harriet (1895–1967), leading exponent of modern English piano music and friend of many English composers, including Elgar, Bax, Ireland, and Vaughan Williams, who dedicated his Piano Concerto to her.

Davison, Archibald T. (1883–1961), American scholar, professor of music at Harvard from 1940 onwards, whose interests lay particularly in the field of choral music.

Dearmer, Percy (1867–1936), Anglican clergyman, scholar, art connoisseur, and sociologist who persuaded Vaughan Williams to become musical editor of *The English Hymnal*. His great interest in the place of the arts in religious worship and his profound knowledge of liturgics greatly influenced the shape of the book, and he later collaborated with Vaughan Williams on *Songs of Praise* and *The Oxford Book of Carols*.

Desmond, Astra (1898–1973), English contralto singer for whom Vaughan Williams wrote the solo part in the Magnificat. Her versatility is shown by the fact that she also gave the first performance of the solo part in *Five Tudor Portraits*.

Douglas, Roy (born 1907), English composer and arranger who, in addition to becoming a member of the Committee for the Promotion of New Music, of which Vaughan Williams was president, has written much music for film and the BBC. Towards the end of Vaughan Williams's life Douglas was his trusted copyist.

Duncan, Isidora (1878–1927), American-born dancer who repudiated 'artificiality' in favour of a 'return to nature'—a form of dance as natural as the rhythm of the waves. Her first success in Europe came in Paris in 1902. She toured the continent and visited Russia in 1905, where she greatly impressed Fokine. She was one of the first dancers to 'interpret' symphonic music in dance; her favourite composers included Gluck, Brahms, Wagner, and Beethoven.

Ellis, F. Bevis (?–1916), patron and conductor who did much to promote the cause of younger British composers, such as Vaughan Williams and Bax, by financing and organizing concerts featuring their music. On the outbreak of the First World War, he joined up almost immediately and was killed in action in 1916.

Elwes, Gervase (1866–1921), English tenor singer. He served from 1891 to 1895 in the British diplomatic service. A great interpreter of English religious compositions, such as Vaughan Williams's *Five Mystical Songs*.

Epstein, Jacob (1880–1959), English sculptor, originally of American nationality, who (at his own request) did the well-known bronze head of the composer.

Falkner, Keith (1900–91), English bass-baritone singer who lived for several years in the United States and did much to develop interest in Vaughan Williams's music in that country. Director of the Royal College of Music from 1960 to 1974.

Fuller-Maitland, John A. (1856–1936), English scholar, composer, and pioneer of the folk-song revival in England, translator of Spitta's *Bach* and music critic of *The Times* from 1889 till 1911. He collaborated with Lucy Broadwood on *English County Songs* and, together with William Barclay Squire, edited the *Fitzwilliam Virginal Book* in 1899. He also served on the editorial committee of the Purcell Society.

Gladstone, Francis Edward (1845–1928), English organist, teacher, and composer who was responsible for Vaughan Williams's first instruction at the Royal College of Music. He was a prolific composer of organ music, songs, part-songs, choral, and church music, professor of harmony at the Royal College of Music, a celebrated cathedral organist and choirmaster and a first cousin of William Ewart Gladstone.

Gray, Alan (1855–1935), English organist and composer, conductor of the Cambridge University Musical Society from 1892 till 1912, and organist of Trinity College from 1892 till 1930. He originally studied to be a lawyer before turning to music after taking two degrees in his original subject.

Gurney, Ivor (1890–1937), English composer who was also a talented lyric poet. He studied under Stanford and Vaughan Williams and showed great promise as a song-writer. He enlisted in the 2/5 Gloucester Regiment in 1914 as a private, was gassed and shell-shocked, staged a partial recovery after the First World War but became permanently mentally disabled in 1922.

Haig Brown, William (1823–1907), headmaster of Charterhouse, who took a double first at Cambridge (classics and mathematics), became a fellow of Pembroke College and took Holy Orders in 1852. After being headmaster of a school in Kensington he was chosen as headmaster of Charterhouse in 1863. It was under his direction that the school emigrated from Smithfield to Godalming, and it was for this that he became known as the school's second founder.

Holst, Gustav (1874–1934), English composer and teacher who studied at the Royal College of Music under Stanford, where he met Vaughan Williams. His experience as an orchestral player and teacher, his breadth of interests and his fearless criticism were invaluable to his friend. There is no need here to mention his many fine compositions, since they are still regularly performed, but Vaughan Williams's most extended tribute to him occurs in the *Dictionary of National Biography*, and his life has been described by his daughter Imogen.

Howells, Herbert (1892–1983), English composer and scholar, professor of composition at the Royal College of Music and King Edward Professor of Music in the University of London. Vaughan Williams dedicated *Hodie* to him.

Hull, Arthur Eaglefield (1876–1928), English organist, writer on music, composer, teacher, and patron. After settling in Huddersfield, where he did much to stimulate musical teaching and activity, he founded the British Music Society in 1918, which aimed at bringing forward interesting contemporary British works for performance. He wrote a number of books, including studies of Scriabin and Cyril Scott.

Irving, Ernest (1878–1953), English conductor who worked mainly in the theatre and the film studio, becoming musical director for Ealing Films Ltd in 1935, a post he held till his death. Vaughan Williams's *Sinfonia Antartica* is dedicated to him, and he was in charge of the orchestra for the film *Scott of the Antarctic*, from the music of which the symphony originated.

Jacob, Gordon (1895–1984), English composer, pupil of Vaughan Williams. He taught at Birkbeck and Morley Colleges and joined the staff of the Royal College of Music in 1926. He was Collard Fellow of the Worshipful Company of Musicians from 1943 to 1946. His music is notable for impeccable craftsmanship and superb orchestration.

Keynes, Geoffrey (1887–1985), English scholar and surgeon whose enormously varied interests included a wide and profound knowledge of literature. House surgeon at St Bartholomew's Hospital from 1913, he was chief assistant there in 1920, and Hunterian Professor at the Royal College of Surgeons in 1923, 1929, and 1945. He edited the writings of Blake, Sir Thomas Browne, and Izaak Walton, and compiled bibliographies of writers ranging from the seventeenth-century naturalist John Ray to Rupert Brooke. He was knighted in 1955.

Lambert, Constant (1905–51), English composer, critic, and conductor; one-time pupil of Vaughan Williams at the Royal College of Music, where he had won a scholarship from Christ's Hospital. Besides writing a number of highly original compositions, he also arranged the score of Vaughan Williams's *Job* for its first stage performance, and his work as a ballet conductor was in considerable measure responsible for expanding the appreciation of ballet in this country. His *Music Ho!* remains one of the most brilliant and stimulating critical accounts of modern trends in early twentieth-century music.

Lang, Craig Sellar (1891–1971), composer and teacher, like RVW a pupil of Stanford's, whose beliefs in the innate musicality of the ordinary schoolboy led him as Director of Music at Christ's Hospital (1929–45) to compose or adapt a number of choral works so as to include a part for massed unison voices. Scornfully dismissed by those masters who did not approve of 'community singing', this approach much impressed RVW when he visited the school in 1938.

Maconchy, Elizabeth (1907–94), English composer and pupil of Vaughan Williams. She studied at the Royal College of Music and in Prague. Although she is known mainly for her chamber music, her opera *The Sofa*, to a libretto by Vaughan Williams's widow, was well received on its first performance.

Mathieson, Muir (1911–75), Scottish conductor who won the Boult and Leverhulme conducting scholarships at the Royal College of Music and later specialized in conducting for the film studio. He was musical director to the J. Arthur Rank Organization from 1945 and was responsible for persuading many eminent composers (among them Vaughan Williams) to write scores for feature films.

Morris, R. O. (1886–1948), English composer and scholar who married Vaughan Williams's sister-in-law. He was professor of counterpoint at the Royal College of Music and wrote many standard textbooks on that subject.

Mukle, May (1880–1963), English cellist, active both as a soloist and as a chamber-music player. Vaughan Williams dedicated his *Six Studies in English Folk Song* to her.

Mullinar, Michael (1895–1973), pianist and composer who studied composition under Vaughan Williams at the Royal College of Music and later became his copyist. The Sixth Symphony is dedicated to him, and the piano part in the *Fantasia on the Old 104th* was written for him.

O'Sullivan, Seumas (1879–1958), Irish poet; editor of the *Dublin Magazine*.

Parratt, Walter (1841–1924), organist, teacher, and composer who held a long list of distinguished posts culminating in that of Master of the King's Musick from 1893 till his death. He also succeeded Parry as professor of music at Oxford in 1908 and was the first professor of organ at the Royal College of Music. His interest in counterpoint induced him to draw attention to works by such composers as Reger who were virtually unknown at that time in England.

Parry, C. Hubert H. (1848–1918), English composer, scholar, and philosopher. Among the first musicians in England to develop an interest in the later works of Wagner, he had been trained as accountant (despite early evidence of his musical gifts). A many-sided man whose gifts ranged from athletics to great administrative ability, he composed voluminously as well as holding the posts of director of the Royal College of Music (from 1894), professor of music at Oxford (1900–8), and teacher of advanced composition at the Royal College of Music. He was knighted in 1898.

Sargent, Malcolm (1895–1967), English conductor who was also a brilliant pianist; first appeared as a professional conductor in the 1920s, although he had already conducted Gilbert and Sullivan operettas with amateur casts as a boy. Chief conductor of the Liverpool Philharmonic Orchestra from 1942. He conducted the Henry Wood Promenade Concerts from 1947, the year in which he was knighted, and was principal conductor of the BBC Symphony Orchestra from 1951 to 1958.

Sedley Taylor, Charles (1834–1920), distinguished mathematician and expert on acoustics who became sixteenth Wrangler in 1859 and a fellow of Trinity College, Cambridge. He was one-time president both of the Cambridge University Musical Society and of the University Music Club, and wrote books on such subjects as *Science and Music*.

Sharp, Cecil J. (1859–1924), the most famous of the pioneers in the rediscovery of English folk-song, an inspired teacher, and a tireless worker on behalf of the subject to which he dedicated his studies. He was educated at Uppingham and Clare College, Cambridge, and after spending some time in Australia, where he was assistant organist of Adelaide Cathedral from 1889 to 1891, returned to Britain, where he taught music in schools. It was in 1899 that he first realized the beauties of traditional song, and from then onwards he travelled far and wide—even to the Appalachian Mountains of the United States—in search of material. A vigorous and forceful personality, he always regarded scholarship as a means to an aesthetic and educational end.

Shaw, Martin (1876–1958), English composer and scholar who collaborated with Vaughan Williams on *Songs of Praise* and *The Oxford Book of Carols*. His songs are perhaps the most successful of his compositions, but he also wrote two musical plays for children, much church music, and an oratorio, *The Redeemer*.

Shove, Fredegond (1889–1949), Georgian poet, the wife of G. F. Shove, Reader in Economics at Cambridge, whom she married in 1915.

Stanford, Charles V. (1852–1924), Irish composer, teacher, and scholar, who was a choral scholar at Queens' College, Cambridge, organist of Trinity College, conductor of the University Music Society and the Bach Choir in London, musical director of the Leeds Festival, professor of music at Cambridge from 1887 to 1924, and professor of composition at the Royal College of Music from its inception. A superb teacher and a gifted though derivative composer, he wrote seven symphonies, several operas, and a large number of songs, choral, and chamber works, but is now best known as the teacher of such composers as Vaughan Williams, Bliss, Ireland, and Benjamin.

Stewart, Jean (born 1914), English violist who played in the Menges Quartet and the Richards Piano Quintet and often appeared at the Leith Hill Festival.

Stoeckel, Carl (1858–1925), American philanthropist who was active in founding and financing music festivals and societies in his native region, one of which, the Norfolk Music Festival, became internationally famous.

Toye, Geoffrey (1889–1942), English conductor who devoted much attention during his career to the popularization of contemporary English works. An interest in the stage—thanks to his experience with the D'Oyly Carte Opera Company—is shown in his compositions.

Waddington, Sidney P. (1869–1953), English composer and teacher who studied at the Royal College of Music, in Frankfurt, and in Vienna, worked as *maestro al pianoforte* at Covent Garden, taught harmony and counterpoint at the Royal College of Music and became master of the opera class there. His compositions include a setting of *John Gilpin*, a piano concerto, and a body of chamber music.

Walthew, Richard (1872–1951), English composer who studied with Vaughan Williams as a pupil of Parry and Stanford.

Wood, Charles (1866–1926), Irish-born teacher and composer who was one of the first scholars of the Royal College of Music, where he studied with Parry and Stanford, later becoming organist scholar of Selwyn College, Cambridge, and organist at Caius College, where he was elected to a fellowship in 1894. On Stanford's death in 1924 he became professor of music at Cambridge. He was a prolific composer.

Wood, Henry J. (1869–1944), English conductor who founded and directed the famous Promenade Concerts at the Queen's Hall (and latterly at the Royal Albert Hall) which bear his name. A stalwart champion of contemporary music, and particularly of contemporary British music. He was knighted in 1911.

Wood, Ursula (born 1911), gifted writer and poet who became RVW's second wife. After being privately educated in England and Brussels, she was a ballet student at the Old Vic, married Michael Forrester Wood (d. 1942), and worked as a BBC verse programme compiler, translator, and reviewer. Her books include *No Other Choice, The Fall of the Leaf, A Wandering Pilgrimage*, and a biography of RVW. Her first collaboration with RVW was in 1938. They were married in 1953 and both before and after their marriage she contributed substantially to the texts of a number of his later works, including *Hodie* and *The Pilgrim's Progress* as well as the poem *Silence and Music* and the poems of the *Four Last Songs*. At the time of RVW's death, they were working on an opera together.

Appendix D

Select bibliography

SOURCE MATERIALS

Palmer, Roy (ed.), *Folk Songs Collected by Ralph Vaughan Williams* (London, 1983).
Vaughan Williams, R., and Lloyd, A. L., *The Penguin Book of English Folk Songs* (Harmondsworth, 1959).

CORRESPONDENCE AND LECTURES

Foreman, Lewis (ed.), *From Parry to Britten: British Music in Letters, 1900–1945* (London, 1987).
Ralph Vaughan Williams, National Music and Other Essays (2nd edn., ed. Michael Kennedy, Oxford, 1987).
Moore, Jerrold Northrop (ed.), *Music and Friends: Letters to Adrian Boult* (London, 1979).
Vaughan Williams, Ursula, and Holst, Imogen (eds.), *Heirs and Rebels: Letters written to each other and occasional writings on music by Ralph Vaughan Williams and Gustav Holst* (London, Oxford University Press, 1959).

LIFE AND WORKS

Arblaster, A., 'A London Symphony and Tono-Bungay', *Tempo*, 163 (1987), pp. 21–5.
Banfield, Stephen, *Sensibility and English Song: Critical Studies of the Early Twentieth Century* (Cambridge, 1985), pp. 74–87.
Blom, Eric, *Vaughan Williams*, in *The Book of Modern Composers* (New York, 1942).
Butterworth, Neil, *Ralph Vaughan Williams: A Guide to Research* (New York, 1990).
Cooke, Deryck, 'Vaughan Williams's Musical Language', *The Listener* (7 April 1960), p. 639.
—— *The Language of Music* (London, 1959).
Dickinson, A. E. F., *An Introduction to the Music of Vaughan Williams* (London, 1928).
—— 'The Legacy of Vaughan Williams, A Retrospect', *Music Review*, xix (1958), pp. 290 ff.
—— 'Toward the Unknown Region', *Music Review*, ix (1948), pp. 275 ff.
—— *Vaughan Williams* (London, 1963).

Foss, Hubert, *Ralph Vaughan Williams: A Study* (London, 1950).

Fox Strangways, A. H., 'Ralph Vaughan Williams', *Music & Letters*, i (1920), pp. 78 ff.

Frogley, Alain, 'Composer of the Month: Ralph Vaughan Williams', *BBC Music Magazine*, i, 11 (July 1993), pp. 31 ff.

—— 'Vaughan Williams and Thomas Hardy: Tess and the Slow Movement of The Ninth Symphony', *Music & Letters*, lxv, 1 (January 1987), pp. 42–59.

—— 'Hardy in the Music of Vaughan Williams', *The Thomas Hardy Journal*, ii, 3 (October 1986), pp. 50–5.

—— 'The Genesis of Vaughan Williams's Ninth Symphony: A Study of the Sketches, Drafts and Autograph Scores', D.Phil thesis (Oxford, 1989).

—— 'H. G. Wells and Vaughan Williams's "A London Symphony": Politics and culture in fin-de-siècle England', in *Sundry Sorts of Music Books: Essays on the British Library Collections* (ed. Banks, London, The British Library, 1993).

—— (ed.) *Vaughan Williams Studies* (Cambridge, 1996).

Hawthorne, Robin, 'A Note on the Music of Ralph Vaughan Williams', *Music Review*, ix (1948), pp. 269 ff.

Heißenbüttel, Helmut, 'Versuch der Rekonstruktion einer musikalischen Land-schaft: Englische Musik und Ralph Vaughan Williams', *Musika*, xxxi (1977), pp. 557 ff.

Hesse, Lutz-Werner, *Studien zum Schaffen des Komponisten Ralph Vaughan Williams* (Regensburg, 1983).

Hollander, Hans, 'Ralph Vaughan Williams', *Neue Zeitschrift für Musik*, xxxiv (1973), pp. 153 ff.

Howes, Frank, *The Dramatic Works of Ralph Vaughan Williams* (London, 1937).

—— *The Later Works of Ralph Vaughan Williams* (London, 1937).

—— *The Music of Ralph Vaughan Williams* (London, 1954).

Keller, Hans, 'Film Music', in *Grove's Dictionary of Music and Musicians*, iii (5th edn.; London, 1954), pp. 98 ff.

Kennedy, Michael, 'The Unknown Vaughan Williams', *Proceedings of the Royal Musical Association*, xcix (1972/3).

—— *The Works of Ralph Vaughan Williams* (London, Oxford University Press, 1964; and 2nd edn. Oxford, 1980; rp. 1995).

—— *A Catalogue of the Works of Ralph Vaughan Williams* (2nd edn.; Oxford and New York, 1996).

Knorr, Alexander, 'In memoriam, Ralph Vaughan Williams', *Musica*, xii (1958), pp. 623 ff.

Lambert, Constant, *Music Ho! A Study of Music in Decline* (London, 1934).

Laurie, C. Steven (ed.), *The International Dictionary of Opera* (Detroit, London, and Washington DC, 1990).

Lindlar, Heinrich, 'Ralph Vaughan Williams, der Sinfoniker: Impressionen und Reflexionen zur englischen Musik', *Zeitschrift für Musik*, cxiv (1953), pp. 457 ff.

Mellers, Wilfrid, *Vaughan Williams and the Vision of Albion* (London, 1989).

Moore, Jerrold Northrop, *Vaughan Williams: A Life in Photographs* (Oxford and New York, 1992).

Murrill, Herbert, 'Vaughan Williams's Pilgrim', *Music & Letters*, xxxii (1951), pp. 132 ff.

Ottaway, Hugh, *Vaughan Williams Symphonies* (London, 1972).

Ottaway, Hugh, 'Vaughan Williams', in *The New Grove Dictionary of Music and Musicians*, xix (London, 1980), pp. 569 ff.

Pakenham, Simona, *Vaughan Williams: A Discovery of his Music* (London, 1957).

Palmer, Christopher, *Impressionism in Music* (London, 1973), pp. 152–9.

Pannain, Guido, 'Ralph Vaughan Williams', in *Modern Composers* (London, 1932).

Pirie, Peter J., *The English Musical Renaissance* (London, 1979).

Schwartz, Elliot S., *The Symphonies of Ralph Vaughan Williams* (Amherst, Ma., 1964).

Smith, Cecil, 'The Pilgrim's Progress', *Opera*, ii, 7 (June 1951), pp. 373 ff.

Starbuck, P. R., *A Bibliography of Vaughan Williams's Literary Writings and criticism of his musical works* (High Wycombe, 1970).

Stradling, R., and Hughes, M., *The English Musical Renaissance, 1860–1940: Construction and Deconstruction* (London and New York, 1993).

Temperley, Nicholas (ed.), *The Blackwell History of Music in Britain: The Romantic Age, 1800–1914* (London, 1981).

Tovey, D. F., *Essays in Musical Analysis* (OUP, 1935–9; new edn. in 2 vols, Oxford, 1981).

Young, Percy M., *Vaughan Williams* (London, 1953).

BIOGRAPHICAL BACKGROUND

Bliss, Arthur, *As I remember* (London, 1970; rp. with additions, 1989).

Boult, Adrian, *My Own Trumpet* (London, 1973).

Douglas, Roy, *Working with R.V.W.* (London, 1972).

——*Working with Vaughan Williams: The correspondence of Ralph Vaughan Williams and Roy Douglas* (London, The British Library, 1988).

Fifield, Christopher, *Max Bruch: His Life and Works* (New York, 1988).

Kennedy, Michael, *Adrian Boult* (London, 1987).

——*Barbirolli, Conductor Laureate* (London, 1971).

Kirk, H. L., *Pablo Casals, A Biography* (London, 1974).

Rothwell, Barbara Yates (ed.), *The Leith Hill Music Festival: a Centenary Tribute* (Prologue Promotions, 1972).

Short, Michael, *Gustav Holst: The Man and his Music* (Oxford and New York, 1990).

Vaughan Williams, Ursula, *R.V.W., A Biography* (London, 1964).

——and J. E. Lunn, *Ralph Vaughan Williams, A Pictorial Biography of Ralph Vaughan Williams* (London, 1971).

This list is of necessity partial, selective, and subjective. It will immediately be noted that it virtually ignores any commentaries on RVW's music from before 1939. Those wishing for a far more comprehensive list should consult the hardback edition of Michael Kennedy's *The Works of Ralph Vaughan Williams*. In addition, useful articles on certain of Vaughan Williams's works can be found in various Penguin guides such as those on *Chamber Music* (1957, article by David Cox, pp. 338–56) and *The Concerto* (1952, article by William Mann, pp. 422–5).

Index

327

Index

Beethoven, Ludwig van, 16, 39, 62, 88, 102, 106, 178, 183, 199; Bagatelles, 230; *Fidelio*, 171; String Quartet, Op. 95: 245; Op. 133: 131, 230; Op. 135: 98, 152; Mass in D (*Missa Solemnis*), 257; Overture, Leonora No. 2: 171; Symphony No. 3: 6, 99, 213; No. 5: 99, 202, 203, 255; No. 6: 194; No. 7: 80; No. 9: 72, 98, 135, 198; RVW's essay on No. 9: 72, 75, 198, 209–10, 252, 254

Beggar's Opera, The, 158

Bellini, Vincenzo (*Norma*), 91

Bemerton (Wilts), 3

Benjamin, Arthur, 51, 153, 197

Bennett, Mary, 82

Bennett, Richard Rodney, 88

Bennett, Sir W. Sterndale, 11, 14

Benson, F. R., 37, 146

Benson, Lionel, 295

Berg, Alban (*Wozzeck*), 89

Bergamo, 93

Berkeley, Sir Lennox, 199

Berlin, 21–2, 49, 175

Berlioz, Hector, 107; *L'Enfance du Christ*, 119

Bernard, Sir Anthony, 226

Bianco da Siena, 31

Birley, Sir Robert, 75

Birmingham
    Clarion Singers, 89; *Daily Post*, 37, 67; Town Hall, 289, 293; University, 176, 184

'Birth of the Saviour' (folk-carol), 309

Bizet, Georges
    Carmen, 13, 157; *L'Arlésienne*, 238

'Blackthorn Stick' (folk-dance), 182

Blake, Carice Elgar, 66

Blake, William, 60, 89, 116, 149–50, 282, 300

Bliss, Sir Arthur, 50, 51, 75, 106; 'Lie Strewn the White Flocks', 153; Music for *Things to Come*, 75

Blom, Eric, 67

'Bloody Gardener' (folk-song), 311

'Blow away the morning dew' (folk-song), 306

Boito, Arrigo, 15, 162, 272

'Bold Princess Royal, The' (folk-song), 147, 306, 311

'Bold Young Farmer, A' (folk-song), 306

Bolm, Adolf, 148

Bolm Ballet, 58

'Bonnie Banks o'Virgie-O' (folk-song), 311

Boosey & Hawkes (publishers), 286, 288, 289, 298, 301, 306, 307

Booth, General William, 31

Bordon, (Hants), 46

Borrow, George (*Lavengro*), 89

Borsdorf, Adolph, 236

Boston (Ma.), 96; Symphony Orchestra, 63

Botticelli, Sandro (*Marriage Feast*), 149

Boughton (Rutland), 91, 169–70, 316–17

Boulestin, Marcel X., 37

Boulez, Pierre (*Pli selon pli*), 247

Boult, Sir Adrian, 35, 47, 51, 64, 67, 75, 81, 85, 86, 107, 161, 181, 192, 197, 207, 230, 248, 249, 277, 279, 282, 316; on RVW's performances of the Bach Passions, 107; on RVW's Fourth Symphony, 67, 197

Bournemouth Daily Echo, 90

Bournemouth Municipal Orchestra, 90, 174, 273, 287, 302

Box Hill, 41

Boyce, William, 309

Brahms, Johannes, 10, 13, 19, 28, 29, 38, 39, 107, 183, 184, 189, 192, 199, 217, 224, 225, 237, 247; Clarinet Quintet, 256; *German Requiem*, 14, 125, 152, 180; Symphony No. 1: 15, 183; No. 2: 206; No. 4: 247

Brainard, John G., 310

Breitkopf & Härtel (publishers), 285, 290, 295

Brentwood, 23, 26

Bridge, Frank, 40

Bridges, Robert, 299

Briggs, Canon G. W., 77, 141, 297

Bright, John, 292

Bristol opera school, 281

Bristol University, 89

British Broadcasting Corporation, 64, 70, 73, 75, 78, 80, 91, 141, 153, 288, 289, 292, 300, 302, 304; Dance Orchestra, 181; Symphony Orhcestra, 64, 84, 85, 91, 207

British Federation of Competitive Music Festivals, 82, 142

'British Grenadiers, The', 284

British Musical Society, 50

British National Opera Company, 50–1, 56–7, 161

British Symphony Orchestra, 50

Britten, Benjamin, 6, 36, 71, 75, 97, 100, 105, 136, 141, 155, 158, 159, 176, 181, 191, 199, 215–16, 217, 228, 247, 248, 250; on RVW's *Five Mystical Songs*, 118; on scoring of RVW's Fourth Symphony, 199; *Billy Budd*, 89, 106, 119; Chamber operas, 70; Folk-song arrangements, 120, 248; *Gloriana*, 90, 106; *Les Illuminations*, 106; *Noye's Fludde*, 143, 181; *Our Hunting Fathers*, 70, 71; *Peter Grimes*, 83, 106, 158, 176; Piano Concerto, 232; *Rape of Lucreia*, 83; *Serenade* for tenor, horn and strings, 208; *Songs and Proverbs of William Blake*, 118; *Spring Symphony*, 88, 143; *War Requiem*, 139, 214–15; *The Young Person's Guide to the Orchestra*, 217, 256

Index

Index

Index

338

[1] Originally written for a nativity play devised by Simona Pakenham